PARTIES AND POWER IN MODERN ARGENTINA

PARTIES AND POWER IN MODERN ARGENTINA (1930-1946)

by Alberto Ciria

Translated by Carlos A. Astiz
with Mary F. McCarthy

STATE UNIVERSITY OF NEW YORK PRESS
Albany 1974

Parties and Power in Modern Argentina

First published as Partidos y poder en la Argentina Moderna (1930-1946) by Editorial Universitaria de Buenos Aires in 1964
© 1964 by Alberto Ciria

First Edition

Published by State University of New York Press,
99 Washington Avenue, Albany, New York 12210

Translation © 1974 State University of New York
Printed in the United States of America

Library of Congress Cataloging in Publication Data

Ciria, Alberto.
    Parties and power in modern Argentina (1930-46).

    Translation of Partidos y poder en la Argentina moderna.
    Includes bibliographical references.
    1. Argentine Republic—Politics and government—
1910-1943. 2. Argentine Republic—Politics and
government—1943-1955. I. Title.
F2848.C5413   320.9'82'06   70—129642
ISBN 0—87395—079—8
ISBN 0—87395—179—4 (microfiche)

Contents

Tables

Foreword

The period between 1930 and 1946 is essential to an understanding of modern Argentine politics; while other writers have already perceived its significance, none has studied it with the depth, understanding, and meticulosity of Alberto Ciria. His findings have been assembled in the book *Partidos y Poder en la Argentina Moderna*, which is now being presented in English, after having been widely read and cited throughout Latin America. Ciria's book shows that, given certain conditions, Latin Americans can carry out high level scholarly research and make meaningful contributions to the knowledge and understanding of their own nations. It is unfortunate that the necessary conditions are seldom present and that students of Latin American countries have often lacked the ability to discriminate between significant "native" works, of which Ciria's book is a prime example, and less consequential accounts. It is my hope that this English version will enhance such selectivity.

At the risk of stating the obvious, it should be emphasized that these brief introductory remarks are not addressed to the specialists in Argentine history and politics; they are already familiar with the background information provided here. It is my hope, however, that this study will reach many English language readers who are not specialists. They are likely to find these general references to certain characteristics of Argentina's political history helpful in bringing into sharper focus the period covered in the main part of this book.

The territory occupied by today's Argentina was unquestionably a low-priority area within the Spanish colonial empire in the Western Hemisphere. Among other reasons, there were no precious metals, as in Mexico and Peru, and the natives were very difficult to get along with. While its importance grew toward the end of the eighteenth century, a fact confirmed by the creation of the Viceroyalty of the Río de la Plata in 1776, in general the attention paid by the Spanish crown and the care placed in the selection of its officials was minimal. There is no reason to believe that the Creole upper and middle classes and those Spaniards who identified with them failed to perceive the weakness of the Spanish presence. This weakness became totally obvious in the first decade of the nineteenth century, when, owing to events in Europe, Spain was unable to provide military support to its colonies. The English invasions of Buenos Aires and Montevideo and the failure of Spanish officialdom to offer effective resistance reinforced this perception and played an important part in the independence process which started in 1810, although it was not formally declared until 1816 and not militarily assured until the end of that decade.

As is true elsewhere in Latin America, Argentine independence did not bring about a drastic redistribution of economic, social, or political power. Most of the bureaucrats sent from Spain disappeared, and their places and privileges were taken over by those already holding power who threw in their lot with the new nation. The most troublesome political conflict developed, not on the proper place of the Catholic church, as in many of the other Latin American countries, but on the question of the distribution of rewards between the upper class of the city of Buenos Aires and its provincial counterparts. This conflict was to decide whether each provincial political elite was going to inherit the power taken away from the Spanish crown, with Buenos Aires acting as some sort of *primus inter pares,* or whether the future capital was going to dominate the country-in-formation.

The struggle lasted until late in the nineteenth century; the legal basis for its settlement was outlined in the constitution adopted in 1853, which provided for a federal government with certain powers reserved to the provinces (that is to say, to the political elites of the interior). Behind that constitutional facade, however, Buenos Aires extended its power and its upper class took over the country.

Having settled to its satisfaction this power struggle, the Buenos Aires upper class, which was now in the process of becoming Argentina's upper class, embarked on a policy of increasing the labor force by encouraging European immigration. Table 1 shows some of the direct effects of this decision. Its results were not readily apparent, but had profound political consequences for Argentina.

The objective of the traditional upper class was to enlarge the narrow labor pool from which it could draw the rural workers it needed to control and exploit the land already nominally in its possession, as well as that which the Argentine army was taking away from the Indians and placing under government control. It is now apparent, however, that many of the immigrants were not prepared to spend the rest of their lives in the pampas, farming in semi-isolation. They

TABLE 1: IMMIGRATION IN ARGENTINA, 1857-1958

Period	Net Population Growth Through Immigration	Percentage of Total Population Who Were Foreign-born at the End of the Period
1857-1880	173,000	16
1881-1900	958,000	27
1901-1920	1,389,000	24
1921-1940	951,000	18.4
1941-1958	591,000	14.1

Source: Prepared by Astiz from data published in Gino Germani, *Política y Sociedad en una época de transición; de la sociedad tradicional a la sociedad de masas,* chapter 7.

preferred the paved streets of Buenos Aires and other provincial cities; thus, many of those who immigrated never reached the farm, and a large number of those who actually became farmers did not stay very long. Once located in the urban areas, the immigrants and their descendants founded or took over shops and stores and provided the basis for an urban middle class generally acknowledged to be proportionately larger than that of any other Latin American country, with the possible exception of Uruguay. Elements from that middle class did not take very long in demanding unrestricted participation in politics as well as a greater share of the socioeconomic rewards available in Argentine society. The creation of the Radical party in 1890 (under the name Civic Union) signals the first attempt by the more highly politicized elements of the middle class to form a nationwide political organization.

The new and more stringent demands placed on the political system by the newly organized middle class, with some labor support and with support from many urban workers and from other sectors of the society,[1] led to violent confrontations, attempted coups d'état, and terrorism. The traditional ruling elite was, on the whole, able to resist the different methods employed by those demanding greater participation in national politics. However, the challenges to the legitimacy of the system were on the increase and the traditional ruling elite decided to open the system (at least to the middle class) in exchange for the retention of its basic economic features. The effective electoral reform act (known as Sáenz Peña Act after the president who had it drafted and who put it through a reluctant congress) was passed in 1912 and, properly enforced, made possible the Radical party victory of 1916, as table 2 shows.

TABLE 2: SELECTED ARGENTINE PRESIDENTIAL ELECTION RESULTS IN PERCENTAGES, 1916-1973

Party	1916-1937		
	1916	1931	1937
Radical party (including splinter groups)	49.35	6.80*	41.05
Socialist party	8.88	0.35*	2.50
Conservative parties	26.09	60.31	53.77

Party	1946-51; 1973		
	1946	1951	1973
Peronist	52.40	62.49	61.85
Radical	43.56**	31.81	24.34
Socialist	- -	0.72	1.57
Conservative parties	1.53	2.33	12.11

Party	1958-63	
	1958	1963
Peoples Radical	28.80	25.15
Intransigent Radical	44.79	16.40
Socialist	2.91	0.10
Neo-Peronist	1.33***	1.38***

Source: Prepared by Astiz from data published in Darío Cantón, *Materiales para el estudio de la sociología política en la Argentina.* Vol. I (Buenos Aires: Editorial del Instituto Torcuato di Tella, 1968) and 1973 returns.

The Radical party was in control of Argentine electoral politics until 1930, when the depression, the party's inability to carry out some of the reforms demanded by many of its supporters, and widespread political corruption, brought about its overthrow by the Argentine military establishment.[2] Professor Ciria's account takes it from there.

It is convenient to review here some constitutional features of the

* *The main Radical organization abstained.*
** *Includes total votes for anti-Perón coalition (which included Radicals and Socialists) as well as splinter Radicals.*
*** *Peronist organizations were in fact prevented from participating.*

Argentine polity. This is not to say that they have always been observed; as table 3 shows, ten out of the sixteen presidents the country
has had since 1930 gained power through other than constitutional
means, and very few informed observers would dare forecast that
this ratio will diminish in the future. Nevertheless, Argentine basic
institutions have existed, at least in theory, for more than one
hundred years, and I believe that they have influenced the actors,
whether they as individuals enforced or violated the formal rules
of the political game.

The Argentine constitution approved in 1853 lasted, with a few
amendments, until 1949, when Perón had it replaced by another
document which made it possible for him to seek reelection constitutionally.[3] The Peronist constitution lasted only as long as its
creator remained in power. The military government which replaced him returned the country to the 1853 document which,
with one more amendment, is said to be in effect today. Whether
or not the Argentine constitution has ever been fully in force, the
fact remains that it has provided a vision of what the country's
political institutions ought to be. Even such obvious violators of
the institutional system as those who brought General Onganía to
power claim to subscribe to the 1853 document and proclaim it to
be at least partially in operation.[4]

It has been widely recognized that the Argentine constitutional
system was significantly influenced by the American Constitution
and by writings such as de Tocqueville's *Democracy in America* and
Hamilton's *Federalist Papers.*[5]

There are, however, significant differences, both in theory and in
practice, from the model. Although the country accepted the federal
system, the central government was specifically given the power of
intervención. Regardless of the background, objectives, and limitations of the constitutional provision in question (Art. 6),[6] in practice the central government has used it to appoint federal administrators who superseded those provincial authorities who failed to get
along with those in power at the federal level. Obviously, the mere
existence of such a mechanism has made provincial administrators
extremely cautious in their political dealings with the central government. Federal interventors were supposed to remain in control of
provinces for brief periods, but this has not always been the case.
Furthermore, while they were in control, the interventors often
took steps to insure the election of friendlier provincial governments
to succeed them.

The power of *intervención,* plus the economic resources controlled by the federal government, have converted Argentina into a

TABLE 3: ARGENTINE PRESIDENTS SINCE 1862 AND MODE OF ACCESSION TO OFFICE

Name	Period	Mode of Accession to Office
Bartolomé Mitre	1862-68	military victory
Domingo F. Sarmiento	1868-74	election
Nicolás Avellaneda	1874-80	election
Julio A. Roca	1880-86	election
Miguel Juárez Celman	1886-90	election
Carlos Pellegrini (v. p.)	1890-92	president resigned
Luis Sáenz Peña	1892-95	election
José E. Uriburu (v. p.)	1895-98	president resigned
Julio A. Roca	1898-1904	election
Manuel Quintana	1904-06	election
José Figueroa Alcorta (v. p.)	1906-10	president died
Roque Sáenz Peña	1910-14	election
Victorino de la Plaza (v. p.)	1914-16	president died
Hipólito Yrigoyen	1916-22	election
Marcelo T. de Alvear	1922-28	election
Hipólito Irigoyen	1928-30	election
José F. Uriburu	1930-32	military revolt
Agustín P. Justo	1932-38	election
Roberto M. Ortíz	1938-40	election
Ramón S. Castillo (v. p.)	1940-43	president delegated authority
Arturo J. Rawson	1943	military revolt
Pedro Pablo Ramírez	1943-44	coup d'état
Edelmiro J. Farrell	1944-46	coup d'état
Juan D. Perón	1946-55	election
Eduardo Lonardi	1955	military revolt
Eugenio P. Aramburu	1955-58	coup d'état
Arturo Frondizi	1958-62	election
José M. Guido	1962-63	coup d'état
Arturo Illia	1963-66	election
Juan Carlos Onganía	1966-70	military revolt
Roberto Marcelo Levingston	1970-71	coup d'état
Agustín P. Lanusse	1971-73	coup d'état
Héctor J. Campora	1973	election
Juan D. Perón	1973-	election

Source: Prepared by Astiz from public records.

pseudo-federal nation. The Onganía, Levingston, and Lanusse administrations have, for the time being at least, dispensed with the formalistic aspects of the federal system adopted by the 1853 Constitution: since 1966 the executive branch of the federal government has not only removed, but also appointed, the provincial authorities. Thus, under these administrations, Argentina has become a unitary nation *de jure*.[7]

Another important difference is the greater power given the Argentine executive branch, both at the national and provincial levels. This theoretical recognition of the preference for a strong chief of state has been reinforced by political custom. The result has been the widespread belief that, in Argentine politics, things get done by the executive branch, if they get done at all. The predominance of the executive branch and the other provisions mentioned above have made it possible for some *de facto* regimes to develop sophistic arguments showing that they were not exceeding the provisions of the constitution.

A third significant difference between the American and Argentine constitutional documents is the recognition, in the latter, of the preeminent position enjoyed by the Catholic church. According to the Argentine Constitution and enabling legislation, the federal government is responsible for supporting Catholicism, and the president and vice-president must be Catholic. These and other provisions confirm the fact that the church has been, at least until recently, an important element in Argentine politics; it was, and perhaps still is, quite capable of articulating its interests. In any case, it seems apparent that the church's interests were effectively articulated at the constitutional convention.

The Argentine constitution reflected the essential political features found in the country in mid-nineteenth century. While it made certain changes possible, they could only be adjustments to the broad status quo. The period covered in detail by Professor Ciria's study showed what happened when the demands placed on the Argentine political system exceeded the constitutional framework. The epilogue has not yet been written.

Carlos A. Astiz
State University of New York
at Albany

Part One
The Political Facts

1 Uriburu

The situation of the country before 6 September 1930

Federico Pinedo has said that "the 1930 Revolution was not a bolt out of the blue."[1] We may agree with his metaphor for reasons other than those he presents, but we must certainly accept his conclusion. As is always true when dealing with historical phenomena, the explanation for the events of 1930 must be sought in the past. In this specific case there were numerous contributing causes. Let us review some of them.

The forces opposing the Radical party leader Hipólito Yrigoyen could not have felt satisfied with the result of the so-called "plebiscite" of 1928, which carried the old caudillo back to the presidency for a second term. The returns for the most popular candidates are outlined in table 4. It should be noted that the Progressive Democrats and the Communists were left far behind in the voting. Years later, Pinedo went so far as to say that in reference to the 1928 election,

> the word "plebiscite" could be used not only in the sense in which this classic term is employed in everyday political jargon, that is, to describe an overwhelming victory, but also in the sense of a mandate by the "plebs," by the disinherited mass of the people. The latter followed the caudillo with unswerving loyalty, and they were justified in feeling that many of the Radical party candidates elected represented their interests.[2]

The Conservative forces driven from power in 1916, described by Yrigoyen as that "deceitful and discredited" regime (in contrast to his own "cause") did not seem to accept defeat in the gentlemanly manner they displayed in other fields such as social life or fencing. Instead, they adopted an attitude of uncompromising opposition and criticism. They sought political alliances with related groups and even tried to knock on the doors of some representative military men. For example, it does not seem to us a mere coincidence that the apparent leader of the coup d'état of 6 September 1930, Lt. Gen.

TABLE 4: ELECTION RESULTS 1928

Ticket	Party or Coalition	Votes
Hipólito Yrigoyen and Francisco Beiró *	Radical	838,583
Leopoldo Melo and Vicente Gallo	Sole Front	414,026
Mario Bravo and Nicolás Repetto	Socialist	64,985

José F. Uriburu, had some years earlier been a Conservative deputy from his province, even though he eventually came to lose faith in "the politicians." There would always be a Justo at hand to continue maneuvering.

In considering the contacts with other political forces, we find that there were many efforts to cause a split within the Radical party, between the "personalists" and the "antipersonalists" (these efforts had become apparent in 1924 even within the Congress and would continue to gain strength in later years) and to support the Socialist schism of the *libertinos* (so called because the newspaper *Libertad* reflected their interests) who would later become the short-lived but influential Independent Socialist party of Federico Pinedo, Antonio De Tomaso, Héctor González Iramain, and others,[3] The three groups were to form a coalition that became known by the special name of *"el contubernio,"* later to be one of the key factors in the process that led to the coup d'état of 6 September 1930. Its role in Congress was to attempt to lend the projected movement an aura of popular representation. One of their pronouncements made clear that their purpose was

> to coordinate...opposition action outside Congress, throughout all districts, in order to acquaint the public and the electorate of the respective parties with the illegal acts of the executive branch and of the majority party and to foster a spirit of civic resistance to those abuses and outrages. To plan a course of action intended

* Beiró died shortlythereafter and was replaced by Enrique Martínez.

to achieve the objectives stated, and, if necessary, to solicit and accept the adherence of all those citizens who desire a constitutional and democratic government for the country and who wish to contribute their sober and disinterested efforts to that end.[4]

The opposition campaign could not have been carried out with such intensity had it not had the support of the "responsible press," which gave it unusual publicity. The evening daily *Crítica* was in the forefront of the papers that openly incited to the violent overthrow of the regime. The editor of this paper, Natalio Botana, acted as liaison man between the political and military groups involved in the coup. It must be acknowledged that many student groups belonging to the University Federation lent themselves to these activities. Politicians kept in close contact with the Federation through people like Roberto J. Noble, Independent Socialist deputy, and with student leaders such as Raúl Uranga (Law), who coined what became a celebrated insult when he called Yrigoyen "a barbarous and senile caudillo." Many years later, Uranga was elected governor of Entre Ríos Province in the 23 February 1958, elections; at that time he was not above considering himself a perpetuator of the authentic Radical tradition.

An attempt was made to bring into the conspiracy as many sectors as possible by taking advantage of the opposition-controlled Senate's obvious delaying tactics during the consideration of the proposed oil nationalization law approved by the lower house. The imperialist oil interests which Enrique Mosconi had courageously dared to denounce were not uninvolved in this. A national campaign made the whole country aware of the existence of the government-owned oil company, *Yacimientos Petrolíferos Fiscales,* and of its initials, YPF. There was danger that at the next elections in Mendoza and San Juan (set for 7 September 1930) the numerical balance in Congress might be upset and the law might finally be approved. Needless to say, the opposition had time to conspire, as it did on 5 September in the office of the presiding judge of the First Court of Appeals on Civil matters.[5]   In view of the place where this meeting occurred, the fact that the Argentine Supreme Court later recognized the leaders of the coup as the government of the nation should not cause any surprise; we will deal with this subject later. The plotters also had the opportunity to organize a booing campaign and demonstrations against Agriculture Minister Fleitas at the traditional Rural Society Cattle Show on 28 August 1930. Even the opposition victories in the March 1930 congressional election helped to exacerbate the feelings of those implicated in the conspiracy, instead of calming them. This was especially true of the Independent Socialists, who became the visible leaders of the coup d'état in spite of having triumphed in the city of Buenos Aires; thanks to the support of the Antipersonalists, they received 109,292 votes, against 82,713 for the Radical party and 83,076 for the Socialist party.

The opposition had every opportunity to carry on its campaign "...without systematically suffering at the hands of the authorities the brutal repression that became known later."[6] Things were not going so well within the party in power that they could oppose the onrush of the movement. In fact, two members of the cabinet, Elpidio González, minister of the interior, and Horacio Oyhanarte, minister for foreign affairs, had entered into a struggle to succeed President Yrigoyen as party leader. Their partisans vied with each other in trying to influence the "last caudillo" toward one or the other. To this end each side even used partisan physicians.

This struggle could not fail to weaken (as indeed it did) the authority of a government that every day did less and that was subject to the procrastination of a president who insisted on reviewing everything personally, but who, because of age and disease, succeeded only in delaying government business indefinitely.[7] At the same time, and perhaps because of the self-confidence he had displayed throughout his political life and because he considered himself the one chosen to carry out the great program of the "Constitution," Yrigoyen neglected to take the precautions that would have made impossible even the planning of the 6 September uprising; even worse, he prevented others from taking such precautions. On 3 September the resignation of the minister of war, Gen. Luis Dellepiane, became known. He resigned because it was impossible for him to carry out properly what he understood to be his duties, since obstacles were placed in his way by Vice-President Enrique Martínez (who had his own plans in view of the situation) and by Minister of the Interior González, among others.[8] On the other hand, the indifference of the labor movement vis-à-vis developments before 6 September 1930 helped smooth the way for the conspirators.[9]

The outcome of the plot was a foregone conclusion; all the conspirators had to do was to go to the Plaza de Mayo, enter the Casa Rosada, and demand that the government be handed over to them. This was done.

6 September 1930: the conspiracy

Following the majority of those responsible authors who have written about the subject,[10] we shall consider the factions that promoted the September coup under two headings:

a) The *Uriburu faction,* a minority within the movement, very closely allied with nationalist agitation since the end of the 1920s. The military and civilian leaders who advised them (Carlos Ibarguren,[11] Juan P. Ramos, José María Rosa, Leopoldo Lugones, Alberto Viñas) were admirers of Mussolini and Primo de Rivera, knew Maurras, and wished to apply a reform program with corporative tendencies to the federal Constitution. They sought the repeal of the Sáenz Peña Act and its replacement by a system of qualified voting. Such a process would naturally require reorganization of the country by a dictatorial regime.

b) The *Justo-Sarobe faction* included most of the military officers involved in the movement and had notorious ties with the center-right political parties: the Conservatives, the Antipersonalist Radicals, and the Independent Socialists. Rodolfo Moreno, Leopoldo Melo, and Antonio De Tomaso, who were quite representative of the various groups, appeared on the long list of its civilian leaders, though there were many others. They sought to change the personalist position of Yrigoyen, to hold immediate elections, and to uphold the enforcement of the Constitution and of the Sáenz Peña Act. Sarobe was very clear in this connection: "Therefore, the *men,* not the institutions nor the parties, were the objective of the revolution."[12] This sector favored the interests of the landholding bourgeoisie and the various strata of the urban middle class and pinned its hope for electoral victory on the idea that the loss of prestige suffered by Yrigoyen's followers (something they had themselves conspicuously contributed to creating between the years 1928 and 1930) would make the whole nation turn out in their favor in future elections. After the Radical victory in the election held in Buenos Aires Province on 5 April 1931, it no longer mattered to this faction whether elections were free or not.

As related by José María Sarobe in his *Memorias sobre la revolución del 6 de setiembre de 1930* (an essential source of information on this subject), the backstage maneuverings that brought both factions into apparent harmony were bizarre and ranged from the sublime to the ridiculous. In brief, there was a confrontation between the two most prestigious military leaders of the uprising: José F. Uriburu, the apparent head of the movement, and Agustín P. Justo, the *éminence grise* of the most numerous group, who intervened through his friend and subordinate Sarobe. Justo's participation was not limited to being "one more soldier," as he claimed among his friends; he was actually setting in motion (even before the success of the uprising was assured) the mechanisms that were to carry him to the presidency in 1932. Uriburu grumblingly acceded to Sarobe's demands on the objectives of the movement and allowed changes of substance to be made in the text of the proclamation to be addressed to the people of Buenos Aires. This is how it happened that Lieutenant Colonel Sarobe corrected the text drafted with such enthusiastic fervor by the poet Leopoldo Lugones. This was not the least of the successes achieved by Justo, the power behind Sarobe.

This brings us to the eve of Saturday, 6 September 1930, with the conspiracy still far from completely organized. The chaos in the organization has been acknowledged by Sarobe, and the then Capt. Juan Domingo Perón has added clarifying details that show the precariousness of the situation.[13] However, on the morning of the sixth, Uriburu, at the head of the Military Academy cadets, started what was to be his triumphal march (that "military stroll" the Buenos Aires populace so graphically described) to the seat of government, interrupted only by the shooting in Congress Square.

Sarobe has given the roster of the forces that took part in the action:

In the beginning only the Military Academy and the Communications School joined Uriburu and marched with him to the capital. The Second Army Division did not move from the Campo de Mayo Base because the Infantry School under the command of Colonel Alvarez was opposed to joining. In the meantime, the forces of the Ciudadela Base did not move: the Eighth Cavalry Division, under Lieutenant Colonel Bosch, did not do so because they were against the Revolution and the First Artillery Regiment because they were restrained by the attitude adopted by the other unit. In the Palermo Army Base, the First and Second Infantry Regiments at first remained loyal to the government, and the Third Regiment delayed somewhat in joining the small marching column until it was within the precincts of the capital. The Fourth Infantry Regiment and its detachment at the War Arsenal also remained loyal to the Government, and the Mounted Grenadiers' Regiment did not go over to the Revolution until noon. As we had foreseen, the enthusiastic, generous, and unequivocal collaboration by the civilians was a decisive factor in our success.[14]

Despite Sarobe's exaggerations, there is no doubt that Dellepiane's resignation and his replacement by Elpidio González weakened the outward defenses of a government that had been assailed but not conquered. And the attitude of Vice-President

Martínez (had he been led to believe there was a possibility that he might be left in control, after the changes in the cabinet he attempted to carry out the very morning of the sixth?) destroyed any possibility of recovery.

A eulogist of the regime, Julio A. Quesada, did not hesitate to say that:

> Lt. General Uriburu's entrance into Buenos Aires to popular acclaim is worthy of being immortalized by more forceful and inspiring engravings than the famous ones of the French Revolution, since the Argentine Revolution of 1930 was superior in every respect.[15]

This enthusiasm is not surprising, since Sarobe himself, usually so restrained, gives free rein to his feelings and writes that:

> The people and the army together were writing a new and shining page in the annals of democracy. A deep joy filled our hearts. One hundred and twenty years after the immortal exploit of May, civilians and military men were advancing together toward the historic Victory Square, to proclaim in front of the May Pyramid and near the ancient stones of the Buenos Aires Town Hall the immortal slogan of all Argentines: "The people want to know what is going on."[16]

The Government of General Uriburu

On 8 September the provisional government took the oath of allegiance to the Constitution and the laws before a crowd filling the Plaza de Mayo. Let us quote two paragraphs of the speech made by the new minister of the interior,   Matías G. Sánchez Sorondo:

> The sixth of September 1930 marks óne of the great national dates, together with 25 May and 3 February. These are liberating revolutions. And the last is the only one that has been victorious after having been organized on a national scale, in contrast to the other uprisings, since, not being of a political or partisan nature, it is concerned only with the unavoidable necessity of saving national institutions. . .
>
> I speak to you in the government's name in this house from whose balconies for many long years the voice of the holders of power has not been heard to address the people. And I say to you: "We have sworn before God and the Sacred Scriptures faithfully to observe the Constitution ourselves and to see that others

observe it. We ratify and explain this oath before you. We engage our word and our lives to see that the republic returns to institutional stability. None of our acts will deviate from this sacred objective. We shall return intact to the new Congress the constitutional and legal patrimony of the nation. And after we have installed in office the future government elected by the people in the full exercise of their prerogatives, there will not be, nor can there be, any better reward than that of observing from our retirement the greatness of the nation developing peacefully and effectively.[17]

The new cabinet of the provisional government was then made known to the people, as follows: President, Lt. Gen. José F. Uriburu; Vice-President, Enrique Santamarina; Minister of the Interior, Matías G. Sánchez Sorondo; Minister of Foreign Affairs and Worship, Ernesto Bosch; Minister of Finance, Enrique S. Pérez; Minister of War, Gen. Francisco Medina; Minister of the Navy, Rear Adm. Abel Renard; Minister of Public Works, Octavio S. Pico; Minister of Agriculture, Horacio Beccar Varela; Secretary to the Presidency, Lt. Col. Emilio Kinkelin.[18]   Manuel Gálvez, an author who cannot be suspected of being a leftist, has this to say on the composition of the cabinet:

> The cabinet could not be improved upon intellectually and socially; but one is struck by the fact that three of the eight ministers are associated with foreign oil companies, and all, with the exception of two or three, with various European and American companies. The initial acts of the Uriburu government leave no doubt that the revolution will be, if it is not so already, a restoration of the regime. The sixth of September is a sort of Thermidor in our history.[19]

That same day there was a short-lived subversive attempt, with random shooting between the Presidential Palace and the Post Office Building, that may be attributed to the state of confusion, perhaps fostered by some Yrigoyenist groups, in which the capital still lived. That night, forestalling future complications, General Uriburu offered General Justo (and the latter accepted) the position of commander in chief of the army, which he would occupy only until 24 September. His aspirations went further, and he could not let a position of such importance shackle him to the decisions of the government. However, his request to the relieved of his post was made to seem a sacrifice.

In the meantime, on 10 September, 1930, the Supreme Court handed down a far-reaching decision that would establish a precedent on the problem of recognition of de facto governments. The complete text read as follows:

Buenos Aires, on the tenth day of September 1930, the justices of the Supreme Court, José Figueroa Alcorta, Roberto Repetto, Ricardo Guido Lavalle, and Antonio Sagarna, and the attorney general of the nation, Horacio Rodríguez Larreta, meeting in extraordinary session in order to consider the communication addressed to them by the president of the provisional executive branch, Lt. Gen. José F. Uriburu, informing this Court of the constitution of a provisional government for the nation, decided:

First. That said communication officially brings to the knowledge of this Supreme Court the constitution of a provisional government resulting from the victorious revolution of 6 September of this year.

Second. That this government is in possession of the military and police forces necessary to ensure peace and order in the nation, and, consequently, to protect the life, liberty, and property of all persons and has, moreover, declared in public that it will uphold the supremacy of the Constitution and of the basic laws of the country while it exercises power.

That the foregoing facts undoubtedly represent a de facto government as regards its nature and that the officials who now constitute it, or who may be appointed in future, partake of said nature, with all the consequences derived from the doctrine of de facto governments with regard to the possibility of carrying out validly the necessary acts for accomplishing the objectives it seeks.

That this Court has declared, with reference to de facto officials, that constitutional and international doctrine is uniform in the sense of considering their acts valid, whatever the deficiency or defect in their appointment or election, on the basis of public order and need and for the purpose of protecting the public and the individuals whose interests may be affected, since the latter could not carry out inquiries nor challenge the legality of the appointment of officials who are in apparent possession of their offices and functions (Constantineau, "Public Officers and the de Facto Doctrine," *Fallos,* v. 148, p. 303.)

That the provisional government that has just been formed in the nation is, therefore, a de facto government, whose title cannot be successfully challenged judicially by individuals since it exercises administrative and political functions derived from its possession of power as the key to social order and safety.

That this notwithstanding, if, once the situation is normalized
in the course of the activities of the de facto government, the officials constituting it should ignore personal or property guaranties
or others safeguarded by the Constitution, the court charged with
enforcing compliance with such guaranties would restore them in
the same manner and with the same effect as it would have done
under a de jure executive branch.

This conclusion, mandatory under the organization of the judicial branch itself, is confirmed in this case by the declarations of
the provisional government which on taking office has hastened
to take an oath to comply with, and to make others comply with,
the Constitution and the basic laws of the nation, a decision that
entails the consequence that it is ready to lend the support of the
force at its command to obtain compliance with judicial decisions.

In view of the above considerations, the court decided to acknowledge receipt to the provisional government of the said communication by means of the forwarding of the note agreed upon,
ordering that it be published and entered in the corresponding
volume. Signed before me, to which I bear witness. Figueroa
Acorta.—Repetto.—Guido Lavalle.—Sagarna.—Rodríguez Larreta.—Raúl Giménez Videla, Secretary,[20]

This is not the place to go into a legal critique of the decision
transcribed above and, in any case, it has been done with recognized
authority by Rafael Bielsa.[21] Here we can only point out the dangerous position assumed by the Court vis-à-vis individual rights and
guaranties, when it leaves them to the sole decision of the de facto
executive branch, since, if the latter does not lend its power to the
execution of the sentences, what value will judicial decisions have?

Moreover, these words spoken by Sánchez Sorondo in the Senate
are pertinent:

... since 6 September, we have been living outside the Constitution, we are in full revolution and while as the senator [Pala-
cios] has reminded us, the men in the provisional government
have promised, as far as possible, to follow the dictates of the
Constitution in their exercise of the government, this does not
mean, cannot mean when dispassionately considered, that they
should submit to the Constitution. Where has there ever been a
case of a revolutionary power that has submitted to a Constitution, since the very fact of its existence implies a violation of
that same Constitution? [22]

That disaffection for the Constitution which General Uriburu had so often expressed before the outbreak of the Revolution (and which was shared by some of his closest assistants) characterized the acts of a sector of the provisional government still intent on corporative reforms and the repeal of the Sáenz Peña Act. One proof of this, and not the sole one, was given by the administration of Carlos Ibarguren as federal interventor in the province of Córdoba.

These goals of the head of the government are reflected (aside from the 1 October manifesto) in two important speeches delivered at the Higher War College (13 December 1930) and at the Infantry School (18 December 1930) in which the political role is disparaged and the institutional reforms considered essential are emphasized. A ringing speech was delivered by Ibarguren in the Rivera Indarte Theater in Córboda on 15 October 1930, supporting Uriburu's original plan.

The National Democratic Federation (an entity responsible for coordinating the Conservative parties of various provinces, the Indepent Socialists, the Antipersonalist Radicals of Entre Ríos, and the recently established small groups)[23] on 15 October replied to these statements in the same locale, insisting on "returning to normalcy as soon as possible" and calling for elections; De Tomaso, Miguel A. Cárcano and Rodolfo Moreno were among those who spoke. The future *"Concordancia"* was on its way despite the fact that the federation soon ceased to exist when it encountered opposition from the powerful Conservative party of Buenos Aires Province and from its able advocate in the cabinet, Matías G. Sánchez Sorondo. The preparations for the pilot experiment of elections in that district, set for 5 April, 1931, were already under way. Elections in Santa Fe, Córdoba, and Corrientes Provinces were to follow.

Ibarguren had no qualms about confessing what his attitude had been. He wrote:

> For my part, as far as Córdoba is concerned, *I tried to delay fixing the date for elections as much as I could,* giving as a reason the need of preparing new voting lists to take the place of the invalid ones of the previous regime: that was what I advocated at the Interventors' Conference held in December 1930.[24]

Finding it necessary to support a candidate for the future presidency of the nation, Uriburu started by favoring Lisandro de la Torre, to whom he specifically communicated his intentions. But de la Torre, displeased by the turn of events and knowing the latent corporative intentions of the dictator, refused the offer. As a good liberal, perhaps the last great liberal in our political history, he preferred to accept a losing nomination, that of the Civil Alliance, which included the Socialist party, to renouncing his ideas.[25] His basic anti-Yrigoyenism forced him to try to rescue what could be rescued from the 6 September movement, despite Uiruburu's equivocations and those of his cohorts, and to proclaim himself the revolution's legitimate successor. On 13 September 1931, in a campaign speech made at the Coliseo Theater in Buenos Aires, he said:

> We come, in fact, to save the revolution, because we are the interpreters of its popular spirit. We come to channel it by getting from the ballot box a verdict consecrating the will to renewal that on 6 September beat in the hearts of all Argentines, even in those of the defeated, not all of whom were insensible to the dreadful chaos in which the nation lay! We come to take up a banner mistakenly abandoned by the revolutionary government, a banner the people have made their own; and we come, in the name of the people, to reestablish the harmony and fraternity that have disappeared from our national life. We want to carry out the work the people expected on 6 September. Who but a madman would attempt to restore the deposed regime? [26]

However, it must be made clear that Lisandro de la Torre, leaving aside the euphoria of the campaign speeches, had no illusions about his real chances of election. In a letter to Elvira Aldao de Díaz, dated 22 October 1933, he wrote:

> What was offered me was really a losing nomination. Uriburu was not the man to draw back from any excess — if there was anyone who knew this, it was I who knew him so intimately and so well. That is why I accepted, because I was rendering a service to civilian and democratic sentiment without thought of myself, and because it pleased my old Santa Fe friends who found their electoral strength increased when joined to a national movement. Also, it was my understanding that I was entering into a temporary obligation and would return to my retreat at the end of a campaign that would last no more than two months. I had my eyes on the national stage and did not see that the victory of the Progressive Democrats in Santa Fe would make it almost impossible for me to leave them to their fate.[27]

After 6 September Radicalism had begun a decline that would continue throughout the decade. The message whispered to his faithful by Yrigoyen, who was being arrested and humiliated, was that "Marcelo must be surrounded," but conditions were not favorable because the Personalists were no longer in office and did not have the same freedom of movement.

Marcelo T. de Alvear, from his habitual residence in Paris, had taken charge of drawing up hasty newspaper statements full of charges against his former mentor and the popular currents he had supported. But this was immediately after the September coup, under the influence of euphoria and distance. Alvear decided to return to Argentina and on 25 April 1931, he arrived in Buenos Aires. General Justo, who had been his minister of war, was at the port to receive him. So was the aide-de-camp to Lt. General Uriburu, an old friend. But their paths, which at first sight seemed to be the same, were soon to diverge.

After refusing to entertain Uriburu's suggestion that Yrigoyenism be disregarded in any political maneuvering,[28] Alvear joined other important figures of both sectors of the Radical party in setting up a "Reorganizing Board." Leopoldo Melo (later Justo's minister of the interior), who had since 1928 aspired to higher offices, was the one conspicuous omission.

The uprising led by Lt. Col. Gregorio Pomar in Corrientes Province (20 July 1931), although quickly suppressed, led to Alvear's deportation, the arrest of the leaders of the opposition, and eventually helped to bring about the long-awaited announcement of presidential elections. Justo devoted himself to putting the finishing touches on his political machine, from then on to be known as the *Concordancia*, and bent all his efforts to being named candidate.

Some events that materialized at the right time must be mentioned: One was the definitive annulment of the elections for governor of Buenos Aires Province that had confirmed the victory of the Honorio Pueyrredón-Mario Guido ticket and another was the vetoing of the Alvear-Adolfo Güemes presidential ticket nominated by the Radical party convention on 28 September 1931, the practical result of which was to exclude the party from the elections. The 8 November elections no longer presented any problem for Justo.[29]

Despite the anxious efforts of Vicente G. Gallo to have the Radical party present a ticket acceptable to the provisional government (presumably with Vicente G. Gallo, the frustrated 1928 vice-president, at its head), the die was cast and abstention from voting by the Radicals was a fact. The main beneficiary of the process, President-to-be Justo, had carried off a great political maneuver. His only adversaries were the candidates of the Alliance, Lisandro de la Torre and Nicolás Repetto, whose total vote would be appreciably increased by the Radicals' abstention.

The faction Sergio Bagú has described as "the friends of the British Empire, given to fraudulent electoral maneuvers and to Curia-like legalism, rather than to the open use of truncheons and clubs,"[30] decided that Gen. Agustín P. Justo was the best possible candidate. Federico Pinedo has recorded part of the parturition process resulting in the selection of the candidate (gestation had started quite some time before).[31] The National Democratic party — a new organization uniting the Conservatives, Democrats, Liberals, Autonomists, and some smaller groups — together with the most extreme Antipersonalist factions and the Independent Socialist party, strengthened the coalition. According to Pinedo, it was only a relative strength since "... every once in a while disunion became more apparent than union, discord than harmony. This is how the double candidacy to the vice-presidency was conceived, which despite the accompanying difficulties and the efforts made to avoid it, it was impossible to abandon until the end."[32] In effect, after the attempts to make Eduardo Laurencena the running-mate, two different candidates to the vice-presidency were named: José Nicolás Matienzo, supported by the Entre Ríos Radical party, and Julio A. Roca, by the National Democrats, who did not want to add to the presence of Radicals on the ticket. (Justo always knew how to employ his Radical Antipersonalist convictions very effectively when he found it necessary to effect a rapprochement with that faction.) Humorists of the time said that General Justo had committed "political bigamy."

The fact is that the elections (as could have been expected) definitely confirmed the Agustín P. Justo-Julio A. Roca team. Many "responsible" groups showed preference for this combination. The magazine *Criterio,* which acted as spokesman for an active group of Catholic thinkers, went so far as to say:

> We believe we have been sufficiently explicit. The apolitical nature of our magazine has not changed during the difficult times the Republic is experiencing. On 8 November, a civic contest will take place that is without precedent because of its bearing on the future and because of the special circumstances under which it will take place. Abstention by the Radical party (certainly very regrettable) leaves the field to two heterogeneous parties, one of which, the Alliance, because of its principles and its men, represents an undoubted danger for the country. The honest citizen already knows what the facts are.[33]

The Argentine episcopate had already done its part by issuing a pastoral letter (certain to be quoted in the political field for many years) on "modern laicism and the present duties of Catholics" a month before the elections. This document gave Catholics precise guidelines to follow in voting. They were told not to vote for parties urging the separation of church and state, lay schools, and legal divorce. These guidelines were obviously directed against the Alliance candidates. Soon after 8 November 1931, Nicolás Repetto, the Socialist candidate for vice-president for the Alliance, confessed that:

> The Radical party members having been prevented from taking part in the elections with their own candidates, the 1931 elections for president and vice- president were the most fraudulent of any ever held in this country and were used to give an appearance of legality to the usurpation of power carried out against the Radical candidate. In these elections, decided upon by one general to favor another general, those in power carried to extremes the system of methodical fraud, and the rights and liberties of the citizens were subject to increased restrictions.[34]

The Radicals' abstention was the deciding factor that allowed the Socialist party to elect forty-three national deputies and two senators (Alfredo Palacios and Mario Bravo) and the Progressive Democrats to take the governorship of Santa Fe for its candidate, Luciano Molinas, and send some legislators to Congress, of whom Lisandro de la Torre was the most outstanding.

On 20 February 1932, General Uriburu delivered the insignia of office to his successor, General Justo. But the former. "a genuine representaive of our patrician class,"[35] also transferred to Justo a proposal he had carefully prepared for reforming the Constitution of the nation. The "citizen engineer," Agustín P. Justo, "by vocation a politician, by nature ambitious, liberal, restless, cautious, and an 'operator' when it was necessary to become one to attain his object,"[36] received it graciously and then consigned it to limbo.

Uriburu had stated his government objectives with some precision:

> (1) To clean up and rebuild the administrative and financial sectors speedily; (2) to bring order to the country and the universities; (3) to prepare the institutional reorganization of the nation through constitutional reforms that would protect us in the future from the dangers of personalism, centralism, oligarchy, and demagoguery; (4) to stimulate the formation of great civic forces to provide the solutions necessary for a return to normalcy, without my goverment taking a partisan stand.[37]

Gabriel del Mazo has this to say about the first point:

From the Conversion Fund, 170 million gold pesos were taken (that is, 40 percent of the gold reserves); the floating debt of the Treasury was increased and 300 million paper pesos were put in circulation. New taxes amounting to over 15 percent of the national budget were established. The government was characterized first by nepotism and then by electoral favoritism.[38]

In connection with the second point, it is interesting to recall the attempts at subversion by noncommissioned officers in Córdoba Province (27 November 1930), by General Severo Toranzo (20 February 1931), the already-mentioned attempt by Lt. Col. Gregorio Pomar (20 July 1931), the frustrated revolt in Tucumán Province (27 August 1931), and the uprising by armed civilians led by the Kennedy brothers in La Paz (Entre Ríos Province, 3 January 1932). Also, martial law was imposed, new criminal laws were passed, and old ones amended by proclamation; the death penalty, which had been abolished by the Penal Code, was reestablished. There were executions, persecutions, tortures, and deportations. Elections were annulled and political slates were vetoed. Fraud was rampant in the presidential elections, especially in the provinces of Buenos Aires and Mendoza. Under the pretext of correcting "university anarchy" universities were placed under the control of governmental delegates, reactionary by-laws were promulgated for them, and student leaders who showed signs of recovering from the September euphoria, which had done so much harm, were persecuted and jailed.

The third point on Uriburu's list of objectives is covered by the proposed constitutional reforms to which we have already referred.

As for the fourth point, perhaps it is meant to refer to the systematic opposition to Yrigoyenist Radicalism, undeniably a "great civic force," which was prevented from participating in the political process. It was preferred to give official recognition to the Civic Legion (20 June 1931), a quasi-military organization with the functions of a praetorian guard, which had been "armed by the Ministry of War" and the disarming of which "for a long time, even after the provisional government had gone out of office, . . . posed a difficult problem."[39] Ibarguren, who considered the Civic Legion an indigenous Argentine phenomenon, deplored the fact that "it did not have time to develop throughout the nation nor to attain the size and influence of a powerful force capable of achieving the objectives sought by the head of the provisional government."[40]

However, the Uriburu government has left its imprint on the Argentine political scene chiefly because it fostered the renaissance of a nationalist ideology with aristocratic tendencies (the above-mentioned Ibarguren was one of its precursors). This ideology was to be revised and expanded in later years by an intellectual team noted for brilliance rather than depth, with the resulting changes and restatements of that ideology. The sixth of September 1930 cannot be ignored in connection with the appearance of the military on the political arena, but it does not represent the first milestone. Nineteen thirty was merely the culmination of an earlier process. This must be kept in mind in order not to view history as an irrelevant succession of incidents. The 6th of September also gave impetus (unfortunately not always well-directed) to the Argentine university movement, a side effect of some importance because of its special growth since then.

The political parties did not rise to the challenge. This does not refer to the winners (the Conservatives, Indepent Socialists, and the Antipersonalists) nor to the losers (the Radical Yrigoyenists). Rather it refers to those who adopted seemingly "neutralist" attitudes, as the Socialist party and the Progressive Democratic party did, yet did not hesitate to claim they were the authentic heirs of the revolutionary movement and to criticize dictatorial excesses, and to the Communist party, which exhibited a deplorable lack of understanding of Radical ideology and of the role of its most representative figure, Hipólito Yrigoyen.

This chapter started with a quotation from Federico Pinedo and will close with another by the same author. As time went by he came to ask himself whether:

> Taking for granted that Yrigoyenism had to be eliminated, was it wise to appeal to the armed forces to achieve it? Many doubted the wisdom of such a course in view of what it had cost to break the habit of military uprisings that was so widespread in our Latin American world and of which Yrigoyen was the unsuccessful exponent for thirty years. *Can we conclude that the revolution was wise? The fact that after seventy years of an uninterrupted succession of governments (1860 - 1930) we have had a series of uprisings in the last quarter of a century affords grounds for doubting such wisdom, if what has happened can be viewed as a consequence of the 1930 operation.*[41]

2 Justo

Economic aspects

José Luis Romero, in speaking of the "infamous decade," said that "fraud and privilege were the characteristics of this period." [1] Economically, the main distinguishing feature of Justo's government was that he placed the country in a position of colonial dependence on Great Britain, thus favoring the traditional upper class. Justo's experiments included state intervention; the Regulatory Boards, which controlled production in various fields, are an example of this. Needless to say, they favored the privileged and did not foster the interests of the community. What seems paradoxical is that this president who owed his office to fraud and who favored returning to nineteenth century liberalism did not hesitate to use unorthodox measures to attain his objectives. It should be remembered that former Socialist Antonio De Tomaso was Justo's agriculture minister and that he was responsible for much of what happened in agricultural production.

Justo's initial cabinet was made up as follows: Interior, Leopoldo Melo; Foreign Affairs, Carlos Saavedra Lamas; Treasury, Alberto Hueyo; Justice and Public Education, Manuel M. de Iriondo; War, Col. (later Gen.) Manuel A. Rodríguez; Navy, Navy Capt. (later Rear Adm.) Pedro S. Casal; Agriculture, Antonio De Tomaso; Public Works, Manuel Ramón Alvarado. [2]

The 1929 world crisis continued to have important repercussions years after its inception. As a meat-exporting country, Argentina was profoundly affected by the conference held between Great Britain and its dominions in the Canadian city of Ottawa in 1932, which considered granting preferential treatment to Empire products. Great Britain never gave up this sort of protectionism whenever it suited its interests, even though it made constant verbal references to free trade. This protectionism aroused great uneasiness in the cattle-raising circles of the Argentine Rural Society because of the possibility that purchases by our traditional client, the United Kingdom, would be reduced in favor of its colonial dependencies.

This situation led the Argentine government, under pretext of returning the Prince of Wales's visit, to send a mission to London headed by Vice-President Julio A. Roca. His entourage included men of prestige such as Guillermo Leguizamón, who was attorney for the British railroad interests; Conservative Deputy (later agriculture minister) Miguel Angel Cárcano, and Raúl Prebisch, counselor to the Ministries of the Treasury and of Agriculture, who later became manager of the Central Bank. A document that was to be a subject of controversy for years to come resulted from this trip: the Roca-Runciman Treaty, signed by Roca and British Board of Trade President Walter Runciman on 1 May 1933.

The executive branch sent this treaty to the Chamber of Deputies on 3 June, urging its approval with a haste worthy of a better cause. Carlos Ibarguren has outlined its main provisions as follows:

Great Britain did not undertake any substantial obligations toward Argentina; on the other hand, Argentina contracted all those commitments I shall list hereafter: Great Britain was given the right to restrict its meat purchases according to its interest and, what is worse, to allocate 85 percent of our meat exports to Great Britain among those exporters it selected within Argentina; only the remaining 15 percent was allowed to be exported to Great Britain by nonprofit Argentine enterprises, provided that such shipments were placed in the market by normal means (that is, British vessels and merchants), and taking into consideration the coordination of the commercial interests of the United Kingdom. For its part, Argentina agreed to: 1) Continue to maintain on the same status coal and all other merchandise that was then imported duty-free; 2) To return to the rates and valuations in effect in 1930 on those British imports on which the United Kingdom sought a reduction of import duties, the Argentine government committing itself not to impose any new duties and not to increase the existing ones under any guise whether through changes in rates, valuations, or in any other manner; 3) To follow a policy of maintaining railroad fares; 4) To allocate for the benefit of British commercial interests all the foreign exchange earned from British purchases. In no case was the exchange rate for remittances to Great Britain to be less favorable than for remittances to other countries; 5) To give favored treatment to British-owned public services and to other British enterprises in Argentina, whether providing national, municipal, or private services, and to protect the interests of the same.[3]

Opinions on the treaty differed greatly. Guillermo Leguizamón, who had much to do with negotiating it, stated that "the Roca-Runciman agreement represents the most important event in the financial history of the nation in this century.' "[4] On the other hand, Lisandro de la Torre, speaking in the Senate about one of the stipulations of the treaty, asserted that:

> Under these circumstances it cannot be said that Argentina has become a British Dominion, since Great Britain does not take the liberty of subjecting the British Dominions to such humiliations. Each British Dominion has its own quota and each administers it. . . . Argentina cannot administer its quota; New Zealand may do so; so may Australia, Canada, and even South Africa. Great Britain has greater respect for these communities, which have restricted international legal personality and are part of her Empire, than she does for the Argentine Government. I don't know whether we can continue to say: "Greetings to the great Argentine people."[5]

Alberto Hueyo resigned as minister of the treasury because of "disagreements with its stipulations."[6] His post was taken by Federico Pinedo, who carried out the program of economic subordination to British interests very effectively from 24 August, 1933 to 30 December 1935. The Independent Socialist party was in its death throes: De Tomaso's death, Pinedo's official involvement, the part played by Roberto J. Noble as minister in the Fresco provincial government, all hastened the process. There no longer was any difference between Conservatives and Independent Socialists, not even as to labels.

The Roca-Runciman Treaty bore the germ of many measures that would later be adopted in the field of economics and finance and that were to embody what Arturo Jauretche, a member of the Force of Radical Orientation of Young Argentina (an organization of young, nationalistic members of the Radical party, known as FORJA), has fittingly dubbed "the legal expression of colonialism."[6]

On 1 September 1934, Senator de la Torre submitted to the federal Senate a draft resolution on the meat industry; this resolution gave rise to the most notable debate of the decade in the Argentine Congress. It read as follows:

> An investigating commission composed of three senators, having all the powers inherent in such commissions, is hereby appointed to ascertain the situation of the Argentine meat export industry and to verify whether the prices paid by meat-packing plants in

Argentina are in consonance with those they obtain in their sales abroad.

The Senate approved this investigation and appointed Senators Laureano Landaburu and Carlos Serrey (majority) and de la Torre (minority) as members. Despite deficient reporting by the major newspapers, the course of the debates (the "meat debates") was followed with growing interest by large intellectual and political sectors that considered the senator from Santa Fe an incorruptible voice clamoring in the wilderness of the regimented majorities of the decadent Senate. Needless to say, both exaggerated idealizations and presumptuous negative views in judging de la Torre's attitude are out of place: *within the system,* he was a penetrating critic who did not abjure his liberal background nor the confused ideas that led him to equate fascism and communism in certain aspects, and yet he very casually suggested that a state monopoly might be the answer to the complex meat problem, something he had done on previous occasions in discussing the same subject (1922-23 debates). His great value lay in that he publicized the conditions existing at the time (the volume of his *Collected Works* containing his speeches is an essential document for the study of Argentine economic history), but he could not be a thorough reformer. In the struggle between the large and the small cattle breeders, he sided with the latter. In doing this he was only voicing the claims of his native Santa Fe Province; we must not forget that he was president of the Santa Fe Rural Society in the early years of the century. He hurled accusations at the cattle raisers who were the accomplices of the meat-packing monopoly, at venal officials, at a do-nothing government. He was alone in the midst of a hostile Senate that treated him as if he were a mad old man, among ministers that threatened him and colleagues that indulged in what he considered petty interruptions.

His denunciations brought to light the imperialist connections of some lawyers who were then or had formerly been in the cabinet: Horacio Beccar Varela, the former minister of agriculture under Uriburu, was shown to be the attorney for the Anglo meat-packing concern as a result of the arrest of Richard Tootell for withholding rolls. [7] Clandestine shipments of documents that had been requested by the commission de la Torre guided were traced to the SS *Norman Star.* The inaction of Agriculture Minister Luis Duhau in not curbing the maneuvers of the winter-pasture and meat-packing interests was investigated. As minister of the treasury, Pinedo attacked this investigation in a heated exchange with de la Torre that became famous:

Lisandro de la Torre: If the Senate investigation had not brought these facts to light, they would have remained unknown. The minister of the treasury and the minister of agriculture look on impassively and so do the counselor to both [Raúl Prebisch] and the president of the Republic who, like the Tax Board, seems to be in limbo...

The Minister of the Treasury: The senator will answer for all this, item by item!

Mr. de la Torre: I did not hear what the minister said.

The Minister of the Treasury: He will answer dearly for all the statements he has made! We will not interrupt him now, but we will answer all his words.

Mr. de la Torre: If that is all, I shall proceed, and I hope he will reply. [8]

In short, it was through de la Torre's work that the existence of a meat-packing monopoly that ranged from the purchase of cattle on the ranches to the sale of meat in the consumer markets was exposed. This monopoly had been responsible for the disappearance of specialized establishments either by putting them out of business or by mergers. It enjoyed unusual opportunities for carrying out its activities in Argentina, manipulating the laws to its own advantage, and depending on the protection of high official circles.[9]

But the investigation of the meat industry had not yet been completed. The murder of Enzo Bordabehere (senator-elect for Santa Fe Province, who was in the Senate to follow the debate) on the floor of the Chamber, broke the spirit of his teacher and friend, who refused to proceed with his accusation. De la Torre ventured only to say:

The damage suffered by the prestige of the government would not amount to anything if in the future it were possible to avoid the continuation of the other damage, the one that strikes a death blow at the most important source of wealth in the nation, consciously subjected to the interests of foreign capitalism. [10]

In commenting on this subject, writers such as Arturo Jauretche and Raúl Scalabrini Ortiz were aware of the thread that bound these issues together, and that must not be lost sight of when isolated instances are considered. Jauretche wrote:

The issue was not an isolated one, as de la Torre thought in the course of the meat debate, when Bordabehere's corpse lay on the Senate floor simply because he had lifted a corner of the curtain. It was not a question of the railroad or street-car interest in one case, of the interest of a meat-packing plant or two in another, nor of that of a group of banks or of a given financial enterprise; nor was it a question of benefiting a group of wealthy people, made solvent again through the Mobilizing Institute, nor of benefiting a few industrialists through the limitations on production established through the Regulatory Boards. All these were aspects of a policy intended to limit the development of the country, to keep it a monoproducer, to restrict its capacity to participate in free competition abroad, and, as a consequence of this, to deny upward social mobility to the masses in order to keep the consumer market limited so it would not add the competition of internal demand to the price of what they called our *exportable* balance.[11]

With this in mind, the creation of the Argentine Central Bank (included in the proposed legislative package on money and banking), which the administration urged the Senate to approve in 1935, makes more sense (it should be remembered that the electoral abstention of the Radical party had just come to an end). The haste demonstrated led Socialist Senator Alfredo Palacios to remark:

This proposal has come to the Senate by a process which violates all parliamentary procedures: on Saturday, the tenth of this month, it was received at an extraordinary session and a day later the bill was reported by the committee with twenty-one amendments. Insofar as we know, no study has been made, the banks have not even been consulted, nor have the university finance professors and former Treasury ministers who undoubtedly would have been able to contribute some information to those of us who approach the study of this matter without considerations of a partisan nature.[12]

This matter was handled in this way because the creation of the Argentine Central Bank had been decided upon beforehand and not by the minister of the treasury alone. The state of mind of the congressional majority that approved the bill in question has been described by Pinedo in a masterly manner:

There was rather excessive partiality in favor of the British proposal [that of Sir Otto Niemeyer] from which we drew not only many ideas but also the phraseology, when we thought there was no serious objection to doing so, even though we may have felt that better texts could have been adopted. We did this because we did not want to create serious obstacles to the approval of the bills and we knew that, by a curious characteristic of the collective

mentality, *at that moment adoption of the government's proposals would be facilitated if we could make them appear to
coincide to a great extent with what the foreign expert had
advised.*[13]

The key to the dangers involved in the creation of the new Central
Bank ("which was not of the Republic" as José Luis Torres graphically pointed out), had already been emphasized by Ibarguren as
consulting attorney to the Bank of the Nation in an opinion given on
17 April, 1933:

> I pointed out the dangers that Mr. Niemeyer's Bank, later to
> become the Argentine Central Bank, entailed in that the econom-
> ic sovereignty of the Republic would be delegated to a corpora-
> tion in which the state did not have effective participation or con-
> trol; and I mentioned the danger that the meetings of stock-
> holders, made up mostly of foreign banks, might be controlled by
> entities that would look only to their own interest, and that the
> economic government of the country, directed by those alien to
> the state, might suffer the extraneous influence represented by
> the interests of the majority of the foreign banking community.[14]

The Mobilizing Institute of Bank Investments, created by Law
No. 12,157, received "a fabulous amount of money to cover poor
bank investments, whether now existing or future."[15] In this way
the government solicitously went to the aid of the financial oligarchy, channeling resources to them that might have profitably been
used for other purposes of general interest.

The Production Regulatory Boards in the fields of meat, wine,
cereal, milk, cotton, and other products fulfilled a double purpose:
they centralized in the city of Buenos Aires the direction and control
of the basic industries of the country, and they contributed to the
consolidation of the existing production and distribution monopolies. Wine was poured down the gutters (this actually happened in
Mendoza Province) in order to improve the price of the wine reserves
held by monopolistic consortia. The state, through a new neoliberal
Keynesian style of intervention, supported corporations to the detriment of the small producers. Not only was the destruction of raw
materials authorized, but even the limiting of production was per-
mitted, as well as the fixing of minimum prices and the regulation or
prohibition of exports and imports.[16] Law N⁰ 12,139, standardiz-
ing internal taxation, in practice represented "a powerful contribution to the abolition of municipal autonomy by the federal government"[17] and also favored well-known antinational interests. Thus,

for example, "abolishing the power of the Mendoza and San Juan provincial governments to tax wine, and that of the Tucumán, Salta, and Jujuy provincial governments to tax sugar, furnished permanent organic bases for strengthening of the trusts trading in these noble products."[18] The voices usually raised in defense of an outworn federalism merely muttered some weak arguments and the law was passed, thus forging another link in the invisible chain that bound the interests of an oligarchical local minority to the imperialist metropolis.

Approval of the "Coordination of Transportation" bill was a foregone conclusion when a deputy such as Carlos A. Pueyrredón could assert during the congressional debate that:

> If the railroads, which are the structural base for the whole transportation system of the country, are not protected by adequate legislation that will place them on a level of equality with the other means of transportation, it will be difficult to acquire new capital, their development will be hampered, and their progress consequently will be brought to a standstill.[19]

British capitalists welcomed with satisfaction the victory their local representatives had achieved vis-à-vis the headlong advance of North American imperialism which backed highway transportation. Palacios confirmed these facts in the Senate when he stated that:

> I can cite a personal experience to show that the laws now being debated would benefit only foreign capital established in the Argentine Republic. The speech I delivered in this Senate on 2 August 1936, in order to record my protest against the intervention of the British government and diplomatic corps in favor of the laws we are considering, was summarized in the great London daily *The Times* [3 August, 1936]. A footnote was appended for the information of the readers: "The coordinating laws to which the Argentine legislator refers have for their purpose the protection of the railroads and street-cars of Buenos Aires, in which much British capital is invested."[20]

The railroads and street-cars were protected.

In two other basic sectors of the economy, oil and electricity, the imperialist impact was also felt. The process has been studied in detail and, given the nature of the present work, there is no point in going over it again.[21] The venality and corruption brought to light in the 1936 proceedings for extending the ordinances regulating the Argentine Electrical Company (CADE) and the Italian-Argentine Electrical company (CIADE) were displayed by both Conservatives and Radicals, after the latter had given up abstention and forgotten their Yrigoyenist tradition. Only the Socialist block of councilmen (together with one or two Progressive Democrats and José Penelón of *Concentración Obrera*) upheld the principles of national sovereignty. FORJA also carried out an in-depth analysis of the problem and every day had less to do with the Marcelo T. de Alvear brand of Radicalism.

The nationalistic Gen. Enrique Mosconi was no longer directing the Argentine Government Oil Company (YPF); this fact may help to explain the 1937 contracts signed between the YPF, Royal Dutch Shell, Standard Oil Company (the latter participated in this because of one of those truces that rival imperialist interests sometimes accept in order to solve some common problem) and the smaller companies. "Full direct control of the oil market by the state is relinquished. The YPF ceases to be the executor of the national oil policy to become a mere commercial enterprise, and control of the market passes to a trust made up of the YPF and the private enterprises, a de facto mixed-capital company."[22]

So far we have mentioned various economic proposals that were certain to be implemented under the presidency of General Justo. In order to present a complete picture, it is necessary to mention other aspects of the economic structure of the country.

On the subject of unemployment, for example, at the time the banking laws were being debated, Socialist Deputy José Luis Pena addressed the legislators on the government side as follows:

> This government has been unable to take care of the unfortunate situation of thousands of men who cannot find work and live in shanties along the railroad tracks, no one knows how; this government has not come up with a program to alleviate the unfortunate plight of this enormous mass of workers, yet this same government has conceived a plan to improve the situation of a few privileged people.[23]

Over a year earlier — in 1933 — the executive branch had sent to Congress a bill creating the National Unemployment Board. In the preamble to this bill it was stated that:

> According to these figures [the census made by the National Labor Department] the total of unemployed in the whole country amounted to 333,997, but disregarding partially and seasonally unemployed, it is evident that true unemployed amount to 263,265, that is, approximately 2.40 percent of the total population.[24]

The industrialization then under way was going to require cheap labor, very cheap labor if possible, and a discreet number of unemployed on the market might help to maintain wages at low levels. This was true in the urban and industrial centers. In the "poor" (at the time the euphemistic term "underdeveloped" had not yet been coined) provinces the situation was equally desperate. Again we quote Palacios:

> There was always the same ominous word: hunger. Hunger, gentlemen, in those regions where the true Argentine people are found, the native leaven, the spiritual reserves of our country. Argentine hunger vis-à-vis the meat packers, who despoil the small producers and enrich themselves increasingly through exorbitant profits, vis-à-vis foreign capitalism that knows no fatherland and has no soul. This distressing situation has never merited as prolonged and passionate a debate as the one we have just finished. Where are the plans, the proposals to improve the living conditions of the people who constitute the very foundation of our nation? We are all guilty and no one should try to evade his responsibility.[25]

Certain regions of the country were beginning to feel the impact of industrialization, with its most important effects: internal migrations, concentration in a few sections (in the provinces of Buenos Aires, Santa Fe, Córdoba, Entre Ríos, and Corrientes), concentration in large industrial establishments, and adjustment to new living conditions. But in other regions — in the Northwest, for example — the opposite was true. David Efron, an author who has studied the subject, gives us this view of the situation:

> With the exception of the sugar-producing districts of Tucumán, Salta, Jujuy, and some small and isolated agricultural zones in La Rioja, Catamarca, and Santiago del Estero, the Argentine Northwest constitutes, from the economic point of view, one of the most backward and abnormal regions of the country. From the social point of view, the region is characterized by extreme maladjustment and poverty that cry out for immediate help. There are many districts in which a semifeudal land and labor structure places serious obstacles in the way of rational use of the resources. In other regions this situation is aggravated by adverse natural conditions.[26]

Table 5 shows the figures for this deplorable situation.

TABLE 5: INDUSTRIAL RETRACTION, 1914-1935

Province	Number of Plants			Personnel (Blue and White Collar Workers)		
	1914	1935	Net Change	1914	1935	Net Change
Santiago del Estero	624	301	-323	7,919	3,303	-4,616
La Rioja	1,101	156	-945	3,906	1,401	-2,505
Tucumán	789	693	-96	15,159	11,070	-4,089
Salta	2,297	241	-2,056	6,312	4,501	-1,811

Source: Adolfo Dorfman, "La industria argentina através del último censo industrial" *Revista de Ciencias Económicas* (Buenos Aires), *April 1939.*

However, if we consider the country as a whole, the situation appears very different because of the industrial increase in some privileged zones. Table 6 shows the improvement attained in the years 1935-37, in comparison with the 1914-35 period.

Adolfo Dorfman explains that industrialization was already vigorously developing the the mid-1930s because of the following: (1) decrease of Argentine exports, both in value and tonnage; (2) devaluation of the currency; (3) increase of import duties beginning in 1931 (especially by 10 percent surcharge, which by itself accounted for two-thirds of customs revenue); (4) government regulations of imports, to adjust them to the level of Argentine exports; (5) the existence of a plentiful, cheap, and skilled labor force; (6) the existence of a relatively important consumer market (to the extent that it gave rise to certain industries); (7) the existence of certain developed auxiliary industries (certain raw materials, manufacture of industrial machinery, etc); (8) the dismantling of plants in the more developed countries such as the United States, that left inactive valuable plants that had to be put to use elsewhere; (9) conditions in those countries conducive to the export of capital and technicians available because of the business and unemployment crisis; (10) the greater profit expected from industrial activity in an economically under-developed country that allowed the use of a lower proportion of fixed capital; and (11) the need to adjust production to the tastes of the consumer in order to be able to offer him welcome flexibility.

[Around 1940] most Argentine . . . manufacturing produced consumer goods. Even automobile plants limited themselves to assembling imported parts and those making machinery worked

TABLE 6: CHANGES IN INDUSTRIAL ACTIVITIES IN ARGENTINA, 1914-37

	1914	1935	1937	Increase 1914-35	Increase 1935-37
Plants	39,200	40,600	49,300	1,400	8,700
Labor Force	383,000	590,000	734,000	207,000	144,000
HP electric motors	86,000	517,000	630,000	431,000	113,000
HP primary motors (not using electric energy)	202,000	483,000	555,000	281,000	72,000
Value raw materials in millions of pesos	1,082	1,964	2,881	882	917
Value product in millions of pesos	1,823	3,458	4,708	1,635	1,250
Value added in millions of pesos	741	1,496	1,927	755	431

Source: Adolfo Dorfman, "El desarrollo de la industria argentina" Cursos y conferencias, Year X, Nos! 1 - 2 - 3, April - May - June 1941, p. 129.

cast iron also brought from abroad. There was no heavy industry, which is the very blood of the industrial life of more developed countries.[27]

A majority of the internal migrations were channeled into those industries, most of which were concentrated in and around the city of Buenos Aires, and, to a lesser extent, along the northeastern part of the country. Table 7 provides supporting evidence regarding the movement of internal migrants as of 1947. This process had started prior to World War II and grew significantly between 1943 and 1947.

TABLE 7: PLACE OF RESIDENCE OF ARGENTINE MIGRANTS, 1947

Region	Percentage of Migrants
Buenos Aires Metropolitan area	50.4
Northeastern Provinces	27.8
Northwestern Provinces	7.6
Central and Western Provinces	4.3
North-Central Provinces	5.6
South	4.3

Source: Gino Germani, Estructura social de la Argentina (Buenos Aires: Raigal, 1955), p. 63.

In the 1931-40 period immigration from abroad reached its lowest levels since the 1860s. The net inflow, after making allowance for those leaving Argentina, is indicated in table 8.

TABLE 8: INFLOW OF IMMIGRANTS INTO ARGENTINA, 1857-1954

Period	Net Population Gain
1857-1860..	11,100
1861-1870	76,600
1871-1880	85,100
1881-1890	637,700
1891-1900	319,900
1901-1910	1,120,200
1911-1920	269,100
1921-1930	878,000
1931-1940	72,200
1941-1946	33,000
1947-1954	747,000

Source: Germani, *Estructura social,* p. 82.

If we look into the average yearly inflow of migrants (both Argentines and. foreigners) into the Buenos Aires metropolitan area, between the years 1895 and 1947, as indicated in table 9, the growing preference for this part of the country is clearly documented.

TABLE 9: AVERAGE YEARLY INFLOW OF INHABITANTS (NATIONALS AND FOREIGNERS) INTO THE BUENOS AIRES METROPOLITAN AREA, 1895-1947

Period	Net Average Yearly Inflow
1895-1936	8,000
1936-1943	72,000
1943-1947	117,000

Source: Germani, *Estructura social,* p. 76.

At that time various bills were presented dealing with the decrease of inflow from abroad (specifically from Europe). One bill was sponsored by Conservative Deputies Carlos A. Pueyrredón, Aquiles M.

Guglialmelli, Adrían C. Escobar, Daniel Amadeo y Videla, Rogelio J. Solís, and Dionisio Schóo Lastra. The first section provided that: "Immigration of foreigners seeking work or coming to occupy salaried jobs or offices is prohibited for a term of five years," though the preamble (written by Pueyrredón) qualified this by stating that "I wish to leave on record that the prohibition I propose arises not from their being foreigners, but from their being unemployed."[28] When Ernesto Sammartino introduced a draft resolution in 1938, he referred to this subject in the following terms:

Our 1876 immigration law, instead of being improved or complemented by a basic settlement law, has been vitiated and impaired by restrictive decrees and regulations opposed to the vital interests of the country and to the express provisions of the Constitution. Among such restrictive measures are the decree of 16 December 1930, imposing new duties or fees on the consular processing of the documents of immigrants; the decree of 26 November 1932, directing consular agents abroad to discontinue issuing landing permits and visas to immigrants not having a fixed destination and occupation, something the government tries not to give them, as though immigration concerned only the immigrants and not the country; the decree of 17 October 1936, prohibiting the entrance into the country of any person who might constitute a danger to the physical and moral health of the population or who might conspire against the stability of the institutions created by the national Constitution.[29] [See table 10]

The interests opposing immigration sometimes betrayed another attitude, as when the journal *Criterio* in an editorial entitled "The Wild Beast" made a reference to Jews: "We uphold the right to protect ourselves, to limit the entrance into the country of a race that does not adapt to ours . . ."[30] Once again we quote Dorfman's analysis of workers' wages; these were the workers whose wages were suppoed to be protected by prohibiting the entrance of foreign workers into the country, as we have seen above:

Taking into account the cost of living, we arrive at a figure for the real wage of the industrial workers showing that it has suffered a marked decline in the last decade. The cost of living in the most privileged spot in Argentina, the city of Buenos Aires, has gone from 100 in 1933 to 120 at the present time (mid-1940). The real salary index of 100 in 1929, and about the same in 1935, varies between 96 and 97 in 1938-39 and is perhaps down to 90-92 at present.[31]

If the conditions described above held true in Buenos Aires, consider what must have been the conditions of rural employment in zones with a very low consumption level, what this situation meant in the sugar, *mate*, and cotton plantations (and in some cases still means today). This will give a general idea of the difficult labor situation in those days, not to mention work in the ubiquitous meat-packing plants and the repeated complaints brought by their workers year after year because of the unbearable conditions.

The regional concentration factor we have already mentioned must be added to the above. This allowed the entrepreneur to obtain, in view of the situation in the rest of the country we have outlined, an efficient and cheap labor force. The case of the textile industry is quite significant. According to the 1935 Industrial Census, this industry employed 80,000 workers who made up about 17 percent of the total Argentine labor force. Therefore, the maximum concentration around the federal capital and environs represented a total of 87 percent of the textile production of the country and ". . .92 percent of the country's textile workers are found within a radius of 20 kilometers from the Argentine Congress Building."[32]

TABLE 10: FOREIGNERS ENTERING AND LEAVING ARGENTINA:
1928-1937

Years	First Class			Second and Third Class		
	Entered	Departed	Net Change	Immigrants	Emigrants	Net Change
1928	11,328	9,330	+1,998	129,047	54,262	+74,785
1929	11,603	9,783	+1,820	140,086	58,357	+81,729
1930	11,395	9,268	+2,127	124,006	59,734	+64,272
1931	8,589	7,024	+1,565	56,333	53,677	+ 2,656
1932	6,359	5,641	+ 718	31,267	43,386	−12,119
1933	7,296	6,147	+1,149	24,345	35,066	−10,721
1934	8,753	7,073	+1,680	27,554	27,104	+ 450
1935	9,853	8,693	+1,160	35,006	19,844	+15,162
1936	12,073	10,372	+1,701	35,560	17,328	+18,232
1937	12,756	11,321	+1,435	41,469	14,303	+27,166

Source: Argentine Chamber of Deputies, *Diario de Sesiones,* 14 July 1938 session, p. 769.

Bearing all this in mind, it will not seem strange that because of these favorable circumstances the corporations quoted on the Argentine Stock Market showed high profits for those years and saw the amount of capital devoted to stock market operations increase, as table 11 indicates.

TABLE 11: CAPITAL INVESTED IN THE ARGENTINE STOCK MARKET 1927-1937

Years	Millions of Argentine Pesos
1927	622
1928	690
1929	658
1930	605
1931	546
1932	423
1933	672
1934	803
1935	883
1936	1,250
1937	1,420

Source: Revista de Economía Argentina, Year 9, No. 237, March 1938, p. 81.

Over and above the partial explanations we have touched upon in this section, there stands the vital fact that Argentina had from 1869 (date of the first national census) to 1947 (fourth national census) changed from a rural to a predominantly urban country, with all the consequences that that change entails (see table 12). The period of Justo's presidency saw the process begin to accelerate that was to reach its peak in the 1940s.

The country was taking great strides toward industrialization (the war in 1939-45 helped the process by reducing imports), the "twilight oligarchy"[33] controlled the basic resources of the economy and of finance as representatives of British imperialism, while American imperialism awaited its turn, soon to come. The resources of the state were used to benefit the privileged, as we have indicated above, and this "liberal" interventionism seemed to help solve the internal and external crises of the system. For how long? Many years ago Arturo Frondizi summed it all up as follows:

TABLE 12: URBAN AND RURAL POPULATION, 1869-1947

Census Year	Total Urban	Rural	Percentage Urban	Rural	Total Yearly Increase Urban	Rural	Average Percentage Yearly Increase Urban	Rural
1869	492,600	1,244,300	28	72				
1895	1,488,200	2,466,700	37	63	38,000	47,000	4.63	2.30
1914	4,152,400	3,727,900	53	47	140,000	66,000	5.55	2.18
1947	9,932,100	5,961,700	62	38	175,000	68,000	2.67	1.43

Source: Gino Germani, Estructura social de la Argentina, p. 67.

(1) The juridical forms of the economy evolve slowly when an equilibrium is maintained in socioeconomic relations; (2) Each economic group protects its own interests without abiding by principles, since it accepts state intervention when the latter means protection, while refusing such intervention when the same means limitation, even of its own excesses; (3) A type of economic policy and its accompanying juridical framework is quickly abandoned under pressure of certain economic situations; (4) Some dominant economic forms live and develop within different legal frameworks; (5) Juridical evolution by itself, while it contributes to diminishing the gravity of some socioeconomic problems, does not imply a fundamental solution of the same, as long as the relationship of the social forces regulated by the laws is not modified. [34]

Political aspects

The period between 1932 and 1938 was notable for fraud under all its guises: "patriotism" was not the only mask it wore. The facts themselves were disgraceful and they were publicized in Congress by the repeated charges brought during the examination of the credentials of legislators whose legitimacy was in doubt. Interventions of the provinces were common when it was desired to circumvent any possibility of free expression of the popular will: those carried out in the province of Buenos Aires (Manuel A. Fresco was elected governor in an election that followed the intervention) and in Santa Fe (against the Progressive Democrat government of Luciano Molinas) may serve as examples.

Leaving aside value judgments, Rodolfo Moreno presents the situation with conceptual clarity:

The emotional climate in the country has changed: the popular mass that on 6 September 1930 surrounded the revolutionary government and gave the impression that the defeated bureaucracy had disappeared forever from political life seems to be shifting its posture in order to return to its former demagogic loves; in so doing, it threatens to restore the already defeated system, with all that it implies.

The forces in power feel the approach of danger and resort to measures forbidden by law in order not to lose their positions. Distinguished and patriotic citizens, some of whom were politicians, some not, representatives of business, banking, and industry, of various Conservative factions with different origins and objectives, prelates, military men, law and order people in general, *claim it is imperative that they protect themselves and at all costs uphold the government positions.*[35]

In view of this, it is not surprising to read Moreno's subsequent statements on the inadvisability of the secret ballot, which "tends not to educate democracy, but to corrupt it," and on the need to control political parties: "There is no doubt that among us great parties are lacking and that the organic body of laws for the purpose of governing them is also lacking." It also explains his desire for the future transformation of the Senate, in order to "organize it as a representative of the country's interest groups in an intellectual and productive sense."[36]

Since the capital city of Buenos Aires had a margin of electoral honesty greater than that in the provinces, the mathematical forecasts for the whole country did not fail to take into consideration a possible opposition victory in Buenos Aires. Because of this and because there were a few opposition legislators in Congress, it was possible to give the impression (particularly outside the country) of a certain political maturity, a certain status as a representative democracy. Of course, the situation in other districts such as Tucumán was significantly different. José Luis Torres has left us this record of the situation:

There, those who controlled the wealth also controlled the government. And the province was governed, no matter what the party label, by the merchants and for the merchants, who always subordinated political principles to their individual business interests, with complete disregard for the public interest and with professed contempt for the life of the humble workers, whose existence was held in less regard than that of the beasts of burden. There, the oligarch controlled all the resources of public life. The legislatures were always made up of the most obsequious employees of the mill owners affiliated with the

various parties, who after the electoral scramble joined together
to vote for the laws prepared by the loyal servants of the
masters, or even by the masters themselves. The latter were then
appointed national senators, naturally according to what had
previously been decided by the Sugar Producers' Association,
where the high posts were apportioned; the deputies who said
they represented the people of Tucumán in the federal Congress
were also selected, before the party conventions took place, by
the owners of the mills; those officials who because of the importance of their duties in the courts or in public administration
needed the approval of the provincial Senate in order to fill
their posts, had, first of all, in order to be nominated, to give
clear proofs of subservience to the oligarchy, and then had to
produce results in order to stay in their positions. In this way,
not only the laws, but even executive and court decisions were
closely adapted to the business interests of the powerful and
these interests were never restricted within the framework of
the laws, even though the laws were always manufactured to
please the powerful.[37]

Without naming them, Torres sketches the portraits of parliamentary figures such as Deputy Simón Padrós or Senator Robustiano Patrón Costas, who defended as though they were their own
(they were) the interests of the provincial sugar mills. Tucumán
was not the only place where all this happened.

Not all those in Congress occupied their seats rightfully. Some
did so through fraud, others because the strong Radical party
abstained; the fact is that there were more congressmen than really
needed.

Verbal exchanges and mutual recriminations (especially between Conservatives and Socialists) were commonplace. For example:

Solari (Juan A.): We can understand that the deputies belonging to the Conservative Right may feel a lively and real admiration for the events of the 6th of September. They constitute a
political party that has intervened directly or indirectly in those
events and has reached the government as a result of the
same. . .

Solano Lima (Vicente): . . . We are not interested in the opinions
of the Socialist sector on the events of the 6th of September.
They hold a special place within Argentine politics: they have
grown at the expense of the revolution, they have reaped some

of the benefits accruing from the fact that in this country we have unfortunately had a defeated party, though it was not defeated by us but by its own defects and its own responsibilities. [38]

The truth is that the functions of the opposition in Congress implied, whether they wished it or not, an aspect of collaboration with the government that had come into being through fraud and the abstention of an important political force. Nicolás Repetto acknowledged this at a Socialist party meeting held toward the end of 1932:

We participated in the general elections of 8 November of last year and we have collaborated with the government consecrated or, rather, imposed by those elections, because in that way, rather than by abstention or revolution, we hoped to overcome the serious difficulties of the moment in order gradually to achieve the institutional normalization and political pacification of the country. *We must confess that the fruit of our collaboration does not satisfy us.* [39]

Until those members of the Radical party who had already adopted a stance of open electoral participation were incorporated into the Congress, the functions of the opposition had devolved on the Socialist and Progressive Democrat members, who descended to their own rightful levels when they did not benefit from the consequences of the Radicals' abstention. They were never again to have the numerical strength they enjoyed in the first years of Justo's presidency, except in their ephemeral flowering in the 7 July 1963 elections, due above all to the proportional representation system used at that time. Américo Ghioldi offered another version of the collaboration theme in 1935:

We are not part of an opposition sector or party. We do not understand the opposition to mean constantly and permanently opposing the work of the men in control of the government. We have demonstrated throughout our nearly forty years' existence as a party and our twenty-three years in congressional activity that the Socialist party rises above the outworn concept of the term opposition and at all times knows how to allow necessary action to proceed without interruption, protecting its prestige as a party and always leaving the seed of an idea to germinate when the environment becomes propitious. [40]

Socialist Deputy Rogelio L. Ameri in 1936 painted a somewhat less idyllic picture:

What has happened to the country since the 6th of September? I must confess, since deeds are more eloquent than words, that that event produced a general sensation of relief. But what came afterwards? . . . We are undergoing a dictatorship; elections were held and the decision of the ballot-box was ignored; Santa Fe was intervened without any reason; student and worker harassment was started and still continues; press and speech censorship was imposed; and even radio broadcasting (that magnificent expression of technical progress) is used only to flatter the ears of office-holders with words pleasing to them, but is closed to the expression of the opinion of men who are in the opposition. We witnessed that great national disgrace that was the murder committed in the Senate; and we come to these elections with the knowledge that besides reducing our political rights, those few freedoms that can still be enjoyed on election day, the attempt is being made to eliminate the voting booth, to adopt qualified voting, to *make fascist* our institutions and cut liberty to shreds.[41]

The Federal Police's Special Bureau seems to have become a regular appendage of the Interior Ministry during the last decades of Argentine political life, although its name has been changed from time to time. That "Special Bureau for the Repression of Communism," as it was originally called, prompted a request for information by Socialist Deputy Luis Ramiconi. In justifying his request, Ramiconi stated that:

I said at the beginning, referring to my fellow party member Nemirowsky, that the prisoners at the Villa Devoto prison do not question certain punishments; they take slaps and kicks for granted. The Villa Devoto prisoners complain only in serious cases of torture. In the presence of two federal deputies, four lawyers, and the prison authorities, those prisoners have accused the Special Bureau of burning their fingers, crushing their fingers with presses, placing lighted cigarettes in their nostrils, beating their heads brutally with a copy of a thick edition of Marx's *Das Kapital* . . . forcing them to swallow pamphlets edited by Communist or non-Communist organizations, it does not matter which, Mr. President. I, who have heard these accusations, cannot but bring them to the floor of this Chamber.[42]

A note by Minister of the Interior Leopoldo Melo in answer to the request for information reads in part as follows:

I must explain that in view of the training of the personnel, of the discipline that is in effect within the police force, of their understanding of their respective duties, and in view of the severity with which any fault or omission in the service is sanctioned, any possibility of torture or harsh treatment must absolutely be ruled out. Such accusations are a well-known device suggested by the Red International Assistance as a propaganda means. [43]

What is undoubtedly a "well-known device" is that employed by lawyer Melo; he answers by denying the facts through appeals to good manners, to training and morality; he does not offer to prove the truth of his statements *(magister dixit)* and follows up with charging the victims themselves with the responsibility for the tortures, or, according to Melo, charging those who *pretended* they were tortured. Their accomplices would of course be their defense attorneys: Enrique Corona Martínez, Nydia Lamarque, José Peco, Rodolfo Aráoz Alfaro, José Katz, and others, those "professionals who according to the police report form part of the legal aid organized in this capital by the Red International Assistance." Business as usual and let Congress continue to attend to its legislative functions.

Political violence reached new heights. At a public gathering in the city of Córdoba, unknown persons assassinated the Socialist Deputy José Guevara (1933). In many sectors there was heated discussion concerning the criminals' connection with high official circles. On 28 June, 1932 in the city of Curuzú-Cuatiá in Corrientes Province, "cowardly aggressors protected by the police and the government"[44] shot to death Maj. Regino P. Lascano, an Yrigoyenist, while he was on a mission assigned to him by the head of the current Radical conspiracy, Lt. Col. Atilio Cattáneo. But the most notorious crime of the decade was the assassination of Senator-elect Enzo Bordabehere during the 23 July 1935 session, at the very height of the meat debate. Ramón Valdéz Cora, a professional killer who had been following the debate for some time, was the actual assassin, but the responsibility for the crime involved individuals high in government circles for whom the president of the Republic vouched. It was never made clear what part had been played in the affair by Minister of Agriculture Luis Duhau, or by his private secretary, Ernesto Duggan, or by two witnesses — out of the 180 who testified — with prodigious imaginations, who declared they had seen Bordabehere, *gun in hand,* struggling with Duhau, something that had escaped the attention of all the others present. This cause célèbre resulted in a petition, sponsored by Radical and Progressive Democrat deputies and presented at the 5 August 1937 session, that malfeasance charges be brought against Federal Judge Miguel L. Jantus. The evidence on file in the case adjudicated by Judge Jantus provides a clear view of how it is possible for the judicial process to come to a halt. [45]

In 1936, when the repercussions of the outrage had not yet died down, a young Radical deputy, Ernesto Sammartino, pointed an accusing finger at that embodiment of sangfroid, President Justo:

A few hours after Dr. Bordabehere had been barbarously slain on the floor of the federal Senate (an unprecedented deed that shook the nation, but did not have the results it would have had in a country with greater culture and greater democratic sensitivity than ours, where such an event would have caused the immediate fall of the government and would have sent the crowds into the streets to determine those morally responsible for the crime) a few hours after this deed, the president of the Republic occupied his box in the Colón Theater with an impassive countenance, in this manner trying to prove a courage he had not had occasion to display up to then, and, thank God, also his old, but still virgin, sword as a general of the nation. [46]

President Justo also assumed the responsibility for the decree intervening the province of Santa Fe after the end of the ordinary session of Congress and after the meat bill had been approved by the Senate (29 September 1935). In this connection, Minister of the Interior Leopoldo Melo acted as his legal advisor. Melo,

... not lacking some presidential aspirations, lent himself to the maneuver. This explains how a citizen who had throughout his life been ostensibly respectful of provincial autonomy; how a citizen who had drawn up a bill in which it was stipulated that such interventions were the exclusive prerogative of Congress; how a citizen who had more than once served as a counterpoise against the impulsive conduct of the executive branch, suddenly emerged as the leader of the attack against the autonomy of Santa Fe Province.[47]

Though this intervention was carried out under the pretext of abstruse legal questions connected with the validity of the 1921 provincial constitution, its true short and long-range objectives were, first, to bring the district over to the *Concordancia* by securing a loyal governor for the province (former Interventor Manuel

M. de Iriondo would become such a governor) and suitable national legislators, and then to make sure of the presidential electors
for future elections. By implication, the measure struck at de la
Torre, the leader of the Progressive Democratic party in Santa Fe
Province. Federico Pinedo gives an authoritative opinion that turns
out to be surprisingly candid:

> The loss of Córdoba Province by the Democrats and the coalition
> in the gubernatorial elections immediately preceding the presiden-
> tial elections was what gave significance and scope to the federal
> intervention in Santa Fe Province in 1935, to which I have re-
> ferred before *and which I shall not try to justify even though I
> may bear responsibility in connection with the legislative "half
> sanction" on which it appeared to be based and with the decrees
> by which it was approved.* I refuse to accept the claims of the
> legend special interests have tried to propagate that the adminis-
> tration Santa Fe had at that time was in any way prodigious;
> but *I do not hesitate to acknowledge that that province,* then
> governed by political opponents of the National Government,
> *had, in my judgment, although others have denied it, a local
> government as good as other good provincial governments then
> in existence,* outstanding among wich were those considered by
> general public opinion respected and progressive administra-
> tions, such as the Radical government of Entre Ríos Province
> and the Democratic governments of Córdoba and Mendoza Pro-
> vince.[48]

In one of his letters de la Torre confesses that:

> My candidacy to the governorship (a candidacy I had such good
> reasons for not wishing to accept) was the main reason for the
> attack. Aside from the hatred they have felt for me since the
> meat debate, it would seem that they attached fantastic signifi-
> cance to the fact that I had that theater of action for my activi-
> ties. And I was so unaware of any such significance.[49]

When the controlled elections of 21 February 1937 took place,
the Alvear Radicals still (still!) trusted that Justo, the great elector, would ensure fair play and went to the polls expecting a favorable result. The Progressive Democrats knew that they were already defeated by a carefully prepared and fraudulent political
plan. De la Torre himself, who had shortly before resigned his seat
in the Senate, again confesses that:

Your impression that the Progressive Democratic party did not try hard to get voters out in the 21 February elections is correct. I myself did not take the trouble to go to Rosario to vote. Countless friends did the same, being full of indignation because of the farce being perpetrated; as the poll watchers were driven from the polling places, abstention was declared.[50]

The intervention of Buenos Aires Province was the starting point for the process that secured the governorship of that state for Manuel Fresco, a physician who had long been in the service of the British railroads and did not feel there was any incongruity between that post and his professed sympathy toward the Italian Duce. This intervention and the bizarre incidents that led to the impeachment of the then governor, Martínez de Hoz, a traditional Conservative, together with the "reform of the electoral law carried out to legalize a priori the formidable fraudulent plan being prepared"[51] made possible an episode of a corporative and fascist cast with Argentine overtones. Félix Luna writes that "of his [Fresco's] government it may be said that it was full of ostentation and violence: religious instruction was imposed by decree, the electric cooperatives were persecuted, gambling was legalized, and the administration was characterized by systematic intimidation.[52] Fresco's end was distressing, though less permanently so than that of his much admired Mussolini: another federal intervention during the presidency of Roberto M. Ortiz removed him from office.

The "systematic intimidation" of Buenos Aires Province which Luna describes was also felt in the rest of the country under various guises and carried out by various agents. The persecutions of "communists" (the quotes are used to indicate the latitude in this term's use which has persisted during later periods) were common occurrences. The Special Bureau grew and included among its chores surveillance of students and laborers, who were subjected to torture and illegal arrest. But even court proceedings violated basic guarantees. The criminal proceedings against Héctor P. Agosti are a case in point that show the passion and zeal employed in carrying out the slogans of the day. On top of the irregularities of the trial itself, defense attorney Peco was subject to a sanction which certainly is not included in the Argentine Criminal Code; he was fired from his teaching position at the Law School of the University of Buenos Aires . . . because he had carried out his professional duties. We were truly in the *days of the republic.*

The zeal for legalistic procedures led to revival and debate in 1936 of a forgotten bill for the control of communism that Senator Sánchez Sorondo had sponsored. Lisandro de la Torre once more (for the last time) confronted the arrogance of that "orator notorious for his bad taste, who covers with bombastic phrases his lack of ideals."[53] De la Torre answered the swollen periods of Sánchez Sorondo ("We believe in the virtue of this law; but if that were not enough — it must be enough — we must seek efficacious remedies for the supreme defense of society, even though for this purpose we may have to declare the necessity of putting the Republic on a war footing! ")[54] by an analysis he had made of the situation, throughout which the Santa Fe legislator's traditional respect for the concept of freedom of thought is evident. Senators Eduardo Laurencena and Alfredo Palacios supported him though they were not so effective as de la Torre. When the bill came to a vote, seventeen voted for approval and four against (de la Torre being absent, Palacios, Laurencena, Atanasio Eguiguren and Mario Bravo voted against the bill).

But the Chamber of Deputies refused to consider the bill and Senator Sánchez Sorondo looked to other latitudes for a climate more propitious to his anti-communist zeal, ". . . invited by his Excellency Signor Mussolini to visit Italy, and by General don Francisco Franco to travel through the areas of Spain under his command."[55]

Congress debated, debated at great length, and after 1936 (and until 1938) its level of productivity went down. The Radical party interrupted its prolonged abstention on 3 January 1935 and took part in provincial and national elections. The Party was able to elect the governor of Entre Ríos and the Amadeo Sabattini-Alejandro Gallardo team (1936-1940) defeated the Conservative candidate, José Aguirre Cámara, in Córdoba. Sabattini became the exemplar of the good administrator, of the honest functionary in a country that had patiently endured embezzlement, bribery, misappropriation of funds, and other forms of fraud for so many years. In the Congressional elections, the Radical party won many seats. Radical members elected to the Buenos Aires City Council took part in the discussion of the concessions to the CADE.

Alvear managed the party machinery with the FORJA young people being practically the only ones who harassed him. Hipólito Yrigoyen had died on 3 July 1933 and popular mourning was sincere. A great political figure had died and with him had passed a whole era and a series of basic positions that require careful analysis. Not until tango singer Carlos Gardel's funeral was another such crowd to be seen. Nicolás Repetto spoke in the Chamber of Deputies, as follows:

> I do not know whether Yrigoyen labored solely for glory or in order himself to enjoy the improvements that he might bring about by his own efforts in the political evolution of the country. For the sake of his honor, I would like to assume the latter. If this be so, it must be admitted that Yrigoyen had the privilege of knowing the greatest satisfaction that a man of his type could aspire to: he helped to overthrow the old oligarchical regime and inaugurated the first government of democratic origin in the country. This single accomplishment is sufficient to secure him an outstanding and lasting place in Argentine history.[56]

The death of the old caudillo and the failure of the Radical uprisings made the efforts of the *concurrencistas* easier. None of the uprisings achieved their objectives. That of the Kennedy brothers before Justo became president (January 1932) failed, as did the frustrated revolution of Lt. Col. Atilio Cattáneo, which inexplicably miscarried in Buenos Aires on 21 December 1932. The interesting history of the latter may be found in the book already mentioned, *Plan 1932*. The revolt led by Lt. Col. Roberto Bosch in the city of Paso de los Libres in 1933 also failed. Arturo Jauretche, the FORJA soldier-poet, sang about this revolt in gaucho stanzas:

> The fatherland is being taken
> by Yankees and Britishers;
> it seems wrong to the people
> but they are not being heard.
> Since Yrigoyen has left us
> the country can't hold its own! [57]

As usual, the disclosure of the various conspiracies brought on arrests and imprisonments, from which not even Yrigoyen had been immune in the last months of his life. Alvear, Pueyrredón, Ricardo Rojas, and other Radical leaders personally experienced the repressive measures instituted by a government that knew how to be strong.

The Radical party, in 1935, was disposed to take part in elections. Del Mazo has explained why:

> The leadership that had favored the raising of the Radical abstention asserted that its program was based on three objectives:
>
> 1) to test the sincerity of the government's insistent invitation

to participate in legislative elections, under a solemn promise of honest elections; 2) to organize a congressional opposition to check the omnipotence and impunity with which the government handled every aspect of federal and provincial administrations; and 3) to begin occupying positions in the deliberative bodies so that when the Radical party took over the national administration in 1938 it would have experienced majorities.[58]

Is there any need to add that none of the three objectives was achieved? "Honest elections" continued to be conspicuous by their absence; "the opposition" ceased to be such; and the Radical party did not take over the "federal and provincial administrations."

In 1936 the Radical deputies bungled an opportunity to uphold what has historically been one of their uncompromising positions, that of demanding free elections, when they agreed after a long interregnum to return to Congress, without considering the problem of the fradulent credentials held by legislators from Buenos Aires Province.[59] The *Concordancia* again interrupted the workings of the legislature in 1937 (the Ortiz-Castillo team had already been elected) when it refused to provide a quorum in the Chamber of Deputies. Américo Ghioldi, who was usually not critical, reproached the government coalition, saying that:

> They are the deliberate, conscious, willing architects of the institutional collapse that for some time has been deliberately provoked. We have a state of subversion in the province of Buenos Aires; the initial fraud in February of this year in the province of Santa Fe; the September presidential fraud; the trafficking in justice; the implication of university people, of men who profess the Catholic religion; the broad panorama of a minority that calls itself a select minority, but about whom we can say that no one will deny they are a minority, but that we all doubt that it is select.[60]

The Alvear brand of Radicalism gradually left behind other traditional Yrigoyenist principles. They seemed to be attempting to play both sides when they drew closer to the Socialist and Progressive Democratic parties in the manner of the "Popular Fronts" then in vogue throughout the world. The Communist party manifested great interest in participating in the movement, but its illegal status aroused the apprehension of the other groups' leaders. A public gathering took place on 1 May 1936 at which Repetto reports representatives of the General Confederation of Labor, of the Radical party, of the Socialist party, and of the Progressive Democratic party spoke.[61] The parties Repetto has dubbed "legalitarian" also held a joint meeting, on 22 August 1936, to reaffirm the concept of free elections (the monument to former President Roque Saénz Peña was being unveiled) and Alvear, de la Torre, Repetto, and Pueyrredón spoke. Interparty contacts did not cease even after the 1937 presidential elections.

Official circles had early begun to consider names for the slates the *Concordancia* was to support at the time of the elections. Julio A. Roca, the vice-president of the country, and the veteran presidential hopeful, Vicente Gallo, who had been rector of the university of Buenos Aires since the middle of 1936, sought agreement between the executive branch and the government forces in Congress. The hopes of various candidates were dashed: those of Leopoldo Melo, for example, because General Justo preferred Roberto M. Ortiz, his minister of the treasury, who had an Antipersonalist Radical background and was held in high esteem by the great British interests (he had been attorney for their railroads). A National Democrat was wanted as the second member of the team: Justo would have favored naming Miguel Angel Cárcano, his minister of agriculture, but when the party demanded that the spot be given to Robustiano Patrón Costas, a deal was made between the two factions, and the beneficiary was Ramón S. Castillo, Justo's minister of the interior, a former judge and dean of the Law School of the University of Buenos Aires.

The Radicals again insisted on Alvear, with Enrique Mosca for his running mate. The Progressive Democrats were not very pleased by the naming of the latter, since as governor of Santa Fe Province (1921) he had vetoed the provincial constitution on which the de la Torre partisans had placed such high hopes. The Socialists chose for their team Nicolás Repetto a~d Arturo Orgaz. The Communists and the short-lived Workers' Socialist party supported Alvear.

Again we quote Pinedo, this time for an opinion on the 5 September 1937 presidential elections: *"The way those elections were conducted,* something for which the former ministers can hardly be blamed, *makes it impossible to include them among the best or the good or even the average elections the country has experienced. . ."*[62]

Félix Luna has stated that:

The government was quite willing to let the opposition rave on. Let the poor creatures give vent to their feelings. . .It was enough that the government had won. At the beginning of October the complete returns were published: the *Concordancia* had won 248 electors as against the 128 for the Alvear-Mosca team. The latter was credited with 815,000 votes as against 1,100,000 for the government. The Radical party had won in the federal capital and in the provinces of Córdoba, Tucumán, and La Rioja. The *Concordancia* had taken the rest of the provinces including Entre Ríos, where the attitude of the Yrigoyenist faction of the Radical party had led to the defeat of the combined Radicals.[63]

Conservative authors (among them the one we have so often quoted as being a participant and an authoritative witness of the events of this period, Federico Pinedo) insist on emphasizing the positive nature of the legislation adopted during the first four years of Justo's administration. Without going into a detailed analysis, but taking into consideration objectively useful measures, such as the extension of the highway network, the introduction of the one-half working day on Saturday, and the improvement of business clerks' working conditions (which were later painstakingly reduced by court decisions that showed no inclination to extend this improvement to other workers), it is impossible to ignore the antinational and antipopular nature of much of the basic legislation passed without hesitation by a subservient Congress. The subject has been dealt with to some extent in the first part of this chapter, and we refer the reader to that account. Between 1936 and the time elections were held the following year "the vigorous and creative phase of Justo's government came to an end."[64] Congress devoted many sessions to electoral disputes (fraud, credentials), but what really mattered was the outcome of the approaching presidential elections. Given the politico-economic conditions existing in the country at the time, the winners could be predicted, and Agustín P. Justo could look forward to a possible return in 1944. Scalabrini Ortiz has said some things that needed saying, and his trenchant remarks of 1937 bear repeating: "In the whole course of Justo's presidency there has not been a single measure born out of a sense of concern for public welfare, a single measure that tended to protect the economy of the nation from foreign rapacity."[65]

Note on international policy

We agree with Sergio Bagú that "the international conduct of a state constitutes an integral part of the national history of the country in question."[66] In the case of Argentina, the truth of this statement is, if possible, more obvious than in others. Also, the international relations of a country such as Argentina make it possible, when a little effort is made to understand them, to observe very clearly the interimperialist struggle and the pressures and maneuvers to which governments are subject on occasion. Justo's term of office signaled for the United States of North America the beginning and gradual development of the Good Neighbor policy practiced by President Franklin D. Roosevelt and Secretary of State Cordell Hull. That policy was to have new applications as a result of World War II.

Cordell Hull's *Memoirs,* covering the period between 1933 and 1944, constitute an essential source for understanding this subject.[67] We will follow these *Memoirs* in writing this section. Hull recalls vividly what happened at the 1928 Pan-American Conference in Havana, where there was a "pyrotechnic clash" between the United States and Argentine delegations over the issue of intervention, and adds: "The statesmen and politicians of Argentina had for some years undertaken to assert leadership of the hemisphere by rallying all possible elements against the United States."[68] At least verbally (during the presidential terms of Yrigoyen no Pan American Conferences were convened and Bagú states that this was not an oversight) [69] Alvear's administration upheld the traditional positions of the old Radical leader.

At other international meetings this was not true to the same extent. At the Pan American Conference in Montevideo in 1933, Hull, who led his country's delegation, and Saavedra Lamas, the Argentine foreign minister, who headed ours, held various personal conferences. Hull mentions that Spruille Braden "of New York, a businessman in Chile,"[70] was among the North American delegates. Ten years later we will meet him occupying more important positions.

According to the American secretary of state, the meetings with Saavedra Lamas were to have positive results in aiding him in his task of spreading the somewhat discredited official doctrine of Pan Americanism. Hull let Saavedra Lamas know that the conference ought to approve two broad resolutions: the first covered a constructive economic program to foster business recovery; the second provided that each delegation present should try to engage its government to sign the five main treaties that would make possible maintaining the peace in the Western Hemisphere.[71] Hull also told Saavedra Lamas that he had prepared drafts of both resolutions, but that he preferred that the Argentine foreign minister should submit the peace proposal because of his acknowledged gifts in the field of foreign relations and because he was known as "an advocate of peace." Hull added: "Of course, if you should not see fit to do so, it will be necessary to select the next most suitable person for this outstanding task."[72] The head of the Brazilian delegation, Afranio de Mello Franco, was the likely candidate.

In less than twenty-four hours, Saavedra Lamas met again with Cordell Hull and accepted his conditions. The draft resolution was only slightly modified and Lamas had already prepared the speech he was going to deliver in the assembly. He added: "And I'll support your economic resolution, although my government is not very favorable to certain portions of it." Cordell Hull, who had chosen his man well, comments that "this last [point] was doubly important because Saavedra Lamas was chairman of the committee in which the resolution would be presented."[73]

The system employed by Hull was neither new nor unpremeditated. Let us see what he has to say:

> ... I firmly believed in the principle that "there are no real triumphs in diplomacy." I felt that true success could come only by inducing our opponents to become our allies *through convincing them that basically our ideas were their ideas.* Occasionally this meant giving statesmen of other countries credit for the ideas I myself entertained. I have already pointed out how, in Congress, I often permitted fellow Members to make use of my ideas and information and christen them with their own names. I transplanted this practice into diplomacy as well. I could have introduced into the conference the peace resolution I had prepared, rather than give it to Saavedra Lamas, and perhaps I could have secured a majority in its favor. But, had I done so, Argentina doubtless would have fought it on some technical ground, and the unanimity it needed would have vanished. I believed it wise in the circumstances for the head of the Argentine delegation to offer it.[74]

With some variants, Federico Pinedo, who was then a deputy, seems to have had a similar method of operating, as he confesses that:

> for this reason ... I adopted a stance of relative resistance that was at the time especially unpopular, but that I believed justified. I was so committed to this that *I took the trouble, in order to avoid gross errors, to draft the bills of the various groups in*

*the Chamber, both of those I intended to vote for and those I
opposed with all my might.* This attitude, which I also adopted
on some other occasions, brought down upon me a long series
of bitter criticisms, but I still believe that there was no foundation for them, since I see nothing wrong in using the legal
knowledge or the writing ability a person may possess to try to
give the best possible legislative expression both to one's own
opinion and to that of others. [75]

To return to the Montevideo Conference, after the trial of
strength between Hull and Saavedra Lamas, everything went very
smoothly. The Argentine foreign minister merely censured "the
transgressions of the United States government in the past" when
referring to nonintervention, and Hull signed the resolution submitted by Saavedra Lamas (which, after all, was his own). The
economic resolution also was approved. Henceforth, Cordell Hull
— he says so himself — was to urge the candidacy of Saavedra
Lamas for the Nobel Peace Prize, until the Argentine foreign minister finally obtained that distinction in 1936. [76]

Disregarding the fighting during the 1932-35 period between
Bolivia and Paraguay because of the magnitude of that armed conflict and because of the interimperialist overtones of the developments in that war (brought to an end by the signing of the Protocol of Buenos Aires on 12 June 1935), we shall make some observations on the "Inter-American Conference for the Maintenance of
Peace" that met in Buenos Aires in 1936. By their presence, President Roosevelt and his secretary of state lent prestige to this conference. Sumner Wells, another important member of the delegation, recalled the great welcome given the North American president on his arrival and during his stay in Buenos Aires, [77] but he
omits any reference to what perhaps provided a discordant note.
We will let the hero of the episode tell the story:

> When the time came, on the day of the solemn opening session
> of the extraordinary conference, at the very moment when the
> president of the United States was about to voice his lie, I felt
> that 150 million Latin Americans, who some day would repeat
> the gesture by other means, were expressing themselves through
> my condemnatory voice, which resounded fully from the gal-
> lery within the locale of the National Congress where the cere-
> mony was being held and was heard clearly by radio throughout
> the length and breadth of the continent. Three words were
> enough then to express all: "Down with imperialism! " And the
> brilliant ceremony was interrupted for an instant.

This was the romantic gesture of a leftist militant using the native pseudonym of "Quebracho." His real name was Liberio Justo, and he was the son of the president of Argentina.[78]

Hull was no romantic and he had no space to devote to mentioning this daring interruption, but he did take care to record his displeasure at the change in Saavedra Lamas's attitude. The latter had "receded from the friendly cooperation he had shown me there [in Montevideo]. This despite the fact that on the day before my arrival at Buenos Aires he had been awarded the Nobel Peace Prize, for which I unofficially had recommended him and virtually managed the movement in his behalf."[79] It is not strange that Hull attributes Saavedra Lamas's behavior to the latter's interest in the League of Nations, which continued to meet in Geneva. After all, Geneva is in Europe. So is Great Britain.

The secretary of state confesses that President Justo, who is "considered to be more or less a dictator and the representative of that section of the population which favored a dictatorship,"[80] supported — or at least did not interfere with — the "obstructive" course of his foreign minister. The results of Saavedra Lamas's reticent attitude were reflected in one of the main agreements signed during the conference. It was desired that the twenty-one American republics agree to consult and collaborate together in the event of a menace to their peace from any source, or in the event of war or virtual state of war between American republics, or if war outside the American continent threatened the peace of the American republics. Hull's comments are not to be missed:

The Monroe Doctrine protected them from dangers overseas, but that doctrine had come to assume in the minds of many of their leaders a connotation of domination of the Western Hemisphere by the United States. Under the new convention, the American Republics took one step in the direction of a hemispheric Monroe Doctrine. We were to go much further at the Pan American Conference at Lima two years later, and at the Havana Conference in 1940. The Argentines, however, were able to emasculate this resolution by inserting four words between two commas in the clause providing that the American Republics, in the event of war outside America which might menace their peace, should consult to determine the proper time and manner in which they might eventually cooperate in some action tending to preserve the peace of the American Continent. The words were, "if they so desire."[81]

O. Edmund Smith, Jr., a specialist on the relatións between the United States and the Latin American republics, confirms Hull's feeling when he summarizes the problem of the Buenos Aires Conference as follows:

The landed oligarchy of Argentina feared that an agreement committing the American republics to adopt a solidary attitude in the event of war outside the hemisphere might result in one or more European powers' taking offense toward the New World community; the *estancieros* were convinced that Argentina's (i. e., their own) best interests could be served only by maintaining friendly relations with all the leading Old World nations.[82]

New Pan American Conferences would take place in years to come. They would provide opportunity to contemplate new diplomatic skirmishes, aggravated by the outbreak of World War II.

3 The Ortiz-Castillo Administration

Roberto M. Ortiz, the ailing president

The year 1938 marked the beginning of the end for the Spanish Republic in its struggle against the fascism of the rebellious generals supported by Adolf Hitler's Germany and Benito Mussolini's Italy and by the culpable indifference the European "democracies" showed with their *no intervention* policy. The republic had only the friendly solidarity of some Latin American countries (with the Mexico of Lázaro Cárdenas in the lead), the heroic romanticism of the Brigades, and the support of the Soviet Union. In this connection, Stalin's attitude has not been studied in depth in relation to Spain; despite the collapse of the cult of personality, only crude pamphlets by defectors or Johnny-come-latelies have been published.

The reference to the Spanish Civil War is not out of place here, since after the beginning of that war the domestic politics of many countries became entangled in international politics. Domestic attitudes toward a given problem or series of problems came to depend on the participants' reaction to the foreign scene. When World War II started, the interrelation of national and international politics became more evident. In Argentina there was much discussion and argument and sides were taken according to the Allied or Nazi sympathies of the moment. To be more accurate, it must be said that this was true of one sector of Argentina. Another sector, that of the working man, especially the industrial worker who was serving his apprenticeship in the capital city metropolitan area, and of the perennially forgotten rural worker, was oblivious to the war except insofar as it affected the basic needs of the sector (scarcity of certain products, for example). Socialist and Communist leaders took refuge in the workers' organizations of the time and these organizations were conscious of foreign problems, but no one is in a position to assert that they were really representative. A massive, vertical, and nation-wide union movement did not come into being until after 1943.

In the years 1938, 1939, and 1940, events overseas affected Argentina. The consequences were to be evident in the diplomatic field and were to intensify in subsequent years. Ortiz came into office on 20 February 1938 and his cabinet was composed as follows: Interior, Diógenes Taboada; Foreign Affairs, José María Cantilo; Treasury, Pedro Groppo; Justice and Public Instruction, Jorge E. Coll; War, Gen. Carlos D. Márquez; Navy, Rear Adm. León L. Scasso; Agriculture, José Padilla; Public Works, Manuel R. Alvarado.[1]

As table 13 shows, the process of industrial growth to which we alluded in the previous chapter continued despite the war; in fact, it increased because of the reduction in imports. New industries started to spring up, requiring more workers, and the old ones increased production. Foreign labor was not available because of the obstacles placed in the way of immigration by the government during the thirties and later because of the effect of what was first a European conflict and then a world-wide one. However, a plentiful supply of labor was available from the interior of the country. These migrants, who had not yet been branded "dark heads,"[2] came to the city in increasing numbers. The political parties and the oligarchical sectors were slow in becoming aware of this movement from the interior; a few years afterwards it was too late.

In discussing the regional distribution of population in Argentina, Dorfman remarks that "there are provinces that inexorably become depopulated and others that languish in a forlorn stagnation that lasts decades. "[3] It is obvious that the process of industrial concentration has much to do with this phenomenon. Table 14 shows the population increase of the ten largest cities in the country (Buenos Aires, Avellaneda, Rosario, Córdoba, Mendoza, and the rest) in relation to the remainder of the country.

If the occupational distribution figures of the economically - active population (both industrial and agricultural) are taken into account, the impressive growth of the industrial workers becomes apparent.

According to Germani, the "disparities in the geographic distribution of the population are the natural result of the internal and external migrations. The northeastern and federal capital regions have received the greatest number of foreign immigrants and at the same time have proved a magnet for those Argentines born in other regions. In fact, it is the latter aspect that has characterized the process in the last two decades."[4] This may be understood as the result of immigration plus normal growth; the figures make it

TABLE 13: INDUSTRIAL ACTIVITY IN ARGENTINA 1935-1943

Year	No. of Plants	Number of Workers	Wages and Salaries Paid by Industry (Absolute Figures) (Millions of Argentine Pesos)[1]	Value of Raw Materials Used (Millions of Argentine Pesos)	Value of the Production (Millions of Argentine Pesos)	Power Used (H.P.)
1935	40,606	590,000	782	1,964	3,458	2,750,000
1937	49,375	730,000	1,001	2,881	4,709	3,048,000
1938	*	760,000[2]	1,046[3]	2,997o	4,900[4]	*
1939	53,927	785,000	1,123	3,002	5,127	3,370,000
1940	*	813,000[2]	1,150[3]	3,100[4]	5,327[4]	*
1941	57,978	918,000	1,285	3,858	6,341	3,603,000
1942	60,500	955,000[2]	1,450[3]	4,550[4]	7,300[4]	*
1943	65,000o	980,000[2]	1,575[3]	5,100[4]	8,100[4]	*

1. Workers, employees, directors and managers, and families of the owners employed in the industry. It excludes craftsmen and those who work in small plants not included in census.
2. Figures based on the occupational indices.
3. Figures based on the salary indices.
4. Figures based on the publications of the Argentine General Bureau of Statistics and Census.
* No data.
o Estimated
Source: Revista de Economía Argentina, Year XXVI, No. 315, September 1944, p. 206.

clear why Ezequiel Martínez Estrada called the capital a "Goliath's Head" in one of his books.

Germani traces the rhythm of migration toward Buenos Aires to a "traditional" centralizing tendency with ancient Hispanic roots and to the universal process of urbanization, without isolating these factors from the political and social history of the country. He continues:

It is important to point out that on the eve of a series of political and social changes that took place from 1943 on, the population of the Buenos Aires metropolitan area was made up of a

TABLE 14: CHANGES IN THE URBAN POPULATION OF ARGENTINA 1869-1939

Year	Ten Largest Cities		Rest of the Country	
	Absolute	%	Absolute	%
1869	300,000	16	1,450,000	84
1895	1,000,000	25	3,000,000	75
1914	2,500,000	31	5,400,000	69
1939	4,400,000	34	8,600,000	66

Source: Adolfo Dorfman, Evolución industrial argentina (Buenos Aires: Losada, 1942), p. 360.

TABLE 15: OCCUPATIONAL DISTRIBUTION OF THE ECONOMICALLY ACTIVE POPULATION OF ARGENTINA 1914-1938

Year	Industrial Workers	Agricultural Workers
1914	1,246,000	880,000
1930	2,156,000	1,137,000
1938	2,600,000	1,050,000

Source: Adolfo Dorfman, Evolución industrial argentina, p. 360.

large proportion of people who had migrated from the interior of the country and had done so very recently.[5]

He estimates that by 1943 the number of persons who had migrated from the interior within the previous ten or eleven years must have amounted to 800,000, a figure that, in his view, represents

a very high proportion if it is considered that these immigrants were especially concentrated within a social class — the working class — and a given age group — adults, or at least those over fourteen years of age. It is perfectly logical to assume that the relatively sudden inflow of this new population mass, having psycho-social characteristics different from those of the long-time city dwellers, may have significantly affected the manner of thinking and acting of the urban masses, especially in the working class sector.[6]

TABLE 16: POPULATION OF BUENOS AIRES METROPOLITAN AREA : 1867-1947

Year	Population	Percentage of Total Population of Country	Total Increase	Annual Increase
1869	225,000	12.9	542,000	21,000
1895	767,000	19.4	1,232,000	65,000
1914	1,999,000	25.4	1,458,000	66,000
1936	3,457,000	26.7	593,000	85,000
1943	4,050,000	27.0	568,000	142,000
1947	4,618,000	28.7	555,000	111,000
1952	5,173,000	28.7		

Source: Gino Germani, Estructura social de la Argentina, p. 74.

This growth of the working class was dimly sensed by some Conservative deputies. Reynaldo Pastor was one of these, but he could not discard his accustomed thought patterns and so wrote in a paternalistic tone that:

> *When our workers become accustomed to have the wealthy, the great industrialists, the high government officials and high-level politicians listen to and show that they are aware of the needs of the workers and thus prove that their minds are open to attempts to solve them,* then so many rebellions will no longer be encouraged and the Argentine worker will realize that he has a noble mission to perform within our society and will be aware that he, too, is a factor for progress, a factor worthy of respect, a factor for work and culture within our country. I say this because I harbor the hope that these words will reach the bosom of some Argentine homes and the conscience of men who may contribute to guiding the present social situation.[7]

Of course, this did not satisfy "our workers." They wearied of sending petitions and memorandums demanding justice to the National Congress and having such justice systematically denied them on all sides. To take only one example, José Peter, secretary general of the Council of the Labor Federation for the Meat Industry, signed a vigorous protest against the inhuman working conditions in the meat packing plants (again the meat packing plants!).[8]

Does it not seem strange that congressional insensitivity was such that it failed to foresee that by a logical reaction the meatpackers would take the lead during the events of October 1945? Their leader then would not be the Communist Peter, but Cipriano Reyes, a union man.[9] Congress did not foresee this change either.

During the years that Ortiz (and later Castillo) occupied the presidency, Congress acquired all the hallmarks of decadent collective bodies. Conservatives and Radicals united to support shameful reports, such as the one on the results of the investigation of electric concessions in the federal capital. The text is an indictment of those who signed it:

> That the study of the background of the discussion and approval of Ordinances Nos. 8,028 and 8,029 does nòt indicate any irregular procedures entailing any legal or moral responsibility on the part of the persons involved in these acts; that the said ordinances, considered as a whole and insofar as their direct and indirect results and effects vis-à-vis the general interest and that

of the consumers are concerned, are advantageous in relation to the legal and de facto conditions existing prior to their approval.[10]

The legislators who concurred in the above opinion were Emilio Ravignani, Faustino Infante, Juan I. Cooke, Ricardo A. Moreno, and Reynaldo A. Pastor.

On 5 January 1939 Lisandro de la Torre had died by his own hand. In a letter to his closest friends (in reality his last will), he wrote:

> I beg you to take charge of the cremation of my body. I do not wish for any public funeral procession, nor any lay or religious ceremony whatever, nor do I wish the curious and the photographers to be allowed to view the body, with the exception of those persons you yourselves may especially authorize. If possible, my body should be deposited today at the Crematorium, and it should be cremated early tomorrow morning, in private. Many good people respect and love me and will sorrow for my death. That is sufficient recompense for me. Excessive importance should not be attached to the final denouement of a life, even though vulgar preoccupations may do so. If you do not disapprove, I would wish my ashes scattered to the winds. It seems to me an excellent way to return to nothingness, commingling with all that dies in the Universe.[11]

The similarity to the will of Luigi Pirandello, another agnostic, is striking.[12] That gentle sorrow, that consciousness of being alone — and strong — like the Ibsen hero in *An Enemy of the People* (whom de la Torre quoted in Congress) — did not abandon de la Torre until he left this world. He was not a builder, he was a man faithful unto himself, even in his errors. In the 1930s his self-sacrifice (and it was a time of suicides: Leopoldo Lugones, Alfonsina Storni, Horacio Quiroga) was perhaps the last warning against the general insensitivity of the milieu. First, World War II, then political events within the nation, in time obscured the memory of his gesture.

Some deputies referred to his death, among them José P. Tamborini, Benjamín Palacio, Plácido C. Lazo, and Ernesto Sammartino. Sammartino did not employ a very felicitous figure of speech when he said that:

> The people who inundate the race tracks, the football fields, and the stadiums and those who spontaneously come together like a tide to do homage to *payadores* and movie stars live deaf

and dumb to the drama and dedication of the worthiest citizens of the Republic, when they do not abandon them to persecution and to the teeth of the mastiffs.[13]

This figure of speech is unfair, and it does not reflect the real situation since Congress is regarded with almost complete indifference by the sectors alluded to, and it is not the fault of the latter.

In the Senate the dull resentment of the Conservatives — evident as much as or more than when Hipólito Yrigoyen died, the other great death of the decade — received in silence the tributes of its representatives. Alfredo Palacios said of de la Torre that he "was the perennial castigator of the demagogic farce that pretends to be democratic; the implacable enemy of those who exercise power without standards or control; of those who proclaim the need to deceive in order to rise."[14] Senator Fernando Saguier, a member of the Buenos Aires Radical party, also spoke. "With Lisandro de la Torre," he said, "the spiritually youngest man the Republic could count upon has disappeared."[15]

Almost from the beginning of his term, President Ortiz had been suffering the effects of a serious illness that brought about first his withdrawal and delegation of powers to Vice-President Castillo, then his resignation as president, and, finally, his death. Two political events marked those first years. One was the intervention of the province of Catamarca — the birthplace of the vice-president — which offended the members of the governmental coalition (Conservatives and Antipersonalists); and the other was the intervention of Buenos Aires Province as a result of the fraudulent February 1940 elections, arranged by Fresco, the retiring governor. Fresco's candidate was Alberto Barceló, the Avellaneda boss, who wished to broaden his field of activity. He succeeded in defeating Antonio Santamarina for the Conservative party nomination, but the intervention frustrated Barceló's aspirations. However, he was eventually able to obtain a Senate seat representing the same district.

These and other factors began to bring groups of Alvear Radicals into line behind Ortiz because of their recurring desire to get into power by playing along with the regime. At that time, Ortiz was considered a democrat who sought to erase the stigma accompanying his own accession to power and to support the right to the secret ballot and clean elections. But in economic and social attitudes and all else that did not relate to the limited subject of suffrage, he was not too different, at least in essentials, from his predecessor Justo. Many years later a Conservative accurately defined President Ortiz's position by saying that "he constituted *a true inclined plane toward Radicalism,* which he openly protected, so much so that he intervened Catamarca Province (among others), the political seat of his own teammate, who was unfairly affronted by this measure, and Buenos Aires Province, which was considered a bulwark of the conservatives."[16] The author's silence as to whether the measures were justified or not is significant. This was not an isolated instance of the institutional problem being reduced to an interparty struggle.

In 1940 Congress devoted much of its time to the affair of the El Palomar lands, which "despite its narrow scope when compared to recent immorality — only a few hundred thousand pesos — implicated even some circles close to the executive branch" (Martín Aberg Cobo).[17] What matters is not the size of the deal nor whether legislators were implicated (one of them committed suicide and the other one was expelled from the Chamber of Deputies), nor whether the sensibilities of the minister of war, General Márquez, and of the president himself were hurt. What matters is that the system allowed such irregularities, that the legislative machinery tolerated such serious faults. All the rest are mere incidents, soon forgotten.

To indicate his displeasure with the findings of the Senate Investigating Committee (Palacios, Gilberto Suárez Lago, and Héctor González Iramain), Roberto M. Ortiz sent his resignation to Congress. At a joint session held on 24 August 1940, over which Senator Robustiano Patrón Costas presided, the government legislators and the opposition vied with each other in extolling the chief executive's keen sense of honor and voted not to accept his resignation. Only one voice was raised in dissent — that of Sánchez Sorondo. In voting to accept the resignation, he explained his stand as follows:

> Here is the dilemma: either the transaction was lawful and the Senate was wrong, or the transaction was unlawful and the Senate was right. If the transaction was lawful, the president of the Republic has the right, he even has the duty, to protect his minister and defend the conduct of his government. But if the transaction was unlawful, the president cannot make a show of solidarity [with the minister] and do the Senate an injustice on the basis of that, and the Congress of this nation cannot accept such solidarity and injustice as the reason for his resignation.[18]

The following remarks by Carlos Ibarguren set the tone for much that was written during this period:

The political and administrative sphere suffered a loss of prestige as a result of episodes that had public repercussions and demonstrated widespread corruption such as the deal for the purchase of the El Palomar lands for the army, in which the state was defrauded of considerable sums of money and in which Radical and Conservative legislators were implicated, the shady dealings in the National Lottery, and other events that indicated the moral crisis existing in political circles.[19]

As it is becoming a commonplace to say in this book, Congress continued to debate about fraud, about anti-Argentine activities (an investigating committee was created which gave some deputies — Juan A. Solari and Raúl Damonte Taborda among them — an opportunity to employ sensationalist methods, reminiscent of the Buenos Aires newspaper *Crítica* when directed by Natalio Botana, to denounce the seriousness of the Nazi infiltration into broad sectors of the life of the nation and to question the credentials of some of its members. For example, the above-mentioned Barceló was investigated in 1942. During this debate, the president of the National Democratic party, Gilberto Suárez Lago, acknowledged that:

We are guilty of grave errors, gentlemen, of grave faults, of grave offenses. Not everything has been clean from 1930 to now in electoral matters. It is not easy to come out of a revolutionary state resulting from the corruption that reached all the spheres of the official life of the nation. Let the country remember this! [20]

Barely twelve years had elapsed and a return to normalcy was not yet possible.

In the 1940 elections the Radicals obtained eighty seats in the lower chamber. But that majority, with very minor exceptions, did not help them and matters continued as before. The loss of prestige suffered by the party (except for some small segments which were attempting a renewal of leadership) led to its 1942 defeat in the federal capital by the Socialists.

"Argentine Action" had been founded in 1940 to bring together the partisans of the European Allies in World War II. Its first Central Executive Board was composed of Juan Carlos Palacios, Raúl C. Monsegur, Federico Pinedo, Jorge Bullrich, Alejandro Ceballos, Alfredo González Garaño, Raúl Moltedo, Julio A. Noble,

Victoria Ocampo, Rafael Pividal, Emilio Ravignani, Nicolás Repetto, Mariano Villar Sáenz Peña,and Juan Valmaggia.[21] The following year, on 22 May 1941, Argentine Action organized an open forum of the organization, which took place in the City Council of the federal capital, in order to discuss subjects related to the war and to the "nazi-fascist infiltration" of the country. The speakers at the opening session were Alvear, Repetto, Bernardo Houssay, and José María Cantilo. As may be observed, contacts between representative figures of the various political parties (and also with independent figures) were frequent. A few years later, these contacts, plus other factors such as the Popular Front strategy of the Communist party, made possible the appearance of the Democratic Union.

However, at that time the political subject most discussed in Congress, in the press, on the street, and everywhere was naturally the illness of the chief executive and the problems that his legitimate succession would entail. He seemed almost a symbol of the "republican times" that were coming to an end. The presence of Castillo signified a direct return of the Conservatives to the administration, and the Radicals had some idea of what this would do to their electoral aspirations. When the vice-president took more or less permanent charge of the executive branch and named a new cabinet (in September 1940), matters seemed to come to a head, even though there is not much evidence of this, and whatever exists seems inconclusive. In one case, Félix Luna speaks of a conspiracy "designed to return Ortiz to the presidency," of which General Márquez, the minister of war, was aware and in which the then Maj. Pedro Eugenio Aramburu and Radical deputies like Emir Mercader were implicated.[22] Alvear disclosed the plot to Ortiz and they both agreed "to repudiate the movement for ethical and constitutional reasons." The ailing executive himself saw to it that nothing happened at a meeting of the cabinet called for that purpose. Of course, all this happened before the cabinet renewal by Castillo.

According to Ricardo Rodríguez Molas, this is the way things happened:

> The possibility that Castillo would mean a change in the anti-Nazi and liberal attitudes initiated by Ortiz worried the prodemocratic political and military circles. With the consent of President Ortiz, it was secretly agreed that a triumvirate made up of Alvear, the Socialist leader Mario Bravo, and General Márquez, the minister of war, would take charge of the government and elections would be called. This was not carried out because

of Alvear's legal scruples which led him to renounce his participation in the project though he had originally agreed to do
so.[23]

Nevertheless, the role of the army at the political level was
becoming progressively more essential, and many military men
with "Justista" tendencies (with their experienced technical director at their head) and also those with nationalistic tendencies were
beginning to devote themselves to activities that were increasingly
less their specific professional ones. This topic will be discussed
later.

The Radicals had already lost their historic opportunity, and
their bungling during this decade has led Félix Luna, a writer who
was originally a Radical, to write while trying unsuccessfully to
vindicate Alvear's name, that "the imperialistic interests knew that
Argentina would be more certain to be on their side through a
Radical government (or a government supported by the Radicals)
than through a Conservative one."[24] He then adds a rather uncon-
vincing excuse, "Probably Alvear did not think of this when he
threw himself into supporting the Allied cause with all his
strength, without any reservations."

The reaction of the Conservatives became apparent. It was
obvious that they could not present to a world at war the mask of
"democracy" as successfully as the Radicals, who missed no
opportunity to proclaim themselves the nation's majority party.
But this was not 1932, and the process that was started by Castillo, first as acting president and then as president, was not characterized by its orthodoxy. This process favored the army and
certain industrial interests. (We refer to objective facts, not to
personal intentions, which are sometimes not easy to ascertain
clearly.) Castillo liked to meet for dinner with high military officers and he was in the habit of making restrained speeches
couched in the language of a judge and university professor (which
he was). It soon became evident that he would not be able to
finish his term.

Ramón S. Castillo, a step forward

The resignation of President Ortiz's cabinet led the vice-
president to effect a complete reorganization. The various portfolios were distributed as follows: Interior, Miguel J. Culaciati;
Foreign Affairs, Julio A. Roca; Treasury, Federico Pinedo; Justice
and Public Instruction, Guillermo Rothe; War, Gen. Juan N.
Tonazzi; Navy, Rear Adm. Mario Fincati; Agriculture, Daniel

Amadeo y Videla; Public Works, Salvador Oría.[25] This was during the last few months of 1940. The appointment of at least two of the men (Pinedo and Roca) bore witness to the ties the new ministers had with British capital. The treasury minister himself recalls that a certain sector of the press and of the nationalist ideologists went so far as to refer to "the British cabinet."[26] This seemed to him a coarse way of looking at things. He added that "that first cabinet was completely pro-Allied, and for this reason was criticized and attacked from the beginning, with the lack of consideration and respect that nazism had made fashionable throughout the world."[27]

Pinedo's short term prevented the putting into practice of his proposed "economic plan," but he nevertheless entered into private consultations with Radical legislators on both that subject and the restoration of free elections. Their conversations culminated in a famous interview (which took place in the city of Mar del Plata on 3 January 1941) between Pinedo and Alvear that might have led to a "patriotic agreement." According to Pinedo's memoirs, Conservative opposition to this possibility led to his withdrawing from the cabinet. His confession is rather touching: "Although I did not represent the Democratic party and was not a member of the same, I was not ready to keep my post without the collaboration of that sector, which had always supported me."[28]

Carlos A. Acevedo took Pinedo's place and Enrique Ruiz Guiñazú that of Foreign Minister Roca. Ruiz Guiñazú was to direct the foreign relations of Argentina in a very different manner. On 7 December 1941 elections took place in Buenos Aires Province, which had been intervened by Ortiz. The victory of Rodolfo Moreno (who, as we have seen, made no secret of his rejection of the secret ballot) recalls the events of Manuel Fresco's *belle époque*. The carrying of Buenos Aires Province by the Conservative party confirmed the two key policies that, according to Félix Luna, characterized the activities of Ramón Castillo during his term in office. They were; "to maintain neutrality and not to deliver the government to the Radicals."[29]

Prior to the Buenos Aires Province elections, the federal government on 10 October 1941 had closed the City Council of the nation's capital. The action generated rhetorical protests from the opposition parties. A young nationalist, Marcelo Sánchez Sorondo, called the measure a "plausible hygienic decree."[30] Perhaps his phrase is colored by memories of the power industry concessions and the exactions to which privately owned bus lines were subject, events which had brought the council into such disrepute.

Castillo governed under a state of siege decreed on 16 December 1941, but he also promoted the development of the Argentine merchant marine and the nationalization of the port of Rosario. His neutralist attitude vis-à-vis the war brought him both praise and criticism. But the problem was not that simple, and we prefer to deal with it elsewhere. In his memoirs, Gen. Franklin Lucero makes reference to a frustrated plot in April 1941, which had as its objective the overthrow of Acting President Castillo. Two of those implicated in the plot were Gen. Juan Bautista Molina and Lt. Col. Roberto Dalton.[31] The struggle between the neutralist and pro-Allied factions, the existence of a movement of General Justo's partisans within the military establishment (such as Tonazzi, then minister of war but later replaced by Ramírez), and the rejection of the increasingly more concrete presidential bid by Robustiano Patrón Costas constitute elements that must be taken into account in order to arrive at a proper assessment of those difficult years. Marcelo T. de Alvear, head of the Radical party, died in March 1942; the Socialist leader Américo Ghioldi said in his eulogy that:

> The last decade of his existence constitutes a patriotic, valuable, and noble contribution to the solution of our political drama, in that he put himself at the head of an extensive and numerous force (but one that did not have the necessary ideological cohesion), endeavored to encourage the masses to return to the polls, and exerted himself to speak to the leaders of the potential dangers of deceiving and abusing the public with a methodical and systematic consistency worthy of a better cause, and in that he gave proof of possessing an adaptable mind capable of contemplating without blinking new political and social ideas.[32]

This was the epitaph of a Radical-Socialist . . . a French one. Events took their course, and on 27 June 1942 the assembled upper and lower chambers, in a joint session, unanimously accepted Ortiz's resignation. He died a few days later on 15 July 1942. In a message explaining his resignation, Ortiz stated that:

> In my isolation as a sick man, I was sustained by the hope of renewing my interrupted labors for the welfare of the people by the strengthening of democratic norms and the uplifting of civic practices, thus stimulating the morality of the citizen and the ethics of the members of political parties, confident that in this way I repelled the danger of ideas and tendencies contrary to

our institutional system and to the traditional customs of the Argentine people.[33]

The gulf between Ortiz's good intentions and political realities (Moreno's election in Buenos Aires, the coming balloting for presidential renewal) is pathetic. In the meantime, General Justo was making a strong comeback. As Luna so effectively puts it:

Justo had declared himself pro-Allies from the first moment and had even offered his own precious blood for the defense of the sacred principles of liberty and democracy. Vis-à-vis the Nazi military groups, the pro-Allied sectors could find no better solution than to go along with Justo.[34]

His military representatives continued to try to create a propitious atmosphere within the ranks of their institution. The United States looked upon him with favor; Great Britain was farther away and had ceased to be the only center of power. Within the Radical party (naturally!) there were groups ready to stake their reputations on the theory of the lesser evil. Since 1942 there had also been frequent contacts between the Socialist party, the Progressive Democratic party, Argentine Action, and some Radical leaders, with a view to a future "Democratic Union" of related parties. But on 11 January 1943, Agustín P. Justo died as a result of a cerebral hemorrhage. The Conservatives seemed to have been left masters of the field, and the eyes of many, including a large part of the army, were attentively fixed on the National Democratic party. The name that led all others was that of Robustiano Patrón Costas, considered by public opinion to be pro-Allies (or, more specifically, pro-American) and in favor of breaking relations with the Axis. Rodolfo Moreno was forced to give up his aspirations to the presidency and what is more, under pressure from Castillo, he resigned as provincial governor. In order to complete the ticket, it was decided not to neglect the Santa Fe Antipersonalists, and to this end the name of Manuel M. de Iriondo, a veteran of Argentine politics, was proposed. The University of Buenos Aires faculty felt obliged to give its opinion:

The university professors who sign this statement of adherence are of the opinion that, as a candidate for the presidency of the Republic, Dr. Robustiano Patrón Costas represents a solid factor for the unity of the Argentine people, since he equally and deservedly represents both the educated sectors based on the universities and the centers of culture and the working men to whom he is united by his persevering and untiring efforts as an early advocate of our industrial legislation, a characteristic that has won him the sincere praise of his fellow citizens and that has been recognized even by his political adversaries.[35]

This statement was signed by Martín Aberg Cobo, Carlos A. Ayarragaray, Rodolfo Clusellas, Jorge E. Coll, Ricardo Levene, Agustín N. Matienzo, Luis A. Podestá Costa, Isidoro Ruiz Moreno, José M. Saravia, Orlando Williams Alzaga, Clodomiro Zavalía, and others. Marcelo Sánchez Sorondo was not feeling quite so academic when he said that: "The Patrón Costas-Iriondo ticket is like a little colonial museum in the provinces, paid for by the British, who always have such a feeling for local color."[36]

On the Radicals' part, there was increasing likelihood of a mixed ticket in collaboration with other political groups. There was talk of having José P. Tamborini or Eduardo Laurencena for president with someone like Bravo, Palacios, or Luciano Molinas for vice-president. The Radical party convention approved the bases for an "Argentine Democratic Union" (let us keep this name in mind), but differences of opinion arose between Socialists and Progressive Democrats as to the second member of the ticket. These differences were the result of Communist party pressure to impose Molinas rather than a Socialist. Difficulties continued to increase, even within the Radical party itself. This was on the eve of 4 June 1943. In some circles it was rumored that some Radical legislators had succeeded in interesting Gen. Pedro Pablo Ramírez in being the Argentine Democratic Union candidate to the presidency of the Republic. Castillo demanded explanations. Ramírez gave them through a press release published in the newspapers on 1 June. Castillo did not find them satisfactory and the negotiations continued. There was talk of Ramírez's resignation. It was presented at dawn on the fourth. Aberg Cobo, after confirming the role played by certain Radical sectors in luring some military chiefs by offering them advantageous future positions (with the rather ingenuous intention of avoiding fraud by the Conservatives), adds that when the coup took place "the Radicals thought that it was a movement in their favor, and later experienced a rude awakening when they realized that they too had been used as mere pawns in a game of chess."[37]

More on international politics

Before the start of hostilities in Europe, a new Pan American Conference met in Lima in 1938. An Argentine delegation led by Isidoro Ruiz Moreno attended. Argentina's foreign minister, José

María Cantilo, was present during the first sessions, but later travelled to the Chilean lakes on leave of absence, thus abandoning the theater of deliberations. Cordell Hull, who was also in Lima, does not hide the difficulties he experienced in that city, where no concrete accord was achieved on inter-American solidarity, and the days were spent instead in prolonged informal conversations between the various delegations. The explanation Hull gave was after all quite direct:

> Ruiz Moreno promised to telegraph his Government for instructions. I spoke to him privately and suggested he let his Government know that he was being severely criticized because he was offering nothing constructive toward an effective declaration. *Following the meeting I telephoned our Embassy in Buenos Aires to contact President Ortiz directly and at once and request him from me to instruct the Argentine delegation to submit a substantial declaration on behalf of Argentina.* Fortunately I had known President Ortiz as a personal friend for some years and admired him as a good financial and economic authority. *In making this move I was going over the head of the Argentine delegation and of Foreign Minister Cantilo;* but I felt fully justified in view of the fact that that delegation was completely hamstrung and Cantilo had deliberately placed himself beyond contact with the conference.
>
> President Ortiz managed to get in touch with Cantilo. Several days later *Cantilo,* still among the Chilean lakes, *sent to Ruiz Moreno the draft of a new declaration. It was in general accord with the draft of the proposal I had given him before he left Lima,* except that it did not provide for the regular meetings of Foreign Ministers which I suggested, and contented itself with calling for such meetings whenever any Republic took the initiative.[38]

At the First Meeting of Consultation of Ministers of Foreign Affairs of the American Republics held in Panamá in 1939 there were no great difficulties, since "it was desired to formulate a neutrality agreement of continental scope."[39] We again quote from Hull for an account of the Second Meeting of Consultation at Havana in 1940:

> Dr. Melo personally was most cooperative. I saw at once, however, that he had come to Havana with rigid instructions from his Government, from which he could not budge. All my arguments would be of no avail as long as this condition persisted.

I therefore *felt it necessary,* as I had done at the Lima Conference, *to go over the heads of the Argentine delegation to the President of Argentina, Dr. Ortiz. I went to see Dr. Melo and asked him to send a telegram to Dr. Ortiz, outlining my thought on the action we should take to safeguard the European colonies and stating my suggestion that Dr. Ortiz send instructions to Melo to work with the United States and other delegations supporting decisive action.*

When Dr. Melo hesitated, I said that what I had in mind was a cable in my behalf which he would transmit. He thereupon agreed. *In sending his cable we were actually going over the heads of the acting Argentine Government. President Ortiz, seriously ill, had retired to a seaside resort, and Vice President Castillo was acting in his stead.*

The answer was not long in arriving. It was substantially in the form of instructions such as I had sought.[40]

The above seems to be at variance with Bagú's impression that "the Argentine Foreign Ministry, while Ortiz was president, was not in the habit of giving in readily to the suggestions of the Department of State."[41] As we have seen, Cordell Hull did not agree. It seems to us that this discrepancy arises from the tendency of certain very responsible authors to be indulgent toward Ortiz, because of his illness and because of the perspective of free elections he offered, and to regard Castillo as an undercover Nazi agent because of his pro-German neutrality, without taking into consideration what will be shown later, that his neutrality was also pro-British.

On 7 December 1941 the United States was attacked at Pearl Harbor; this was the start of the war with Japan and consequently with the Axis powers. O. Edmund Smith, Jr., thus summarizes the new turn of events:

The attack upon Pearl Harbor ended neutrality for the Western Hemisphere in the Second World War. The possibility that the Latin-American community might maintain neutrality, with the United States as a belligerent, never really existed, when the governments of Cuba, Panama, the Dominican Republic, Haiti, Nicaragua, Guatemala, Honduras, El Salvador, and Costa Rica declared war on the Axis a few days after the United States entered the conflict. Mexico, Colombia, and Venezuela severed diplomatic relations with the Tri-Partite powers, and in early January, 1942, Brazil and several other South American repubblics apparently were ready to join in breaking relations.[42]

Castillo's government was beginning to face the most difficult stage of its foreign policy. The pressure of the United States on Argentina to break its ties with the Axis countries continued to grow until it culminated in the dark days of 1944. Foreign Minister Enrique Ruiz Guiñazú, who not undeservedly was considered a Germanophile (his ideological antecedents predisposed him to such an orientation) was the apparent leader of the old executive's neutralist policy. He found support in key sectors of the army and in small groups of nationalist civilians. Most of the traditional parties (except for minority groups such as FORJA people, who were already rather alienated from the official leaders of the Radical party) favored the Allies. Some industrial sectors (in which sympathy toward Great Britain and points in common with the Third Reich mingled confusedly) saw in that policy a possible strengthening of their interests. From 1943 on, the army was the instrument through which that state of affairs was maintained.

The Third Meeting of Consultation, held in Rio de Janeiro ·in 1942, aroused Hull's ire toward Sumner Welles, who had been left in charge of the American delegation and had consented to the signing of the "Declaration" on the breaking-off of relations with Japan, Germany, and Italy. What had happened was that Foreign Minister Ruiz Guiñazú succeeded in introducing into the text of the document the statement that the Declaration was to be regarded as a "recommendation." This would make it extremely difficult to enforce the resolution with respect to countries choosing to disregard the advice. Hull states this clearly:

> The Declaration that was signed did not achieve the purpose we had in mind in going to Rio, namely, to obtain a complete break of the Western Hemisphere with the Axis. Argentina and Chile continued their diplomatic relations with the Axis, and Argentina did become a hotbed for Axis activities. We were to pay heavily in the future for this failure at Rio.[43]

On 14 October 1941, a short time before the Rio Meeting, the first commercial agreement between the United States and Argentina in ninety years was signed. This reinforcement of economic ties, which would be strengthened in future years at the expense of Great Britain, was not a coincidence. An Argentine military mission seeking war matériel made a trip to the United States in December 1941. The State Department tried to subordinate the request to the broader aspects of World War II; this entailed Argentina's taking an active part on the Allied side, as was indicated in a strong note, dated 13 May 1942, from the State Department to the Buenos Aires government. In that note Cordell Hull deplored that the Argentine authorities were not ready to cooperate effectively in the cause to which nineteen of the American republics (Chile had not yet broken its ties to the Axis powers) devoted their activities. The American government viewed with alarm the Nazi movements and propaganda taking shape in Argentina under cover of official toleration. On 28 September 1942 the Chamber of Deputies approved a resolution recommending breaking off relations with the Axis, and President Castillo informed the presiding officer of the Chamber that the conduct of foreign affairs was the prerogative of the executive branch. As may be seen, the lines were clearly drawn. O. Edmund Smith, Jr., summarizes these events from his own point of view:

> In Argentina, the Castillo regime had moved to prevent the neutrality issue from becoming "a subject to divide Argentine public opinion." A state of siege was declared, and Argentine newspapers were forbidden to discuss the government's foreign or domestic policies. Pro-Ally organizations such as *Acción Argentina* and *Junta de la Victoria* were strictly regulated . . . President Castillo made few public declarations concerning foreign policy, but no steps were taken which suggested that a break in relations with the Axis governments was contemplated.[44]

Though he wrote in 1941, Marcelo Sánchez Sorondo was referring to this period when he stated that "the vice president [Castillo] cannot devote himself to domestic policy and consider it apart from foreign policy. There is no other policy than foreign policy," and he calls this era the "years of decision."[45] Bagú, when comparing Yrigoyen's attitudes with those of Castillo, passes a severe judgment on the latter:

> The inspiration of President Castillo's neutrality was radically different from President Yrigoyen's since the international orientation of a country is always closely allied to the chapter of its history it is experiencing. The neutrality of President Yrigoyen was that of a democracy, not yet organic, but full of energy and faith in its creative energies, which feels entitled to establish an ethical norm for the great world powers. That of President Castillo is the neutrality characteristic of a hybrid regime, nervously awaiting the outcome of a struggle among the powerful in order to pledge itself to the winner when the latter becomes clear.[46]

At the bottom of all this lay the undeniable fact that the foreign policies of Argentina, Great Britain, and the United States did not always follow the same line. After 7 December 1941, the United States was engaged in a world struggle and needed to have all Latin America fall behind them as a solid block, opposing the Axis by breaking off relations and declaring war. Economic interests were not disregarded in this proposal, since it left the republics south of the Rio Grande more susceptible to the pressures of Yankee imperialism, naturally to the detriment of traditional British hegemony. Britain itself preferred, in the case of our country, to continue to receive the products essential for its survival, rather than to have Argentina become a belligerent with the result that shipments would diminish or cease. In this instance though the two nations were engaged in a death struggle on the battlefield, British and German interests in Argentina were not opposed to each other. Britain needed supplies, Germany was attempting to infiltrate Latin America — Argentine neutrality seemed to favor both desires.

At the suggestion of Norman Armour, the American Ambassador in Buenos Aires, Cordell Hull (who continued to try to subvert the neutralist attitude of the Argentine government) indicated to Undersecretary of State Welles that he should obtain some declaration to the effect that the British government would look with favor upon Argentina's discontinuing its overly close relations with the Axis powers. Welles contacted Lord Halifax, the British ambassador in the United States, on 26 December 1942. The undersecretary of state

> . . . remarked that, notwithstanding the official statements made by the British Government to the Argentine Government, many of the most important commercial and financial figures in the British colony in Argentina were consistently and publicly stating that Argentina should not break relations with the Axis, and that British interests favored the Argentine position of "neutrality."[47]

Hull was aware of the situation:

> Britain's economic ties with Argentina were appreciably stronger than ours. Her annual purchases of Argentine products were almost double ours. Furthermore, British subjects had made large investments in Argentina over a period of several generations, and the British colony in Buenos Aires enjoyed consider-

able prominence. After the European War broke out, and especially after the German conquest of most of Western Europe, Britain's dependence upon Argentina for food and other supplies became yet more acute.[48]

Summer Welles, who on other matters disagreed with Hull, was in complete accord with his superior on Argentine-British relations.[49] The fact of the matter is that the economic issues were no less important than the political ones, despite the fact that we were dealing with a world war. An able British diplomat, Sir David Kelly, His Majesty's ambassador in Buenos Aires during the years between 1942 and 1946, recognized this. The pungent chapter in his memoirs, *The Ruling Few*, which he devotes to his stay in Argentina must be read for a full appreciation of the situation.[50] This is just a sample:

> While the Americans were very resentful of the Argentine Government's refusal to line up with the other South American Governments by at least breaking off relations with the Axis, they were quite reasonably doing everything possible to build up the trade supremacy for which their geographical situation and the virtual cessation of British exports afforded a solid foundation.[51]

Sometimes Mercury proved stronger than Mars.

4 Perón

4 June 1943

We have already seen that the June 1943 movement that over-threw President Castillo was not, and could not be, either pro-Conservative or pro-Radical. Marcelo Sánchez Sorondo, as spokes-man for the nationalists, asserts that they were not involved.

If collective entities have senses, perhaps the Army sensed some-thing without realizing how to react. There is no conclusive proof that the 4 June coup d'état derived from nationalist proselytizing. Instead, it is true that that event took place while we, for whom the grapes of the military vineyard were always unattainable, were no longer considering a military solution.[1]

The above was of course no obstacle to having various national-ist elements infiltrate the revolutionary government to gain their own ends. Some Radical leaders did so too, among them Santiago H. del Castillo, the former governor of the intervened province of Córdoba, when he occupied a high position in the municipal trans-portation company of the city of Buenos Aires.

But we are getting ahead of our story. First we must consider those involved in executing the military coup of 4 June and how they went about it. As is true of all recent events in the history of Argentina, interpretations vary between absolute denial of military involvement as such and wild idealization of their motives, be-tween labeling the coup "nazi" and claiming that the purpose of the military in June was to reform the corrupt institutions of Argentina. This variety of interpretations is compounded by the fact that the pertinent documents and sources of information have been scattered.

Writers whose works have dealt with Argentine politics have devoted chapters or sections to the 1943 coup d'état and the sub-sequent events that culminated in the 17 October 1945 episode and the elections of February 1946. The first thing that becomes evident in these writings in that an aura of inner mystery surrounds the activities of the GOU, the military lodge that was the motivating force behind the changes. This is obvious when we realize that there is no agreement even as to the meaning of the initials: some interpret them as *Grupo Obra de Unificación;* others as *Grupo de Oficiales Unidos.* Similarly, there is no agreement on other particulars.[2]

The fact is that within the forces which covered the distance from the Campo de Mayo military base to the executive mansion (with only one violent incident, which took place in front of the Navy Mechanics School), there were Axis partisans who were opposed to Patrón Costas's anticipated candidacy (the National Democratic Party Convention that was to name him was meeting that very day), because they considered him to favor breaking relations with the Axis, and there were partisans of the Allies who were showing their disgust at the prospect of fraudulent elections, in which they would be expected to act as guardians and accomplices, as they had been doing for the last ten years. The skill of the GOU men was demonstrated by the way they turned both attitudes to their own advantage. The presence of Gen. Arturo Rawson, considered pro-Allies, at the head of the military column, is evidence of this. The partisan struggle that started the very day of the coup, in an anxious endeavor to provide an *a posteriori* content and program for it (this would seem to bolster the theory of the purely military origins of the episode), served only to prove that the army at that time was in a state of unstable equilibrium. Bonifacio del Carril, one of the civilians who was invited to collaborate with the authorities, corroborates this when he writes that:

> I have taken part in long discussions . . . on this subject, the main purpose of which was precisely to determine which had been or should have been the revolutionary objectives of the Revolution that *had already taken place.* This attitude and this uneasiness were of course shared by many military chiefs who had taken part in the 4 June action and who in good faith were part of the GOU. However, this problem never troubled Colonel Perón, who knew perfectly well what he wanted to do with the Revolution that had taken place if he had a chance to take total control (as in fact he did) of the newly created regime.[3]

The GOU preparations for the coup were conducted through the Ministry of War, where Cols. Juan D. Perón and Enrique P. González operated. The latter were able, while remaining within the letter of official regulations, "to withdraw from the posts near the capital those commanders who might be disaffected to the uprising that was being prepared."[4] This, together with the prose-lytizing among the military chiefs and officers mentioned above, made the conspiracy completely successful.

When news of the military advance was received, President Castillo and his ministers took refuge on the minesweeper *Drummond* of the Argentine Navy, escorted by some ships from the river fleet. There was a rumor that the sea fleet was proceeding at full steam toward Buenos Aires to support the government (actually its chief later became minister of the navy in the revolutionary cabinet). Aberg Cobo, in a display of political solidarity with his fellow Conservative, first attributed to the elderly Dr. Castillo an unlikely intent to resist, but almost immediately added that:

> At that moment one of those episodes occurred which are in-explicable to those who did not know the thoughts of the pro-tagonists — the presidential order [to sail North] was disobeyed; and the ships, once in the middle of the channel, dispersed, leaving only the *Drummond,* which finally entered the port of La Plata, for the purpose of the subsequent capitulation and resignation of the president.[5]

On 5 June 1943 the cabinet of the government headed by General Rawson was announced. Rear Adm. Sabá H. Sueyro was vice-president, and the various portfolios were distributed as follows: Interior, Vice-Adm. Segundo Storni; Foreign Affairs, Gen. Domingo Martínez; Treasury, José María Rosa; Justice and Public Instruction, Horacio Calderón; War, Gen. Pedro Pablo Ramírez; Navy, Rear Adm. Benito Sueyro; Agriculture, Gen. Diego Luis Mason; Public Works, Gen. Juan Pistarini. Aberg Cobo has this to say about some of the members:

> Furthermore, the publication of the cabinet named by the latter [Rawson] had caused a painful impression: it included Generals Ramírez and Martínez, who had, according to the official an-nouncement, originally excused themselves because of their sta-tus as former collaborators with Dr. Castillo, but later had changed their attitude at the request of the provisional presi-dent and for "patriotic" reasons.[6]

General Rawson was the first victim of the uprising he had led (or had been allowed to lead), and his ephemeral cabinet did not even take the oath of office. The young officers decided to with-draw their confidence from him. It was asserted that Rawson in-tended to break relations with the Axis powers within a short time and his first statements on foreign policy did not satisfy the colonels and majors. His substitute was no other than Pedro Pablo Ramírez, the former minister of war in the cabinet of President Castillo and in the stillborn Rawson cabinet.

O. Edmund Smith, Jr., the American international relations expert, has offered an interesting interpretation, which would seem to have been confirmed by later events, of the role Ramírez played among the revolutionary officers:

> Undersecretary Welles believed that President Ramírez possessed no real authority within the Argentine government. While a few generals and admirals, such as General Rawson, apparently favored breaking with the Axis in order to obtain U.S. military aid, it was increasingly evident that the Buenos Aires government was actually controlled by an ultranationalistic clique of army colonels (the G. O. U. —*Grupo de Oficiales Unidos*) which opposed the abandonment of Argentine neutrality. These younger officers dominated the army and gave orders to the generals. The G. O. U. wished to secure Yankee armaments, but was unwilling to submit to U. S. dictation in Argentine foreign policy. President Ramírez attempted to stand between the two "extremist" groups; but, as the colonels gained increasing power, he became more and more of a puppet, and his early promises to sever Argentine ties with the Axis countries could not be honored.[7]

Ramírez reorganized the cabinet as follows: Interior, Col. Alberto Gilbert; Foreign Affairs, Vice-Adm. Segundo Storni; Treasury, Jorge Santamarina; Justice and Public Instruction, Col. Elbio C. Anaya; War, Gen. Edelmiro J. Farrell; Navy, Rear Adm. Benito Sueyro; Agriculture, Gen. Diego Luis Mason; Public Works, Vice-Adm. Ismael Galíndez. Sabá H. Sueyro continued as vice-president.[8]

As has become customary in military movements in recent years, individuals connected with imperialist and conservative interests seem to have infiltrated this cabinet. José Luis Torres has this to say:

> It was a joke played by some imp intent on interfering with God's plans. The board of directors of ANSEC, the electric power monopoly which was a subsidiary of one of the greatest holding companies with imperialist capital — the Electric Bond and Share Company — was obliged to accept the resignation presented by Admiral Galíndez as president of that company so that he might take charge of his high post in the revolutionary

government. As for Santamarina, he was, and continues to be, one of the most capable men of the regime that the revolution had come to oust.[9]

The differences of opinion on the 4 June coup could have been foretold; they resulted from the position on international policies of the groups or individuals holding them, rather than from their position on domestic policies. Pinedo does not hesitate to say that:

> When José Luis Pena, an old Socialist party comrade with whom I have clashed many times, but whose high ideals, erudition, and capacity for work I have always acknowledged, came to see me around the middle of the afternoon of the fourth of June to ask my opinion about the events, I replied without hesitation that *this was a case of a nazi movement.* We were in agreement. The avalanche of revolutionary statements and manifestos and *our own satisfaction at the ending of a regime with which we had nothing to do* could not blind us.[10]

Repetto is more specific:

> Uncertain at first, it did not take long to reveal itself as a coup intended to stifle the democratic and pro-Allied opinion of the Argentine people and to bring into being a government of a more or less totalitarian type, animated by imperialist purposes.[11]

Many years later some young Conservatives were to say that "that of 1943, on the other hand, was the anti-Conservative revolution *par excellence,* even though rightist and even Conservative elements took part in it, brought together by deceit and treachery."[12]

Del Mazo spoke of the repercussions aroused by the candidacy of Patrón Costas, who was

> an anti-neutralist, a partisan of the United States, and connected with the Standard Oil in Salta Province . . . English and German interests vetoed the attempt, and the 4 June 1943 coup broke out on the same day that that candidacy was to be announced, the definition in foreign policy being replaced by a bristling anti-Americanism, neutrality for the duration of the war, and restoration of full English influence. The fourth of June was therefore an effort to assure the continuity of Argentina's foreign policy in view of the possibility that such continuity might be broken by the accession of Patrón Costas.[13]

Alfredo Galletti summarizes his views as follows:

The 4 June movement was strictly military and had no economic or social content. It was only a totalitarian coup for the
purpose of denying access to power to democratic forces and
continuing the international line traced by Castillo.[14]

Enrique Rivera attempted to give a more profound explanation:

Just as an individual is not judged by the concept he has of himself, but by what he really is, the 4 June revolution should not
be judged by what Rawson and Ramírez believed it to be, but
by what it really is. Perón and the young officers who surrounded
him articulated more cogently the economic forces that pro-
pelled them, and this was the reason they forced their army
comrades out. The defeat of the Axis and the loss of prestige of
fascism, whose external ideological trappings inspired the first
acts of the revolution, placed them in a difficult situation and
forced them to find new structures to support them and a new
ideological cover. They found these in democratic and petit-
bourgeois Yrigoyenism, as it was inevitable that they would.[15]

Bonifacio del Carril, in his book, *Crónica interna de la Revolución Libertadora,* gives some interesting details of the internecine
struggles that culminated in the victory of Colonel Perón and his
adherents. He has this to say on the subject:

What happened was simply that the military who held the
power and lent it to Castillo decided that they, not Castillo's
successor, should be the ones to establish the conditions and
stipulations for entering or not entering into the war.[16]

Incidents such as that of the exchange of letters between Minister Storni and Cordell Hull, to be discussed further on, will only
confirm this view.

The official Communist position was that "the coup was carried
out by a coalition of heterogeneous forces in which there were
democratic elements, with fascist military and civilian elements
predominating, and it was the latter who supplied the program-
matic content."[17]

With exception of the oligarchic and clerical nationalist groups
that supported and joined the government, one of the few political
sectors that attempted to take a broader view of the question was
FORJA, which at that time acted with considerable independence
from traditional Radicalism, stating that:

(1) The overthrow of the regime constitutes the first stage in any policy for the restructuring of nationhood and authentically expressing sovereignty. (2) The establishment of a moral system to govern the institutional development of the country and the conduct of its people and leaders is an essential principle; any possibility of creating a nation based on the indigenous genius of our people and its desire for economic emancipation and social justice must rest on it. (3) The gradual and balanced enforcement of a program for the economic, political, and cultural emancipation of the country is a basic demand of the people in order to assert its historical personality and for the Argentine nation to participate on equal terms in the free play of international relations.

This declaration ended by emphasizing the obligation the new authorities had contracted to "repair the moral dissolution in which our politics lay struggling and to create a system based on ethical norms and clear principles of responsibility and sovereignty."[18] We have quoted some paragraphs at length because we believe this will show the similarity in the wording of this resolution and the vocabulary employed later by the Peronist movement (which some FORJA men joined), to which were added concepts derived from the old Yrigoyenist tradition. The effort made by this small group to understand the national situation is worth more than the facile labels of "nazi" (Pinedo) and "fascist" (Communist party) applied to the 4 June 1943 coup.

From June 1943 to October 1945

Shortly after the events of 4 June, the Argentine Supreme Court on 7 June issued a decision that echoed (and not only in its form) the old days of Uriburu. Its text read as follows:

. . . in order to consider the note by which the president of the provisional executive branch of the nation, Gen. Pedro Pablo Ramírez, informed this Supreme Court of the constitution of a provisional government for the nation arising from the successful revolution of 4 June of this year, and whereas a situation has arisen analogous to that envisaged by this Supreme Court in its decision of 10 September 1930, which reads as follows. . . [the terms of the decision given above on pp. 10-11 were transcribed]
Be it resolved: On this day to acknowledge receipt to the provisional government of the note to which reference has been made, with a transcription of this decision, which shall be pub-

lished and entered in the corresponding volume. Signed: Roberto Repetto, Antonio Sagarna, Luis Linares, Benito A. Nazar Anchorena, Francisco Ramos Mejía [Supreme Court Justices]. Juan Alvarez [attorney general]: Esteban Imaz, Ramón T. Méndez, secretaries.[19]

Repetto and Sagarna had already signed the 1930 decision. The 1943 one is almost reduced to a procedural matter.

Juridical discrepancies were also characteristic of the period between 1943 and 1946, even after Perón had become president of the Republic. Within the Supreme Court we find that Judge Tomás D. Casares (named to the Court by the *de facto* government), a militant Catholic, argued for a greater latitude in interpreting the powers of the executive, opposing the strict construction of the other members of the court. Casares's opinion on the validity of the decree-laws, without need for subsequent sanction by Congress, finally prevailed. Magistrates who had previously served the government of the day, and would do so afterwards, hastened to hand down decisions favorable to those now in power.[20] Decree No. 773 of 18 June 1943 provided "that the word 'provisional' be struck from the official documents on which it may have appeared, and it is hereby forbidden to apply it to the authorities of the government of the nation."

In the early days of the Ramírez government, various decisions were taken that indicate the mental confusion that reigned in the military sectors of the June coup. One of these was the decision to consider Uriburu's coup a "liberating" one. This is reflected in the decree dated 2 September 1943, the preamble of which states:

> That this is the anniversary of the civilian-military movement brought about by the deeply and intensely repressed popular anxiety to bring back the rule of the Constitution and to return to the people the enjoyment and full exercise of civilian institutions.
> That it is the duty of the government to commemorate the generous sacrifice of those who fell on that historic occasion and to honor the memory of its prestigious chief, Lt. Gen. José F. Uriburu, who headed the liberating movement.[21]

This was followed by memorial services, laying of wreaths, and granting of a legal holiday. Two months later, the same administration (there had been ministerial changes already) made public Decree No. 15,074 of 27 November 1943, by which the Secretariat of Labor and Social Security was created. The preamble affords a convenient opportunity to parade the roots and theoretical influences that later will continue to be mentioned in the labor legislation inspired by the most dynamic figure of the administration, Colonel Perón.

Whereas: The problems relating to capital and labor should receive preferential attention on the part of the government because of their direct connection with the general welfare and the economic development of the nation; *Whereas:* To make more efficient the work of the agencies charged with enforcement of the labor laws, it is necessary to create an organism that will centralize and control such state activity, sponsoring in due course the proper measures for a greater harmony between the productive forces; *Whereas:* Experience in countries where the various aspects of the social activity of the state have been centralized proves the advisability of adopting such a system; *Whereas:* In so doing, national unity will be strengthened by the prevalence of greater social and distributive justice, which is the basic and enduring aim of the present government, and will bring about the practical acknowledgment in all sectors of the country of the supreme dignity of labor; *Whereas:* By means of a central supervising agency for all the activities conducted by the state in favor of the material and moral improvement of the laboring class, it will be possible to decide, on the basis of an over-all judgment (which is the most suited to the complexity of the social reality), upon those measures that will lead to a prompt and effective raising of the standard of living of those who depend solely on a slender salary to support that standard; *Whereas:* It will only be possible to satisfy the expectations of the present moment through an organism that will allow comparing and remedying the multiple needs that afflict working-class homes, exercising the most perfect control on the application of the special legislation in force and preparing the development of a social policy; *Whereas:* Neglect of the social duties that in varying degrees are incumbent upon both the owners of wealth and the laboring populations is a primordial cause of the evils that disturb the functioning of modern societies, it is fitting that the state should proceed to develop an intentisve publicity campaign intended to infuse into the conscience of the Argentine people the conviction that it is not lawful for anyone to elude the said duties; *Whereas:* Compliance with the same will bring about the mutual rapprochement of the productive forces, a condition necessary for peaceful coexistence within the Christian principles that constitute our historical tradition; and *Whereas:* A goverment measure that, while leading to the achievement of the general welfare, may in the main contribute to the strengthening of the Argentine family, which is the foundation of the greatness of the Fatherland, should not be postponed;

Now Therefore: The president of the Argentine nation, with the concurrence of the entire cabinet, decrees: *Article 1.* The Secretariat of Labor and Social Security is hereby created as a dependency of the Presidency of the Nation.[22]

The fact that this decree recognizes (as the numerous later legal texts of the 1943 - 1946 period continued to do), though in a vague and inconclusive manner, that the labor sector has an undeniable importance in the social life of the nation is perhaps what gives it historical value. The rest (the examples of fascist, Bonapartist, and even Marxist-style phrases and the touches borrowed from the Papal encyclicals that are revealed by a careful analysis of Decree No.15,074/43) is window-dressing. Of course, it is truly amazing that veterans of Argentine political life did not see in these measures anything except what they wanted to see, without separating the wheat from the chaff, namely, what was demagogic in the manner of presentation from what constituted the real basis of that demagoguery. Repetto went so far as to say that

. . . under the pretext of introducing into the country the social policy that according to him had been ignored by all those who had preceded him, *the colonel was looking for converts and he prepared his following by means of a vast electoral organization which he called the Secretariat of Labor and Social Security.*[23]

As may be seen, two aspects of the question are confused: one is the actual fact of the work the Socialists did in Congress in the field of labor legislation, and the other is the new element of effective and efficacious enforcement both of that and later legislation. If a distinction is not made between these two aspects, the likelihood of misunderstanding is great. The Communists, though their concern with and activity in the labor field cannot be denied, were blinded by their narrow outlook on the problem (new unions were being formed, controlled by those devoted to the "colonel," in which there was no room for the party), and they also indulged in rhetoric:

In view of the constant increase in the fighting spirit of the masses, the fascist-dictatorial regime gradually became aware that

repressive measures were not sufficient to prevent the struggle
of the workers and the popular masses for their socioeconomic
claims and for a democratic regime; this is why in December
1943, at the request of Colonel Perón, *it created the Secretariat
of Labor and Social Security, thus employing repression and
social demagoguery as an instrument of government.*[24]

Is there any reason to justify the subsequent amazement felt
when it was realized that the working masses, whose advent on the
Argentine social and political scene characterizes those still recent
years, were indifferent to the abstract, liberal, formal slogans of
the Democratic Union, when the parties of the left were so off
course?

The program of the Ramírez government on which the military
factions continued to work, was not confined to the decree creating the Secretariat of Labor and Social Security: another decree,
the effects of which were to outlast many administrations, was that
on the reduction and then the freezing of rents, which brought up
for discussion the controversial question of housing, still a live
issue after more than a quarter of a century. By a coincidence that
may be more apparent than real, that same day (31 December
1943) two decrees of very different tenor were made known: political parties within the territory of the republic were dissolved and
the teaching of the Catholic religion was declared compulsory in
primary, postprimary, secondary, and special schools, thus breaking the lay tradition that had prevailed in these matters from the
time of the Avellaneda Educational Act (1884).

The Catholic church, through authorized publications such as
the influential journal *Criterio*, gave its approval to *both measures.*[25] The Catholic hierarchy and intellectuals were ready to
play a dominant role in the governing process. Monsignor Gustavo
J. Franceschi spoke in defense of the national authorities, when
they were accused of totalitarianism:

First, we have the word of the president of the Republic, of his
ministers, of his official spokesman, Colonel González, secretary
to the presidency. The latter, in referring to this subject before
some Buenos Aires newsmen less than fifteen days ago, pointed
out to them that totalitarianism is pagan and that, on the contrary, the government has just restored religious instruction in
the schools. Second, we have the facts themselves. Has the
present government at any time tried to absorb the total human
person, interfere with the family, with religious matters, with
domestic life? One of the characteristics of totalitarianism is

the sole labor union imposed by the state; the professional association organized from top to bottom as a state institution; now, then, recently Colonel Perón, the secretary of labor and social security, has proclaimed free unionization, has opened wide the doors of his offices to the professional associations organized by private initiative, and has taken measures to strengthen their activities. There is nothing that savors of totalitarianism in the present government.[26]

This wavering between different courses of action, this internal contradiction between the measures and their executors, this lack of a concrete plan for implementation (made more evident by the very existence of isolated and sometimes contradictory implementations) was also observable, for example, when the investigating commissions were set up. The two most important ones were the Investigating Commission on the Electric Concessions in the Federal Capital, headed by Col. Matías Rodríguez Conde; and the Investigating Commission on the Bemberg Case, headed by J. Alfredo Villegas Oromí. Both, in the end, found the free conduct of their investigations hampered by administration interference.[27]

In an "Address to the Military" Marcelo Sánchez Sorondo thought he could lay down conditions for the military:

> Today revolution consists of deeds and of the motivation for our action. The state at this time takes an active part in events. This is the first sign that the revolution has started. But woe to deeds without political theology! Woe to action without doctrine! Everything may degenerate into the worst of materialisms, the materialism of false efficiency, into truth destroyed by efficiency or by resentment, according to Marxist tenets. Beware of the letter without the spirit. This has to be said: your responsibility, our responsibility, the responsibility of all in the fourth of June is enormous. The fourth of June is the decisive date of a decisive year. The country has already been committed. Either we achieve national unity or anarchy will engulf us. You, the military, now have all the authority. You, the military, who make your lives a profession of honor, on the fourth of June made a profession of faith.[28]

Nationalism, too, demanded a program of action to suit its interests. Jorge Abelardo Ramos, a writer affiliated with the Nationalist Left, summarizes the measures taken by the 1943 military government that he considers positive:

> It dissolved Congress and political parties, reorganized the judi-

ciary, intervened the provinces, reaffirmed the policy of neutrality. It created the Industrial Credit Bank made necessary by economic expansion, it searched the offices of the power companies and investigated their accounts. It intervened the Buenos Aires Transport Corporation, expropriated the Natural Gas Company, initiated a study to revise import tariffs, promoted military industries . . .[29]

On the debit side he places the following:

In the first six months of military government a harsh offensive was promoted against the labor movement; unions were closed, their leaders and active members were arrested, the revolutionary press was suppressed . . . The universities fell into clerical hands, which subordinated all teaching to St. Thomas's battle cry.[30]

Internal problems and international pressures (with the United States Department of State and Secretary Hull taking the lead in applying the latter) led to the breaking of relations with the Axis countries on 26 January 1944. Palace intrigues were soon to claim a new victim: President Ramírez, who had signed the decree breaking relations with the Axis. Gen. Edelmiro J. Farrell, who had the confidence of the military lodge and especially of Colonel Perón, replaced Ramírez first provisionally, then permanently. Whitaker has this to say about the change:

Again Perón followed Farrell up the ladder, becoming Minister of War on 26 February and Vice-President on 7 July. He continued to occupy both these positions, as well as the Secretaryship of Labor and Social Security, until October 1945. The combination of these three offices enabled him to build up the twin supports of army and labor upon which his regime has since rested.[31]

Perón's struggle to become minister of war constitutes one of the key points in his political rise to power. As related by Bonifacio del Carril, the candidate the majority of the GOU members (ten out of the total seventeen) supported was Gen. Juan C. Sanguinetti, but Perón was skillful enough to impose his own name as provisional minister (his lack of seniority as a colonel precluded his aspiring to permanent tenure). In this way Sanguinetti's aspirations and those of the sector that backed him were blocked.[32]

Farrell's administration, at least until the early days of October 1945, may in great measure be considered Perón's administration because of the important part the latter played as minister and vice-president. The uncertain situation led to numerous cabinet changes as well as to the reorganization and creation of various secretariats.[33]

On the national scene events moved rapidly, while on the international scene an Allied victory over the Third Reich began to seem certain and American pressure on Argentina increased. The San Juan Province earthquake on 15 January 1944 created a feeling of solidarity in the nation and led to the famous "Collection" that made an obscure second-rate actress, María Eva Duarte, known to the public in roles very different from those she had usually played before. She was to be an important figure in the rapid climb to power of her friend Colonel Perón. On 1 March, Lt. Col. Tomás A. Duco led his abortive coup attempt from Patricios Park to the Buenos Aires suburb of Lomas de Zamora. The United States abstained from entering into official relations with the Far- rell administration "awaiting future developments" (for this, read: "the entrance of Argentina into the war"). Some nationalists (Federico Ibarguren and Santiago de Estrada among them) reacted violently to the breaking of relations. This was especially true in Tucumán. Colonel Perón gave almost daily speeches before differ- ent audiences; many people were alarmed by what he said on 10 June at the Universidad Nacional de La Plata on the occasion when the Chair of National Defense was inaugurated. But most traditional organs of opinion, and especially the traditional politi- cians, did not take note of the many speeches he made to the workers, or if they did so they dismissed them with vague epithets such as "laborism," "demagoguery," and so forth. Neither had they noted the phenomenon of the internal migrations nor the human consequences of industrial concentration and growth of a national proletariat. Some politicians preferred exile, and they started a campaign against the Argentine regime from Montevideo. In the Uruguayan capital they joined in a movement which even- tually led to the formation of the "Democratic Union." Nicolás Repetto, who was one of the exiles, has confessed that: "I left Buenos Aires of my own volition, since at that time no one was threatening or persecuting me."[34] His activities in Uruguay lasted until 1945. An important document drawn up by the "Junta of Argentine Political Exiles" on 30 June 1945 demanded continen- tal solidarity against the admission of Argentina into the United Nations at San Francisco. It was signed by Repetto (Socialist par- ty), Julio Noble (Progressive Democratic party), Agustín Rodrí- guez Araya (Radical party), José Aguirre Cámara (National Demo- cratic party), and Rodolfo Ghioldi (Communist party).[35]

Let us return to the events of 1944. During that year there were many arrests of political leaders. Newspapers were closed or their publication suspended. The liberation of Paris led to some celebrations in the federal capital, although the government tried to neutralize them. After the 24 August 1944 testimonial, Generals Ramírez and Rawson (the latter had long since resigned his post as ambassador to Brazil) were urged by the demonstrators to speak out. The opposition started to use the defense of public liberties as a rallying cry and to unite behind charges of nazism in the government's orientation. The publications favorable to the Axis, either by changing their names (the pro-Nazi newspaper *El Pampero* became *El Federal*), or because of the ineffectiveness of the repressive measures the government felt obliged to take on occasion, continued their now pointless propaganda; the defeat of Germany and its allies was a foregone conclusion, and the only question was the exact moment of their collapse.

The year 1945 started with a Decree on the Security of the State issued on 15 January; its provisions were Draconian. The declaration of war against Germany and Japan finally came on 27 March. This was later diplomatically useful, for it made possible Argentina's participation in the United Nations, much to the chagrin of Cordell Hull, who had already retired from his high post because of illness. In May the legislation regulating political parties was published and challenged by the traditional groups, who were to become habitual challengers in the years that followed 1945.

Repetto writes that

> General Farrell's statements at the annual solidarity dinner of the armed forces held on 7 July 1945 were received with evident satisfaction by the Argentine exiles in Montevideo. It could not be otherwise. At a military meeting, the de facto president, himself a military man, had engaged his word of honor that: "there will . . . be free elections before the end of the year and the country will have a legal government." These words were interpreted as the expression of General Farrell's firm intention to bring the revolutionary adventure to an end and to return to a constitutional governmental regime.[36]

By 3 September almost all the politicians were back from exile. They were faced with two immediate challenges; the figure of Perón loomed large and had to be removed from the scene, and their own forces had to be organized for the upcoming elections which they were confident they could win. The "anti-Perón" blindness prevented a redefinition of their own positions and a realization that things were changing in Argentina. This led to the defeat of the Democratic Union.

In May 1945, American Ambassador Spruille Braden, in his praiseworthy effort to eradicate the last vestiges of nazi-fascism from Argentina, made the opposition the beneficiary of his dubious support. An account of Mr. Braden's activities properly belongs in the international section of this chapter and will be discussed in detail there. Here we merely mention the nature of his activities. On 6 August 1945 the state of siege was lifted: the anti-Perón sectors (hereafter referred to by this name) organized a public show of force to attempt to make the government aware of the dangers inherent in its lack of popularity. On 19 September the demonstration known as the "March of the Constitution and Liberty" took place. It started at Congress Square and wound its way to France Square. Alfredo Galletti had this to say about the march:

> Those of us who were witnesses to these events became aware of the constantly increasing polarization of forces and of the absence of most labor sectors from that extraordinary gathering made up mostly of students, professionals, business men, and the middle class in general. The [labor sectors]. . . were gradually being awakened by the ideas of social justice expressed demagogically by official circles, and they were moving under slogans of proved effectiveness, which later were adopted by vast sectors of the population.[37]

It seems to us that when Galletti again talks of the "demagoguery" and the "slogans," he forgets to mention the concrete benefits the working and rural sectors were receiving. If the individual flesh-and-blood worker is not kept in mind, it becomes impossible to understand the sociopolitical climate of that period. A Radical author has left a more realistic account of the matter:

> In addition to the temporary measures taken, such as the increase in salaries, the improvement in working conditions, and the ordinances intended to protect various unions, the legal apparatus was established that created labor courts, regulated professional associations, unified the system of social security, and extended the benefits of the dismissal law (No. 11,729) to all workers (Decree No.33,302).[38]

Besides making substantial innovations in labor matters, the Farrell government devoted some thought to the problem of industrialization. At the "Day of Argentine Industry" celebration (2

September 1944) Secretary of Industry and Commerce Gen. Julio C. Checchi, declared that:

> [The government of the nation] created the Argentine Industrial Credit Bank, issued, by general decision of the ministers, the Decree on Promotion and Protection of Industry; took measures to facilitate the education of minors and industrial instruction; studied the situation in our poor provinces; created the National Rationing Council; and organized the Secretariat of Industry and Commerce, a post I have the honor of occupying as secretary.[39]

President Farrell emphasized in his speech that:

> . . . it is essential to industrialize those products, to create work in the city, to achieve self-sufficiency, so that in the future we may be in a position to take advantage of the situation as we should have done during the 1914 War and failed to do later for reasons on which I do not dare pass judgment, but which I am sure had nothing to do with your dedication as industrialists.[40]

The military sectors opposed to Colonel Perón were not inactive during the years 1944 and 1945. They tried to find an opportunity to get the upper hand, but when they did, the opportunity was wasted. The traditional parties did not rise to the occasion; the university students, on the other hand, lived through days of activity, fighting against government intervention in their halls of learning. In August 1945 a subversive movement was quelled in the city of Córdoba. However, the most important events took place in October of that year. The spark that set off the train of events was the attempt to appoint Perón's candidate, Oscar Nicolini, as director general of the Post Office and Telecommunications Department. The Campo de Mayo garrison was displeased by the news and made a demand through its commander, Gen. Eduardo Avalos, that resulted in Perón's resignation from all his posts. Numerous meetings of the military (army and navy) with politicians took place. They were held at the Círculo Militar and at the Naval Center. For his part, General Avalos sought an understanding with the political parties; that understanding was to be based on a proposed list of three names from which a civilian president was to be chosen.[41] The feeling in the navy and other military sectors favored entrusting the government to the Supreme Court after Farrell's resignation. They went so far as to appoint "a committee composed of Adms. Héctor Vernengo Lima, Leonardo Mac Lean and Francisco Clarisa, and Gens. Alberto Guglielmone,

Ernesto C. Quiroga and Orlando I. Peluffo to appear before the president"[42] and present the demand. In the meantime, Perón was taken into custody at the Buenos Aires suburb of Tigre and transferred to Martín García Island. His faithful partisans (Eva Duarte, Cipriano Reyes, Domingo Mercante, and Filomeno Velazco) went into action to change the situation. Avalos refused to accept the idea that the Supreme Court should take charge of the government, since in his judgment such a course would represent a loss of face for the armed forces. In the maelstrom of those days (from 8 to 17 October), President Farrell called Attorney General Juan Álvarez and entrusted him with the mission of forming a new cabinet. Álvarez, with provincial slowness, set himself to the task; he failed to understand the situation around him now as in earlier years he had failed to understand Argentine history in his pioneering essay *Las guerras civiles argentinas*.

Matters came to a head: many people gathered at San Martín Square to take part in the military deliberations. "When Rear Admiral Vernengo Lima wanted to address the crowd from the balconies of the Círculo, there were insistent cries from the square of 'the government to the Court.' 'I am not Perón,' the sailor said gravely."[43]

On 16 October Álvarez announced the cabinet. Among the members there appeared Jorge Figueroa Alcorta, Alberto Hueyo, Isidoro Ruiz Moreno, Tomás Amadeo and Álvarez himself. Though he favored this course, Bartolomé Galíndez in his book *Apuntes de tres revoluciones* comments on the bizarre backstage deals that went on during those October days and feels constrained to add that ". . . they were worthy men, but they lacked political resourcefulness, the very essence of a revolutionary situation."[44] José Luis Torres is more specific:

> While on the one hand Attorney General Juan Álvarez, with the authorization of the Supreme Court (and aided by Federico Pinedo, who climbed to the public rostrum to announce the good news), devoted himself to the formation of a *patriotic* emergency cabinet, on the other hand, the person that now [1947] occupies the presidency of the nation was obliged to resign and was jailed. The name of the chairman of the Power Company Board of Directors, Alberto Hueyo, was suggested for the Treasury portfolio in the improvised cabinet, while that of Public Works had been offered to Atanasio Iturbe, the almost perennial chairman of the local board of directors of the British public services enterprises.[45]

The uncertainty felt as time passed is thoughtfully reflected by Galíndez:

> The civilians had not defeated Perón arms in hand; the military, who had raised him to power, had themselves eliminated him. His removal from three important posts was in itself a victory. The rest would come later. With Perón's disappearance, there was only the problem of democratic coordination left, and any demand might cause everything to collapse.[46]

Enrique Grande, speaking at a round table, declared that:

> It was then, while the political leaders engaged in Byzantine disputes over whether power should be entrusted to the Court, or to a group of men of science, or to some illustrious personage, or to some descendant of the Incas; it was then, I say, that the collaborators of this new power that had become popular on the strength of their achievements while in power brought into being the act of 17 October 1945.[47]

On the above date Perón, alleging reasons of health, but refusing to be checked by a medical commission that traveled out to Martín García Island, requested Farrell to change his residence. On the morning of 17 October he was taken to the military hospital. In labor circles there was great evidence of unrest. The day before, the Central Committee of the General Confederation of Labor had met to consider calling a general strike that had already been approved in principle on the fourteenth of the month. The discussion that took place is not too widely known, but Alberto Belloni, an union activist who has given a lively account of the labor movement from the point of view of the forces that supported Perón, has recorded it.[48]

In brief, by twenty-one votes for and nineteen against (at the last moment Libertario Ferrarri, an old-time member of FORJA, was the one who succeeded in swinging the majority) it was decided to call a general strike *beginning on the eighteenth*. But there had been workers on the streets since the sixteenth and increasingly throughout the seventeenth. They moved from their places of work, mostly in the industrial suburbs of Buenos Aires, toward the presidential palace, to demand the freeing of Colonel Perón. Great crowds collected there during the night of 17 October. The army troops and the police forces did not interfere with the people's movement and in this way facilitated the gathering of the populace.

During this time Perón was holding conversations at the military hospital with government emissaries. Armando G. Antille, originally a Radical, who had entered the Farrell cabinet around the middle of the year at the same time as J. Hortensio Quijano and Juan I. Cooke, visited Perón repeatedly. The colonel's supporters both within the government and outside it were ready to bring about his return.

Those gathered near the presidential palace continued to wait in what was unseasonable heat for an October day.[49] Mercante and Avalos tried to address the workers, but they were not allowed to speak. Perón was transferred from the military hospital to the presidential palace. As Galíndez has written:

> Vernengo Lima made a last attempt to break up the crowd; Farrell opposed this. Perón arrived and the expected embrace took place . . . Vernengo Lima, betrayed, left the executive mansion and boarded a ship. He gave the order to the fleet. It was short, a decision in a few words; but he immediately countermanded it by another statement which made clear that the army did not go along with the navy. The uprising was put down without a fight.[50]

Perón addressed the assembled crowd in a short speech and urged them to go back home. A witness to the event states that "the approval and rejoicing with which his words were received cannot easily be forgotten."[51] The comments by the opposition played up the sweat of the "descamisados," the rabble, the washing of feet in the fountains of the square, the men, women, and children lying on the grass in the park, the bribery, the official inaction.

Raúl Damonte Taborda (though years later he did not hesitate to travel to Madrid to curry favor with former President Perón) writes that "Chief of Police Mittelbach and Assistant Chief Molina guaranteed *protection to the mobs from Berisso, Avellaneda, Valentín Alsina, Ensenada, and industrial centers contiguous to the capital.*"[52] The official Communist position was confined to recording that ". . . on the seventeenth and eighteenth of October 1945, police and army forces, supported by a sector of the people, restored Perón to the government, even though nominally General Farrell continued to occupy it."[53] They then go on to attempt a theoretical and almost psychological explanation:

> The support that one sector of the labor and popular movement gave to the forces that restored Perón to power was due to the belief that the fall of Perón signified the reconquest of power

by the oligarchical and reactionary forces and, therefore, the annulment of its socioeconomic victories and of its right to fight for better living and working conditions in the future. That belief also arose from the fact that at the moment the democratic parties did not present a united front, making known to the people what the democratic and progressive answer was for the purpose of substantially improving the living and working conditions of the working class and of the people and making Argentina take part in the world concert of democratic and peace-loving nations.[54]

The Communist party did not bear in mind that large sectors of the workers had already obviously improved their "living conditions" and that the "democratic parties" had not been responsible for the measures that had brought about that improvement. José Luis Romero saw deeper into the 17 October phenomenon; he distinguished two aspects of it:

On a general scale, the movement had the same internal structure as others which the police had previously organized to lend a little popular warmth to the public appearances of the revolution of 1943 government; but it was unmistakable that *now there was also a spontaneous movement of the popular masses for whom the name of Perón had become the symbol of a social movement.*[55]

It was the second aspect that lent an air of political myth to that date, which from then on was commemorated every year with government support. Its detractors and eulogists were soon to proliferate. Its importance is due to this very fact.

After Colonel Perón had spoken and while the crowd was dispersing, the negotiations continued to solve the crisis once and for all. The two groups, General Avalos and other chiefs of the Campo de Mayo garrison on the one hand, and, on the other, General Pistarini, Colonels Velazco and Molina (among others) continued to exchange ideas in the overheated atmosphere of the presidential palace.

During this interval, a few shots were fired (at the building housing the newspaper *Crítica* and at El Molino teahouse), and there was danger of worse. Perón's supporters took over the federal police headquarters and the third infantry regiment command posts.[56] The disturbances were put down, and the next day the appointment of Gen. José Humberto Sosa Molina as minister of the army, Rear Adm. Abelardo Pantín as minister of the navy, and

Col. Filomeno Velazco and José Domingo Molina as chief and
assistant chief, respectively, of the federal police were made public: they were all Perón men. Sir David Kelly, the English ambassador, points out in his memoirs that:

> Some of the Opposition had on that day [17 October] decided
> to accept the situation and came to General Farrell with their
> proposed list of ministers, only to be waved aside and informed
> that Colonel Perón had returned. Thus, the Opposition, after
> having by Braden's campaign been whipped up into a frenzy
> which was probably responsible for the temporary disappearance
> of Colonel Perón, had thrown away their one chance of regain-
> ing power and of permanently excluding their future dictator.
> From that day onwards, until the elections early in 1946, affairs
> marched swiftly to what appeared to me, though not to an
> Opposition blinded by hatred and wishful thinking, their inevi-
> table end.[57]

International Policies in Decisive Years

On 11 June 1943, shortly after the 4 June coup had taken
place, the United States recognized the Argentine government presided over by Ramírez and continued to exert upon him the increased pressure and coercion that had become familiar to Argen-
tinians·during Castillo's term. Hull points out that:

> In conversations with Ambassador Armour, Ramírez and Storni
> indicated that, given a comparatively short time in which to pre-
> pare the country, the new Government intended to break rela-
> tions with the Axis. Ramírez thought this would be done by
> August 15 at the latest. The Argentine Government, they said,
> intended to implement a policy of close inter-American cooper-
> ation based upon the inter-American pacts in force.[58]

Chile, another country that had been remiss, had already broken
relations with the Axis on 20 January 1943. But Washington was
not very pleased with some of the measures adopted by the new
authorities such as the postponement of the elections, which was
announced on 19 June, the dissolution of Congress, the steps
against "pro-Allied" publications and organizations, and the presence of notorious Axis sympathizers in important government
posts. The exchange of letters between Minister of Foreign Affairs
Storni and Secretary of State Hull (the texts were published in
Washington and Buenos Aires on 6 September 1943, but they
were dated in August) raised a storm of criticism because of the

uncomfortable position in which it placed the administration officials. Storni had appealed to Hull for "a modification of the coercion program"[59] and for Argentina to be allowed to participate in the Lend-Lease program, so that the South American balance of military power should not be altered (Brazil received those benefits).

> Hull replied in a scathing note that the United States took no part in balance of power politics in South America and would consider the question of military and other aid to Argentina after the new regime had fulfilled its overdue obligations to aid in the war effort against the Axis.[60]

Storni resigned his post on 9 September, and in October Sumner Welles (who had opposed many aspects of Hull's policy with respect to Argentina) resigned as assistant secretary of state. In the eyes of the Department of State the picture was complicated in December by the outbreak of the Bolivian revolution, in which it was claimed prominent GOU and Argentine government figures were implicated. As a result of this, in a memorandum to President Roosevelt on the subject, dated 8 January 1944, Cordell Hull suggested that:

> . . . a step that would have a most healthy psychological effect would be to provide Brazil with certain additional arms and equipment. This would show the Brazilian Government and people that we were standing behind them in a realistic way and would permit Brazil to move forward with her preparations to send an expeditionary force overseas.[61]

It was Hull's opinion that the "present military gang in control of Argentina would understand at once the import of this action." We do not know whether he remembered that only a few months earlier he had asserted that the United States had nothing to do with balance of power politics in South America.

The coup by Gualberto Villarroel in Bolivia mentioned above and the Oscar Hellmuth affair (Hellmuth was an Argentine agent implicated in a proposed exchange of German light arms and ammunition held on the island of Trinidad by British Intelligence Service agents) led some American government circles to assume that Argentina and the Axis would soon break relations. They did on 26 January 1944. On this O. Edmund Smith, Jr., comments that:

> Information which later reached the State Department revealed that President Ramírez and Foreign Minister Gilbert carried out

the rupture over the strong opposition of most of the Colonels' clique, when several cabinet members opposed to severing ties with Germany were absent from a crucial meeting on the night of January 25. A G.O.U. countermove against the *rupturista* faction appeared to be inevitable.[62]

Foreign Minister Gilbert resigned on 15 February 1944, and later President Ramírez was removed and replaced by General Farrell. The United States, in a change of tactics, refused to recognize him, on the basis of the so-called "Guani formula" (a doctrine formulated by the Uruguayan foreign minister, requiring "prior consultation" among the members of the Pan American Union before proceeding to recognize a new government). Hull complained bitterly about the measures adopted by the Farrell[63] government to favor German interests and stated that "in the face of these developments we could not remain inactive. Silence gave a species of acquiescence in the dangerous course of the Farrell regime, and we had no intention to acquiesce."[64]

On 22 June 1944 the United States recalled Ambassador Norman Armour to Washington. The Argentine government replied by doing the same with Adrián Escobar, its ambassador in that country, who returned to Buenos Aires. The Department of State took advantage of the occasion to suggest that the remaining Latin American republics withdraw their ambassadors accredited to Argentina within a period of fifteen days. The suggestion was also made to Great Britain. On 23 June 1944 the United States recognized the Bolivian government, by then "purged" of its nazi sins. Argentina was the last unregenerate sinner. Smith adds that:

> On August 15,1944, the Washington government took the step long advocated by Treasury Secretary Morgenthau: Argentina's gold reserves in the United States were frozen. U. S, merchant vessels were prohibited from calling at Argentine ports, and extensive restrictions were placed upon exports to the River Plate republic.[65]

Diplomatic pressure continued to mount, but the attitude of the United States did not achieve its purpose of changing the foreign policy of the Argentine government. The latter, somewhat paradoxically, found an unexpected ally in His British Majesty's government. Hull refers to this fact in many passages of his *Memoirs,* though he does not acknowledge its true nature as an interimperialist phenomenon (in the midst of a world war!) For example the secretary of state says that:

We desired a consistently strong attitude toward the Argentine Government, including refusal to recognize the Farrell regime. The British, fearful of an interruption in their meat supply, wanted to reach an agreement with the Farrell regime and to recognize it.[66]

This explains Hull's desperate efforts to get Prime Minister Churchill to agree to his own position. Argentina had taken care to maintain commercial relations with Great Britain, even during Ramírez's presidency. For example, on 21 August 1943, a treaty was signed with the United Kingdom agreeing to sell all surplus meat to the latter until 30 September 1944. During this time, Hull, in long interviews with Lord Halifax, the British ambassador in Washington, endeavored to force Great Britain to take a common stand with the United States. Churchill, in a message addressed to President Roosevelt, states that "cessation of Argentine supplies would disrupt military operations on the scale planned for this year. Before we leaped. . . we really had to look."[67] When Hull was shown this reply, he said to Halifax that

. . . the British were interested primarily in one situation in Argentina — meat supplies — while the United States was interested primarily in breaking up the ever-increasing pro-Axis elements based in the Argentine and steadily moving up the continent with the idea of overthrowing other Governments and setting up pro-Axis Governments as in Bolivia.[68]

However, the secretary of state went on to counsel the British ambassador about the meat problem, saying that:

The Argentines want a four-year contract with the British at a certain price. I suggest that Britain make contracts on a thirty-day or sixty-day basis, renewing them every month or two. This will bring the Argentine Government to reason and send it running after the British.[69]

Finally, responding to a request from Hull, Roosevelt sent a personal message (dated 30 June 1944) to Churchill requesting him to take a common stand with the United States in the Argentine matter and also to recall Ambassador Kelly. The British prime minister "very reluctantly and almost angrily agreed,"[70] pointing out the very difficult position in which Great Britain was placed by this measure. Of course, this gesture was as far as Churchill was prepared to go.

One of the severest critics of Hull's conduct was the British ambassador in Argentina, Sir David Kelly, when he reported his interview with Hull en route to London via the United States. Hull devotes seven pages of the *Memoirs* we have been quoting to a meeting that lasted forty minutes, in a last attempt to justify his policy. Kelly says that:

> To anyone reading this chapter in Mr. Cordell Hull's memoirs, without any other knowledge of the circumstances, the attitude of the British Government must appear both wooly and selfish. But in fact events, including the obvious one that the American and the other Ambassadors all returned to Argentina within nine months or so without their absence or return having in any way influenced the situation, showed that the British Government's hesitations, though they could not give adequate reasons for them, were entirely sound.[71]

Hull's illness and later resignation brought Edward Stettinius to the fore as the new secretary of state, beginning on 30 November 1944. He appointed Nelson Rockefeller assistant secretary of state for Latin American affairs, and the latter played an important role in the formulation of American policy with reference to Argentina. Sumner Welles summarizes the situation up to the time of Hull's retirement very well:

> The situation is due primarily to the effort of the Department of State to use the act of recognition as a diplomatic weapon, and as a means of exerting pressure in order to shape political developments in Argentina ... No one with any knowledge of Spanish-American psychology, and particularly of Argentine psychology, could have favored such a course. There can only ensue one of two possible results. Either the Farrell Government will be overthrown, in which event even the most democratic elements in Argentina, and those most opposed to that obnoxious dictatorship, will be greatly embittered against the United States for thus flagrantly interfering in their internal affairs; or else the reaction of all elements in Argentina against an attempt at coercion on the part of the United States will be so strong that the Farrell dictatorship will be strengthened. In either event the hostility against this country which our recent policy has created throughout Argentina will persist for years to come.[72]

With new people in the State Department the chances of an accommodation between the two governments increased, since neither one of them could fail to benefit from the cessation of such an uncertain situation. The United States was pressured by public opinion and by some Latin American governments; Argentina, by the need to line up with the rest of the continent in the already discernible new era about to be ushered in by an Allied victory over fascism. Smith confirms this when he writes that:

> In any event, the progress of World War II in favor of the Allied cause dictated, by early 1945, that the Argentine government align itself with the United Nations, especially since plans for the creation of a world organization were nearing fruition. Argentina felt that she might rely upon Latin-American support in a bid for diplomatic recognition and readmission into the hemispheric councils, but not at the price of submission to Yankee dictation.[73]

There was an unsuccessful attempt to call a meeting of foreign ministers within the Pan American Union, requested by Argentina on 27 October 1944 in order to deal with the situation existing between the Argentine Republic and other American nations. Hull opposed it from the hospital and his successor Stettinius attempted to have Argentina excluded from that meeting. Consequently, Farrell's government refused to participate under those conditions. In February of the following year, a State Department mission arrived in Buenos Aires and held secret conversations with Perón, Juan I. Cooke, and other officials for the purpose of resolving the stalemate. If Argentina complied with the obligations of the 1942 Rio de Janeiro Meeting, the United States would abandon its coercive attitude.[74]

This understanding started to take public shape during the Inter-American Conference on Problems of War and Peace held at Chapultepec (Mexico City) in February and March 1945. Resolution LIX

> ... invited [Argentina] to adhere to the Final Act of the Mexico City conference, and it was understood that a declaration of war against Germany and Japan was also expected. In return for these "last hour acts of solidarity," the American republics, including the United States, were unofficially pledged to grant diplomatic recognition to the Farrell administration and to support Argentina's right to membership in the United Nations Organization when the San Francisco meeting assembled.[75]

By decree of 27 March 1945 Argentina declared war on Germany and Japan. On 4 April 1945 the Argentine representative in Mexico signed the Final Act of the Chapultepec Conference. On 9 April 1945 the United States, Great Britain, and the Latin American republics who had adhered to the nonrecognition policy, reestablished diplomatic relations with the Argentine government. The final step in this international phase of Argentine policy was represented by the San Francisco Conference (25 April 1945). The Latin American block at that time held 40 percent of the votes in the assembly, and the United States could not do without them. They agreed to Argentina's admittance to the United Nations (this point continues to be debated, as to the Americans responsible for this attitude, as we see from Hull's *Memoirs*)[76] in exchange for regional support on other problems which faced the capitalist world vis-à-vis the Communist block. Hull himself believed that Argentina's admission to the United Nations was "the most colossal injury done to the Pan American movement in all its history."[77]

With the reestablishment of diplomatic relations, the ambassadors who had left nine months earlier began to return, Sir David Kelly among them. There were new faces, too: Spruille Braden was the new United States representative.

Braden or Perón

The American author we have been quoting on foreign policy matters comments on the activities of Ambassador Braden, which lasted only a few months. He says that:

> Demanding that the Farrell government restore basic civil liberties to the Argentine people, *Spruille Braden abused the privileges of his diplomatic post by touring the interior of Argentina, delivering speeches against the government to which he was accredited.* The Nationalist government had scheduled a presidential election for early 1946; but *it appeared to many Argentineans that the election campaign had already begun, with Braden as one of the candidates.* Braden dismissed the Farrell government's protests concerning his activities by stating that as U.S. Ambassador to Argentina he was accredited to the Argentine people as well as to the Argentine government.[78]

Braden collaborated openly with the Democratic Union then being formed and which in the end supported the Radical presidential candidates. Its *leit-motiv* was democracy:

> Our objective is to support the democracies, and we would wish for democratic governments in all parts of the world. It was out of need and not out of preference that the United States recognized governments that had assumed power without the consent of their peoples.[79]

Braden's stay in the country lasted only a few months, but his concentration on Argentine problems increased as he achieved new and more important positions in the State Department. President Truman on 2 July 1945 appointed James F. Byrnes secretary of state, after Stettinius had resigned from the post. Byrnes looked for a specialist on Latin American affairs and found him in the person of Braden, who took Rockefeller's place as assistant secretary of state in charge of Latin American affairs on 25 August.

There could be little doubt that Braden planned a return to Hull's program, except that economic sanctions would not be employed. Powerful financial interests persuaded the Washington goverment against a resumption of economic coercion, but the ban on armament shipments to the Buenos Aires regime was not lifted.[80] José Luis Torres quotes documents that support his statement that:

> [Braden], the Yankee diplomat who had turned Argentine political leader in order to bring to an end a failed revolution that had represented a national hope, achieved even the impossible. The Radical party, which named the candidates on the presidential ticket that was later adopted by the parties that formed the Democratic Union under the ostensible auspices of the United States Embassy, went so far as to expunge from its electoral platform the principles that had animated its activity during the whole course of its civic endeavors, namely, the defense of sovereignty.[81]

The explanation is to be found in the fact that at the level of the leaders who controlled the party organization Radicalism was committed to a posture of active militancy in union with the other groups opposing Perón. Only the Intransigence and Renewal Movement then being formed opposed the democratic front, demanding a return to early principles. The FORJA people (who since 1940 had dropped the earlier requirement of affiliation with the Radical party in order to join its cadres) greeted the new forces which entered Argentine public life on 17 October 1945 by saying, among other things, that:

> In the debate established before public opinion the line between the oligarchy and the people is perfectly delineated, no matter what temporary banners are displayed, and FORJA, in line with its Argentine and Radical duties, expresses its unequivocal support for the laboring masses who are organizing for the defense of their social achievements.[82]

On 15 December 1945, the group passed a resolution dissolving itself, "leaving its members in complete liberty of action," in view of the existence of "a popular movement with the political and social conditions that are the collective expression of a national will to self-fulfillment, the lack of political backing for which led to the creation of FORJA as a result of its repudiation by Radicalism."[83] Arturo Jauretche and Darío Alessandro signed this resolution.

The other parties resumed the negotiations that had started before 4 June 1943, with a view to achieving a program and electoral agreement to oppose the presumed (after 17 October 1945 there was no room for doubt) official candidate: Perón. Repetto was one of those who relied most heavily on the opportunity offered by the promise of free elections. As he writes:

> In my book, *Deber cumplido,* published in 1943, I have given in chronological order all the memoranda, writings, and speeches pronounced by me during six years, calling for the union of parties in order to reestablish the constitutional regime and counteract the growing nazi influence. It was an effort full of good will, but fruitless, which I renewed with the same determination, after a short interval, when General Farrell's promises authorized us to hope that there would be a prompt call to elections in order to give the country a constitutional government.[84]

Repetto, who was a veteran Socialist leader, was in the forefront of the conversations which were renewed during the last few months of 1945. The decree dissolving political parties was rescinded on 30 October. Traditional parties were also allowed to reorganize themselves along familiar lines instead of having to follow the recent Organic Statute for Political Parties. As Whitaker says:

> They were then given a considerable measure of freedom in conducting their campaigns through the mails and public meetings as well as by press and radio. For the first and last time in Argentine history, provision was made for the equal treatment of all parties   by the radio broadcasting stations.[85]

During the course of the electoral campaign, incidents and problems arose in connection with the application of legal norms. These incidents and problems increased when the Democratic Union became aware of its defeat, after the elections. But there were fields in which the democratic forces had notoriously greater support for their candidates than the Peronist forces: the press (the great dailies compared to *La Época*) and the radio (the private stations compared to the government stations).

The Democratic Coordination Junta was the immediate precursor of the Democratic Union. It was "made up of personalities with various ideologies and social positions, some of them associated with the oligarchy and the imperialist monopolies."[86] It published manifestoes calling for "the immediate surrender of the government to the president of the Supreme Court of Justice,"[87] and this demand was viewed with favor by the Radical party, the National Democratic party, the Socialist party, the Progressive Democratic party, the Anti-Personalist Radical party, and the Communist party; also by the Argentine University Federation, among other institutions. Another forerunner of the Democratic Union was "Argentine Action," which had for some years worked for the union of the "democratic" parties against "nazism." When Peronism came to be somewhat inaccurately identified with nazism, the opposition was extended to the new movement. Whitaker is clear on the subject:

> Gradually, however, the growing seriousness of the domestic threat from Axis sympathizers led some of the leaders of Acción Argentina to try to develop it into a coalition of all the anti-Axis parties and groups in Argentina, under the name of *Unión Democrática,* for the defense of democracy in Argentina itself.[88]

During this interval, Braden had not been idle in his new post in Washington. His superior, Secretary of State Byrnes, on 27 November 1945 hastened to endorse enthusiastically a Uruguayan proposal (the Rodríguez Larreta doctrine), a few days after the Uruguayan had officially formulated it. Welles comments wryly on Byrnes's speed in approval, pointing out that the proposal had not "even been digested in the other Foreign Offices to which it had been sent."[89] The Rodríguez Larreta doctrine urged "collective action on the part of the American nations in cases where a continental country does not fulfill its obligations."[90]

Argentine Foreign Minister Cooke hastened to denounce the proposal as a dangerous perversion of the "fundamental American principle of non-intervention." The United States also refused to take part in the 20 October 1945 foreign ministers meeting in Rio de Janeiro to convert the Act of Chapultepec into a permanent treaty. Braden undertook to persuade important members of the

Foreign Affairs Committee of the American Senate, explaining to them how inconvenient the presence of the Farrell regime at the conference would be for the United States. The Pan American Union had no objection to postponing the meeting until 1946, but it actually did not take place until 1947, when Gen. George C. Marshall had already taken Byrnes's place at the State Department. Braden resigned his post in June 1947.

Within Argentina, the forces that were to participate in the 24 February 1946 elections were aligning themselves. On the one side were the Democratic Union parties that eventually agreed on a presidential ticket. Repetto mentions Radical leaders who supported or rejected the Democratic Union: Enrique Mosca belonged to the first camp; Amadeo Sabattini, Honorio Pueyrredón, and Elpidio González to the second.[91] Despite the opposition of the Intransigent delegates, the national convention of the Radical party met on 27 December 1945 to approve the platform, ratify the "democratic union" (in effect since 14 November between the Radical party and the Socialist, Democratic Progressive, and Communist parties) and elect candidates for president and vice-president. José P. Tamborini and Enrique Mosca, respectively, carried the day. The Conservatives did not present a ticket of their own, but they supported the Radical one.

Three groups had joined forces on the Peronist side: the Labor party, organized on the basis of union leaders favorable to the new policies set in motion by the Secretariat of Labor and Social Security, such as Luis F. Gay, Cipriano Reyes, José Tesorieri, Alcides Montiel (the former Socialist Joaquín Coca, who joined the movement, became one of the presidential electors); the Radical party (Renewal Board), made up of activists separated from the party, some of whom were already in the Farrell cabinet; and the Civic Centers, which were of secondary importance. The Labor party elected Perón as its candidate for the presidency; the Radical party (Renewal Board) was to do the same for the vice-presidency. When everything seemed to indicate Armando G. Antille had been elected, a maneuver in the assembly (the Radical origins made this almost predictable) led to the naming of Jazmín Hortensio Quijano, an eccentric-looking lawyer from Corrientes Province. [92]

The candidates traveled from one end of the country to the other in the midst of tremendous electoral euphoria. There were some attempts at violence against the Democratic Union's "Liberty Train" and against the Labor candidate.

A pastoral letter issued by the Argentine episcopate on 16 November 1945 repeated earlier texts (this is something that has not always been kept in mind) and was generally interpreted as discreet support of Colonel Perón by the ecclesiastical hierarchy. From the pulpits, atheism was attacked and the religious instruction law was praised.

The ranks of the Democratic Union exuded optimism. Overwhelming victories against their opponents were predicted. Ambassador Kelly made a famous statement:

> I was convinced that Perón was going to win, a belief in which I was nearly alone with the exception of the sagacious *Times* correspondent, Hinkson, and the extremely well-informed Papal Nuncio, Monsignor Fietta.[93]

But the opposition parties seemed not to notice certain facts: Perón himself had taken skillful advantage of Braden's open intervention in Argentine affairs, whether in Buenos Aires or from Washington, by hurling his challenge: "Braden or Perón"; the refusal of the most important management group, the Argentine Industrial Union, to implement the labor regulations that Perón had promised and that had been approved around the end of 1945 (the government threatened heavy fines and finally broke down entrepreneurial resistance): and the Supreme Court attitude in denying the validity of resolutions passed by the Secretariat of Labor and Social Security.

And, of course, there was also the famous *Blue Book* episode, of which Smith says that:

> On 12 February 1946, the U.S. government took a step which was tantamount to open intervention in the Argentine election, when it published the *Blue Book on Argentina,* making public the evidence at its disposal that linked Colonel Perón and several of his G. O. U. aids with the Nazi regime in Germany.[94]

Much of the material collected came from documents captured in the Chancellery of the Third Reich; however, their interpretation has been disputed. Smith comments that:

> Argentinean public opinion, in the judgment of most competent observers, reacted to the publication of the U.S. memorandum in a ˙manner contrary to what was hoped for in the State Department. Most Argentineans [sic.] did not doubt the veracity of at least some of the charges made in the *Blue Book,* but the general feeling was that the facts so presented had been generally known throughout the hemisphere for more than a year.
> The Argentines [sic] wondered why the State Department withheld its publication until two weeks before the presidential elec-

tion. The almost unanimous judgment of the State Department's action in Argentina and throughout Latin America was that the issuance of the *Blue Book* constituted an unmistakable and unwarranted intervention in the election scheduled for February 24. . .[95]

An author favorably disposed toward the Democratic Union ("it constituted a last attempt to bring the country back to constitutional ways"), when commenting on the subject of the *Blue Book,* contents himself with deploring the unfortunate timing. It is his opinion that:

> The document should have been published much earlier and then its effects would have been fully felt. At this time its effects were not only rendered inoperative, but it even influenced minds susceptible to nationalistic formulas that had been subjected to official repetitions in rough and lying language *ad nauseam.*[96]

The Communist party (some of whose leaders were defending the forming of the Democratic Union as late as 1958)[97] in its official history reduces practically all Braden's activity to a short paragraph:

> Using as a pretext the attacks directed against him by North American Ambassador Braden, Perón stepped up anti-Yankee demagoguery and in this way intensified even more the conviction of the masses that, if he achieved a majority of votes in the elections, once in power he would fully satisfy all their aspirations for social justice and would defend national independence.[98]

University students known as the "generation of forty-five" supported the democratic unity movement; they went further, they became one of the pillars of the movement. Tulio Halperín Donghi stated that:

> . . .the cause defended by the university, that of the democratic order against the attempts to imitate the fascist example, tended to become confused with other causes, especially with that of the economic forces that defended the status quo in the social field against the attempts at renewal inspired by administrative circles.[99]

Enrique Grande, who was a candidate for national deputy in the February 1946 elections, was more trenchant:

. . .the Democratic Union was born out of necessity, as a position between the sword and the wall of all the men who had fought against the abstract idea of the birth of nazism, without realizing that the possibility of reaching the working people lay on the other side.[100]

This is why the *Libro Azul y Blanco* (Buenos Aires, 1946) that Colonel Juan Perón published as a reply to Braden's *Blue Book* barely aroused the curiosity of many opposition sectors. The same was true about the colonel's speeches, which were written off as "demagogic." A foreign commentator analyzed the preelection scene much more clearly when he wrote several years later that:

While the Democratic Union promised Argentinean workers "social justice," Perón was able to call attention to concrete gains for which he claimed credit, including wage increases, yearly bonuses, and rent decreases, with the intimation that these benefits were only a token of what might be expected were he elected to the presidency.[101]

The presidential elections took place on 24 February 1946. Of the 2,734,386 votes cast, 1,527,231 (56 percent of the total) were for Perón and 1,207,155 (44 percent) for Tamborini. These figures became known after several days of counting. Whitaker says that:

From all the evidence, the election appears to have been free and honest, as the government had promised. Just after the polls closed, the opposition leaders themselves, including Tamborini, described it as a model of democratic rectitude and the best election ever held in the history of Argentina . . . [102]

Elpidio González congratulated President Farrell on the conduct of the elections,[103] but there were lamentations later when the democratic groups were faced with the cold figures that spelled defeat. The victory of the Peronists (due among other factors to the provisions of the Sáenz Peña Act) was even more overwhelming in the number of elective offices carried (congressmen, governors, provincial legislators) than in actual figures. The opposition — aside from the "Radical block of the 44" in the Chamber of Deputies — only got the governorship in Corrientes Province and the two national senators from that province. However, the province was intervened and the two men elected, Luis F. Bobbio and Mariano Gómez, never sat in Congress.

Perón reached the presidency with a greater aggregate of political power than any other executive before him, greater even than that of the Yrigoyen of the "Plebiscite." The use he made of that power is part of the recent history of Argentina. Our work ends in 1946, as it had begun in 1930, in a somewhat arbitrary manner. The historico-political process transcends all the limiting dates we may attempt to fix.

Part Two
Around The Centers of Power

5 Political Parties, Political Forces

Function and dysfunction of Congress

The legislative crisis in Argentina has roots that go back much further than is generally supposed. It is common to condemn solemnly many of the Peronist Congress's shortcomings. According to these accounts, the story begins in 1946 with the gradual reduction in numbers of the Radical opposition. They include the same tiresome details about the eccentric parliamentarians, the cloture motions, the systematic "party line" the majority block followed. . .The criticism is usually extended to include what we would call the "Frondizist" Congress (1958-1962), because that congress also showed a low level of representation and a fundamental lack of results. The congress of President Arturo Illia's (1963-1966) unfinished administration has represented what is up to now the nadir in the gradual deterioration of congressional representation in Argentina.

Is there nothing more to be said? Many pages of this monograph will give an account of the work done by the legislators of the 1932-1943 period, because we have used the *Diarios de Sesiones* of both chambers as a constant reference source in writing this book. We believe that in this way we can reconstruct what has been tentatively outlined in the preceding chapters in such a manner as to extend the period of the "crisis" to include the end of the twenties and all of the thirties.

Before the revolution of 6 September 1930, the Chamber of Deputies was the scene of two episodes that rather accurately set the tone for the period. The first was the speech by the Radical party deputy for the province of Buenos Aires, Raúl F. Oyhanarte, in which he asserted that:

> Radicalism, because it is young, is not afraid of vote counting nor does it feel itself called upon simply to add up votes, nor to obtain favorable balances; let all those take their place in this Chamber who are entitled to do so in their own right — those

112

who have won. Without odious exceptions or sterile rancours, let us be reconciled, gentlemen, within legality! All the latent aspirations of the dynamic life of a people can find room within the latter. The oppressed are awakening and rising up like a living mass. Under the fraternal roof of Radicalism there is no room, there can be no room, for anyone or anything that is not sanctified by legality; if this is not so, let the defeated be regarded as martyrs and let us blush for the winners! . . . Let no one, no matter who or what he is, attempt to strike blindly at the prickly beehive without taking into consideration the rich honey-combs it affords as the result of its patient, industrious, collective, and anonymous efforts![1]

The second episode involved the famous speech delivered by Nicolás Repetto on 28 August 1930. In this piece of oratory (which takes up sixteen pages of the *Diario de Sesiones*) the Socialist leader touches upon various subjects of then current interest and also strays somewhat afield into the political history of our country. He states his position on the revolution of 1890 and on the Radical party in the following terms:

The Revolution of 1890 failed, but we all breathed easier when we were sure that, while the Revolution had failed, the reins of government remained in the same hands that had held them, since that government was the only one that had support that was massive, widespread, and well-established enough to assure us of stability. . . . If [the government] had not been controlled by Pellegrini and if it had not been assured of General Roca's collaboration, this country would immediately have fallen into chaos because the revolutionary force of 1890 was not an organization of political ideas and more or less homogeneous principles, but rather an adventitious grouping, a conglomerate of different political forces, which came together from all directions, which were each motivated by ambitions, purposes, and hatreds of their own and out of which it would have been impossible to fashion a great governmental effort.

I, who have been an enthusiastic supporter of the Radical party, who as a youth poured out irreverently so many offensive epithets on General Mitre's politics of consensus, I now want to take this opportunity to express my admiration for the common sense, foresight, and sensible patriotism of that policy.[2]

Repetto had this to say about the Radicalism of 1930 and its leader:

Instead of leading a government of free citizens and institutions, he attempts to order, direct, and permeate everything according to his will. . . but I maintain that he is not a man of strong will. He is a man of obstinate will and the deputies know that obstinacy and strength are two absolutely different things. Energy allows adjustment and adaptation to events, difficulties, and inconveniences; energy bends, but it does not break. Thus, this man has neither energy nor will; he has obstinacy, a desire to control the political conscience of the citizens. . . There is nothing more serious for a bourgeois government (let the deputies understand that when I say a bourgeois government, I mean a government established to defend the economic status quo),for a bourgeois government like this one of Yrigoyen's, of the Radical party, there is nothing more dangerous than to forsake legality because if a bourgeois government, which must naturally be one of order, forsakes normalcy, it breaks precedents and says: "Well, I am paying no attention now to the basic rules, and I proceed according to my own inclination," when a bourgeois government does this, at immediately finds itself faced with two consequences: the working class (which is a reality and which today, especially in urban centers, is moved by the impulse of the philosophic and social ideas that are shaking the world) as soon as it discovers that a bourgeois government has overstepped the bounds of legality, it immediately concludes that it too can go beyond those bounds. This is a problem which is discussed, which is studied, and which has already become the primer of the political and social conscience of the men who are active in the labor movement. "If the government does not respect the law, neither will we." Moreover, if the government does not respect the law, if it believes that it can impose on the army of the nation the unseemly and ignoble functions (I qualify them according to my own feelings) that the president has imposed on the army of the nation in San Juan Province, when an officer of the army feels that he is obliged to perform such functions, knowing that his main mission is to maintain the territorial and constitutional integrity of the nation (the army does not exist to maintain only the territorial integrity but also the constitutional integrity) unavoidably it must ask itself: "Does not my mission as a military man lie in defending constitutional integrity also, as well as in defending the integrity of the Argentine soil? Can I lend myself, can I be the instrument, can I descend to such lowly occupations, so incongruous to the essence of the functions it behooves me to perform?"[3]

After predicting a revolution in Argentina if the government did not change its course, the Socialist deputy ended his discourse in this way:

Therefore, let your voice be heard by those who should hear it, and who should submit to these dictates of common sense, these dictates of the law, these dictates that should arise from the innermost being of any real Radical. Let your voice be heard and let it be soon! Let there be a radical change and let the country move with enthusiasm and alacrity, since in politics we do not want the quiet of the grave; let interests clash, let the heat of passion be felt occasionally, since that too is good, that sublimates impulses and often reveals what is inside a human consciousness! Let the heat of our former democratic struggles reappear! Let us return to that permanent condition of restlessness that disturbs the sleep and digestion of the proper bourgeois, but which gladdens the heart of good patriots who know that in the struggle and in the continuous clashing of these opposed interests lies the health and progress of peoples![4]

This is the way Nicolás Repetto felt. In one of the passages of his speech he took time to direct his criticism toward the very institution of which he was a part:

Let us now talk, gentlemen, about the decay of this body. I do not intend to disparage any one person, but I do have the obligation of declaring before you that this Congress betrays a marked decline in its capacity for work, its method, and the daily activity of the legislators who compose it, as compared with the one that I found in 1913 when I was first elected.[5]

Interestingly enough, here we find the Socialist Repetto eulogizing the Conservative oligarchy that had been in power at the time of his initial election to Congress. Since these words were spoken in 1930, criticism of Congress has been widespread on all sides. Of course, this general criticism includes that which was motivated by the self-interest of those who wished to implement a corporative structure based on the European model. The fact of the matter is that there were many voices raised to censure a body that was rapidly ceasing to fulfill its traditional function.

In a lecture given at the University of the Littoral in 1933 entitled "The Spiritual Crisis and Argentine Thought," Saúl Alejandro Taborda devoted some meaningful paragraphs to this subject. For example, he said that:

We have lost confidence in our legislative organ. For a long time now Congress has lacked the internal cohesion that provides the sinews and vitality of an institution. In relation to Congress the same thing has happened to us that has happened to other countries that have tried it under more favorable conditions than we, since they had at their service a tradition nourished and elaborated throughout long centuries of culture. It is not mere coincidence that the day after the 6th of September uprising, through the columns of *La Prensa* of Buenos Aires, Lloyd George revealed to us the intrinsic vices of the institution and the desperate delusion of the British people faced with its increasingly more pronounced and notorious inefficiency. In referring to the burning question of unemployment, the eminent statesman recognizes that the lack of solution [of the problem] has made the public aware of "the impotence of Parliament," and he concludes by asserting that "there is something improper" in this, using the customary forced euphemism of the parliamentarian.[6]

The charges Taborda brings against Congress are serious, since he affirms that it is a "ponderous machine that today dictates an emergency law long years after the need for it has passed, as proved by the condition of agriculture, left unprotected and at the mercy of speculation by international banks; as proved by the oil situation; as proved by the condition of the lower classes; as proved by all our unresolved problems."[7]

Deodoro Roca, another voice from the interior, is trenchant in his comments on the assassination of Senator-elect Enzo Bordabehere. He said that "Liebknecht called Congress 'the fig leaf' of autocracy. We could very well call it 'the fig leaf of the monopolies.' "[8] José Luis Torres sums the situation up in these words:

Both the Congresses with a Radical majority and the Congresses with a Conservative majority were burdened by the same decisions from on high, imposing upon them from the shadows the hasty approval of ignominious laws favoring supercapitalism, while the complaints provoked by the prevailing uncertainty and the most legitimate anxieties of the people were allowed to sleep in the desk drawers of the committees and the demands of those who were hungry and thirsty for justice were thrown into the wastebaskets.[9]

Provincial legislatures and the Buenos Aires Municipal Council did not lag far behind Congress in this. As the same Torres has expressed it:

In this way, within less than a week, the Legislature of Buenos Aires Province approved the law providing for the conversion of the public debt, which was carried out in a seemingly clandestine manner and the results of which were approved by another law pushed through despite the fact that the operation left the state with a deficit of over 30 million pesos, after having handed Bemberg more than 15 millions by way of improper commissions and expenses for which they never accounted. The laws of Coordination and Incorporation of Transportation were approved within a fortnight...; in little more than a week the laws on Banking and Currency were approved after the bills had been submitted to Congress, in violation of all parliamentary rules. In the twinkling of an eye concessions authorizing S.O.F.I.N.A. (an entity representative and typical of supercapitalism without a country and without a flag) to exploit the people were approved until the year 2002.[10]

Some experts in public law have also commented on the failure of the legislative institutions. Perhaps Carlos María Bidegain has best indicated the nature of the problem:

Quick action is what people want and the president is made to act and not to talk, while Congress continues to be bound by old formulas that permit it to talk a great deal but act little. In any case, the work had to be done and since Congress was ill-prepared to carry it out well, it has carried it out very badly. Even before 1946, the pressure of the president on Congress could not be resisted when it represented an abuse. The failure of Congress has given rise to the growing influence of the organizations representing interest groups, making the idea of the "economic and social councils" appear ever more seductive. Congress is running the risk of being the victim of what Ayala pointed out as the fate of institutions that do not adapt to the changes of the times: to be discarded and become fossilized, while new and different institutions arise to perform its task.[11]

However, the legislative body itself seldom seemed to be concerned about its own fate. Some reform bills (like that of 1940) merely provided for relatively formal improvements, the effects of which were lessened by the habits of the legislators, such as reading interminable speeches despite the rule against it, abusing the time limit set for having the floor, bringing up points of privilege indiscriminately, and so forth.

The dissolutions of Congress decreed by Uriburu and Ramírez in 1930 and 1943,[12] were merely the prelude to later events that do not fit within the time limits of this study: the "Liberating Revolution" of 1955 also closed the Legislature; in the end something similar happened as a result of the 18 March 1962 elections and the coup d'état that followed: Congress ceased to exist after some months of much-discussed death throes. No one was too concerned about it, not even the legislators themselves. The center of political power had for some time been lodged in other sectors. This was fully confirmed by the most recent closing of the Argentine Congress on 28 June 1966, when Illia was deposed by the self-styled "Argentine Revolution."

The majority

During the period when Congress did function (1932-1943), the conservative forces and their allies (Pinedo's Independent Socialists and the Anti-Personalist Radicals who still had some standing in provinces like Entre Ríos and Santa Fe) became the main political support of the executive branch, except for occasional, soon overcome, differences such as the death of Ortiz, which was a rude blow for those who were counting on his turning toward traditional Radicalism. Patrón Costas's failure to obtain the nomination indicated that the Conservatives no longer were satisfied with secondary posts but were aiming at the leading role. However, saying no was up to the army, not the political groups.

Galletti has summed up accurately some characteristics of the conservative sectors, which varied in nuances according to the different districts in which they were active: the Democratic party of Córdoba, for example, was not exactly the same as the Conservative party of Buenos Aires.[13] Among other differences, their attitudes toward fraud distinguished them, at least formally. Buenos Aires Province was the great bastion of the Conservative party and produced leaders as representative of an era as boss Alberto Barceló in the city of Avellaneda and the fascist Manuel Fresco clinging to his governorship. Many years after he left office, Fresco recalled those days with a certain pride:

> I produced an honorable and active government, nationalist and Christian in tone, such as did not exist in the country at the time. As a minor sin, I had to accept the accusation of fraud, which led to the Ortiz administration. *There was no such fraud, only a stratagem to end the Radical government, a process the 1930 revolution started. The Radicals were legion, and they always constituted a threat.*[14]

Fraud was tenaciously cultivated — and defended — by authorized Conservative spokesmen, to such an extent that it may be said to have been the characteristic of the period in its political aspect. In 1931 out of the ruins of the National Democratic Federation, which had been based on the "acceptability of coalitions in a country with a presidential system"[15] and had aspired to coordinating Conservative, Independent Socialist, Radical Anti-personalist, and local party groups, arose the so-called National Democratic party, made up of provincial nuclei with a certain freedom of maneuver: the Corrientes Province Autonomists, the Entre Ríos Province Popular Concentration, the Buenos Aires Province Conservatives, the Córdoba Province Democrats, the San Luis, Mendoza, San Juan, Tucumán and Corrientes Liberals, the Provincial party of Jujuy and the Salta Provincial Union.[16] The Congressional Records of both houses make clear to even the most undiscerning reader that the *leit-motiv* of the sessions was the repeated charge of electoral fraud brought by almost all sectors. On occasion the Conservatives took the offensive in replying:

> We owe the country a word of truth. We have discussed at length the electoral processes that took place on 6 March [1938] in almost all the provinces. We are charged with defending fraud; but we have not defended fraud, the existence of which we do not acknowledge, only a political and civic conviction that we can place before the country in all sincerity and truth.[17]

Eduardo Laurencena, an anti-Yrigoyen Radical, who, as governor of Entre Ríos Province, was not affected by the 6th of September coup, has outlined the psychosocial mechanism of the Conservative mentality with respect to fraud. Of this he says that:

> The whole process is a typical example of the sort of politics that has prevailed in the leadership of the country for years, the outstanding characteristic of which is the constant contradiction between words and deeds, between the ideas expressed and those practiced. Fervent democrats in their verbal expressions, they scorn democracy in practice; when clean elections are most emphatically promised it is because they are already prepared for trickery, fraud, and, if necessary, violence; while religious observance of the laws (especially of those admittedly bad) is proclaimed because the cult of legalism forbids violating them, flagrant violation of the most fundamental clauses of the Cons-

titution has already been planned; when the supreme and sacred interests of the people are mentioned, it is because some paltry political interest is to be defended.[18]

During its brief existence, the Independent Socialist party proved the most faithful ally of Conservatism. The group led by Federico Pinedo and Antonio De Tomaso came into being through a disagreement that arose within the Socialist party in 1927. Pinedo is clear about this:

> Although on both sides there were some who were bound to find deep philosophical causes for that disagreement, I hereby declare, as I did at the time, not without incurring the disapproval of some esteemed colleagues, that *I saw no other reason for divergence than personal reasons or at most temperamental ones.* In the long run, the old party has managed to adopt, in its internal life and in its relations with the outside world, a good many of the practices and procedures that we, the dissidents, wished to implement and which led to our separation.[19]

In short, the Independent Socialist party came into being as a bridge between the right wing of traditional Socialism and the Conservative right, in an attempt to give the latter greater flexibility of movement within the country's political structure. When the Socialist party devoted itself to its task as an opposition on the European model (the comparison to His British Majesty's Loyal Opposition comes naturally to mind), which of course did not exclude cooperation with the administration on many matters,[20] the raison d'être of the Independent Socialists came to an end. It was for this reason that after their 1930 victory in the city of Buenos Aires elections, they won eleven seats in 1932 in the Chamber of Deputies, six in 1936, two in 1937, and so disappeared from the scene. The ferocious anti-Yrigoyenism which the Independent Socialists displayed at the beginning of their activities allowed them occasionally to obtain the votes of sectors that were not strictly Conservative but were guided by outward appearances. Outwardly, the Independent Socialists seemed to some to be authentic "socialists." In reality they were liberal Conservatives, something which is made quite evident by a glance at Pinedo's career — the same Pinedo who, as an Independent Socialist legislator, eulogized the old days he has not ceased to regret:

> The charge that this country has been governed by a brutal and selfish oligarchy, that has only prospered in power without concern for the lot of the people, is infamous. What the country

fortunately had in its early years was an enlightened oligarc
like few others, an oligarchy so enlightened and generous that it
called men born in other lands to share political leadership and
economic and financial control of this country. And the proof
of its generosity and moderation is that all the wealth escaped
from its hands and was concentrated in the hands of the immigrants' sons, whose ancestors had found here a great opportunity to express their personality and to develop their aptitudes.[21]

The funeral eulogy delivered by Miguel Angel Cárcano on Antonio De Tomaso (whom he succeeded two years later as minister of
agriculture, continuing his policy) sounds more like the tribute of
a comrade who shared De Tomaso's ideas than the prescribed
words of formal tribute that might be expected under the circumstances.

> During the last fifteen years there has been no economic, politi-
> cal, or social problem that he did not study and consider with
> his great mind and his great heart in order to enlighten, orient,
> exalt, calm, or instruct the masses of the people. For this rea-
> son, he was an imponderable factor in the preparation of the
> revolutionary movement of the 6th of September, which the
> warmth of his advocacy encouraged and the balance of his judg-
> ment guided in order to come later, logically and naturally, to
> the government of the Republic.[22]

Anti-Personalist Radicals "became an important nucleus that
gave allegiance to the government of General Justo. They attained
a maximum representation of sixty deputies in 1934."[23] The Conservatives knew how to go about courting them skillfully, exploit-
ing their traditional anti-Yrigoyenism and on occasion yielding to
them important government posts such as the presidential nomination of Roberto M. Ortiz. Their lack of ideological homogeneity
was notorious, but gradually their existence became an anachro-
nism, in view of the paralled development of Alvear's Radical
leadership and the emergence within the Radical party of sectors
demanding a greater adherence to the Yrigoyenist roots, as
FORJA did in the thirties (though it later became independent of
the party apparatus) and the Intransigence and Renewal Movement in the forties. It is almost a tradition with the Radicals that
when a sector or group that is in the opposition attains the official
party leadership, it betrays the very principles which it had earlier
paraded and to all intents and purposes follows the very same political line that it had earlier challenged with very "radical" fervor.
This, together with the more or less permanent and outwardly

very deep schisms, represents a constant in the Radical party that has not been sufficiently analyzed.

The Conservatives did not waste any opportunities to praise their congressional and governmental allies. Adrián C. Escobar sets the tone of this approach to political seduction, which character-ized a considerable portion of the period under study. In a speech made during the celebration of the Ortiz-Castillo victory, held in the city of Santa Fe, the Conservative lawmaker, in speaking of the Anti-Personalist Radical party of that province, asks:

How could a party with a select nucleus of leaders of great capac-ity fail to prosper? The experienced statesmen, called to take part in the operations of the provincial government; the res-pectable figures of advisers forged in the experience acquired in civic struggles and sacrifices for the welfare of this land that has for many years been the scene of arduous labors; the talented politician who has sought the explanation of social phenomena objectively, garnering from observation the philosophical conse-quences and explanations of problems; and the men who have proved their disinterested and unselfish devotion; all these have contributed their time and their efforts to their fellow citizens of the province, in many cases without taking heed that the time when life begins to decline would arrive without their having assured their personal economic future, not thinking about their own families in order to think about the life of all. The member bursting with enthusiasm and civic ardor who plunges into the melée of the committee and the public square; the intelligent, fluent, lively newspaperman, overflowing with passion, who involves his concerned mind in the collective wel-fare; the lawmaker who in the national Congress or in the pro-vincial legislature upholds brilliantly, intelligently, and with un-equaled knowledge and energy the political principles that cons-titute his program; the intelligent and patriotic young men who everywhere spring up spontaneously and enthusiastically; and the noble and hard-working people who understand and encour-age their leaders; all these are elements that constitute a respect-able and weighty political force, that show that here in Santa Fe you are the majority and that the arguments and pretentions of those who have thought they could lead public opinion as-tray are worth nothing, that public opinion would not allow it-self to be misled, that it knows the truth, and that it has passed judgment on them definitively and permanently.[24]

We have already referred to the Santa Fe political processes of that time and the facts in no way resemble the enthusiastic version of them given by Escobar. There are dangers in indiscriminate praise.

Radicalism: its abstention and later history

The decade of the thirties is almost certainly one of the culminating points in the evolution of the Radical party, a period that explains many later developments. A number of important events occurred during this time; the Radical party ceased to be the party in power because of the 6 September coup; its leaders were persecuted (including Yrigoyen himself and intellectuals such as Ricardo Rojas); the Radicals were prevented from following the electoral way (the Alvear-Güemes ticket was vetoed) and decided to abstain; some groups tried the way of revolution (Pomar, Cattáneo. . .); Alvear directed the party along a conciliatory path (gambling always on his capacity to maneuver and on the undeniable popular support enjoyed by the Radical party); a group opposing the official leadership emerged (FORJA); from the beginning of World War II the idea of a "Democratic Union" with Socialists and Progressive Democrats began to take hold. After 1943 incomprehension of contemporary socioeconomic problems on the part of the Radicals made them (with internal opposition by the Intransigents) one of the bases on which the opposition forces regrouped to face the Peronists in the 1946 elections. The Communists supported the new alliance, and the Conservatives counseled voting for the Tamborini-Mosca ticket. The Yrigoyenist influence was conspicuously absent.

Histories of Radicalism have almost all been characterized by their rhetoric, their excessive attention to detail, and their hopelessly parochial spirit. They have suffered, as does the classic work by Gabriel del Mazo, from two main defects: they have knowingly identified the Radical course with Argentine history, and they have believed that party conventions, assemblies, and meetings are the key to the internal processes of the organization. When the historians of the party have not been Radicals themselves, their works generally abound in diatribes and witticisms at the expense of Yrigoyen, instead of searching for deeper causes than the admittedly absorbing personality of a single man. In our judgment, what is important is to point out some characteristics of Radicalism as a party that have a bearing on the recent political history of Argentina.

For example, the correlation between the party's electoral abstention and the Radicals revolutionary attempts is a key element.
After the abandonment of the former and the systematic suppres-
sion of the latter [25] Radicalism decisively infiltrated the congressional opposition, and eventually even achieved a majority in the
Chamber of Deputies. Félix Luna recalls that:

> At the end of March [1940] elections were held in the federal
> capital. When the vote counting ended, the new political aspect
> of the country became apparent. The Radical party had won
> the majority in the elections for deputies carried out in the
> federal capital and in Buenos Aires, Santa Fe, Mendoza, Jujuy,
> Entre Ríos, and Tucumán Provinces. It had carried a new gover-
> norship: that of Jujuy, where Raúl Bertrés had been elected,
> and through the election of Santiago del Castillo had assured
> the continuation of a Radical administration in Córdoba. It had
> its own quorum in the Chamber of Deputies: eighty congress-
> men. The Buenos Aires, Santa Fe, and Mendoza Province victo-
> ries were very representative of the majority position of the par-
> ty presided over by Alvear...President Castillo could not com-
> plain of the Radicals' collaboration in Congress: over sixty laws
> were approved during the 1941 session, even though many ses-
> sions were devoted to discussing the findings of the Anti-
> Argentine Activities Investigating Commission, whose investiga-
> tions in connection with the Nazi penetration of the country
> had some sensationalistic aspects. The attention of the Chamber
> of Deputies was also taken up with the report of the special
> commission appointed to study the matter of the 1936 electri-
> cal concessions, a report that constituted a bill of immunity for
> those implicated, whose culpable actions were only brought to
> light by the work of the 1944 Rodríguez Conde Commission. Des-
> pite the hasty absolution voted in favor of the councilmen who
> five years earlier had approved the extension of the electrical
> concessions, the oppressive atmosphere redolent of a "deal"
> that surrounded some representatives of Radicalism had been
> reinforced by another investigation: that of the demands made
> on the private bus lines of the city of Buenos Aires, an investi-
> gation that was started in June and in which two Radical coun-
> cilmen were implicated. [26]

Though the prestige of the Radicals had been somewhat eroded,
it had still led to an excellent 1940 electoral showing. However, it
did not withstand the pressure of the events of those years such as
the withdrawal from office and the death of President Ortiz, the

Conservative reaction on the part of Castillo, and the 4 June 1943 coup (which in its early days certain sectors of the Radical party applauded). In 1942 the Socialist party won a majority in the elections for national deputies held in the federal capital, and three years later, Radicals, Socialists, Progressive Democrats, and Communists sealed their "democratic union" pact in order to oppose (with the acquiescence of the Conservatives) the emerging Peronist movement. Many of the more apparent than real differences that had separated the parties during the preceding decade (strictly speaking, since 1930) were unobstrusively hushed up in order to allow for common slogans such as "For liberty, against nazism, for an authentic social justice."[27] Other, and in this case real, differences were simply sidestepped only to be exacerbated as soon as the results of the election became known. Radicalism, once it was under the control of the Intransigent faction, monopolized the opposition, especially in Congress, tacitly renouncing any connection with the Democratic Union. At least this was true during the first years of the new regime. This has led an old-timer in the nationalist movement to write, with obvious controversial intent:

> Take a 1943 Conservative, impoverish and embitter him, and you have a Radical; take a Radical, make him a rabid anticlericalist, and you have a Socialist. The common background of all three is last century's *liberalism*, which, by excluding any other party as "against the institutions," becomes a dogma, while at the same time it exudes underneath its natural and true distillation, communism. Therefore, liberalism shows what it has always been, a dogma, that is, a Catholic heresy. What distinguishes the three branches of the "United Tri-Faced Party" is only the hypertrophy of one of its component elements: privilege, opposition, resentment. Consequently, we have an absurd type of Totalitarianism of Liberty or the Church of Democracy, since Radicalism, an offshoot of a federal main stem, quickly lost in the process we have already studied the characteristics impressed upon it by its founder [Leandro N. Alem], the child of the *mazorquero:* traditional federalism.[28]

Though much of the political writing of Leonardo Castellani is characterized by constant exaggeration and gives evidence of a febrile imagination (no doubt a product of his meritorious work as an author of fiction under the pseudonym of Jerónimo del Rey), he does point up the reality that underlies the somewhat diluted Radical posturing of the Alvearists. Something of the sort had been pointed out in 1932 by no less an authority than Repetto in dealing with both the Conservatives and the Radicals in the Chamber of Deputies. An excerpt from the dialogue carried on by the Socialist congressman is given below:

> Mr. Repetto: I am talking in a general sense, sir. We are dealing with two sectors of the Argentine propertied class. The same landholders appear in the Conservative party and in the Radical party, the same property owners. . .
> Several Deputies: And in the Socialist party. . .
> Mr. Repetto: That would only be a rare exception *(Laughter)*. . .
> The same landholders, the same property owners, the same nationalists, the same militarists, the same clericals, appear on both sides. I am not speaking in a derogatory sense, gentlemen. I know the reality in my country and I respect it when that reality imposes itself as a historical phenomenon. These two forces are now engaged in a death struggle. On the 6th of September, the Conservative party, which had been eliminated from the government by the Sáenz Peña Act . . .
> Mr. Bustillo (José María): By violence, because it was dislodged by the arbitrary intervention of 1916.
> Mr. Repetto: . . . has by force returned to power and is now enjoying the fruits of the same.[29]

The fact of the matter is that Radicalism, after it lifted the electoral abstention (the latter did not make political sense without a corresponding subsequent revolutionary uprising), became just one more party within the fraudulent structure of the time — perhaps the single most numerous and popular party as regards the number of its followers. As such, it contributed to legalizing domestically and internationally the anti-national measures that were so common during the period. This is what gave rise first to the FORJA reaction, and then to the Intransigent factions within the bosom of the Radical party.

Radical abstention (a historical phenomenon that finds its only possible parallel in the blank vote cast by the Peronists and the consequences deriving from it from 1955 on, allowance being made for the differences in time) was the palpable proof of the hold that the Radical party maintained on important sectors of the electorate (especially on the middle sectors). Gabriel del Mazo points out that:

> Abstention is not carried out by a political force when it wants to but when it can, and without a deep Radical feeling or deep Radical philosophy, it would lack its most important meaning:

it would appear to be political calculation or political nihilism. For a political force to "be able" with sense and fervor to adopt a program of abstention, a general and individual ethicospiritual process is needed that cannot be produced in a day, but only through a gradual and dramatic formation. Only complète intransigence justifies deciding upon and maintaining abstention. . . *The fact was that 1935, and more particularly 1936, showed even to the point of open scandal that the Radical leadership in general lacked the intrinsic qualities for fighting intransigently,* and that reason would indeed explain the lifting of the abstention.[30]

Alvear and his followers had some years earlier done all they could to frustrate the revolutionary opportunities of the military and civilian followers of Radicalism.[31] Very concrete and powerful interests, such as those of the SOFINA-CADE group, needed a party of the Radical type in the opposition in order to have it back their notorious maneuvers against the country; the Socialists and the Progressive Democrats were sure to oppose (as indeed they did) the scandalous municipal ordinances extending the concessions. Alvear was the man they needed. (One of the men, for on the opposite side Pinedo and Hueyo were the ostensible representatives of the imperialistic electric monopoly). As a result of Alvear's influence, the deal went through.[32] Félix Luna, an author whom we have quoted repeatedly during the course of this work, did not lack sympathy for some of Alvear's attitudes, and in the biography he devoted to this political figure does not hesitate to say that:

Setting aside the possibility of personal profit from the transaction, by elimination we are forced to conclude that *Alvear's conduct was intended to result in obtaining from the companies that benefited the resources that his party needed to face the 1937 electoral campaign.* The struggle for the presidency of the nation was going to be long and costly; it was necessary to cover the cost of tours, to help districts that lacked funds, print propaganda material, subsidize partisan publications, and rent premises for local party headquarters. Alvear knew this well, and he also knew it was difficult to raise among the Radicals the funds needed to cover the great expenses of the campaign.[33]

How is it possible to try to justify Alvear's attitude simply because he did not enrich himself personally? Are we not again

identifying Radicalism with the nation? Marcelo Sánchez Sorondo
appraised realistically Alvear's intended mission. In 1941 Sánchez
Sorondo wrote that:

> As an illustrious survival of the nineties Alvear knows the
> bitterness of exile and is therefore in favor of a collaborationist
> intransigence with a patriotic motive. The lisping gentleman has
> in the highest degree the gift of the trite phrase. His speeches
> seem plucked out of an anthology of democratic common-
> places. But the vintage form of expression does not necessarily
> guarantee innocence. The enormous intellectual vacuum of the
> leader does not decrease the amount of will-power employed in
> the maneuver. Alvear wants a sacred union not only of the
> Radicals, but of all the parties in defense of the famous institu-
> tions. Because of his own mediocrity, he is aware of the appeal
> of a common denominator to the crowd. When a common
> denominator is in question, when an inclined plane affords a
> solution requiring a minimum of effort, then it is claimed that
> things have mended by themselves and God is Argentine.[34]

It was not an accident that the reversal in the Radical party
policy took place under Alvear's leadership. He was, after all, the
most representative figure of the Radical party while it was playing
the role of the French or British opposition; the Radical party
remained within the legal system, a system constantly belied by
fraud and discrimination. After an intraparty struggle, the factions
opposing Alvear followed two roads: they either joined the ranks
of Peronism or they supported the Intransigence and Renewal
Movement within the party, in an attempt to gain control of it.[35]
In the meantime, and throughout the 1932 to 1943 period, the
obvious struggle continued to be that between the *Concordancia*
and the Radical party. The former's presidential candidate,
Roberto M. Ortiz, made it clear that:

> The option is clear and unmistakable: you are either for the
> 1930 governments or for those of 1937, either with the dissol-
> vent and corrupting demagoguery or with constructive democ-
> racy placed at the service of national progress. We are living
> through moments that are too anguishing to permit remaining
> indifferent vis-à-vis the political changes which may come
> about. Any one who during the present presidential campaign
> adopts the merely contemplative stance of one who is witness-
> ing the regular workings of democratic institutions reveals a
> blameworthy insensibility. The coming elections do not simply

represent two parties facing each other, but rather two antagonistic tendencies. One, the one we represent, is inspired by strong
feelings of nationhood; the other, which we will combat with all
our civic energy, is intimately associated with the basest demagogic impulses. We defend Religion, the Fatherland, the Family.
It is for this reason that we feel that we are the interpreters of a
great Argentine cause rather than mere spokesmen for a political program.[36]

Ortiz, the Conservative candidate, was a Radical of Anti-Personalist origin who attacked the "dissolvent and corrupting demagoguery" not of Yrigoyenist Radicalism but of the Alvearist party.

A municipal party and a provincial party

The Socialist party continued to have a respectable electoral following only in the city of Buenos Aires, though on occasion there
were moderate upsurges in other, usually urban, areas. These, however, were not of long duration. During the period we are studying
(Juan B. Justo had died in the 1920s) the most representative figure in the Chamber of Deputies was Nicolás Repetto who, as he
relates in his memoirs, left medicine for politics. With him there
were many congressmen of the same persuasion, including the
then young heir apparent to Repetto, Américo Ghioldi, whose
normal school laurels were still fresh. In the Senate the classic pro-
files of Mario Bravo and Alfredo L. Palacios (the latter had returned to the fold of the "old and glorious" Socialist party)
played the part of the democratic opposition to a fraudulent and
shameful regime.[37] The Socialists very often took pains to make
clear the nonparticipation of their party organization in the preparations leading to the 1930 armed movement. For example,
Repetto asserted in Congress that:

Governments considered bad must not be ousted in order to
equal and even surpass them in vices, errors, and ineptitude.
You, the ministers and deputies, do not constitute a government under a normal order; you are, in a way and to a certain
extent, still the expression of a government of force; you are
the descendants of a movement that has taken the government
from the hands of the one who was legitimately carrying it on
for the people, doing sincerely what he could and was able to
do; but you, who have seized the government from the hands of
the one who legitimately held it, have the obligation, have the
unavoidable duty of showing yourselves in action a thousand

times superior to the man that you evicted from a post conferred by a legal process.[38]

Carlos Sánchez Viamonte, referring evidently to the 1930 revo-
lutionaries, felt justified in saying that:

> If a law student should be questioned as to what a revolution is
> and should answer that it is a victorious uprising, he could not
> be faulted because, in the final analysis, an uprising is usually
> only a revolution that failed. That is the lesson of our American
> institutional history, and up to now there has been no change in
> that norm and tradition.[39]

Senator Palacios, taking part in a debate between de la Torre
and Sánchez Sorondo on the supposed collaboration of the Santa
Fe politician with the September dictatorship, noted that:

> On 6 September I was Dean of the School of Law of the Univer-
> sity of Buenos Aires, and that same day I drafted a resolution
> that I immediately made known to the University, ignoring the
> government of force that had just been installed. So that I not
> only did not at any time accompany the column in which Gen-
> eral Uriburu marched, but from the first instant I repudiated
> the movement that I considered fatal to the tranquillity and the
> institutions of the country.[40]

The Socialist party (which with the Progressive Democratic
party had formed the Civil Alliance for the 1931 presidential elections), apparently aided by the Radicals' abstention, reached the
first congressional sessions of the following year with a numerical
representation that was not unimpressive: forty-three deputies and
two senators, a total they would never again attain. Repetto recognized this clearly:

> Having been denied the right to enter the 8 November 1931
> elections, many Radical party supporters voted for the presiden-
> tial ticket of the Socialist-Progressive Democrat Alliance and for
> the Socialist party slate of national congressmen. Thanks to this
> spontaneous and very valuable contribution, our party obtained
> the two senatorships, the majority of the seats allocated to the
> federal capital in the Chamber of Deputies, and the minority of
> those allocated to the provinces of Buenos Aires, Córdoba, Men-
> doza, and San Luis.[41]

The congressional actitivity of the Socialists is most characteristic of their position during the 1932-1943 period. They were
determined to respect the rules of the game, so they sought allies

among small parties such as the Progressive Democrats, instead of
facing a serious joint effort with sectors of the Radical party as
Joaquín Coca, who later migrated to the ephemeral Socialist
Labor party, wanted to do. From 1939 on they were more concerned with various aspects of World War II than with the needs of
the vast human contingent that was entering political life, to
whom the still obscure Colonel Perón was then turning his attention. For this reason, the Socialists attracted the middle class, non-
radical voter more than the industrial worker who had come from
his province or the rural worker who had no legislative protection.
In the meantime, the Socialist members in Congress debated in
minute detail such bills as the divorce one (1932, approved by the
lower house, blocked by the Senate), presented innumerable petitions for reports, proposed granting political rights to women,
questioned ministers, protested against fraud, requested reductions
in the military and clerical budgets, and supported the capitalist
democracies.[42] At times, though not often, an unlikely creed was
verbally proclaimed:

> Deputy Repetto has already stated it this afternoon: we are an
> essentially democratic party in Argentina; we do not deny our
> long-range final objective, but as long as we are allowed to do so
> we use the method of legality and democratic processes. We will
> have to employ other means if the day ever comes when we lack
> the liberty and opportunity to work within the democratic
> fold.[43]

At the same time, both in the Radical party opposition and
within the *Concordancia,* a few voices were raised to point out the
differences that separated those parties from Socialism. The Radical Carlos M. Noel, for example, stated that:

> The Socialist ideal, which has a respectable background made
> up of profound truths and tremendous errors, in reality clashes
> with our ideals. We agree with them on the respect for popular
> sovereignty and on the belief that all representation must come
> from the clear will of the people; but while their sole objective
> is the passing of control from one class to another, we seek
> social harmony within the present order. Instead of catastrophic
> solutions, we want the joining together of all minds and all in-
> terests. Socialism contains within its doctrine the profound
> errors that gave rise to it. As an abstract concept of theore-
> ticians, it contains the impersonal fiction of its mathematical
> formulas.[44]

During his electoral campaign, Roberto M. Ortiz said:

I do not ignore the merits of our adversaries. I would not be a sincere democrat if I did not know how to respect and discuss them calmly. For example, I acknowledge the beneficial contribution of Socialism, as a minority party, to the perfecting of political and social conditions within our country, although, of course, I do not in the least share its materialistic creed.[45]

The Socialist party, thus reduced to being an opposition party without much of a popular following (except in the capital, as stated earlier), became inflexible in its structures and repetitive in its leadership. The phenomenon was noted by a foreign observer of our reality, Arthur P. Whitaker:

The leadership of the chief opposition party, the Radical, became bureaucratized, developed a kind of oligarchy of its own, and lost contact both with the party rank and file and still more with the general public. Much of the same thing happened to the Socialist party, too; its young men complained that the oldsters kept a death grip on the party.[46]

For a party with a labor background this was especially damaging. Another American author confirms these conclusions:

The steadfast refusal of the middle-sector-led Socialist Party to sacrifice its basic objectives in return for immediate advantages prevented it from cooperating closely with other Center and Left organizations for extended periods of time. Also, *the Socialists' reluctance to use their influence with the labor movement to interfere in the internal affairs of the unions cost them the vote of the workingman who supported groups both to the Right and the Left that favored drastic and direct methods of obtaining his objectives.*[47]

A former Socialist party member, who continues to make confused appeals for the "national integration" proposed by Rogelio Frigerio, has summarized, not without a certain malicious enjoyment, the course of the divisions and subdivisions that have been characteristic of the party throughout its history:

This double personality of the Socialist party, as evidenced by a doctrinaire mask and a reality of opportunism foreign to the concrete reality, set a path of contradictions and internal crises for the party, which had already become apparent within three years of its founding. In fact, in 1899 Collectivist Socialism withdrew from the party; in 1903 the party congress held in Junín expelled the unionists, with the advice, given by Repetto, that they should gain political experience for themselves; in 1915 Alfredo Palacios resigned his seat and established the Argentine Socialist party. Later, the Communist party schism took place, and in 1921 the so-called *"terceristas"* were expelled from a congress held in Bahía Blanca. In 1927 the so-called Independent Socialists left; in 1936 the "labor" socialists did so; during the Peronist regime other fragmentations occurred, the two most important being led by Enrique Dickmann and Dardo Cúneo, and lastly, beginning in 1958, reciprocal expulsions began to occur. . .[48]

During the period we are considering, the Socialist party inaugurated its political plans with the Civil Alliance and closed them by participating in the Democratic Union. On both occasions it was accompanied by the Progressive Democratic party, a group that had roots almost exclusively within the province of Santa Fe. Its immediate origin (the more remote one includes the disillusions encountered by Lisandro de la Torre in his contacts with Yngoyenist Radicalism and the Conservatism of the ranch owners) was the establishment of the Santa Fe *Liga del Sur,* which was "essentially Federalist and municipalist." In some cases, the main ideas of the Progressive Democrats go back to French Radical-Socialism, finding concrete expression in documents such as the Santa Fe provincial constitution of 1921, "unfortunately revoked for minor political motives."[49] The party occasionally recovered strength through the activity in the Senate of its founder, but once de la Torre died, the Progressive Democrats fell into a sort of lethargy attested to by their recent history. Because of Radical abstention, it also suffered a corresponding "inflation" of votes which resulted in its having up to fourteen deputies in 1932-1933.

The Socialist Party-Progressive Democratic Party Alliance, which had Lisandro de la Torre as its presidential candidate in the 1931 elections that General Justo carried, was a frustrated attempt to project the ideas of that group on a national level. Very few voices were raised against the coalition, except for the Radical abstainers who considered the presence of the Alliance in the elections inopportune, since, to a certain extent, it "legitimated" the official fraud faced by the Radical party. Within the Socialist ranks, the exception was the above mentioned Joaquín Coca, who said:

...the Executive Committee of the Socialist party proposes to its members a pact with the Progressive Democratic party. Should we support it? That party is an artificial grouping organized around one man, Lisandro de la Torre. It is a personal party. In the best of cases, it is a group of university people who have invented (or have appropriated, since it is an old story) a recipe for forming "centrist" electoral parties which consists in theoretically occupying the middle ground between the extremists of the Right and of the Left in order to gain partisans from the "exact middle," as it used to be called years ago, and avoid reaction and revolution. In reality, they are conservative-liberal groups, more conservative than liberal and more reactionary than revolutionary. ..., We Socialists are the opponents of Radicalism, because as a labor party we go much beyond the political, economic, and social objectives of Radicalism, but it is obvious that Radical objectives are part of our own, to the extent that for a long time now it has been an axiom of our party that when Radicalism does not fulfill its duty as a liberal bourgeois party we must take its place in that indispensable work of liberalism in order to prepare for the working class a better position which will allow it to progress more effectively and surely along the road to its emancipation. . . Even if it were only for the reason that the Radical party contains a great labor mass, we should be closer to that party than to the Conservative party, since if Socialism is to increase its following and expand its sphere of influence in our country, it will be through the workers who are now Radicals because they do not know Socialism and who will be Socialists as soon as they know who we are and what we want, and as soon as *they do not see us acting in agreement with the Conservatives, their adversaries, and exclusively against Radicalism.*[50]

The founder of the Progressive Democratic party, the group that was so harshly censured by Coca, was himself conscious of the basic uselessness of his political struggle and also, since he was its leader, of the ultimate uselessness of the Progressive Democratic party, always in unstable equilibrium between its theoretical principles and the burning reality. De la Torre states this in his correspondence:

I do not know how far I will put into practice this year your patriotic advice to tell the government annoying truths unceasingly, for the two-fold reason of the uselessness of the effort in an unresponsive milieu and because of that profound distaste for action which I have mentioned to you before. . . . From a distance I must seem to you a combatant inflamed and even drunk with victory. I wish it were so! In reality, I am a slave to a monotonous task that recommences endlessly and obliges me to use my last energies without having faith in anything, almost without a purpose.[51]

A defender of the opposition stance of Socialists and Progressive Democrats has not failed to point out the lack of connection of all this with what was really occurring in Argentina:

> The appearance of the Civil Alliance had a profound significance. It was the last heart-beat. . . of an alert citizenry that demanded the necessary reforms to bring our country up-to-date with reference to a progressive policy. Later, the currents of opinion up to 1945 touched upon other areas of reality: the Spanish Civil War, the World War, all the great events that were taking place in the world, but that were a little remote from our sociopolitical reality. This was because during those years there was little faith in our country and in our institutions.[52]

On the other hand, when we attempt to evaluate the work of Congress, it may be said that Alfredo Galletti's good intentions surpassed the deeds:

> Besides, the attitude of the Socialist and Progressive Democratic parties for some years prevented the abuse of power, made possible whatever critical action was practicable under the circumstances, impelled the government to promulgate laws that were relatively important from a social point of view, and retarded the process of loss of credibility and avoidance of responsibility.[53]

Had all this been true, the Democratic Union would easily have beaten Perón.

The Democratic Union and its program

Some aspects of the Democratic Union's formation and campaign have been considered before in chapter 4. What interests us now is to look specifically at the program that guided the promoters of the movement. We cannot resist the temptation to transcribe it *in toto,* in order to refresh the memory of some and to make it known to those who have not known it before.

PROGRAM OF THE DEMOCRATIC UNION

1. Defense of the juridical order and political system of the Constitution.
2. Respect for provincial autonomy and for the duly elected municipal authorities. Faithful compliance with the Sáenz Peña Act. Strict control of fraud and any actions that may tend to give rise to governments by force or of a nazi-fascist type.
3. Conversion and extension of the rights of the citizenry: freedom of thought, association, and assembly; religious liberty; free union organization; assurance of a fruitful and healthy life.
4. Elimination of all hindrances to foreign immigration coming to the country to work without hating its institutions. Prohibition of racist or anti-Semitic activities.
5. Immediate transformation of all national territories with more than 60,000 inhabitants into provinces. Financial autonomy for the Buenos Aires Municipality.
6. Bringing morality into public administration. Law prohibiting the enrichment of public officials, both civilian and military.
7. Repeal of Law 4,144 on the expulsion of foreigners.
8. Financial readjustment. Balancing of budgets.
9. An economic policy tending to raise the standard of living of the people; progressive suppresion of consumer taxes and those on useful activities. A sound currency.
10. An international policy based on the close cooperation of Argentina with countries with a clear democratic orientation. Effective collaboration with the other peoples of America. Sincere compliance with agreements entered into. Solidarity with the Spanish people in their struggle against the tyranny that oppresses them. Diplomatic and commercial relations with the Soviet Union.
11. Respect for university autonomy, for the principles of the reform of secondary education, and for the system of public education.
12. A policy of nationalization of the public services and sources of power. Use of hydroelectric power.
13. To prevent unemployment, organic public works projects and construction of low-income housing. Regulation of the working day.
14. Repression of maneuvers that tend to monopolize the instruments and materials of production and of labor and to raise the prices of food, clothing, and housing.

15. Minimum or living salary. A system of social welfare and insurance, retirement, and pensions.

16. Protecting, broadening, and perfecting the gains obtained by the workers, so that social justice may be the sure sign of Argentine democracy.

17. Agrarian reform; subdivision of land; stability for the *colono;* protection for the rural worker.

18. Promotion of free cooperation.

19. Protection for children. Coordinated and intensive action against illiteracy. Increased school construction.

20. Promotion of free professional and technical education. Organization of social solidarity for young people without resources and unemployed, so that they may continue their studies, complete an apprenticeship, find a place to work, and occupy their free time advantageously for their education.

21. Political rights for women.

22. A national plan for fighting disease: wholesome, abundant, and inexpensive diet; regular vacations; maternal and child-care service; extension of sanitary services, construction of hospitals, and other welfare and medical centers; mobilization of all professional medical services; improvement of medical procedures and increase in the organizations devoted to such study. Action against tropical diseases on a permanent basis. Cleaning up of insalubrious areas. Health insurance.

Signed: For the Radical party: Carlos E. Cisneros and David Michel Torino. For the Socialist party: Silvio L. Ruggieri and Juan Antonio Solari. For the Progressive Democratic party: Juan José Díaz Arana and Santiago P. Giorgi. For the Communist party: Rodolfo Ghioldi and Gerónimo Arnedo Alvarez.[54]

Critisicm of this alliance has been widespread in recent years, though not in all circles. In a heterogeneous collection of essays,[55] to which men like Silvio Frondizi, Rodolfo Ghioldi, Rodolfo Puiggrós, Jorge Abelardo Ramos, Abel Alexis Latendorf, Esteban Rey, Ismael Viñas and others contributed, the only one who did not critize the Democratic Union was Ghioldi, who referred the reader to his participation in a 1958 round table mentioned above. At that time, Ghioldi said:

What did the Democratic Union represent? There has been much criticism of the Democratic Union. The main defect, it is said, was that it was an attempt to unite different parties. What is overlooked is that it was the one great attempt to unify the Argentine people democratically and save it from ten years of nazi despotism. The Democratic Union has been represented as something oligarchical. Do you know the program of the Democratic Union? It was not wholly satisfactory, but it was quite reasonable. It included agrarian reform, nationalization of public services, breaking relations with the Spanish Falange, and recognition of the Soviet Union. Was this not an acceptable program? [56]

In his discussion of the subject in a paper written in 1946, Silvio Frondizi's judgment seems much more sensible:

Even in the hypothetical case of the victory of Unity, it would be the forces of the Right that would assume power, leaving those [of the Left] betrayed and without popular support. In other words, they would have lost their raison d'être: the people's struggle. Besides, union with reactionary forces, "unity without exclusions," favored the resurgence of the latter. It is painful to behold how the men of 3 June, who were guilty of all the shame that ever blanketed the country, could emerge into civic life after having purified themselves in the waters of the Jordan represented by the struggle against the dictatorship. They fought against the dictatorship, not because they were sincere democrats, but because that dictatorship did not want to accept an arrangement with them. They demonstrated this by their actions throughout one of the most shameful periods ever recorded in the history of Argentina.[57]

This mixture of Radicals, Socialists, Progressive Democrats, and Communists, very closely watched by none other than the Conservatives, did not even come close to being a modest Popular Front (such as the one attempted during the thirties with a different purpose and scope). It mixed Tyrians and Trojans under the same abstract labels, while the masses were receiving concrete benefits (not the Biblical "mess of potage" to which many ward heelers attributed the rise of Perón). One example (though there were many) is the case of the Democratic Union program to which Rodolfo Ghioldi so nostalgically refers, which speaks of "protection for the rural worker," while on 17 October 1944 the "Statute of the Rural Worker" had been enacted by Decree N° 28,169 and had been implemented, thus immediately benefiting a great sector of the rural population who thenceforth would support "Colonel Perón." Moisés Lebensohn, who helped found the Intransigence and Renewal Movement of the Radical party, has explained the options offered by the 1946 elections:

The dictatorship, on the one hand, and the Radical party (reduced to leading the opposition), on the other, played complementary roles. They skillfully confronted the people with an unreal dilemma — social justice on the one hand, constitutional order on the other, as though these were antithetical terms. One brought forth its social justice from an abomination of liberty, the other deferred to an uncertain and murky tomorrow the answer to the questions of the people. The Radicals took refuge in legality, that bastion of the economic and social status quo, and were doomed to fail because the status quo was indefensible; thus it left to *continuismo* (which brandished them as decoys without believing in them) the banners of the emerging world and the traditional watchwords of the Radical party: the struggle against the oligarchy and against imperialisms. On 24 February 1946 the preoccupied and confused man in the street had to choose his future while facing a crossroads.[58]

As it can easily be perceived, Lebensohn was more concerned about the internal problems of Radicalism than about the choice made by the "man in the street." Colonel Perón had known how to reach that man in the street (and the one in the country, too, let us not forget). A concrete proof of the labor and rural support given the Labor party and splinter Radical (Renewal Board) party joint ticket is given by Gino Germani in his analyses of the 1946 and 1948 elections:

Indeed, the position of all occupational groups appears to be much better defined during this second period. Thus, while before 1946 the correlations computed did not reveal the existence of parties with a homogeneous electorate from the point of view of its occupational makeup, after this date the panorama changes radically with the polarization of the popular class (urban workers only in the case of the city of Buenos Aires) on the one side, and the middle and upper class (the owners, professionals, and white-collar workers) on the other. These two categories rallied around the two most important political groups; the majority (the Peronist party) supported predominantly by the popular class and the minority (the Radical party) supported by the middle and upper class.[59]

This phenomenon would afford one of the most substantial keys for the in-depth study of the Peronist period. The democratic Union did not even suspect what was happening. The result — a close victory for the forces that supported Perón — always seems to have eluded even their most pessimistic predictions. Ernesto Sábato has borne witness to this in referring to the answer some leftist political leaders gave him when he questioned their participation in the Democratic Union:

> We were told. . . or we were given to understand with paternal benevolence that we were boys without political experience, that Perón would never win free elections, that there was no such control of the laboring masses, but rather barely of those Marx had called the lumpen proletariat; we were told that the crowds that had marched to the Plaza de Mayo on 17 October were *descamisados* without principles, that the real mass of workers — the working mass of the great unions — had class consciousness and did not allow itself to be fooled by the demagoguery of a nazi who was also a military man; that the strength of Colonel Perón was made up of the formless and classless masses that had recently come in from the countryside, without consciousness, without political preparation, and without a sense of trade unionism.[60]

This was the theory of the Democratic Union, whose most fervent defenders belonged (a paradox?) to the so-called parties of the Left.

Argentine Communism

Subject to practically uninterrupted persecution during the period from September 1930 to 1945 (except in some aspects during the Democratic Union preelection period), the Argentine Communist party has upheld a tradition of struggle and personal sacrifice on the part of its members which should not obscure the reversals of its strategic and tactical lines. The dates 1930 to 1945 offer an excellent opportunity to give examples of this. In accordance with its official publication, which summarizes (though at times it may modify) the process that interests us here, the Communist party has gone through the following stages:

a) Indiscriminate criticism of Hipólito Yrigoyen's government, without taking into account the danger of a reactionary coup such as the one that was already being prepared. The official Communist position even claimed that: "the Yrigoyen Government is a capitalistic reactionary government, as shown by its repressive, reactionary, fascisticizing policy against the struggling proletariat, against whom it increasingly uses terrorist methods." This quotation dates from August 1930. The fact is that more or less word for word, these concepts might serve more precisely to describe the government of Uriburu.

b) In order to place the Uriburu government in context, on the next page it is claimed that "with the military-fascist coup d'état of 6 September 1930, the ranching and agricultural oligarchy and the great monopolistic capital reconquered complete control of the machinery of the state and formed a government to defend their interests. . ."

The Communist party bore heroically the harsh represession meted out by Uriburu and his successor Justo. "However, our party later found that the political results of that period of struggle were not commensurate with the enormous sacrifices made by our members." Extremist positions predominated, ultraleftist attitudes were assumed by many leaders, and it was not unusual to find "workers' and peasants' soviets" being promoted. Luis V. Sommi, then one of the party, even asserted that:

> The Radical party fights to maintain and reinforce the dictatorship of the ruling classes, and the Communist party fights to crush all the political power of the ruling classes and to pass power on to the proletariat and the peasants. This is the basic difference. Any one who does not understand these simple matters does not understand anything about the class struggle.[61]

Of course, all tactical and fundamental interpretations followed the international line that guided local Communism. This line joined the fate of the Soviet Union under Stalin's command too closely (and not exactly dialectically) to our own fate, without realizing that the problem was exactly the opposite: from the particular to the universal, and that the "national question" was what was urgent and had priority. This lack of adjustment to concrete fact on the part of the Communist party (something that has been remarked upon by all those who have commented on its history) had deplorable consequences not only for the party itself, but also for other progressive forces moving forward at the time.

c) The extremist idea prevailed until March 1935, when the enlarged Central Comittee critized errors and ordered changes in the party leadership: the era of "popular fronts" on the world stage was beginning (the Soviet Union thought that in this manner the Nazi danger about which it was so concerned could be neutralized). Of course, this formula had to be applied to Argentina, and the Communist party devoted itself to the search for "the unity of action of democratic forces."[62] Despite some isolated symptoms to the contrary (a trend that later led to the founding of the Socialist

Labor party), the Socialist party did not look with favor upon
the presence of the Communists by its side and preferred "to bring
about a conjunction of *popular and law-abiding parties* in order to
commit it to the defense of public liberties and the reconquest of
an authentically and freely elected regime."[63] The logical candidates for the Socialist "front" (and of course for Communist
efforts, too) were the small Progressive Democratic party and the
Radical party. Alvearist "intransigence" spoiled any chance of
this, and the popular front failed to materialize. Perhaps this failure is to be deplored, especially in view of subsequent events that
led to the Democratic Union, where the joining of political forces
came to a climax. Despite the failure to form an alliance, the Communist party supported first Alvear as a candidate for the presidency, and later Ortiz as president.[64]

   d) In the political activities of the Communist party there is an
interlude that has come to be known as the "neutralist period,"
but no reference is made to it in the official history of the party.
Juan José Real, a former active member, who at one time occupied high posts in the Argentine Communist hierarchy, has acknowledged this indirectly:

> As for us, the Communist and fellow-travelling activists of the
> Left, during the first phase of the war, when it was still con-
> fined to the conflict between the Axis on the one hand and
> France and England on the other, we were neutralists; at that
> moment we agreed with Radical party neutralists and with
> FORJA. But on 20 June 1941 the German troops attacked and
> overran Soviet territory, and the war became worldwide; a de
> facto alliance between the powers that were fighting the Axis
> immediately crystallized into a formal alliance.[65]

Real forgot to mention that the Soviet Union and Nazi Germany had signed the Molotov-von Ribbentrop nonaggression pact in
August of 1939 as a result of the isolation in which the USSR had
been left by England and France (to whom it had unsuccessfully
made overtures for an alliance) and of the pressing threat of Hitler
on its Western flank. The temporary "neutralist" position of the
Argentine Communist party was basically due to this dependence
on the strategic needs of the Soviet Union, something which this is
not the place to discuss.

   e) After Hitler's attack, the scene changed: the USSR became
the ally of England, France, and, later, of the United States vis-à-
vis Nazism; the war was no longer a purely interimperialist problem. The Communist party bent all its efforts to favoring the

Allied cause, something that in itself is not to be censured, though some armchair terrorists would like to have us do so. Let us not forget that nazism cannot be defended. The antinazi struggle is (and was) a just struggle. What must indeed be emphasized is that, paralleling this struggle *(which did not have to lead to the connubial type of association of the Democratic Union)*, the Communist party was distinguished until recently by a rather inadequate understanding of the mass phenomenon generically termed "Peronism."[66] During the 1943-1946 period such errors affected its own structure as a working-class party since, rather than attempting to understand the aspirations of the people, it tried to minimize the friction between its discredited political allies. While the theoretical concept of a union of political forces is laudable, it seems less acceptable that the Communist party did not understand the role that Perón was playing at that time with regard to the masses and the effect of his propaganda.[67] The connection the Argentine Communists had in 1945 with the American Embassy and with the conservative groups whom they had opposed during the preceding decade could not fail to astonish the ordinary voter. Perón knew how to use this contradiction very effectively. The Communist party, for a change, was again using the term "fascist," which it applied successively to Ramírez, Farrell, and Perón (especially to the latter) and tried to solve what was a real problem by the use of an adjective. Unless we want to accept the simplistic explanation implied by the use of the word "demagoguery," we must wonder why the Communist party, rather than asking itself why the majority of the new workers who came into industry and the metropolis did not form Communist cadres but instead supported Colonel Perón, continued to be obsessively preoccupied with unity: "The participation of the parties in the [move for] unity is a peremptory need for the Republic. Democracy must respond by ratifying a common fighting front. Unity, now, this week. On us all, without exception, the tremendous responsibility weighs."[68] After Perón's victory there were some sectors within the Communist party that wished to redefine the party attitude toward Peronism, but they were purged. Rodolfo Puiggrós (1946) and Juan José Real (1953) were among the outstanding men so expelled.

Going back to the 1930s, we must emphasize the unsuccessful attempts to pass anti-Communist legislation which would have covered any citizen who opposed the government. The first bill was introduced in 1932 by the well-known and often mentioned Senator Matías G. Sánchez Sorondo[69] and finally came up for consideration during the famous debate of November and December 1936. Another bill along the same lines is not so well remembered. It was introduced in the Chamber of Deputies by Congressmen Miguel Osorio, Juan F. Morrogh Bernard, Santiago Graffigna, Ernesto M. Aráoz, Raúl Godoy, Reynaldo Pastor, Juan Carlos Agulla, Daniel Videla Dorna, Enrique Ocampo, and Francisco Uriburu. This bill attempted to incriminate "all persons whether or not members of an association, who may profess, teach, or practice ideas included in the platform, program, or objectives of the Communist Third International."[70] However, in order to point out to those who still need proof of the dichotomy between law and reality that has preoccupied juridical liberalism so much, that is, the unavoidable contradictions that existed during the historical period popularly known as the "infamous decade," it will be enough for us to mention the Special Police Bureau that (within the law or outside the law, and preferably the latter) devoted itself to the persecution, imprisonment, and torture of all those it deemed disturbers of the existing idyllic order of things. They carried out this sorry task conscientiously and perhaps even more harshly than in later periods. Communists and non-Communists felt its its rigors, although for the purpose of the Special Bureau everyone was a "Communist." In order to indicate the discredit occassioned by these measures, Radical party Deputy Leónidas Anastasi said in the Chamber of Deputies that "naturally, these useless bureaus are created in an attempt to increase employment. One of these bureaus is the one the deputy for the capital has mentioned — the famous Special Bureau against Communism, which earlier had persecuted Communists and now devotes itself to persecuting the passersby."[71] This *boutade* remains tragically apt in the late sixties even though there have been changes in the organization's name.

During this period the petitions to establish commercial relations with the Soviet Union (introduced by Deputies Augusto Bunge in 1932, Vicente E. Pomponio in 1934, Manuel Palacín and Alejandro Castiñeiras in 1935, and Camilo F. Stanchina in 1942) were never considered. The Communist party would have to accept as a dialectic contradiction the fact that the ruler who would put into effect commercial and diplomatic relations with the USSR would be Perón, soon after the beginning of his presidential term.

FORJA

In recent years various authors have given different interpretations of this movement, which sprang up within the Radical party and later became separate — or independent — from that party. Around the end of 1945, it turned toward the then rising "popular movement" and dissolved itself, leaving its members "at liberty to take action."[72] Juan José Hernández Arregui has defined the essential characteristics of the Force of Radical Orientation of Young Argentina (FORJA according to its Spanish initials), at least in its major features:

(1) A return to the nationalistic, though indecisive, doctrine of Yrigoyen, historically related to the ancient Federalist traditions of the country prior to 1852. (2) Adoption of the ideological postulates of the 1918 University Reform movement as originally stated. (3) Its ideas do not reveal European influences. It is thoroughly Argentine as a result of being rooted in Yrigoyen's doctrinairism and Hispano-American under the influence of Manuel Ugarte and [Victor] Raúl Haya de la Torre and Peruvian Aprism. (4) It supports the thesis of Hispano-American revolution in general, and Argentine revolution in particular, on the basis of the popular masses. (5) It is an ideological movement of the lower income strata of the Buenos Aires University middle class, with later ramifications within the interior of the country. (6) In its anti-imperialist posture, it opposes both Great Britain and the United States in a two-fold national and Latin American perspective.[73]

It is possible to find the key to the history of FORJA in this itemization even though the author has mixed actual deeds and mere good intentions. Originally a reaction to Alvearist control of the party machinery, FORJA counted among its early members some men who appeared again within the Intransigence and Renewal Movement (del Mazo, Luis Dellepiane); later on a political writer of the stature of Raúl Scalabrini Ortiz, who alone would fill a chapter with his accusations against British imperialism, joined the group; and Arturo Jauretche is himself an adequate example of the intellectuals who, having first been Yrigoyenist Radicals, later joined the Peronist ranks in 1945. But by then FORJA had ceased to exist.

The work of the FORJA movement was conducted enthusiastically and hazardously. Not having press or radio support, they relied on their proliferating pamphlets and statements. Street meetings were also frequent (particularly in the capital), as were their propaganda lectures. It is obvious from analyzing some of their documents that the FORJA people had found an expressive and suitable terminology in which to couch their accusations. For instance, they spoke of "the legal expression of colonialism" and they concentrated their fire on the British variety of it that the Republic endured. From the beginning they proved that the leaders of the Radical party did not give much thought to the following:

(1) The creation of the Central Bank of the Republic and of the Mobilizing Institute of Bank Investments, (2) steps leading to the coordination of transportation, (3) the creation of regulating boards for the various branches of industry and commerce, (4) the unification of internal revenues, (5) the London Treaty, (6) the economic sacrifices imposed on the people to benefit capitalism, (7) regulation of foreign exchange operations, (8) the oil policy, (9) the arbitrary military interventions, (10) restrictions on freedom of opinion, (11) wide discretion in the management of public funds, (12) subordination of education to foreign organizations, (13) joining the League of Nations, (14) discontinuing relations with Russia, (15) parliamentary investigations on armaments and the meat industry, (16) the murder in the Senate, (17) censoring the expression of ideas, (18) miscarriages of justice against individual liberty.[74]

FORJA concentrated its propaganda on many of these issues, as well as on others that it later took up (neutrality during World War II; a nationalist position with relation to university reform). Its campaign to educate the public is worthy of praise; however, it does not seem advisable to overstress the movement's scope or its limitations, which in the last analysis were those of the authentic Yrigoyenist traditions supported by FORJA. Its activities may be divided into two distinct periods. The first covers five years, starting from 29 June 1935, the date of its constituent assembly. Hernández Arregui sums up the problem as follows:

As happens in every group, from the beginning there were two trends discernible in FORJA. One was that of the young men who had political aspirations, most of them university graduates with certain literary pretensions, led by Luis Dellepiane. The other had as a definite objective popular proselytizing activities and was determined to make clear the doctrine behind the Radical party program and to make available to the masses this solution of national problems; this trend was represented by Raúl Scalabrini Ortiz and Arturo Jauretche. Around 1940 there was a schism between the partisans of separation from the Radical party and those who wanted to keep working within the party. Immediately after this schism, Gabriel del Mazo and Luis Dellepiane, among others, withdrew from FORJA. After that, Arturo Jauretche remained at the helm.[75]

Jauretche explained the reasons for this "autonomy" of the group:

The term "Radical" had ceased to afford a point of contact with the people when it lost the original meaning and became a mere formal designation. Insistence on the requirement of being a Radical in order to be a member of FORJA, therefore, became an obstacle in relation to the young and also to those Argentines coming from other political sectors that were rapidly being depopulated. The year 1945 bore witness to this fact, to the amazement of all the parties that had been left like empty shells; they failed to realize that the people were abandoning them and would only return to the scene when faced with a new fact and with new men who would express the unrest of the "submerged" Argentina that was evolving socially as well as intellectually. This "submerged" Argentina would only reach its goals on the basis of the national doctrine being worked out by scattered groups, for which FORJA thought it represented a central rallying point.[76]

Nevertheless, Jauretche's rationalization that FORJA might practically be considered ideologically the forerunner of Peronism seems to us somewhat hasty, especially if we consider that an author as favorable to the group as Hernández Arregui has stated that "for this reason, FORJA, on the level of political action, trusted the middle-class youth more than the working masses. It did not see the proletariat, which it diluted within the generic concept of 'the people'."[77]

This lack of understanding was not unusual among the Radical middle-class groups from which the majority of the FORJA people came; it was shared, as we have seen, by the parties of the Left. Nevertheless, FORJA may justly claim to have made valuable contributions to public awareness.

In its second phase, the group, after withdrawing from the Radical party, continued its anti-imperialist work and supported the 4 June 1943 military movement ("the military coup d'état has become necessary because of the ineffectiveness of the civilian forces").[78] Many of its members joined Colonel Perón and, finally, on 15 December 1945, at a general meeting of FORJA members, it was resolved to dissolve the organization in view of the fact that "the purpose and objectives aimed at when FORJA was created have been fulfilled when a popular movement defines itself in political and social terms that are the collective expression of a national will to self-realization, the lack of political support for which led to the creation of FORJA, after Radicalism had abandoned it."[79] An important sector of FORJA joined Peronism and collaborated with the national revolution, "particularly in Buenos Aires Province, where FORJA men ran the provincial economy during the administration of Governor Domingo A. Mercante."[80] Authors who belonged to the Radical party, including former FORJA member del Mazo, tend to be reluctant to concede the merits of this political group. Félix Luna says that "its error consisted in having abandoned the internal struggle, thus allowing the more spurious groups to seize party control." Later on, however, he does acknowledge that "Alvear's despotic leadership liquidated all internal opposition."[81] Where does the truth lie? Rodolfo Puiggrós from his own point of view, concluded:

> FORJA's struggle lasted five years. The group was fought by the government, denied by the Radical party leadership, and accused of being "fascist" by the Socialist and Communist parties, A series of basic studies for the interpretation of the present and future problems of Argentina are the legacy FORJA's extraordinary work has left. While it did not succeed in coming close to the working class and in understanding that the latter is the key to the solution of Argentina's problems, it did leave an eloquent record of the enormous reserves latent in the bourgeoisie and the petite bourgeoisie, which these can contribute to the national liberating revolution. FORJA disappeared because it did not know how to combine its vision for our economic liberation with the working out of a strategy and tactics to be followed for uniting the forces that will make certain the victory of a nationalism with a popular content.[82]

More than twenty years after its dissolution, FORJA continues to provide much material for discussion. Its connections with both the Radical party, within which it was born, and with Peronism, which absorbed it, give rise to stimulating speculations.

The nationalists

The definitive history of the nationalists (it seems preferable to employ this word, rather the hackneyed term "nationalism," in order to indicate the lack of an effective organizational structure unifying the various personalities during the successive stages experienced by the movement) is still to be written. However, there are many partial contributions to such history, and they will be most useful in carrying out this urgent task.[83]

Here we need only point out that the modern nationalist movements (what some authors would call "rightist," "clerical," "aristocratic," or "oligarchic" nationalism) began to take root during the period before the September 1930 coup. Among the important people involved were the poet Leopoldo Lugones, who by then had left his Socialism of the early part of the century far behind, and Carlos Ibarguren. A foreign influence that should be mentioned is that of the Frenchman Charles Maurras. Lugones, in death as in life, continues to be a controversial figure.[84] Ibarguren, a confidant of Uriburu's together with Juan E. Carulla, another September nationalist who had an unusual career,[85] has recorded in his memoirs some valuable observations on the nationalists. With reference to the inheritance of the movement led by Uriburu, Ibarguren states that:

> The revolution meant a leap which was arrested by the action of the political groups that prevented the carrying out of the program its leader wished to give it, something he was not able to achieve because of the lack of a powerful organized and coherent civilian force that would support the new order proclaimed by General Uriburu. But this revolution sired a basic result: the nationalist ideological current that ten years later was able to blaze a new trail for Argentine historical evolution. When the leader of the September revolution retired from the government he seemed to have a presentiment of this, which he expressed in an interview with newspaperman Espigares Moreno: "I believe and hope that the germ of the revolution will not be lost and that, beyond the purely political interests, it will go down into history."

Ibarguren's nationalist concept, which he perfected around the middle of the thirties, includes a harsh criticism of the liberal state and of traditional parties. In this connection, it is well to keep in mind that Ibarguren's earlier political career had taken place within the Progressive Democratic party.

> Nationalism. . . was anxious to have, instead of the oligarchic or demagogic entities known as political parties, that do not genuinely represent national values and that take possession of the state through blind and irresponsible national suffrage, the active production and labor forces and cultural institutions orga-

nized as representatives of the various classes and sectors of the society...[86]

At this stage Mussolini's influence had already become evident, and Franco's also became apparent after the Spanish Civil War. A young nationalist, the son of an old Conservative with fascist tendencies, did not hesitate to speak plainly on this point. Marcelo Sánchez Sorondo said that:

> Our conviction thus began as a religious one. Afterwards we proceeded intemperately to extend it to politics also, with the intemperance of truth. In the aesthetic aspect of politics we were partisans of the monarchy and in what we might call the kinetic aspect, fascists, rabid fascists. When examined closely, this conversion is not as reactionary as it might appear at first sight. Therefore, let it be said for the record that in Buenos Aires there were those who owed their political convictions to their religious convictions; there is a group of men with all the visible and invisible symptoms of a generation that became fascist only because they were Catholics, who through their Catholic awareness were able to understand the greatness of the secular *risorgimento* proclaimed by fascism. In the abstract this route may be disputed, but as an actual happening it is an indisputable fact.[87]

Mario Amadeo, who was Sánchez Sorondo's colleague within the nationalist ranks until after the 1955 "Liberating Revolution," in writing in 1956 about the same subject preferred to be more cautious and throw the mantle of oblivion over the not too distant past:

> ...We reject the diagrammatic interpretation according to which Argentine nationalism was nothing more than a servile imitation, a gross plagiarism of Italian fascism or German national-socialism. The autochthonous elements of nationalism were much more influential than the imported ones in shaping the characteristics of the movement.[88]

This is the result of Amadeo's continuing to use the traditional diagrammatic interpretations of "liberty" and "authority" and wanting to find points to justify his position at that time that would be nearer the former than the latter. How else are we to understand his collaboration and that of other nationalists with the 16 June 1955 movement, whose civilian leaders were of a distincly liberal hue (Adolfo Vicchi, Miguel Angel Zavala Ortiz, and Américo Ghioldi) and Amadeo's participation in the events of September of that same year, in the government of Arturo Frondizi and, lastly, in that of the "Argentine Revolution"? Amadeo, an antiliberal in the thirties (the antiliberal reaction is one of the essential characteristics of the authors we are considering), acknowledged Bloy, Péguy, Maritain, Chesterton, Belloc, Papini, and Maeztu and "the European writers who raised the banner of the antiliberal reaction" as the mentors of his nationalist generation.[89] His Catholic upbringing was of course another basic element. The attitude assumed by the Catholic church toward Mussolini's fascism after the signing of the Lateran Treaty is well known — the *Quadragesimo Anno* encyclical, Catholic Action, and so forth. Some members of the clergy, such as Julio Meinvielle and Leonardo Castellani, appeared among the nationalists as advisers or fellow travellers. While we may justifiably apply to the September nationalists and their immediate followers the conclusion to which Ismael Viñas came that "… they have served as the noisy and daring shock troops of an oligarchy that, as a whole, did not wish to change anything, but had come only to restore,"[90] yet it is a fact that most of the representative figures of the movement fit the description by Jorge Abelardo Ramos: "Full of ultramontane fervor, the nationalists condemned a dying liberalism in the name of an already buried feudalism."[91] Those who succeeded in overcoming these reactionary impediments joined Peronism, where to some extent their elitist "nationalism" was diluted. Some of them, such as the historian Ernesto Palacio, became national deputies for the coalition of forces that was victorious in 1946.

The truth is that the lack of understanding, or the complete disregard, of the labor question that we have pointed out in the case of FORJA, applies equally to the nationalists, only in the case of the latter the failure was even more pronounced. Generally speaking, the few times they referred to the proletariat, they did so only to place it within a more or less corporate concept that would allow the elites (themselves, of course, by divine right) to manipulate political matters more easily. For example, it is very hard to understand the surprise expressed by Amadeo when faced with Perón's plan:

The ideas with which Perón was concerned were, on the one hand, to build up a great political force and, on the other, *to attract the labor sectors.* I considered the latter project to be an *ingenuous utopia, since I must confess that at that moment I could not conceive of a colonel without experience in civilian life being able to make himself the leader of the proletarian masses.* However, his plan to create a political force that would assume and continue in time the "postulates" of the 4th of June attracted me.[92]

Another nationalist, José María de Estrada, analyzes the relations between Peronism and nationalism so vaguely that he barely states the problem:

> There is no doubt that a great part of the initial success of Peronism was due to its having publicly, with fervor and enthusiasm, spoused certain of the ideas and attitudes of nationalism. Perón's achievement lay in his appropriation of a body of ideas that up to that moment had not become known beyond some more or less limited nuclei, but that had the force of great conviction and the merit of having hit the mark with a series of questions about our national being and our historical and social condition.[93]

The same author, speaking in general terms about the "nationalist" ideology (and its international points of reference), reaches the conclusion that:

> During the recent war, important nationalist regimes were toppled. Nevertheless, despite the errors and deviations that they may have fallen into and despite their defeat, some of the ideas or, if you will, some of the attitudes of these regimes remained sound and even triumphant. We mean that, despite the serious deviations that became apparent in some nationalist ideas, the initial attitude — that sincerity in facing facts, that unbiased realism, that decided anti-Marxism, that belief that there are things that are intrinsically valuable independent of any human judgment and rationalization, in short, all those characteristics already pointed out — remains as something positive and valuable.[94]

These are the points that Estrada had already analyzed as a positive contribution to the movement in Argentina, a fact that makes his words clearly polemical. The reference to the "decided anti-Marxism" perhaps deserves clarification. After referring to the *crisis of liberalism,* the author discusses immediately thereafter the problem of *Marxism.* All the criticism that liberalism is found to merit, he also applies to Marxism, so that the two are fused together in an unbelievable amalgam that permits calling any idea or any person a liberal-Marxist with absolute disregard for ideological distinctions. Besides being scientifically incorrect, this lack of discrimination has often turned out to be dangerous to the physical and or intellectual liberty of those so described, since the security and repression forces are in the habit of making the same mistakes.

Thus it was that "nationalism" arose formally in support of a revolution (that of 6 September 1930) that soon ceased to be its own. It survived the time span from 1931 to 1943 by multiplying its periodical publications *(Baluarte, Nuevo Orden, Crisol, La Nueva República, Sol y Luna* — the last a classic example of Hispanic nationalism that is almost viceroyal — *Nueva Política, El Fortín, Nuestro Tiempo, Balcón,* and the dailies *El Pampero* and *El Federal),* and developing an effective proselytizing campaign in some sectors (the military and the university). On 4 June 1943, at the time of the military coup, the nationalists saw their second chance. They modestly offered themselves as the ideologists for the movement against Castillo, once the troops had ousted the old president, and to a certain degree achieved their objective. Marcelo Sánchez Sorondo in his "Speech to the military" advised them, saying that:

> Since 4 June there has been a break in continuity, but it seems as though one had reached a sort of apolitical oasis. The military movement ousted a government that had the appearance of being the end of a regime. Facts still speak for themselves with great impersonality, in their half-crude, half-undeciphered language. *What is missing is an intelligent interpretation of events, what is properly called doctrine... Today revolution consists of deeds and of the motivation for our action.* The state at this time takes an active part in events. This is the first sign that the revolution has started. *But woe to deeds without political theology! Woe to action without doctrine!* Everything may degenerate into the worst of materialism, the materialism of false efficiency, into truth destroyed by efficiency or by resentment, according to Marxist tenets. Beware of the letter without the spirit. This has to be said: your responsibility, our responsibility, the responsibility of all in 4 June is enormous. The fourth of June is the decisive date of a decisive year. The country has already been committed. Either we achieve national unity or anarchy will engulf us. You, the military, now have all the authority. You, the military, who make your lives a profession of honor, on 4 June made a profession of faith.[95]

Buttressed by this "profession of faith," the nationalists consolidated their positions in the fields of education, public administration, and foreign affairs, and on many occasions they showed themselves sectarian and arbitrary.

However, the new stage carried along the ballast of the past, since
the nationalists retained key positions in the administration and
particularly in education. They had entered the latter with self-
assurance. Men like Sepich, Baldrich, Genta, Olmedo, and Obligado confused education with abuse and their convictions with
martial law decrees. Of course, the ultramontane phobia, the
hatred of the French Revolution and of Voltairean principles,
the claim that the May Revolution is more or less a continuation of Philip II, are not proclamations suited to attracting
youth.[96]

We deem it prudent not to discuss at length other characteristics
of the nationalist groups — their admiration for Juan Manuel de
Rosas (and their one-sided attempts at historical revisionism), their
nostalgia for the old days of the Spanish conquest and coloniza-
tion, and their respect for certain traditional values —[97] but we
will say a few words about another characteristic which is peculiar
to the movement: the formation of shock troops devoted to direct
action, among them the Argentine Civic Legion and the Nationalist Liberating Alliance, one belonging to the early part of the
period considered in this study and the other to 1945 and the
years following. The Argentine Civic Legion achieved official recognition by the authorities on 20 May 1931 and was granted juridical personality on 11 January 1932. Ibarguren, being anxious to
find precedents for this organization in Argentine history, attempts to make it seem to derive from Mariano Moreno, the Tucumán Congress, the Directory, and the Confederation, and he vigorously rejects the alleged influence of Mussolini. According to its
bylaws, the Civic Legion was made up of "patriotic men" who embodied "the spirit of the September revolution and who morally
and materially were ready to cooperate in the institutional reconstruction of the country"; the government authorized the members
of the organization to "go to the barracks on Sundays and holidays to receive military instruction and target practice."[98] The
organization was publicly denounced on numerous occasions by
various sectors of public opinion and so were similar groups with a
narrower field of action. Deputy Nicolás Repetto introduced a
draft declaration in the Chamber of Deputies in these terms:

> The Honorable Chamber of Deputies of the Nation declares that
> it is urgent that private groups organized and armed under var-
> ious names that tend to take the place of the legal organs in the
> regulation of public liberties be dissolved, and it manifests its
> deep displeasure upon finding that the executive branch has not

known how to defend public liberties from the aggressions of these groups.[99]

Ibarguren reminds us of the existence of other groups:

Besides the groups existing since the 1930 revolution, such as the Republican League, the Civic Legion, and the May Legion, new ones were formed, such as the Argentine Nationalist Action, directed by my friend, the outstanding writer and professor Juan P. Ramos; the Argentine Guard, organized by the illustrious poet and great patriot, Leopoldo Lugones; the Military College Legion, the Nationalist Civic Militia, and many others. These various entities were not able to enter into a binding agreement that would unite them, even though their objectives were the same, and they were inspired by the same ideologies. The Argentine Civic Legion was perhaps the group with the most members; it later became the Nationalist Youth Alliance, whose original leader was General Juan Bautista Molina.[100]

There is only a step from the National Youth Alliance to the Nationalist Liberating Alliance led first by Juan Queraltó, then by Guillermo Patricio Kelly. In a way, the Alliance was formed as a Peronist shock group and was active on both the political and university scene, had official backing, and at that time was characterized by pronounced xenophobia and racism. In its own way, the NLA was the precursor of Tacuara and other nationalist activist nuclei from the late fifties on.

Hernández Arregui, who sometimes is too indulgent in judging the movement, was nevertheless forced to conclude that "nationalism relied on the past but stagnated in the present. The concept of the present as a return to the past precluded the possibility of the conservative philosophy of nationalism having any connection with a future that was opening up before a world shaken by revolution."[101] However, there were some isolated figures, such as Jorge del Río, José Luis Torres, and Raúl Scalabrini Ortiz (whom some authors group together under the general heading of a hypothetical "democratic" nationalism that might have remotely derived from the Federal *caudillos,* José Hernández and, in this century, Hipólito Yrigoyen), who approached political and economic problems vigorously, but not always (especially in the case of Torres, a combative journalist) with complete consistency.[102] In some aspects they are linked intellectually to the nationalists, although they acted individually. But in the final analysis they are rather the exception than the rule. The rule was, and continues to be, that nationalism tended to be aristocratic, religiously linked, Hispanist, and reactionary.

The University movement

The University Reform Movement that originated in Córdoba in 1918 had already had various ups and downs on the eve of the September 1930 coup. The details of the movement's internal history have already been set forth in other studies.[103] What is of interest here is to sketch in broad strokes the course of the reform movement between 1930 and 1946 and to point out its connections with political activity.

In general, the students' good will and desire for improvements were taken advantage of by reactionary politicians in order to involve student organizations in the agitation preceding the 6th of September. There is no doubt that the mistaken policy toward the university of certain Yrigoyenist sectors who saw "dangerous Bolsheviks" even in their soup, and especially in all centers of advanced learning, contributed to this.

> Reformist students who had until the day before been mistreated by the "Radical Klan" and by the Yrigoyenist police, viewed the fall [of Yrigoyen] with joy. Very few noticed the reactionary and imperialistic background of the coup and the irreversible nature of this institutional break. Most thought that a confused and arbitrary state of affairs had come to an end, that it would be possible to bring order into a "rudderless world" and into a university where immovable specters lingered.[104]

When Uriburu's government started making references to "university anarchy" and got ready to impose order, the students soon came to understand that they had made a mistake (they were not the only ones who made it). In Buenos Aires, Benito Nazar Anchorena, the interventor for the University of Buenos Aires, was the executive arm charged with creating harmony. The persecutions that were to last several years began with attacks on the student reform movements and on "the professors who, for one reason or another and generally because of their activity in Radicalism, were in difficulties with the new government."[105] The consequences of this situation were many. Some activists were arrested (Héctor P. Agosti), some professors removed from teaching posts (José Peco, who had defended Agosti; Gregorio Bermann, and Jorge Orgaz in Córdoba); and some students exiled (Eduardo Howard), and there were hundreds of other cases. The Argentine University Federation (AUF) was denounced as being the agent of International Communism and so were many of its members (this was a device that became a habit). Under Justo's presidency matters did not improve appreciably. The various reform sectors debated their principles at the Second National Student Congress (Buenos Aires, 1932).[106] There were isolated attempts to convert the university reform movement into a political force, as a way of overcoming the difficult university-society antinomy. The best known was led by Julio V. González before 1930 and was called the National Reform party,[107] but what happened in most cases was that university people joined the existing parties. José Peco, Mario Sánz, and Eduardo Araujo joined the Radical party; Alejandro Korn, Carlos Sánchez Viamonte, Deodoro Roca (for a short time), and Julio V. González himself, the Socialist party; and Ernesto Giúdice and Rodolfo Aráoz Alfaro, the Communist party. The Argentine University Federation supported the frustrated attempts to form a popular front that failed, among other reasons, because of the Radical refusal to cooperate. It expressed its solidarity with the Spanish Republic, was on the side of the Allies during World War II, and was among the organizers of the Democratic Union ("the generation of '45").

In 1942 the Third National Student Congress took place in Córdoba during the Radical administration of del Castillo and Arturo U. Illia, which, together with the group led by Sabattini, was neutralist with regard to the world conflict. "It was a vigorous but ineffectual reminder to those who were dragging the country toward evil days; it was also a categorically antifascist demonstration."[108] After 4 June 1943 the universities and primary and secondary education were taken over by the clerical and reactionary sectors. The reformist movement fought courageously against this but the forest could not be seen for the trees (the reactionary trees), and the AUF lost sight of the fact that Perón had the support of the working masses.

The AUF fell into its adversary's trap, sought allies anywhere, and even sponsored the industrial magnates' lockout. It can also be said that it was in the Buenos Aires University Federation that the Democratic Union, a coalition of disparate parties (the Radical, Socialist, Conservative, and Communist parties) united by the sole common denominator of their anti-Peronism, was hatched. The groups of the Left that comprised it committed the error — opportunely pointed out by [Luis Carlos] Prestes and then by Julio V. González — of entering into negotiations with interests that should have been repudiated, thus allowing Perón to place them in the category of those "who sold their country" and who had become subservient to Braden. . .[109]

Those were the days when slogans proclaiming the superiority of the working class to the university community were common. The anti-Peronism of the University movement increased throughout the 1946-1955 period.[110]

As for its antiimperialist tenets, while it is true that the main current of reformist criticism was directed toward Yankee imperialism (which was no small matter in view of the later course of events), it is an exaggeration to claim (as the so-called Argentine National Left has been doing, and as the nationalists had done earlier) that the Reform was a sort of accomplice of British imperialism. This would seem to be an argument resorted to in bad faith. It is true that the reformists have not analyzed the phenomenon of Argentine "nationalism" in depth, but it is also true that the nationalists have ignored the University Reform Movement by conveniently covering their eyes when faced with it and by speaking of it disparagingly. Had the nationalists opened their eyes, they could have read statements such as the one by Deodoro Roca:

> We have kept in mind the memory of Gandhi and of British imperial justice. It cannot be denied that Argentina is a British subcolony, with all the burdens and without all the advantages of the preferential treatment accorded by the metropolis to its "independent dominions." This has been especially true since a planned economy has been in force, implemented by the minister [Pinedo], and the "Niemeyer" brain child has been put into operation. The Buenos Aires elections may perhaps have been somewhat distasteful to the traditional decorum of the British and to their sensibilities as the leaders of Democracy; there is no doubt that this was not what they would have wanted, but when all is said and done, it is a subcolony and the case has only a subimportance. For the time being, it was in the interest of the British system to consolidate, at least formally, the domestic political system of the Conservative *Concordancia*. To do anything else would have been a waste of time. Some day a way will be found to unite the disparate interests of the national groups that take their turns in power in a "higher synthesis." Either a "new *Concordancia*" or a "new Radicalism" fits in with the program of the monopolistic British financial capital; but what matters at this moment is to reassert the political strength through which it has consolidated its hegemony. "We

must keep up appearances," is a very British attitude. This is why when three judges say yes and two say no, everything is saved. You can continue to bargain, and as far as vague threats of popular uprisings are concerned, other means will be found to keep up all appearances. . . . Many of the old officials of the Argentine oligarchy in the service of the British Empire — the judges, lawyers, captains of industry, professors, and all the influential and well-paid fauna — suddenly became rabid nazis, the most terrible adversaries of British "capitalism," of the wicked and newly discovered British "imperialism." It was comic — and tragic. It was in those days that this attitude arose and was initially nourished by this spirit, though a few had vague misgivings. What imminent, immediate danger gave rise to this? The success of nazism and its overflowing into America and the whole world.[111]

Deodoro Roca, who may be considered a true Renaissance man because of the diversity of his interests throughout his full life,[112] is a clear-cut example of one who followed the path from university reform to social action and then to purely political action (not partisan in his case, except for a brief affiliation with the Socialist party and his candidacy for mayor of the city of Córdoba under the Civil Alliance) with a penchant for self-sacrifice. There are some others with a similar history, such as Saúl Alejandro Taborda, who has been even more completely forgotten (except that he is occasionally remembered for his *Investigaciones pedagógicas);* Aníbal Ponce, and Julio V. González, who was to continue to serve his youthful ideals in the ranks of the Socialist party; as a deputy he introduced the university and the oil nationalization bills, which were never passed by Congress.

From his native Córdoba, Roca fought unsuccessfully for the Popular Front that he considered essential for the country. However, it was the official Radical position (though it was not that of Amadeo Sabattini, "a big healthy voice that seemed to come from the masses")[113] that it was possible to achieve power alone, without dangerous allies who would spoil the good public relations of the Radicals. So the opportunity was missed. Roca was later a determined militant against Franco and against the Nazis, and he was on the side of the Allies in the struggle against the Axis. He died in 1942.

Taborda, another Argentine who "lived and thought for his country,"[114] died two years later. Hasty and superficial commentators have dubbed him a "fascist," but the outlines of Taborda's political thought — articulated outside the framework of traditional political parties — are set forth in his communalist thesis, in which he defends interesting and forgotten national precedents and sees the commune as "the essential basis for our federalism," [115] a federalism with a clear social and economic outlook.

Finally, we have a case such as that of Aníbal Ponce, whose journey from positivism to Marxism opened up a new path (which he himself did not travel to the end) for those who are entranced by Leopoldo Lugones's journey from his socialism early in the century to his xenophobic nationalism with the "hour of the sword" and all that. The route glimpsed by Ponce has hardly found any followers, but this does not mean it is not the most promising for the future.

6   The Church

The church and politics: the themes of Catholicism

We want to stress that what we intend to do in this chapter is to consider certain problems presented by the activity of the church (or of certain of its members, both official and self-appointed) in the political sphere. It follows from this that we will only refer indirectly to the traditional problems of Argentine constitutional law treated in a book by an American author that we have found useful in our work.

> Constitutional provisions and historical events and precedents have combined to create at least three separate sets of problems in the study of ecclesiastical-civil relations in the Argentine Republic. These can be identified as (1) the juridical status of Catholicism, (2) the exercise of the *patronato*, and (3) relations with the Holy See.[1]

From 1930 to about 1943, the church and its noninstitutional means of communication (both the documents issued by the hierarchy and Catholic publications, among which the journal *Criterio* merits special attention) focused their activities on a few subjects of interest. The key points were undoubtedly the perpetuation of the legal provisions against divorce and the struggle for religious education. The strongly antiliberal tone of church teaching provided the background for the development of church strategy, which in many cases must be deduced from isolated facts or from specific results. There were naturally some variations, as evidenced by the very different paths followed by Bishop Miguel de Andrea and Father Gustavo J. Franceschi, not to mention Father Julio Meinvielle.

The divorce problem had repercussions in Congress, and the Socialist sector was the one that expressed the liberal point of view on the subject. The same ideological confrontation took place on other related subjects, so that Socialism came to be identified as the anticlerical and secularist party.

161

Américo Ghioldi, who in 1932 was a young congressman, set forth the dichotomy as follows:

It is natural that all the paths of national thought and feeling should cross here in this chamber, but there are only two major ones. Some . . . [members] are consciously or subconsciously motivated by the moral and intellectual forces that emanate from St. Paul's doctrine, from the theory of sin, the concept of horror of fornication, the cult of asceticism (subconsciously the tendency to feel a horror of physical beauty still exerts an influence, even though it has now been modified); by the concept of the inferiority of woman, who continues to be the eternal "rib of man," by the preconceptions about the sacrament; by the idea of the immutability of familiar forms; and by the intellectual tendency to find in the Sacred Scriptures the truth that is to light their way. We follow another path, that of science, love and liberty; we are men who read the Sacred Scriptures as human documents with a high literary value, but who through science try to find an interpretation for phenomena in nature itself and not in written texts. We have a mind adapted to thinking about things and institutions in their constant flux and evolution, not as petrified and fossilized immutable forms. We are influenced by secular achievements, by the creation of romantic love, and by the secularization of life and of institutions. When the problem of divorce is brought up by us or by others, we remain consistent, endeavoring to bring to fruition an evolution that should long ago have been completed, that is, the secular and liberal evolution of the country which was started in the dawn of the Revolution and now demands a divorce law in order to win the separation of Church and State immediately thereafter.[2]

During this 1932 debate, Deputy Enrique Dickmann gave a brief analysis of the historical process that had led to consideration of the matter.

In 1902 the entire episcopate appeared before the chamber with a long and documented petition denying the right of the Argentine Congress to consider and approve this law. . . This time the church as such has not taken an official stand on the subject. While in 1902 the Catholic church appeared before the Congress personally, in 1922 it appeared through a representative. The chamber knows that in 1922 there was an almost unanimous report from the General Legislative Committee in favor of divorce. Only one deputy was against it. The chairman of the committe was one O'Reilly, an Irishman, a Radical, and himself a Catholic. Just as now there are many sincere Catholics who accept the divorce law, they all signed the report and it was the representative of the Catholic church, Hipólito Yrigoyen, who sent an incredible message to Congress, denying its authority to discuss and approve this law....The subject was not discussed any further, and in 1932, a renewed chamber that is harder working, more intelligent, and more responsive to reason discusses divorce with complete freedom. No pressure is exerted now upon the conscience of the Chamber of Deputies by archbishops, bishops, or presidents.[3]

The reason for this was that methods were beginning to change everywhere, not only in Argentina. For example, the setting up of Catholic Action allowed the church greater freedom of movement so that some of the tasks (such as the one they undertook in 1902, as recalled by Dickmann) the hierarchy had performed before devolved upon this association. Ghioldi has this to say in this connection:

> In a secret circular issued by Argentine Catholic Action, carrying the signatures of Martín Jacobi and Rómulo Amadeo, the president and secretary of the same, an account is given of the individual work being done among the deputies. I am not going to give the names of the deputies who have been the object of this "work." The circular reads as follows: "In order to facilitate the work. . . of seeing the national legislators for the purpose of engaging them to vote against the divorce law, we have the pleasure of informing you about the measures taken by the diocesan boards, begging you to use the data with proper discretion, since it is confidential.". . . Later another confidential circular attempted to mobilize all the Catholic institutions throughout the country; on 12 August the same gentlemen informed these institutions that the moment had come to bombard the Chamber of Deputies with letters, telegrams, petitions, and lists of signatures collected against the instituting of divorce. The circular carried an interesting notation: "In view of the makeup of our Chamber of Deputies, it is advisable under the circumstances to employ legal and social rather than religious arguments."[4]

The divorce bill was approved in the Chamber of Deputies by a vote of 98 to 26. It was never approved by the Senate — this was another of the lobby's triumphs.

While the church insisted on maintaining the status quo in relation to divorce (that is, divorce was legally forbidden), in the case of religious instruction in the public schools it advocated changing the legal provisions, and the change was achieved. Numerous examples of concrete proselytizing activities can be cited in connection with some matters related to religious instruction. The ideas advocated by the University Reform Movement (to which obscure extremist objectives were attributed) were virulently attacked, attempts were made to establish private universities (put into practice as recently as 1958), and anti-Socialist charges in varying degrees were brought. The Bishop of La Rioja, the Very Reverend Froilán Ferreira Reinafé, defended religious instruction as follows:

> The Catholic religion has established. . . and indisputable. . . rights in our public school. It is the duty of the legislator to respect these acquired rights, which in turn arise from the very depths of the human soul and have been guarded during the three hundred and fifty years of our existence. How could it be otherwise when the education of the child is less a technical than a spiritual matter and, in order to carry out this function effectively, close communication and real cooperation must be maintained with the powers above? [5]

In the pastoral letter from the Argentine episcopate "on the duties of Catholics at the present moment," dated 15 November 1945, the right already acquired was defended:

> The church has received the right to teach from God himself. It can therefore demand it in God's name, but it can also demand this right in the name of the interest of the child which requires that he be given an integral education, making him aware of his divine origin, his immortal destiny, and the sacred rights of his person. It can demand them in the name of the Constitution, as well as in that of Argentine tradition. [6]

Any effort that tended to give impetus to ideas related to religious instruction was considered by the clergy a partial victory. An example of this is the manner in which the decree of the Buenos Aires provincial government of 6 October 1936, establishing the teaching of the Catholic religion in primary schools during regular school hours, was received. This measure, sponsored by Manuel Fresco, set an important precedent for federal Decree-Law No. 18,411 of 31 December 1943, issued by General Ramírez's provisional government and later ratified by Congressional Act No. 12,978/47. The Archbishop of Santa Fe, the Very Reverend Nicolás Fasolino, and the Bishop of Rosario, the Very Reverend Anto-

nio Caggiano, took pains to define the juridical and moral consequences of the decree on religious instruction:

> Religious instruction in the schools flows from a right of fami-
> lies and of the church that not only does not injure the state
> but renders to it the most profound contribution for the moral
> formation of citizens. It does not suppress nor wound the reli-
> gious liberty of non-Catholic students or parents, who have the
> right to demand that their children not attend the religious ins-
> truction classes; instead, the state offers them instruction in
> ethics, a subject essential to any man and based on the natural
> law of conscience. We are within our rights in defending it, and
> we fulfill an essential obligation of Catholic doctrine. You may
> disagree with us and oppose us, but we should be respected in the
> legitimate use of rights that pertain to us as citizens and as
> Catholic bishops who work along the lines of our apostolic
> mission for the welfare and greatness of our country.[7]

Finally, when Congress was debating the sanctioning of the
decree on religious instruction, the arguments favorable to the
Catholic sector ran as follows:

> "Then," the president of the lower house asked me, "do you
> believe the country will be defrauded if our chamber vetoes the
> religious instruction law? "
> "And also deceived and mocked," I answered.
> "Why? "
> "Simply because it was led to believe that religious instruc-
> tion constituted one of the principles of the Revolution. Any
> majority deputy who now votes against it is purely and simply
> abandoning a fundamental principle of the party that raised him
> to a congressional seat, in order to approve a principle held by
> the opposition sector."[8]

It was not in vain that for years religious instruction had appeared on the program of well-known civilian figures belonging to
the Catholic church who advocated it as necessary for the country.
In 1937 Rómulo Amadeo asserted that "if our democracy wants
to survive, it must seek constitutional reforms," and he listed them
as follows:

> First: To place the origin of sovereignty in God and to adopt
> the Catholic religion as the religion of the state. In this way,
> laws against the precepts of divine and natural law are avoided.
> Second: To establish religious instruction in the schools of the

state. Horace Mann has said that a democracy must be moral or
it will not be; without religious instruction we will have an im-
moral people. If those who elect those who govern and the
legislators have no civic and moral education, the state will
collapse. Third: To place on liberty the limitations of truth and
the general welfare. Liberty is not an end, it is a means, and if that
means does not make for truth and goodness, it becomes an evil
that should be suppressed.[9]

As may be seen, Amadeo intentionally confused the problems
of the country and the needs of the church, and he was not the
only one to do so. In its editorials, the group directing the journal
Criterio fell into a sectarianism as much to be censured as the one
it systematically ascribed to the Socialist party. When the legislators elected in 1946 were sworn in (27 of the more than 150 deputies did not use God's name), the journal, bringing to bear all the
doctrinaire weight it undoubtedly wielded no matter how unofficial it may have been considered, pointed out that:

The atheism of our legislators should not be lost sight of. As a
matter of fact, if they want to be consistent, they must make
every possible effort to establish within the republic an essentially and completely materialistic regime. And we, that is, not
only the Catholics, but all spiritual men, Protestants, deists of
any sort, cannot accept it because it contradicts not just incidental interests, but essential principles of our culture that arise
both from our deepest beliefs and from the tradition of our
country. The matter is much more serious than it may be
thought at first sight, since everything, the school, the family,
the law, the concept of the dignity of the human person, liberty, duty, all is placed in jeopardy. A choice must be made and
no partisan leanings, no political sympathy would justify our
taking what is secondary into account and disregarding what is
essential. When we are faced with individual and private atheism
something more than our common sense and apostolic zeal is
aroused: we suffer at the sight of our brothers straying so deplo-
rably; but when official and public atheism brings the higher
interests of the nation into question, then wholesome social
concepts and properly understood patriotism are involved.[10]

We follow this same journal in our analysis in order to avoid a
dispersion of texts that would not appreciably improve our research. In 1937 *Criterio* took the Radicals to task when they suggested an alliance with the Progressive Democrats in Santa Fe, a
possibility that was definitively blocked by Justo and Alvear.

Therefore, to enter into an alliance with the Progressive Democrats is equivalent to taking a stand against our authentic national tradition and the basic institutions of our country, which the Radical party claims it respects. The Progressive Democratic party represents tendencies that are harmful on two fronts since, while it is crudely capitalistic in economic matters, it professes a rabid atheism in religious matters. We have only to bring to mind the Federal Constitution and the 1921 Constitution of Santa Fe Province to prove this. No truly Argentine and popular political organization can ally itself with [that party], at least not with impunity. Such an operation would not even be beneficial from the immediate electoral point of view. Let the Progressive Democrats vote for anybody they want. Radicals will gain much more by staying free of contact with them.[11]

But the most sustained invective was employed against the Socialist party, and at times *Criterio's* analysis of conditions did not lack an objectivity that went beyond the sectarian intentions of the various writers. Another editorial published in 1940 read as follows:

The Socialist party, reduced by the desertion of those of its elements that abandoned it in order to join either communism or nationalism, *is completing the process of becoming bourgeois and taking shape as a liberal party* with a somewhat reddish cast, but still only liberal. This explains why it loses its social and even its economic revolutionary stance, why it lends itself to the maneuvers of traditional parties, and does not concern itself with anything but fishing for the greatest possible number of voters in order to continue to enjoy some seats in Congress or the Buenos Aires City Council.[12]

Of course, this keeness of perception is not usual and in most cases *Criterio* preferred deliberately to mix communism, socialism, and liberalism into a single bundle, so that its polemics would reach a wider target. We want to emphasize that this was done because antiliberalism was one of the characteristics of the *political* action of the church during this period, and this attitude became aggravated after the Catholic-nationalist irruption into certain positions beginning in 1943. At the same time, Socialist opposition — which was the most consistent during this period — adopted a decidedly liberal stance. Let us look at some concrete facts: the famous speech delivered by Juan B. Justo in the Senate on 23 September 1926, during the debate on whether the Senate should submit to the executive branch the three nominations for archbishop of Buenos Aires, proves beyond doubt what we have stated. Let us make clear that the position he supported was one that remained unchanged throughout the period studied in this work. Most Socialist legislators confined themselves to reiterating certain opinions of the founder of the party, but they did not go a single step beyond that. Justo had this to say about this debate:

> I believe that what the Senate proposes to do in nominating three candidates to the archbishopric is as illegal as if we lent our vote to the appointment of an army marshal. The military law does not mention that grade, nor does it exist within the Argentine military hierarchy, just as that of archbishop does not exist within the Constitution. The intent to nominate three candidates for archbishop is therefore unconstitutional.[13]

Américo Ghioldi, following his mentor during a 1933 debate on the creation of new dioceses and archdioceses, stressed that *"many of us have come to this chamber with a perfectly defined liberal program;* no one who voted for us could have been ignorant of our point of view on religious matters."[14] In the same manner, the bill presented in 1932 by Socialist Deputy Angel M. Giménez and other legislators, which dealt with the regulation of religious orders, is a reflection of Justo's ideas on the subject as expressed in the above-mentioned speech and of the liberal experience during the early years of the Spanish Republic. The Socialist party was the principal opponent of the church during the whole decade of the thirties. For example, it pointed out that:

> Powerful international organizations such as the congregations have brought in their religious faith, their capital, and their industries, and instead of adapting themselves to the Constitution, they have placed themselves outside it in an irregular manner, with the toleration and complicity of the authorities, and they have regularized their situation by taking advantage of the subterfuges afforded by the laws, either by placing their property in the name of third parties, or in the name of associate members of the congregation, under joint-ownership or pseudo-corporations.[15]

The party brought specific charges of religious propaganda in "various elementary and secondary schools" and it requested Minister of Justice and Public Instruction Manuel M. de Iriondo to report on the matter.[16] It opposed the exemption from payment of port duties on ships chartered exclusively for transporting and lodging the members and pilgrims participating in the XXXII International Eucharistic Congress.[17] During the discussion of every budget bill, it took the opportunity to propose the reduction of expenditures for the clergy and the army.[18] At times the closest allies of the Socialists were the Progressive Democrats, who had also remained true to their liberal origins. During the debate on the triple nomination for filling the archbishopric in 1932, Senator Francisco Correa categorically asserted that:

> Of course I harbor no hostile intent: *I am a consistent liberal in the proper sense.* I want liberty to profess any religion, satisfaction and respect for all consciences, and I am not going to be a persecutor of the Catholic church, but that great institution must develop within our laws and our Constitution and these three nominations should not be simply a subject for conversations at the club or for the influence of ladies which senators should view with indifference and vote for one candidate or another merely through deference to a recommendation. It is notorious (and I am not being indiscreet) that the influence of the Nuncio's office makes itself actively felt at the Senate sessions, and I believe that we should react against foreign interventions and see to it that insofar as possible the Argentine church be Argentine and governed by Argentine priests.[19]

Much of the period between 1930 and 1943 was marked by the liberalism-antiliberalism antinomy as far as the relations between Catholics and non-Catholics are concerned. After the latter date the scene is complicated by the influence that the clergy came to exercise in certain sectors of public administration such as primary, secondary, and university education and in foreign relations. To this must be added the totalitarian (especially fascist) tendencies which had been gathering strength for a long time in important church sectors and the latter's attitude vis-à-vis what later came to be called generically "Peronism." Before taking up this subject, let us glance briefly at two important events.

The Eucharistic Congress, Catholic Action

The International Eucharistic Congress that took place in Buenos Aires from 9 to 14 October 1934, aside from its instrinsic significance as an act of religious worship, also served to show the government of General Justo the importance of having some Catholic support for his "fraud and privilege" policy. This was the reason the state generously turned out to help. Gustavo J. Franceschi, an influential clergyman who directed *Criterio,* was one of the first to recognize the Justo administration's support:

It is proper to stress the open collaboration of the government in all the activities of this great assembly. The national and municipal authorities (if we disregard part of the City Council) as well as the military and provincial authorities, have shown on this occasion that they have felt the desire harbored by the great majority of the country. The latter, whether you wish it or not, is Catholic in feeling and impulses. The religious instruction and the moral conduct of not a few may be defective; but under the ashes, the faith has not been extinguished, and the strong breath of the Holy Spirit has brought the hot coals into the open. The leaders of the state, beginning with the president of the Republic, who by his prayer on the last day gave us a magnificent example of piety, recognized this reality and did not wish to differ from their constituents. This is something that will be remembered by God and also by men.[20]

In another issue the journal editorialized as follows, just in case there should still be anyone who did not understand:

General Justo has become the international color-bearer for a great cause and has rendered a service of immense value to those who aspire to save mankind from horrors. The formula: "Christ or Lenin" has in a way become a classic by now; well, the chief executive has announced in a loud voice that a country that respects itself cannot vacillate in its choice: the Kingship of Jesus Christ and not the somber dictatorship of the Soviets.[21]

Franceschi's judgment seemed to have been affected by the religious act performed by Justo. A year earlier he had written a signed article that was somewhat different in tone: "Going to the root of the evil, it has been seen that neither the parliamentary nor the general liberal nature of our institutions will permit an effective defense against communism, the Jewish spirit, the Marxist disorganization, and the general ruin of the economy."[22] The change can doubtless be considered one of the miracles of faith. As could be expected from a Jesuit, Leonardo Castellani approached the question much more perceptively:

The populace of the great cities did not create the daily *Crítica,* on which it now nourishes its spirit; an Uruguayan adventurer [Natalio Botana] created it with the tolerance and aid of those most highly placed in our society. At the Great Eucharistic Congress in 1934, a president of the Republic and general of the national army, who was one of the biggest stockholders in *Crítica,* a blasphemous daily, consecrated the country entrusted to his conscience to the Most Sacred Heart of Jesus, side by side with the Legate of His Holiness, today himself His Holiness, [Pius XII], and with the Cardinal Archbishop — after which he went to dine at Botana's place. Meditate on this fact.[23]

Was the president's prayer a political or a religious act? Ernesto Palacio did not have any doubts about it: "The celebration of the International Eucharistic Congress of Buenos Aires in 1934 showed the existence in the country of an enormous Catholic majority, for which reason *the Justo administration, lacking convictions of its own, thenceforth also adopted a pronounced clerical position.*"[24] The figure of Dionisio R. Napal, vicar general of the Navy since 1926, who acted as the master of ceremonies, was conspicuous during the Eucharistic Congress. His popularity was outstanding and we mention him here because there were some who suggested making him a candidate for senator from the city of Buenos Aires. This is recorded in an anonymous biography of Napal, a document which is useful in understanding the period under study in relation to certain positions adopted by the Catholic clergy.

After the October 1934 Eucharistic Congress, he was one of the historical men consecrated as a public figure who could have collected votes and support in order to occupy the senatorship for the federal capital. While this serves to show Napal's true reputation, considering that his elevation was not due to a political party, which is often managed by a very small group, but rather the result of a marvelous understanding by the crowd, it also served to temper the marvelous fiber that remained upright through good and evil fortune. *It was not the Curia that objected to Napal accepting the possible senatorial nomination; it was Napal himself, to whom such a civilian office meant nothing after God had seen fit to unite him in such an intimate way with the glory of the Eucharistic Congress.*[25]

As may be seen, the effects of the Congress went beyond the specific plane of religious worship. For example, the fact that that year marked the fiftieth anniversary of the passing of the Public Education Act (No. 1420), against which public opinion was being aroused, was not overlooked. The 1934 assembly encouraged some Catholic sectors to intensify their undercover work. Perhaps the most important agent for this was Argentine Catholic Action. Galletti has described the situation as follows: "From the days of the Eucharistic Congress, the influence of the Catholic groups in-

creased. During the European War there was true agreement between the groups of the Catholic Right and nationalist military
groups."[26]

The Catholic Action Movement which was revived for Italy by
Pius XI (as well as its local branches in the various countries) cannot be understood without taking note of the relations between
the Catholic church and the Italian government of Benito Mussolini. These relations were consolidated by the Concordat of 11
February 1929, to which writers of the stature of Antonio Gram-
sci allude.[27] Suffice it to say, by way of example, that the accord
signed between the Holy See and Italy on Catholic Action (1931)
provided that "Catholic Action shall be essentially diocesan, depending directly upon the bishops, who shall choose the ecclesiastical and lay directors. *Persons opposed to fascism cannot be chosen. In accordance with its religious and spiritual nature, Catholic
Action cannot intervene in politics. . . .*"[28] We cannot even begin to
mention the problems that this change of position by the Vatican
created in connection with the *popolari* of Luigi Sturzo and the
Catholic masses.

Argentine Catholic Action was established by a collective pastoral letter of the ecclesiastical hierarchy dated 1 December 1928
and on 5 April 1931 it was again found necessary to explain by
means of another pastoral from the episcopate that

> as long as politics do not threaten the intangible deposit of reli-
> gious and moral principles, whose custody Jesus Christ, by vir-
> tue of his Divine authority, entrusted to the Church and which
> takes precedence and is above all the authorities of the world
> and all the sovereignties of heaven, earth, and hell, then politics
> should not have anything to fear from the Church or from
> Catholic Action.[29]

Professor John J. Kennedy, whose opinions are generally favorable to church activity in the political field, cannot avoid acknowl-
edging that Catholic Action. . . "has been singled out as the apparatus through which anti-democratic and pro-fascist trends were
made effective in the critical years 1938-46."[30] He goes on to
point out that its members are theoretically forbidden to act in
politics. But ". . . the individual is free to join any political party
he chooses, provided that the party is not explicitly opposed to
Catholic doctrine or morality."[31]

This theoretically apolitical attitude becomes quite questionable
when we consider another pastoral letter, that of 30 May 1936, in
which the hierarchy admonishes a wider public, that is, not only
those who are members of Catholic Action, but all Catholics:

The true Catholic, who is consistent in his beliefs·and in his actions and social life, *must also adapt his thinking, in social and
political matters,* to the true and wholesome orientations of his
shepherds, whose desire is for the greatness of the Fatherland
within the arms of Christ.[32]

If we keep in mind the inescapable connection between the bishops and Catholic Action, it seems to us that the conclusions will
be even more obvious.

Various authors have expressed their ideas on the subject of
Catholic Action. For example, Alfredo J. Molinario stressed that
Catholic Action consists of the "organized activity of lay Catholics, developed in a multiform manner, within the life of society
and tending to the integral reestablishment of the Social Kingdom
of Jesus Christ."[33]   According to the organization's own figures,
Catholic Action grew appreciably during this period: from 80,000
dues-paying members in 1940 it rose to over 98,000 in 1943, besides having "several hundred thousand more adherents."[34]   Its
work was varied, but one example is its outstanding performance
as moral censor of publications, which was tolerated and even recognized by important officials such as the mayor of Buenos
Aires, Mariano de Vedia y Mitre.[35]   Catholic Action was the
church's most important lay group in Argentina and the faithful
executor of episcopal instructions. Many young men were formed
within its ranks who later entered "major" politics after 1943 during the Catholic-nationalist epidemic, and from their posts continued to defend the interests of the church, which they internal-
ized. The rightist nationalist groups, as outsiders, and the lay
groups of Catholic Action, in a more official manner, made up the
two wings of the religious strategy. Convincing proof of what we
assert is to be found in a document published by the organization
in 1944 "for the purpose of avoiding errors, wʰich give rise to
public confusion and are the result of a deficient knowledge of. . .
[Catholic Action's] nature and purpose." Some of the articles in
this manifesto point out that:

(8) Thus, Catholic Action is responsible for its own direct activity, exercised organically *in close association with the hierarchy, subordinate to, and under the supreme and immediate
direction of, the latter.* (9) On the other hand, the strictly and
exclusively individual activities of its members that are carried
out under their own responsibility in fulfilling their duties as
Catholic citizens in the field of socioeconomic activities cannot
be ascribed to. . . [Catholic Action]. (10) It is well to remember

that not only the members of Catholic Action, in their joint or individual activities, but also all Catholics, as such, should hold strictly to the clear and precise pronouncements of the Argentine episcopate which, in full accord with pontifical teaching, has condemned modern errors such as atheistic communism, the liberalisms referred to in the encyclical *Libertas*, racism, exaggerated nationalisms, and other totalitarian doctrines in all their known forms. . . (14) In social activities in the broad field of economics and politics, controversies are inevitable and at times fruitful. Members of Catholic Action and other Catholics can also engage in them personally. The norms proclaimed by Catholic Action are those of the church: *occidite errores, diligite homines.* What is honestly considered to be the truth can be defended vigorously, and errors can be energetically attacked, but always respecting persons as sacred. (15) Finally, Catholics when acting personally under their own responsibility are not entitled to act in the name of the Catholics whom they do not represent nor can the spectators justly attribute to Catholic Action or to the church the actions of those who do not act in representation of them.[36]

It is obvious that such a doctrine would lead to the absolute uselessness of any study that may be made of the church as a pressure group or of any of the Catholic associations, whether clerical or lay, and their political or economic correlations. Strictly speaking, only the doctrine of the Pope speaking *ex cathedra* could be considered the official position of the church, something that seems absurd to us. On the contrary, we believe that by examining the documents issued by the bishops, the pronouncements of recognized Catholic entities not condemned by the hierarchy, and the writings of certain Catholic individuals who enjoy special standing or influence, useful inferences may be drawn for an impartial study of the official Catholic position on a given problem or period. We prefer the possibility of error to the easy recourse to dogma.

Of course, the general situation was unsettled and at times there is a certain degree of (accepted) discrepancy between what we might call "official" positions (pastoral letters) and those of private Catholic groups and even of individual priests. If we consider the different positions taken by Bishop de Andrea and Father Virgilio Filippo from the very beginning of Peronism, what we mean will be clear. From his own point of view, Kennedy has this to say:

While it is illogical to think of any sector of Catholic opinion that would work at cross-purposes to the hierarchy or which would defy Church authority, *the area of social thought and action where Church authority commands compliance is necessarily one that is authoritatively defined.* In practice, definitions have not pre-empted a general field of social concern to Catholics. It is therefore entirely possible that Catholic opinion, that is to say a cohesive body of opinion sensitive to Church interests and to the implications of Christian doctrine in a given social context, may react, *not in disharmony with,* but beyond the limits of, an official Church position.[37]

The church and politics: totalitarianism

Kennedy holds that there were two fronts for the church's political action during the thirties "a rightist clergy attacking liberal democracy in the press and in the pulpit" and the already mentioned lay organization, Argentine Catholic Action. The figure that best illustrates the first position is Gustavo J. Franceschi, although Kennedy tends to play down considerably the totalitarian inspiration of this priest. In summarizing his conclusions, Kennedy is forced to acknowledge that "in general *the record does not bespeak what would normally be considered a strong commitment to democracy.*"[38] Quite an understatement! In all his articles and editorials in *Criterio,* Franceschi always expressed himself clearly. For example, referring to Italian fascism he wrote:

I am not dealing here with the worth of its principles nor of its methods; I confine myself to only one of its aspects. It has infused into the sons of Italy an enormous pride in their nationality and a prodigious zeal for its honor. I am aware of the excesses that have occurred and still continue to occur; I am well aware that this nationalism easily adopts forms of hostility and scorn toward everything that is not Italian. But despite all its undeniable defects, I prefer it a thousand times to the indifference or weakness of character of many of our citizens.[39]

He considered Benito Mussolini "not only the first political figure in Europe and in the world at the present time, but also a notable trail-blazer."[40] In 1936 he wrote about the Franco faction in Spain as follows:

I believe that the greatest likelihood of success for the Nationalists lies in the fact that they have leaders: they have a unified command, government, administration, and basic doctrine; they are not weathervanes driven by the wind that blows in the street. Today you cannot exist as a society without this.[41]

Franceschi had traveled to Spain, that is, to the part of Spain controlled by Franco's forces, because he had been "selected by His Eminence the Cardinal Archbishop of Buenos Aires. . . to deliver to its ecclesiastical authorities the ornaments and objects of worship collected among us by the ladies' committee that carried out the Crusade for the Devastated Churches of Spain."[42]

He had the following to say about the church and fascism:

> If [Mussolini] were fully consistent in enforcing his tenets, a revolution would break out within twenty-four hours. The Duce is too intelligent to provoke it. He seeks *a modus vivendi, and the church remains silent if it finds its essential rights respected,* among other reasons because it is indestructible and men and political regimes are transitory.[43]

On strong governments:

> We are witnessing the decline of weak governments. Unhappy are the countries that insist on maintaining. . . [such governments] since they will inevitably be crushed by the nations that will have replaced them. From this point of view, it can be asserted without fear of error that democracies, if they do not disappear, are at least destined to undergo profound structural changes.[44]

The totalitarian streak in Franceschi had anti-Semitic overtones, even though many years later he visited Israel and was to a certain extent reconciled with the liberalism that he had attacked so strongly in his controversies with Lisandro de la Torre:

> I think today as I thought yesterday and as I believe I will think tomorrow. I am not anti-Semitic. I do not desire violence against anyone, but I do assert the impossibility of accepting unlimited Hebrew immigration, in view of its character as. . . a race pledged to keep its ethnic individuality, without placing our predominantly Latin and Christian national character in jeopardy. Nor do I accept the internal warfare that an unassimilated colony provokes.[45]

José E. Assaf, a member of the editorial staff of *Criterio* whose signed articles and editorials we presume were under the control of Editor-in-Chief Franceschi, was even more rabidly anti-Semitic. Let us conclude our quotations with a short selection from Franceschi on the Hitler and Franco regimes:

In short, in coming to the end of this study, we will say that: (1) The church has not pronounced sentence, nor is it up to it to pronounce one, on the present form of *political regime* adopted by Germany at the present time; (2) on more than one occasion it has explicitly condemned the Nazi *doctrine;* (3) it has with similar vigour protested against the *practice* of National Socialism in Germany, both with relation to the rights of the immortal person and to those of the church itself; (4) the continuation of diplomatic relations between the Holy See and the Reich *does not in any way imply approval* of what the latter asserts in the philosophico-religious or social field; (5) in any case of military *collaboration* against a perverse doctrine and practice such as that of communism, the attitude of General Franco is in no way contrary to Catholic teachings.[46]

Our last quotation from Franceschi shows him to be at odds with Father Mariana's classical theory of the lawfulness of resistance to tyranny: ". . . a Catholic, insofar as he is a citizen, while he cannot approve the totalitarian *doctrine* of a regime, must, if he is a member of a country subject to such a doctrine, serve it loyally and fulfill the obligations imposed upon him by the defense of his country."[47] However, another figure within the Catholic church, Bishop Miguel de Andrea, was a contact man with the traditionally liberal sectors and with the so-called "social Catholicism." Ambrosio Romero Carranza has this to say about de Andrea's evolution:

Bishop de Andrea noted that in 1910 anarchist forces attempted to annihilate our constitutional order; that in 1919 atheistic communism emanating from Russia began its work of undermining our basic law; that during the 1930-1940 decade fascism and nazism imported from Italy and Germany despotic institutions to take the place of our democratic customs; and that from 1943 to 1955 totalitarianism took possession of Argentina, practically nullifying our rights and the individual liberties our Magna Carta protects and defends. He fought against all these diseases with the peaceful weapons of his social action and his political ideas. It is not up to me to deal with these achievements here and, as an analysis of his political ideas would take too long. . . I shall epitomize them in two luminous words: *Christianity and democracy.*[48]

De Andrea participated in the general welfare programs intended to improve the condition of urban workers and carried out "apparently. . . with episcopal approval"[49] the memorable Great

National Fund Collection after the "Tragic Week" in 1919. His nomination for Archbishop of Buenos Aires (made by the liberal Alvear) was not supported by the Holy See and gave rise to a *cause célèbre*. After that he was to enjoy a semiofficial status within the Argentine clergy and to redouble his efforts in favor of women workers and office employees. While Franceschi continued to hit the Socialists, de Andrea has not had any objections to writing an introductory note to Carlos R. Desmarás book, *Ley del trabajo a domicilio* (1942), which has a preface signed by Alfredo L. Palacios. But, of course, Bishop de Andrea was not even remotely within the mainstream of the Catholic hierarchy.

The church and political power

While relations between the Radical governments (Yrigoyen, Alvear, and again Yrigoyen) and the church in general have never ceased to be cordial, when Uriburu took charge of the government on 6 September 1930, the sympathy of the hierarchy and the influential members of the clergy toward the work of his government was notorious. An interview with Uriburu, as the head of the movement, quoted him as saying: "I always read *Criterio*, its articles on doctrine and its political editorials. *I belong to the current of ideas that you diffuse and defend...*"[50] The journal seemed to have anticipated this statement when a few days earlier it had published an editorial saying that:

> The regime overthrown, elected under the provisions of the Constitution and through the mechanisms of the Sáenz Peña Act, was destructive and ruinous both because of the men who composed it (who in their own way observed the Constitution) and because it had reached power by way of elections in a contest that may be as democratic as you will and as legal as legal can be, but the results of which could not come as a surprise to any well-organized mind.[51]

The episcopate published a pastoral letter of historic importance shortly before the 1931 national elections won by the Justo-Roca team. It reaffirmed the basic postulates that the church supported in connection with specific questions and referred to contemporary secularism and the duties of Catholics. The part which interests us sets up norms to guide the conscience of the faithful and reads as follows:

> (I) Those who have a right to vote are, as a general rule, obligated to exercise that right, provided that no obstacle of compa-

rable gravity to the importance of religion stands in the way, since abstention would become complicity and responsibility before God whenever such abstention might contribute to the victory of an unworthy candidate or to the defeat of an appreciably better candidate. (II) Among several candidates or slates acceptable from the Catholic point of view, one must vote for those who, in conscience, seem more likely to produce the greatest good for religion and the country, even though they may not belong to one's own party, because the public good is above the good of the party. (III) When the candidates or slates presented are unacceptable from the Catholic point of view, one must vote for the least objectionable, from whose activity less damage to religion and the country is to be feared. In this case, the danger of giving scandal shall be avoided, especially during the campaign period, by reservations [made known] at the proper time as to the conditional nature of the adherence given, without approving the whole program. (IV) *No Catholic can join parties or vote for candidates that include in their programs the following principles: (a) the separation of church and state, in the sense explained above: (b) the repeal of the legal provisions that recognize the rights of religion, and especially of the religious oath and of the words in which our Constitution invokes the protection of God, the source of all reason and justice, since such repeal is equivalent to a public and positive profession of national atheism; (c) secularism in schools; (d) legal divorce.*[52]

As may be noted, this all adds up to an antiliberal program pure and simple. The prohibition against voting for certain candidates was obviously intended for the liberal candidates of the Civil Alliance, though of course no names were named, but was it necessary? We shall see how these provisions continued to be useful in 1945.

It should be emphasized that the church and Uriburu did not disagree on anything; the general himself said in a message to the citizenry: "The Argentine church has continued to exercise effectively the high mission entrusted to it within the state."[53] Justo's relations with the church after he became president have already been mentioned above, especially after the 1934 Eucharistic Congress. The government parties and even the "opposition" Radical party of Alvear tried to pick up suggestions pleasing to the Catholic hierarchy:

. . . it is a fact that Catholic consciousness has received a strong impetus, which will grow stronger from day to day, and that it understand its civic obligations better than before. *Some parties have seen this and become aware of the advisability of adopting slates that will satisfy the aspirations expressed.*[54]

Franceschi undertook to answer some of the objections then being formulated (and which still continue to be heard) to the official ecclesiastical position vis-à-vis political parties:

Nor should [the church] be asked to condemn this or that political group for abuses in the strictly temporal order. I have been asked more than once: "Why does the church not speak a word against those committing fraud? " It could not do so by naming persons or groups without entering into the purely political field; it vigorously sets forth the principles, but their application does not appertain to it, just as in matters of private morals it says: "Stealing is forbidden," but it is not its task, but that of the civil judge, to render sentence that: "So-and-so is a thief." No more and no less than lies within its mission should be required of it.[55]

The church applied this policy with supreme skill, carefully balancing the weight of its veiled official pronouncements and the greater flexibility of its unofficial publicity organs. The position of General Justo's government is summarized in these concepts extracted from a voluminous official publication of the time:

One of the first problems that concerned our present government in the area of relations with the Roman Catholic and Apostolic Church was the precarious state of health of the Archbishop of Buenos Aires, the Very Reverend José María Bottaro. When the latter resigned, the Holy See designated Bishop Santiago Luis Copello to occupy the vacant see. The executive branch, by a message sent to Congress on 26 August 1932, proposed the creation of new dioceses and archdioceses. This bill resulted in Law No. 11,715 of 26 September 1933, by which the dioceses of La Plata, Córdoba, Santa Fe, Salta, San Juan de Cuyo, and Paraná were raised to the status of archdioceses and new dioceses were created in Mendoza, San Luis, La Rioja, Jujuy, Rosario, Río Cuarto, Bahía Blanca, Mercedes, Azul, and Viedma. Steps were immediately taken to obtain the bulls which arrived on 20 April 1934. Archdioceses and dioceses were set up and new and vacant sees were filled by the proper prelates. In October 1934, the thirty-second International Eucharistic Congress was celebrated in Buenos Aires with great pomp and with a large attendance of the faithful. His Holiness

Pope Pius XI was represented by His Eminence, Cardinal Secretary of State Pacelli, as *a latere* legate. Thus, this was the first time not only that the Holy See was represented in this manner at an Eucharistic Congress, but also the first time a Cardinal Secretary of State had left Italy. The Argentine government and people rose to the occasion of this signal honor by cordially entertaining the eminent prince of the church. These manifestations of an unprecedented cordiality toward the Roman Catholic and Apostolic Church culminated in the granting of the cardinal's hat to His Eminence Santiago Luis Copello, Archbishop of Buenos Aires, and the raising of this archbishopric to the rank of the primacy in the Argentine Church.[56]

This cordiality did not appreciably change during the Ortiz and Castillo regime, though it must be stressed that some sectors with a Catholic background (the "nationalists") before 1943 had developed a strong antiliberal campaign that had at that time a nazi cast rather than a fascist one, since Germany had invaded the Soviet Union and the definitive defeat of Communism was expected. The church — that is, its hierarchy — found ways after June to capitalize on the efforts of that sector which, of course, did not represent it "officially." A strengthening of the bonds between the clergy and the armed forces was the result. Shortly after coming into power, General Ramírez addressed a letter (23 June 1943) to the editor of *Criterio,* which this journal promptly published. It said:

I have read your note entitled "Considerations on the Revolution," published in the most recent issue of *Criterio,* with the most lively interest. By means of this letter I want to send you evidence of this interest and of the special attention with which I have come in contact with your reflections on a matter of such lively and intense interest.

The government I head has clearly manifested its true anxiety to promote a patriotic assemblage of the wise and the prudent for the work of national reconstruction which destiny has delivered into its hands. In this sense, your journalistic note on the revolution has value for me as an auspicious contribution to promoting our difficult but honorable work. As such, I esteem it and am grateful. Your illustrious record, Your Excellency, lends all your fruitful labors as a journalist a value commensurate with your high intellectual standing and your undaunted activity in the social apostolate as an interpreter of Christian justice, illuminated from Rome by the effulgence of the Encyclicals. We have assumed the historic responsibility of restoring to the country the traditional values of Argentine culture, which have been upset by a policy of suicidal blindness based on the most disastrous denial of national identity. This is why I have placed my government, in accordance with the most authentic and deepest Argentine reality, under the advocacy of God, who is the source of all reason and all justice. We shall govern under that advocacy, knowing, as indeed we know, that from the very beginning of our history there is projected into any national present aware of itself the august sign of the Cross with which Spain has permanently marked the soul of the continent.[57]

One year before the 4 June 1943 coup, Franceschi had already written:

We cannot leave everything to the good will or the intelligence of our fellow citizens. The experience of many centuries has demonstrated that the two major vices that blind the individual are avarice, or the greed for money, and sensuality, or the excessive appetite for pleasure; both are part of that complex that drives those who in these terrible times think only of profiting from the general poverty to seek exorbitant gains. It is essential that the social authority, what is commonly called the government, despite the weakness that afflicts it as a consequence of the more or less liberal theories on which it is founded, should muster all the resources at its command so that the excesses evident in our country, as well as in all others, should not end by driving some citizens against the others, even to recourse to arms. *This is why we demand a strong state: in order to forestall, first, the advent of a chaotic state, then, of a despotic one.*[58]

After the coup, the same prelate claimed that:

General Uriburu's revolution, which was victorious from the material point of view, failed because it did not dare to carry to its ultimate conclusions the principle on which it was based; it allowed the professional politician to intervene in it, it did not have confidence in its own strength, it sought compromises. This is why two years after the revolution took place there was a return to *normalcy,* that is, to the old politicking, while the general died during a trip that was almost exile. It is also possible that around 1931 or 1932 the consequences of the prevailing regime could not be seen as clearly as they are today. Now we have taken the leap, and this was the opportune moment to do so. God will not permit that it be taken in a vacuum.[59]

In another article he wrote that:

The men who took the initiative in our revolution come especially from the military sector, first, because it is the only one
having the necessary strength to impose and then maintain order; second, because by virtue of the life they normally lead,
they are less contaminated than any others. But as events have
demonstrated, they do not in any sense refuse the collaboration
of the civilian elements, and General Ramírez's letter has
proved this once more. There is only one thing they refuse to
do: to rely again on individuals and groups discredited by politics, whose social ineffectiveness has been made obvious by the
events of the last fifteen or twenty years; they hope that "the
wise and the prudent" will help them gradually to resolve the
terribly complicated problems that arise in this hour of transi-
tion for Argentina and for the world. I am thoroughly convinced that they will obtain this patriotically binding collaboration.[60]

As the spokesman for Catholic thought, Franceschi continued
to be connected with military circles. He addressed the cadets at
the military academy on the occasion of a religious ceremony on
13 June 1943. He also gave a lecture on "Man and War" at the
Higher War College on 23 August of the following year. He ended
his address by saying: "Generals, leaders, and officers who have
had the kindness and patience to hear me, you constitute a Christian army."[61]   After 4 June, the Catholic-nationalist invasion consolidated its forces. The work had been developing on various
fronts even before that date.

There were priests who proclaimed ideas contrary to our institutions and Catholic Action youths who felt themselves swept
along by the New Order. Publications such as *El Pueblo* and
Crisol came under German influence, under that of the brown
demon. It may be said that with cautious skill they seconded *El
Pampero*. It was charged that *El Pueblo* accepted subsidies from
the German embassy, just as other publications and individuals
did, many of the latter belonging to the upper circles. The newspaper *Estrada* was forbidden to publish, and it was a voice for
democracy.[62]

There were some voices, among them that of Father Castellani,
that recorded the complex situation as seen from within the
church:

The case of the Argentine church can be stated in a few words as follows: it is bound by a golden harness to a state that has ceased to be Catholic, or is on the way to doing so; and since it greatly desires that. . . [this state] not cease to be Catholic, it has to cling to the colors of the flag, to the Preamble to the Constitution, to the Catholicity of our founding fathers, to the clergy of independence days, to Sarmiento's catechism, and to the Te Deums and blessings of cornerstones. This constitutes a serious difficulty and a problem that is not to be taken lightly and which has been tormenting us since the time of Estrada. The Socialists say that the solution lies in the breaking off or violent separation of church and state. The Catholics say that the remedy lies in a Concordat. The decision does not lie with us, nor with any man living, perhaps; but circumstances or Providence will one of these days settle the matter. We would wish for an Apostolic Visitor with courage, for a National Synod, and if possible, for an Ecumenical Council. Nothing less.[63]

However, as usual, Castellani's voice was an isolated one. The Chilean newspaperman Alejandro Magnet recalls that:

When the military carried out their coup in 1943, Catholic nationalist groups brought strong pressure to bear and the last day of that same year General Ramírez issued a decree-law reestablishing compulsory religious instruction. The measure was received with rejoicing by ecclesiastical authorities and displeased a minority of Catholics who considered it undesirable that the church should appear to be favored in such a way by officials who were the product of a coup d'état. In their judgment, the law that had been passed by Congress should have been repealed in the same manner and not by an autocratic decision of a military government.[64]

It is not the fact itself that interests us most in this case, but rather the process by which approval of the decree on religious instruction, as well as the more or less absolute control of the three branches of education in the country by Catholic and clerical elements, was achieved. These two achievements represent the fullest political victory for the church — the hierarchy — during the period under consideration.

John J. Kennedy, some of whose opinions we have already quoted, claims that this decree was issued by the revolutionary government without any corresponding "political obligation," but that it was evidently intended to gain Catholic support for the regime. Naturally, those entrusted with fostering the educational policy were priests or lay people of proved fidelity to the official church posture, among them Gustavo Martínez Zuviría, Tomás D. Casares (who became a judge of the Supreme Court in September 1944), Atilio Dell'Oro Maini (federal interventor in Corrientes in 1930, became interventor of the University of Buenos Aires School of Law in 1943), Manuel Villada Achával, Ataliva Herrera, Jesús E. López Moure, Rómulo Etcheverry Boneo, Jordán Bruno Genta, Alberto Baldrich, Carlos Obligado, and Juan Sepich. Kennedy then refers to episcopal activity, to which Bishop de Andrea was the only exception:

> To suggest that the bishops' pronouncements were motivated more by historical factors than by a desire to support the military dictatorship in 1944, and later the Perón presidential candidacy, *does not dispose of the question of whether the effect of the statements was actually to aid first the dictatorship and then the candidacy. Objectively, it is impossible to ascribe a different effect to them. They did not oppose the dictatorship or Perón.*[65]

It is in this light that we must interpret the collective pastoral issued by the episcopate on 15 November 1945, *when the campaign platforms of the political parties that were to take part in the elections of the following February had not yet been drawn up.* The pastoral letter repeated the provisions of a similar document dated 1931, which we have transcribed at pp. 178-179 of this book. What is really significant is the way a commentator on the 1945 pastoral letter defends the legitimacy of the goals achieved:

> The establishment of Catholic religious instruction in the schools of a country does not constitute a free gift of the government to the church, but rather the recognition of the right of Christ to carry, by means of that church, his Truth to the soul of children. . . .It matters little that this recognition be by the Grand Turk, the Emir of Afghanistan, or His Christian Majesty. Would. . . [the church] not react in the same manner if the Soviets were to adopt a similar attitude?[66]

In December 1945 Bishop Antonio Caggiano, the diligent organizer of Catholic Action, was raised to the cardinalate. From his cardinal's see he did "not hide his favorable attitude toward the regime."[67] This did not keep Caggiano from lending his valuable backing to the military regime of General Juan Carlos Onganía twenty years later as Archbishop of Buenos Aires. Casares, who survived the political trial of the rest of the Supreme Court mem-

bers (1947), defended Peronism in the same way. Casares did not
break with the administration until the 1955 crisis between Peronism and the clergy. In short, according to Kennedy,". . . the glar-
ing weakness of the Argentine Catholic position has been a failure
to grasp the essential relation between effective democracy and
free and open elections."[68] However, this author attempts to
disassociate the church as a body from the authoritarian and even
totalitarian posture of many sectors representative of Catholic
thought. Carlos Cossio has best summed up the political course of
the Catholic church between 1930 and 1946:

It is striking to note how the political efforts of the Argentine
church, through its three secular groups, influenced the three
revolutions that comprise the historic cycle through which we
are living. *The 1930 revolution was taken over by liberal Catholics with the old nineteenth century constitutional mentality;*
the first cabinet of General Uriburu (with which the game was
lost) was a star cast of men prominent in national life, almost all
thoroughly devoted Catholics fully trusted by the church. This
was also true of the leader of the government. They were all
authentic representatives of the past and did not know how to
govern in a present that did not belong to them to the extent
that they could not understand it. *The 1943 revolution,* under
General Ramírez and, if possible, even more so under General
Farrell, *was taken over by the Catholic nationalists.* The content of government resolutions, the quotations interspersed
throughout the speeches of the chief executive, the liturgical
pomp with which some provincial interventors took office, all
defiantly bore the stamp of that inspiration. The result was
Perón's constitutional election by a slight electoral advantage
that was attained through the open support of the church after
the candidate had agreed to the sacramental formalization of his
carnal union with Eva Duarte. The church took for granted that
Perón, lacking ideas for governing, would seek them from it in
order to fulfill his commitment. This is what produced the unanimous enthusiasm of all Argentine occupants of dioceses and
the great influence the purple and holy water began to exert
through political courtesy. The old nineteenth century Catholicism outlined by Alberdi had relegated priests to the place
where they had a mission to perform, that is, to the churches;
with Perón they came back in a religious role to Congress and
the university. However, since no totalitarianism can totally
coincide with any other, the takeover by the Catholic nationalists also failed as soon as the tangential arc of coincidence be-

tween them and Perón ran its course. *The 1955 revolution was to have been taken over by the humanist Christian Democratic laymen.* Their admission into the Consulting Board as a political party, without knowing exactly what the electoral following of that handful of men was, shows clearly the weight the church had within the military circles that decided the matter.[69]

Let us state here only that the church has been on good terms with Yrigoyen, with Uriburu, with Justo, with Ortiz-Castillo, with Ramírez-Farrell and, of course, with Perón, on each occasion using the tactic (or tactics) suited to the situation. Using traditional anti-liberalism, whenever convenient (and this was almost always the case), its interests were often well served, whether from outside or from inside the state apparatus. It may be alleged that *directly* the hierarchy was not responsible for this or that measure, but what cannot be questioned is the skill of the clergy in *indirect action.* The authoritarian structure of the Catholic church (consider the dogmas, the infallibility of the Pope when speaking *ex cathedra,* the government of the Vatican) in the majority of cases prevents access to original sources, to the fountainheads. We have to content ourselves with elaborating hypotheses, with analyzing results, which we verify by events. Ours are the first steps taken in this direction, since the political role of the Catholic church in Argentina continues to be a subject that is tabu for the majority of Catholic and non-Catholic authors.[70]

7 The Armed Forces

It is our impression that the period of easy classifications and convenient "anti" positions (antimilitarism, anticlericalism, etc.) is past. It is well to keep this warning in mind when we discuss the role of the *armed forces* in Argentina during the 1930-46 period.

Political scientists are gradually reaching the useful conclusion that it is not possible to elaborate a general theory on the army as a political factor that can have absolute validity everywhere, for developed and underdeveloped, for capitalist and socialist countries alike. Before proceeding with our subject, we would like to refer to two examples of the more recent approach.

S. E. Finer undertook to systematize the "role of the military in politics" on a world-wide scale. On the basis of broad research ranging from Pakistan to Argentina, he analyzes, first, the military will to intervene, taking into consideration the inhibiting and stimulating factors and the correlated tendency to intervene or not, while applying the concepts to the various realities of specific countries. He also distinguishes the levels of intervention of the armed forces and the methods employed, as is shown in table 17.[1] If we delve deeply into our historical experience, we will almost surely find specific instances of political events in Argentina that we can assign to each one of the categories mentioned. The same is true of other countries.

Finer then goes on to analyze the armed forces' opportunities for political intervention, taking into account:

I. Increased civilian dependence on the military
II. The effect of domestic circumstances
   A. Overt crisis
   B. Latent crisis
   C. The power vacuum
III. The popularity of the military

The levels of intervention will vary in accordance with the type of country considered. There will be countries with (a) a devel-

TABLE 17: INTERVENTION BY ARMED FORCES

Levels of
Intervention   Methods

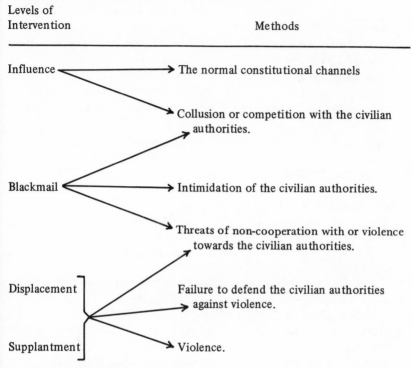

Source: Finer, *The Man on Horseback: the Role of the Military in Politics,* p. 140.

oped political culture; (b) a weak political culture; (c) a minimal political culture. The British author places Argentina under category (b), after analyzing its political process, especially during the years 1930-1962.[2] As may be gathered from the mere enumeration of some of the subjects covered by Finer in his work, the problem of the military and political power has ceased to be treated in the aggregate and by means of schematic concepts.

The same type of approach is being followed elsewhere. In discussing the main types of relationships between civilian and military authorities, Jean Meynaud distinguishes three series of relations: (a) the army as an instrument of the civil power; (b) the army as a factor in governmental decisions; (c) the army as an element controlling politics. Meynaud summarizes part of the problem presented by this crucial issue of the military and power as follows:

Without considering whether it may have happened otherwise at any given moment of evolution, it may be granted that today the schema of the unconditional supremacy of the civil power constitutes an idealization of the problem. The difficulty lies in ascertaining whether the relations between civilians and military follow a *continuum* whose positions would translate into various degrees of military interference in government affairs or whether, on the contrary, it is desirable to introduce qualifying levels between the various types set forth. Of course, this problem can be viewed as a purely academic one; it can also be concluded that any answer is impossible without the prior formulation of many models (industrialized countries and underdeveloped countries, Communist and pluralist countries, Western and Eastern countries). Unfortunately, we do not yet possess all the means to establish them. . . .

In order to approach an acceptable systematization, it would be advisable to examine analytically the relations between the different types of army and the various types of sociopolitical organization. . . .

Specifically, [this study] does not express any global judgment on the social significance of the intervention of the military in politics. This abstention, in part voluntary, arises from a perception of the relativity and diversity of the situations, and from the author's certainty that — in the present state of our knowledge — any generalization is only a doctrinal and even dogmatic prejudgment.[3]

Army and politics: Uriburu, Justo, Perón

Let us now return to the interpretation of events in Argentina. If we define a *practicing politician* as a man who aspires to rise to power, channels his efforts to achieve this end, and finally does achieve it, then it seems proper to us to point out that the three most important practicing politicians of the 1930-46 period in Argentina came from the army. They were José F. Uriburu, Agustín P. Justo, and Juan D. Perón. The latter two may be considered to fit the definition more closely than Uriburu. It is understandable that Alvear. the perennial Radical party "opposition" candidate, should not appear on this list, nor Lisandro de la Torre, alone and stubborn in his seat in the Senate; nor the minor figures such as Ortiz, Castillo, Ramírez, and Farrell.

This first approach to the relations between the army and politics may perhaps err by being too concerned with personalities, but neither is it right to ignore — under the pretext of methodological purity — the influence that certain individual figures exercise on historical processes. Uriburu's political personality has on occasion been excessively praised, usually by those who shared with him the responsibility for the September 1930 movement. Sánchez Sorondo, his adviser and later his minister of the interior, stated in the Senate that:

> Uriburu was a man of destiny. In turbulent and anxious times, when the systematic and deliberate violation of ethical and institutional principles disturbs the political and economic structure, when decentralized forces erupt, threatening to destroy collective harmony, society reels on its foundations, becomes conscious of the impending disaster, and seeks a strong will, a vigorous hand, and a well-tempered heart that will embody its desire for liberty and order. This is how governments of force are born today.[4]

A more moderate assessment is offered by Federico Pinedo:

> Uriburu was an educated man, with enough training to understand the main outlines of the problems of government, even though he was not a scholar; he had some of the characteristics of his military profession (and of a German military man), but he was in no sense a product of the barracks; he had numerous civilian friends and relations, whom he esteemed and respected, and despite his mien, which gave him an appearance of harshness, I considered him an affectionate man responsive to friendship. A patrician from the inland provinces who had numerous strong ties to the traditional Buenos Aires families, he enjoyed the company of people of his class or of his milieu, whose merits he knew how to appreciate but perhaps overvalued. At the time to which I am referring [1930], he was quite under the influence of some ideas of a corporative nature that he had derived directly from more or less fascist publications, then quite fashionable in the circles he frequented, or that had been suggested to him by friends. I do not believe that he intended to transplant European regimes to our country, but the fact is that he was enthralled by some of their institutions, or by the legends about those institutions, such as corporative representation, believing that they might serve as an effective remedy against the evils of demagoguery, toward which he felt a real aversion and which he considered the fatal result of the traditional form of democracy. His political experience was not very extensive, although he had served briefly in the lower house.[5]

Uriburu was the visible head of the 6 September 1930 coup, but we have already seen lurking in the shadows the eventually victorious strategy of General-Engineer Agustín P. Justo. Sarobe's testimony is very enlightening because of his participation in the revolutionary process.[6] Not all opinions on Uriburu are so indulgent. An army comrade, Gen. Severo Toranzo (who had an Yrigoyenist background) wrote him a very violent letter in 1932:

Until 6 September 1930 we had an army that was idolized by the Argentines. Not one of the worst rulers had dared to use it as an instrument of oppression against the people. The army was quietly devoted to preparing itself for the defense of the sovereignty of the nation. You and your followers violated its discipline, corrupting it with bounties and sinecures and using it for the achievement of unavowable objectives. Today the Argentine army is detested by the real people.

On a more personal level, he made the following charges:

Your military career — steering through all the services after your graduation from the Military College: the infantry, the artillery, the engineers, and the cavalry — constitutes the most perfect example of favoritism, without which you would never have reached even the grade of captain. But as the nephew of a president and, through marriage, the recipient of the profits from a section added to the port of Buenos Aires, it was easy for you to obtain, by social allurements and invitations, what you would never have been able to obtain through your virtues and professional abilities. Later, when you lost the fortune you had acquired through marriage, you devoted yourself to usury and to profiting from bribes. A typical example of the dirtiness of your "deals," which relieves me of the need to itemize them, is your close connection with the Finances and Mandates Bank and your participation in the *mate* speculation.

The sixth of September came, a day of mourning for Argentine democracy. Under the protection of a regime of force to which history already applies the most degrading epithets, you and your profiteering collaborators devoted yourselves to sacking the Exchange Fund, our sacred treasure, the symbol of our national wealth and great economic power; it has almost ceased to exist. And today we do not have money even to pay government employees. How could we have, after you had wasted millions and millions to maintain parasitic "civil legions," true armies of voracious spies of both sexes? That is the most visible fruit of the "revolution" and of your tragic misgovernment. . . .

Under the guise of patriotism, you are, in reality, a venal agent of questionable foreign interests. The tax surcharges levied on the people by mere decrees... such as the shameful one on gasoline ostentatiously justified by the need to build highways, but actually responding to pressure from Standard Oil Company (this corporation also has had all the concessions granted by the administrations of Salta Province which preceded and followed that of Adolfo Güemes and the national ones in the Comodoro Rivadavia and Plaza Huincul zone renewed), constitute a significant index of the influence enjoyed in the "provisional government" and its provincial praetorships by the great foreign companies.[7]

Uriburu was placed on retirement status in May 1929, during Yrigoyen's second term. From that moment on "Uriburu's activity was channeled into public affairs and broke through the professional framework to convert him into the leader of a revolution."[8]   Agustín P. Justo was the beneficiary of that revolution. He came into national prominence when the cabinet of President Alvear became known. The facts are all too familiar and Luna sets them forth in his biography of Alvear. The latter was quoted as saying that during a conversation with Tomás Le Bretón (in Paris, of course) he discussed the makeup of the cabinet in his forthcoming administration.

When he came to the Ministry of War, Alvear spoke of Gen. José F. Uriburu. They had been friends in their youth, and he was one of the most senior officers in the army. Apparently, the newly elected president did not consider it important that the candidate for the Ministry of War had been a Conservative deputy in 1914. . . . But Uriburu's name was noticed by Marshal Joffre. In a conversation he held with Alvear, the victor of the Marne pointed out to him that the future minister of war was a notorious Germanophile, something that would not be seen with pleasure by the winning nations in the world conflict. This observation made an impression on Alvear, and he asked Le Bretón for a new name. Le Bretón — who was to be a part of the cabinet as minister of agriculture — said that he knew a military man with a civilian mind, disciplined, an expert in his field, and with wide general culture.[9]

This was Justo. As director of the Military College during Yrigoyen's first term, he had taken the cadets to a testimonial in honor of Bartolomé Mitre during the centennial celebration of the latter's birth and had delivered a eulogy on him. This action stood out in contrast to the official indifference to the celebration. This is not without significance since Mitre was always the model that Justo tried earnestly to imitate: his political ability, his "civilianism," and his love of books are some of the characteristics they had in common. Justo also acknowledged that he was heavily indebted to Gen. Julio A. Roca, twice president of the country. Justo's death early in 1943 prevented finding out whether he would also have achieved that ambition for which he had been preparing, since "... some Antipersonalist committees had nominated him and the Radical party was discussing the possibility of resigning itself to his becoming a candidate."[10]

With important army sectors (led by a man as faithful as Col. Manuel A. Rodríguez, later his minister of war) backing him, Justo maneuvered nimbly among Conservatives and Antipersonalist Radicals, as well as among the independent Socialist group. He was also able to get the support of the Alvear Radicals. Pinedo has seen this very clearly:

> If a ruler's objective can be to obtain a general breakup of the parties supporting him in order to impose upon them any solution that may interest him, without interference from personages of greater or lesser influence on his administration, then it may be said that the objective was achieved when after the opposition was reduced to impotence, the government parties placed themselves at the disposal of the president almost without reservations.[11]

Despite the assertion by his son Liborio (writing under the pseudonym of "Quebracho") that General Justo's greatest ambition was to become minister of war, later events demonstrated a concatenation of circumstances in which their protagonist was not uninvolved: the famous speech on the "hour of the sword" by Lugones was delivered in Lima in 1924 *in the presence of Gen. Agustín P. Justo;* the anti-Yrigoyenism of the latter was taken advantage of by certain political sectors in order to interest him in a movement against the old caudillo, but Justo was to be "one soldier more" among the forces that accompanied Uriburu. According to Liborio Justo, his father took part in the coup:

> *...just so as not to be left behind (perhaps for the purpose of not being discredited before those who had earlier urged him to lead an uprising* with a view to benefiting from the same), even though his attitude and that of his friends in the army, who also took part in this movement, indicated an antidictatorial stand, opposed to Uriburu's intentions.[12]

After finishing his presidential term, Justo traveled abroad, but immediately after the start of World War II he returned home, where

> he assumed the role of the defender of democracy, vis-à-vis the powerful nazi-oriented groups. . . making capital of his relations with the local interests of the Allied powers. To this effect, he drew up repeated statements and even offered his military services to Brazil when the latter declared war on the Axis.[13]

The last of the three men we have selected is Juan D. Perón. He took part as a captain in the 6 September coup. He had an opportunity to become closely associated with Uriburu's minister of war, Gen. Francisco Medina, in whose office he had some duties.[14] Later he became assistant to Gen. Manuel A. Rodríguez, Justo's minister of war; military attaché in Chile (1936-1938); traveled to Italy (1939-1941); and was on assignment in the province of Mendoza until March 1942. The rest is well-known. It is obvious that Mussolini's fascist experience and that of Franco in Spain colored many aspects of Perón's thought, but this should not lead to trying to explain his course *solely* on the basis of fascism. By training and ideology — acquired through such German professors as Lt. Gen. Alexis von Swardz — his sympathies were on the side of the Axis during World War II, although he also profited from Latin American examples such as Vargas's *Estado Nôvo* in Brazil. It is not our purpose here to deal with his work as constitutional president, but rather to refer to his rise to power, accomplished through other individuals who served him as a cover. The most obvious one was the person who took Ramírez's place, Gen. Edelmiro J. Farrell. Perón, by means of his control of the GOU military lodge and of his influence among the workers — especially among the new strata of industrial and rural workers — built up a political and personal apparatus that enabled him to face the powerful Democratic Union in the 24 February 1946 elections. One of the few authors who in 1945 tried to analyze the specific situation that carried Perón to power — outside the framework of traditional parties and also of those of the Left — was Silvio Frondizi, who wrote:

> Vis-à-vis the traditional forces stood the men of the military dictatorship. Since their activity was carried on outside political groups, without any binding allegiance to traditional concepts, attempting to reach power by illegal means and having much to gain and little to lose, they threw themselves into the struggle

with revolutionary methods. In this way they were in consonance with the historic moment through which the Republic was passing, perhaps without conscious orientation and only as a result of circumstances. . . .

We leave aside any consideration of the personal qualities of the leader, a study which merits doing, neverthless, because the negative qualities such as daring, ambition, lack of historical responsibility and so forth, play an important role in the advance of Peronism and in its effects on Argentine society. Those qualities to a great extent explain the transformation of an essentially military movement that was desperately seeking political support, into a movement of a popular character. *The result of this demagogic transformation is really astounding, nothing less than a perfect demonstration that in our country the social question is in full development.*[15]

What we have transcribed seems to us sufficiently clear to need no further comment. We will only add that most of the works dealing with Peronism (the exhaustive study the subject merits is still lacking) choose to stress Perón's demagoguery rather than the social conditions that contributed to the problem.

The Army from 1930 to 1943: rebellions, debates, professionalism

One has only to read the names of the leaders who constituted the revolutionary general staff organized by General Uriburu, with the collaboration of General Justo, during the 1930 revolutionary movement, transcribed by General Sarobe in his *Memoirs,* to notice that the same names keep appearing in 1930, 1943, and 1955; they occupy positions that are sometimes the same, sometimes antagonistic and opposed — but always the same names.[16]

It is not only in the "revolutionary general staff" that names are found that will recur in connection with other coups and uprisings. A not very exhaustive look at the list of personnel of the Military College who on 6 September 1930 started the march toward the Federal Capital gives the following results: the director was Col. Francisco Reynolds and with him there were Lt. Cols. Domingo Martínez and Manuel N. Savio (later the promoter of our metallurgical industry and often mentioned, together with Gen. Alonso Baldrich and Enrique Mosconi, as a true "democrat"); also Lt. Juan I. San Martín (Peronist governor of the province of Córdoba and secretary of the Air Force in the national cabinet after

1946), and Lt. Roberto T. Dalton, who took part in the "Liberating Revolution" of 1955.

In the first company we find Lt. Oscar M. Ladvocat and Cadets Cecilio Labayrú, Diego Mason, Ernesto Cordes, Rosendo Fraga, Juan Carlos Cordini, A. Pons Bedoya, and Enrique Rauch. In the second company, Lts. Juan José Uranga Imaz and Francisco A. Imaz, 1st Cpls. Desiderio Fernández Suárez, Juan B. Picca and Emilio Bolón Varela, and Cadets Federico Gentiluomo, Edgar Landa, Manuel Olascoaga, Carlos Muzio, Ricardo Platter, and Carlos A. Peralta. In the third company, 1st Cpl. Ernesto D'Onofrio, Cpl. Octavio Zenarruza, and Cadets José Spirito, Carlos Túrolo, Armando Martijena, Horacio Rivara, Julio Señorans, and Enrique Mafei. In the cavalry squadron, Cadets Juan Fabri, Federico Toranzo Montero, Paulino Ardanaz, Ricardo Ibazetta, Ventura Morón, Manuel Reimundes, and Víctor Arribau. In the artillery battery, Lt. Arturo Ossorio Arana and Cadets Víctor Hosking, Bernardino Labayrú, Florencio Yornet, and Luis Leguizamón. In the engineers company, 1st Lts. Julio A. Lagos and Juan José Valle, and Cadets Emilio Bonnecarrère, Julio Merediz, and Ernesto Taquini.[17]

It is obvious that 6 September was going to teach various military generations the shortest route to the Executive Mansion; many of the names that appear on the front pages of newspapers in the sixties as occupying high positions started their military careers with a march against the constitutional government of Hipólito Yrigoyen. The consequences of such an attitude have not been sufficiently evaluated when recent historical events have been analyzed.

Counting on the acquiescence of the navy and the collaboration of the military air force personnel to distribute manifestos and proclamations ("In the Palomar Air Base Captains Rosales and Castex Lainfor as well as First Lieutenant Sustaita acted as leaders of the movement")[18] the small forces that General Uriburu brought together achieved their objective of overthrowing the old president, taking advantage of the hopeless internal contradictions of the Radicals, the tolerance or complicity of some and the indecision of others.

In a message to "the people of the Republic," Uriburu had already foreshadowed the thesis of the armed forces' *manifest destiny* as supraconstitutional custodians of governments established by elections.

In response to the clamor of the people and with the patriotic support of the army and the navy, we have assumed the government of the nation. [As] exponents of order... trained in respect for the laws and institutions, we have witnessed with amazement the process of upheaval that the country has suffered during recent years. We have calmly waited in the hope of a saving reaction, but faced with the anguishing reality represented by the country on the brink of chaos and ruin, we assume before it the responsibility for avoiding a final collapse.[19]

In the end, Uriburu was unable to control the forces that had raised him to power. His inevitable political heir was General Justo, who alternated between his never-denied sympathy for Antipersonalist Radicalism — including even the Alvear brand — and the military pressure he hinted at so that the revolutionary government would call for elections. Some of the old-line Radicals have continued to claim that Justo had entered into negotiations with insurgent elements of that persuasion, whom he later abandoned, beguiled by the electoral possibilities that opened up for him, which, of course did not exclude fraud.[20]

Some subversive episodes occurred in opposition to Uriburu and also during the early years of Justo's presidential term, but they all failed. Let us follow Rodolfo Puiggrós's account of them:

Disregarding the unorganized activities of 6 and 8 September 1930, the most important Yrigoyenist movements attempting to recover power were the following: (1) the uprising of the night of 31 December 1930, by the noncommissioned officers of the Córdoba garrison, which spread to Rosario, Buenos Aires, San Luis, Mendoza, Tucumán, Salta, and Jujuy; (2) the uprising of sergeants, corporals, and enlisted men in February, 1931, under the command of General Toranzo; (3) the military and civilian uprising in the provinces of Corrientes and Chaco in July of the same year, led by Lt. Col. Gregorio Pomar; (4) the uprising of the Kennedy brothers in January 1932 at La Paz, Entre Ríos Province; (5) the civilian and military uprising led by Lt. Colonel Cattáneo on 21 December 1932, which covered much of the country; (6) the uprising in Concordia, Entre Ríos Province, in January 1933, which spread to Misiones and Corrientes Provinces with intervention of squads that came in from Brazil; (7) the Puerto Nuevo uprising soon thereafter; (8) the uprisings of December 1933 in Santa Fe, Corrientes, Buenos Aires, and other provinces.[21]

The failure of these attempts was not due solely to the disparity in the number of troops involved or to the government efforts to suppress them. Puiggrós himself gives another basic reason: *"No armed insurrection could triumph without political leadership or with the political leadership being opposed to it.*"[22]

The party leadership of Alvear and his associates never set up any revolutionary objectives for themselves nor even contemplated any uprisings. This has been adequately documented in the work of Atilio Cattáneo, *Plan 1932,* with reference to the movement he led, but the same may be said of that initiated by Bosch. Cattáneo transcribes a letter from Alvear to Justo, sent by the former from his confinement in Martín García Island because of the 1933 uprising:

> Neither can any member of the Radical party invoke the authorization of the party authorities to take part in the events that have occurred. The National Convention met to fix the guidelines for the party. If the preparation of a revolutionary movement had been intended to result from them, you may be sure that it would not be an isolated rash uprising, but rather a great national movement worthy of the Radical party and of the men who today lead it and who in such a case would know how to assume full responsibility. A few months ago the National Committee, in a manifesto against the electoral counterreform proposed by the government, had already foretold the possibility of isolated explosions of popular despair, produced by the economic crisis and the deprivation of democratic liberties. *If I have rendered any service to my country, it is by trying to discipline and guide Radicalism for the good of our country. Your government persists in placing obstacles in the way of this generous work, without understanding what it means to control a great popular force in these difficult times.*[23]

Cattáneo, referring to his own 1932 attempt, speaks of it as follows:

> Our movement was civilian-military. With the same enthusiasm, civic and military virtues were mingled, since all were anxious to overthrow President Agustín P. Justo, not only because of his spurious and antipopular political origin, but also because of his shameful and unavowable government methods such as fraud, impeachment, and other similar immoral acts that brought about the discredit and the dishonor of civic life and of the Argentine army.[24]

Some of the ideas that motivated — perhaps somewhat idealistically — the participants in this abortive attempt were set forth in the unusual manuscript found in the possession of the assassinated Maj. Regino P. Lascano.[25] But the end result was failure.

The bulk of the army responded to the leadership of Justo's minister of war, Gen. Manuel A. Rodríguez, who was preoccupied with technical qualifications, budget improvements, and the concept of "professionalism" which he attempted to infuse into the military ranks. A professionalism that — as will be seen — contributed in a decisive manner to maintaining the existing regime, with its arbitrariness and its defects, as the *non plus ultra* that must be respected. It is easy, once in control of the situation, to invoke "professionalism," and "fulfillment of specific duties" to justify or defend precisely the situation that has been created. Rodríguez, in his own way, also became a forerunner.

Congress, that is, the Senate, recorded a very long-drawn-out debate on the consequences of the so-called Law of Armaments (No. 11,266), passed during Alvear's term as president, and in the approval of which the then minister of war, General Justo, took an active part. Socialist Senator Mario Bravo and Minister of War Rodríguez were the principal participants in the main debate which was based on a draft resolution that Bravo and Palacios submitted in 1932 to the Senate. It read as follows:

(1) To name a special commission of five members to study and report on the administrative, financial, technical, and military conditions under which the law on the acquisition of armaments (Law No. 11, 266) has been carried out. (2) The commission is hereby authorized to subpoena persons, request depositions, arrange for expert testimony, review official documents, take depositions itself within the jurisdiction of the nation, request information and assistance from the civil and military authorities of the nation and examine the documents of the authorities and commissions that have intervened in carrying out Law 11,266 and its regulatory decrees. (3) If during the course of the mission entrusted to it, the commission shall need to use the public forces to subpoena witnesses or to attach private documents or papers, it shall request the necessary authorization from the presiding officer of the Chamber of Deputies. (4) The commission shall render its report on the result of its investigations before 30 September of the current year. (5) The president of the Senate shall make this resolution known to the executive branch and shall request from it the necessary cooperative measures to enable the commission to fulfill its objectives.[26]

Before this draft resolution came up for debate, the conflict between Bravo and Rodríguez had been stated in the following terms during consideration of the 1932 national budget:

The minister of War (Rodríguez); . . . Now I simply wish to leave on record a single fact and that is that the army has always respected the Argentine Constitution and has always been at the disposal of the country, and when on 6 September it started its march toward the Executive Mansion, it was serving the Constitution and its people. (Applause).

Mr. Bravo: It is my wish that this applause may linger in the ears of the minister of war, but the minister has written for the Senate Record two lines of which he will repent some day. *The day when the generals become the arbiters of the enforcement of the Constitution of the country, we shall be living in perpetual subversion.* I deny that the army has the right to say when the Constitution is being enforced and when it is not, because that is for the people to decide, and if there are going to be revolutions here, the sacred revolutions, the only ones, will be those that arise from the bosom of the multitudes! Let the army be a collaborator, let the army submit to a revolution in which the people is the insurgent mass — very good — applause for the army; *but the army as arbiter of legality, arbiter of constitutionality, arbiter of the government, arbiter of the sanctioning of laws, no!* ... [27]

During the same debate on the budget, Senator de la Torre advocated economies in the item for military expenditures, pointing out what in his judgment were excessive outlays (for example, 20 million pesos for the Military College). In his reply, Minister Rodríguez clarified his concept of military "professionalism":

I say to the Senator: unhappy the country where the military can express their political ideas; there the discipline of the army will be at an end and the disappearance of the same will create the greatest danger to threaten liberty: armed men, without an ideal of sacrifice, without an ideal of abnegation, with party ideals: chaos.[28]

Palacios recalled that:

Formerly, we have had a real gang pushing armaments and at present are suffering the consequences. A request was placed for a credit in the amount of one thousand million, to acquire naval and land armaments, buy new units for the navy, construct strategic railroads, and carry out fantastic military constructions, to some of which Senator de la Torre has referred.[29]

Bravo recalled that when the Socialist draft resolution came up for debate:

In this Senate there was only one voice raised against the armament law and a single vote against the armament law, and that voice and that vote belonged to the senator speaking, who at that time represented the Socialist party in this Chamber. The gist of the questions that I then raised was as follows: I wanted to know whether the international relations of the country required such grave measures as those requested by the executive branch. The opinion of the minister was negative; no minister asserted that the international relations of the country were endangered. The other question raised was whether the large amounts requested were motivated by the objective of renewing the old matériel of the army, because, in my judgment, they were excessive. Almost ten years after the passing of the law, we can say with a certain pride that, for example, the artillery matériel purchased in the year 1898 by General Ricchieri and in 1909 by General Duclós is still in use.[30]

Law 11,266 was approved on 30 October 1923, while Marcelo T. de Alvear was president of the nation and Gen. Agustín P. Justo was his minister of war. Col. Manuel A. Rodríguez was secretary to the minister (1923-25, 1928). In 1932, Justo was president of the nation and he found defenders in the Chamber of Deputies of Manuel Fresco's caliber:

At the bottom of this affair there is an intent that it is advisable to uncover. Subtly and skillfully, a malicious campaign is being waged against the Argentine army. During the discussion of the budget we have already witnessed the attempt to make this democratic institution appear like an octopus, like a vulture that absorbs the vital energies of the national economy. We have seen it castigated, an attempt has been made to manhandle it. *In the Senate of the nation an investigation has been started during the course of which an attempt will undoubtedly be made to touch the person of the present president of the nation.*[31]

After defending his draft resolution, Senator Bravo requested that the activities of the Permanent Technical Commission, the Commission for Acquisitions Abroad (the latter presided over by Gens. José L. Maglione, José Belloni, and Manuel J. Costa, in that order) and a special "advance" commission that had left for Europe in December 1923 be thoroughly investigated. The possible existence of irregularities in the negotiation of the contracts with firms furnishing the matériel (Schneider for the artillery matériel) was stressed, as were cases of favoritism that did not accord with law.[32] Rodríguez was invited to the Senate — despite the opposition of Bravo, who maintained that an investigation and not an interpellation was being conducted — and there he defended the interests of the executive branch. He said:

> . . . under these circumstances, I deplore that the senator for the federal capital, who knows that this whole matter that he has brought before the Senate is already being considered by the courts, has not kept in mind that it would have been preferable, in my judgment, not to cast shadows on the reputation of many worthy persons, and that it *would have been preferable also, Mr. President, to wait until. . . the water had settled a little . . . before going to stir it up and make it appear as a special condition involving the whole group.*[33]

The result of the investigation was not taken up until the end of 1934 and the commission issued two reports. The majority one, signed by Senators Mariano P. Ceballos, Carlos A. Bruchmann, and Matías G. Sánchez Sorondo, refers to the fact that all the events examined had already "been the subject of the corresponding proceedings of an administrative or military character," mentions the finding of some irregularities that had actually taken place, and ends with a paragraph obviously intended to please military authorities:

> . . . the conduct of the military commissions that have intervened in the preparation of the purchase plan and its execution abroad has been responsive to the high reputation that the Argentine officer corps has deservedly won for the competence, honorability, and dedication of its members: thus, the majority of the commission advises you to take no further action.[34]

The minority report (signed by Bravo and Eduardo Laurencena) reads as follows:

> Your Special Investigative Commission on Compliance with Law No. 11,266, in the minority, in accordance with your resolution dated May 1932, reports that in view of the data collected to the effect that in the execution of the armament law, due to deficiencies in organization and control and because of the intervention of purchase agents, errors and irregularities have been committed of an administrative, financial, technical and

military nature, to the detriment of the State, of the gravity and
the extent of which you will be informed by the reporter of this
minority commission.[35]

The debate that followed lasted eighteen days, a fact that led
José Nicolás Matienzo to comment that the National Constitution
had been approved after only ten days of debate! The sessions on
the armament law were known as "the battle of the shuttle-
cocks"[36] because of the minutiae of the arguments and the lack
of positive proposals for administrative improvement. Laurencena
was the one who spoke most sensibly after the detailed controversy between Bravo and Rodríguez:

> From the testimony that the Senate has heard up to now, it
> appears that within the . . . commission there is agreement in
> admitting that in the execution of the armament law errors, fail-
> ures, or deficiencies and irregularities have occurred. The dis-
> agreements arise from the number, the extent, and the impor-
> tance or transcendence assigned to those errors, deficiencies or
> irregularities, according to the personal judgment of each one of
> the members of the commission.[37]

The majority of the Senate preferred praise of the army — a sort
of tacit recognition of the most solid defender of Justo's political
regime — rather than critical analysis of the facts. The majority
report received seventeen votes; the minority, four (Correa, Laurencena, Palacios, and Bravo). General Rodríguez had achieved a
new victory.

Rodríguez also referred to the "apoliticism" of the army. Jorge
Abelardo Ramos interprets it as follows:

> The scandalized country was presided over by a general; the
> "apoliticism" that General Rodríguez preached to the army
> consisted of a symbolic defense of the external frontiers that no
> one was attacking. Simultaneously, the oligarchy, through Presi-
> dent Justo, was disposing of domestic sovereignty, the only true
> sovereignty of a semi-colonial country, which does not require
> occupation forces on the part of imperialism, but only facilities
> to exercise its economic and political influence. National de-
> fense, in accordance with this extraordinary doctrine, would
> consist of preparing the army to guard the frontiers and lower-
> ing its presence within its own territory from the industrial and
> social point of view. It is enough to state the problem in these
> terms to understand that only a vigorous industrial economy,
> and not a pastoral agricultural country, can constitute for the
> army the substructure of an authentic national defense.[38]

A personal witness informs us that this work (which can hardly be considered to be in the national interest) was shared by Justo and Rodríguez in the following manner:

General Rogríguez was undoubtedly the greatest collaborator that General Justo had before and during his administration. I have lived through the most difficult moments of their executive activity with both of them, and I can assure you that 50 percent of the work of Rodríguez in the army was due to the honesty, equanimity, and firmness with which he put into practice the directives issued by Justo, and the other 50 percent, to the same honesty, equanimity, and firmness with which Justo supported Rodríguez's initiatives.[39]

With this as a background, the meaning of some statements made by General Rodríguez before the Chamber of Deputies becomes clear:

Militarism does not always arise from the army; militarism is usually a disease, an illness created by political parties when they use the army for what they should not, either to make propaganda in the manner in which some deputies have been doing it or because the political parties use the army for purposes which draw it away from its mission.[40]

Jauretche gives a summary of this theme in his pamphlet, *Ejército y política (La patria grande y la patria chica):*

The military conspiracy that broke out when Yrigoyen returned for his second term was prepared during the period of Alvear's presidency under the direction of General Justo. With the same shrewdness that was to be employed later on, the armed forces were turned aside from their national objectives; in order to do it, the movement was covered with a nationalistic mask that was soon thrown off and replaced during General Justo's government with a political, economic, and social system that was "the legal expression of colonialism," intended to guarantee the maintenance of the economic and social fraud thus established. The armed forces little by little are becoming conscious of the national aberration of which they have been the object, *and they concentrate their activity on technical and industrial development of the sectors of the economy related to national defense.*[41]

However, it was Scalabrini Ortiz who best and most graphically defined the functions of the army during the thirties. In 1935, he wrote that:

The present minister of war [General Rodríguez] has stated in
the Chamber of Deputies that the army is outside politics, thus
displaying a lack of understanding of Argentine reality and the
scarcity of the stuff of which rulers of countries are made. The
minister did not see the political function that the army through
mere inertia performs, even though he is part of a government that
is protected precisely by that inertia. If it could not count on the
protection of the army, what could this government count on,
whose ministers go before the Congress to defend with fervent
tenacity the interests of England and not those of Argentina? If
it did not have the support of the army, whose support would
this government have that is carrying the country to an unknown degree of destitution only comparable with the destitution experienced by some Asian countries such as India? If it
did not have the support of the army, whose support would this
government have that is repudiated by all Argentines who think
like free men and do not agree to fall into servitude to a foreign
nation such as England without even having been defeated on
the field of battle? To separate the army from the people is a
way of contributing to its intellectual mechanization. In this
way a certain automatism might be attained very similar to that
of the occupation armies that some European countries station
in their colonies. The separation of the army and the people is
the ideal of politicians who are not supported by the people,
but by foreign interests.[42]

The position of the army as the supporter of the political regime did not change substantially during the presidency of Ortiz,
who did not let any opportunity to praise the armed forces go to
waste:

I have no objection to stating that the same army, when it left
its barracks on 6 September 1930 to support the action of the
civilians who ran to the streets ready to bring to an end an absolute misrule, has written one of the most austerely beautiful
pages of its history.[43]

Needless to say, the most influential element of this period,
World War II and Argentina's position vis-à-vis this conflict, would
reach a crisis stage under the Castillo administration. Luna has
given his version of events as follows:

In reality, Castillo felt secure, because he had the support of the
army. In September 1941 some problems had developed in air
force bases in the interior. But Castillo and the army had to

come to an understanding. In October a group of colonels interviewed the vice president, making the support of the army conditional to a policy that would be characterized by a strict maintenance of neutrality, no granting of bases to the Allies and the dissolving of Congress and of the Municipal Council in the federal capital. Everything was ready for the overthrow of the government if these conditions were not met. Castillo, after a period of reflection, gave assurances of compliance with all the items except that of dissolving Congress, which he considered dangerous. The conspirators accepted and a tacit pact was formalized. The old vice-president then had a free hand to act. A descendant of old Conservative stock, disdainful of democracy, stubborn and authoritarian, Castillo was an intuitive nationalist whose policy was based on two key items: to maintain neutrality and not to deliver the government to the Radicals.[44]

When Robustiano Patrón Costas, the spokesman for the faction in favor of breaking relations with the Axis, was about to be chosen by the Conservative convention as its presidential candidate, the army withdrew its confidence from President Castillo and the 4 June 1943 coup resulted. Some pro-Allied military men also took part in it, since they were disgusted with the predictable fraudulent procedures that would again be used in the coming elections. The Ramírez-Rawson struggle may be understood as, to a great extent, a show of force by both factions within the armed forces — the pro-Axis and the pro-Allied. Castillo had not foreseen this event:

He thought that perfecting fraud until it became an actual institution was sufficient to insure the continuity of his authority. He did not note that fraud is based on force and that the latter was in the hands of the army which had agreed to enter into the proposed game only in exchange for a predominant position in the life of the country. This situation having ceased or having been disregarded, the army lost interest in the stability of the government.[45]

The army from 1943 to 1946: lodges, industrialization

Throughout our political and military history, lodges have been a more or less permanent part of the Argentine scene. Without going back to the last century and the Lautaro Lodge, it will be enough to mention here the existence of what Juan V. Orona calls a "little known" one,[46] the General San Martín Lodge, which is of vital importance for understanding the events that preceded and

followed the 6 September 1930 coup. This lodge was formed toward the end of 1921 by the merging of two internal military
groups, the San Martín Lodge (with its "Bases") and the General
San Martín Center (with its "raison d'être"),[47] in order to oppose
the drawing of officers into politics and strengthen the feeling of
military duty. As Enrique Ruiz Guiñazú, Jr., has said: "in a word,
in order to banish politics from the army, politics began to be
played within it."[48]

One immediate objective of the Lodge was the control of the
Círculo Militar Board of Directors on the occasion of the elections in that year (1921). It succeeded. From that vantage point
the Lodge developed its plan for future action and, once Alvear
was elected, drew up three demands: (1) that after Alvear took
office, his first visit would be to the Círculo Militar to make
amends for the lack of consideration it had received when the two
notes it had sent to the minister of war denouncing the open intervention of military men in politics had not been answered; (2) that
he should at no time delegate his office to Vice-President Elpidio
González; (3) that he should not name General Dellepiane minister
of war. Alvear honored all three requests. His minister of war was
the then Col. Agustín P. Justo. Orona assures us that Justo "was
never a member of the Lodge," but that indeed "his best friends
and confidential collaborators were Lodge members prominent
in its activities," and . . . "consequently, . . . under the guise of
laws, decrees, resolutions, and regulations, many of the suggestions
and decisions of the Lodge became a fact in reality." The same
Orona explains the disappearance of the San Martín Lodge in
this manner: "The normalcy demanded by the army having been
reestablished during the presidency of Alvear, the Lodge no longer
had any reason for existing." Early in 1926, its activity ended
formally, but not that of the former members who were a prepon-
derant factor in the planning of the September military coup. Col.
Luis J. García, the first president of the group, at that time in
retirement, was one of them.

> For the former members of the Lodge — of course with the ex-
> ception of the traitors — the army was back in the same situa-
> tion that had brought them together in 1921. There was again
> talk of lack of discipline, of disorganization, of politics in the
> barracks, of officers being returned to active service with retro-
> active seniority — which in some cases meant collecting large
> sums — of "deals" and persecutions and even of the possible
> liquidation of the Purchasing Commission abroad.[49]

It must be added that many of those situations had arisen as a result of direct or indirect Lodge action. Gen. Luis Dellepiane, Yrigoyen's minister of war, was not able, despite his desire to do so, to root out the influence of the Lodge members. After 6 September — and the confused events of the eighth — the members of the disbanded Lodge took charge of persecuting or placing in subordinate positions those Yrigoyenist officers — or the ones suspected of being so — who were considered dangerous to the regime's stability, so that there was once again an era of "blacklists" like the one the San Martín Lodge had imposed during its existence. Cattáneo, after pointing out that the objective of the Lodge members was to protect themselves (". . . they had to be appointed to the best posts within the institution") and mentioning their influence in the filling of politico-professional posts such as that of minister of war and military attachés, goes on to say that:

> Another objective, which existed but was not made public, was the elimination from the military ranks of certain leaders and officers who were personal friends of Yrigoyen, and through him related to the civilian-military movement of the year 1905. In justification of this censurable action it was said that its purpose was to "avoid political influence within the army." Some of the military men who were injured by that movement received compensation for their losses during Yrigoyen's administration. This was sharply criticized by the "Lodge members"; but they themselves obtained all manner of benefits through the 6th of September victory, not only by undeserved promotions, but even with funds that were requested from the National Bank for that purpose.[50]

From the General San Martín Lodge we go to the GOU, whom some authors say originated in 1942. Here it is advisable to digress in order to transcribe Rogelio García Lupo's pertinent comments on the subject of military lodges:

> Military lodges are possibly among the institutions most deeply rooted in Argentine life. However, they have never been studied independently of the political events to which they were always linked. The extreme examples of these partial interpretations are to be found in the efforts of liberal historians to present the Lautaro Lodge as a Masonic institution rather than a military one and the GOU as a nazi nucleus over and above its obvious professional organization. For this reason, nobody has been able to explain the presence within the Lautaro Lodge of officers who were not Masons (including San Martín himself, the philo-

sophical aspects of whose personality have not yet been definitely established) and within the GOU of leaders who did not conceal their aversion to National-Socialism.[51]

The GOU, with a board of seventeen officers theoretically equal among themselves, directed the preliminary work of the 4 June 1943 movement. After the takeover by the revolutionary government, it was observed that: " ... four colonels, Perón, Avalos, González, and Ramírez, who occupied the Secretariat of War, the Commandant's Office at the Campo de Mayo Military Base, the Executive Office of the President, and the Office of Chief of the Federal Police, respectively, had the most influence in their decisions."[52] However, the long process that was to lead Perón to become *the power behind Farrell's power* and to control a large part of the military personnel would still include incidents that would be dangerous for the ambitious and energetic colonel. One such was the 8-17 October 1945 episode, when the indecision of his rival Avalos destroyed the "strong man" image the latter had projected. The influence of Colonel Perón, who eventually occupied the Vice-Presidency of the nation, the Ministry of War, the Secretariat of Labor and Welfare, and the chairmanship of the Postwar Economic Council, has been recognized even by his most bitter political and personal enemies such as Reynaldo Pastor (especially since the "Liberating Revolution"):

> In 1943 and 1946 the dictator served as the executive nerve center for the designs of the underground forces that worked for the overthrow of the Republic. He was first involved in Ramírez's betrayal of President Castillo; then he followed Ramírez himself. The same technique was employed by him with those of his followers who did not want his totalitarian dictatorship and with the nation, whose traditions and sentiments are genuinely democratic.[53]

Raúl Damonte Taborda was another one of those who attempted to explain everything by pointing up Perón's nazism (see his *Ayer fue San Perón*) and that of the Argentine military. He seems to have forgotten some of the statements he had made in the Chamber of Deputies in 1941 to the effect that he had "the pleasure and the honor of declaring . . . that, except for some misguided leaders being prosecuted or already arrested, the Argentine army offers a solid bulwark for the republican and democratic institutions of our country."[54]

However, some voices were raised against the GOU from the ranks of the military. One of these was that of Col. Roque Lanús, ideologically and also through family connections in sympathy with Conservative ideas, his brother Adolfo Lanús having been a federal deputy for the *Concordancia*. In response to a request for support for the GOU made by Colonel Perón himself (then still head of the Secretariat of the Ministry of War), Lanús stated that he had answered as follows:

> That it seems to me a mistake to request the support of those who by force of discipline were obligated to obey and that since that was the state of my mind, I would not join this lodge, as I had never joined any other. . . . It is precisely my feelings of camaraderie, my esprit de corps, the respect that I have for hierarchy and discipline that have always prevented my taking part in cliques and lodges, especially since, as in the case of the GOU, their own by-laws organize accusations and spying within the army.[55]

By a decree of 18 April 1945, signed by Farrell and Perón, it was provided that Colonel Lanús be retired from active service, "without request on his part, not for any shameful cause or postponement in promotion, or physical incapacity or any record of arraignment proceedings or even verbal questioning for alleged crimes, without the intervention of proper judges, boards, courts, or councils."[56] The process from 1943 to 1946 in connection with the flux of politico-military events has been summarized by S. E. Finer in these words:

> The 1943 coup of General Ramírez ushered in a military oligarchy which lasted some one-and-a-half years. And here again is seen the push-pull towards and away from open supplantment of the civilian régime. On this occasion, unlike 1930, the army plotters — the G. O. U. — had no intention whatever of holding new elections. They unquestionably envisaged some sort of military oligarchy, though their precise plans are still obscure, and indeed it is very likely that they were both disunited and vague on anything but short-term objectives. What is certain, however, is that they had not long been in power before widespread opposition developed, and thrust them into increasing repression. Their opponents — the press, the universities, the trade unions — were struck down in turn; but the more repressive the régime the more unpopular it became. In June 1945, when the industrialists, merchants and cattle breeders signed an open manifesto against Vice-President Juan Perón, the dismayed military began to give way. Elections were promised in July and in August the state of siege was lifted. There now took place a

massive all-party demonstration in the capital, the "March of
the Constitution and Liberty." Clearly elections boded ill for
the army. The fear of political destruction now prompted the
G. O. U. to arrest Perón, in the belief that he was their Jonah.
Their effort failed. For one thing, they had no clear alternative
to Perón. For another the *descamisados* counter-demonstrated
in favour of Perón. From that point the military took the only
possible way out — the one trodden by General Uriburu. They
decided that there must be elections, and that their candidate,
Perón, must win. He did; and for the moment the political future of the armed forces was secured.[57]

It is evident that Finer shares the view of many Argentine
scholars in the field of traditional parties, though he does not succeed in explaining — and neither do they — the relations between
Perón, the army (not the GOU any longer, since it was too limited
at this juncture) and the new labor unions being formed, which
afforded a base for his maneuvers (the Socialist and Communist
unions indeed were opposed to the colonel, but they made up
only a minority of the organized workers). Not to see this relationship is not to see to the bottom of the problem. Nor can it be said
that the elections of 24 February 1946 which the forces supporting Perón won by a narrow margin, were fraudulent. As long as the
Democratic Union was sure of victory, they brought no charges of
fraud. Sometimes defeat is a bad counsellor.

García Lupo has described the modus operandi of the GOU:

The development of the GOU confirms the thesis that retired
officers are decidedly marginal to any coup with chances of success. The conspiracies led by the untiring Gen. Benjamín Menéndez in 1940 and 1941 did not crystallize. Major Filippi, a
military man of considerable intellectual attainments who took
part in the creation of the GOU, commented at the time that
"it would seem that we will not be able to carry out our revolution until we succeed in getting the Ministry of War. Perhaps the
regimental commanders are afraid to obey those who do not
command them legally." The GOU men then hastened to follow
the traditional tactics: first they placed General Ramírez in the
Ministry of War (Ramírez was Filippi's father-in-law), then they
completed the placing of their men in the best commands, and,
finally, they staged a coup against Castillo's civilian government,
repeating the stratagems that the Logia San Martín men had
used fifteen years earlier. This time, also, they did not waste
one of their prominent members and the provisional stage was

covered by Ramírez and Farrell, who assured the constitutional advent of Perón two years later, without any military difficulties.[58]

In contrast to those who simply use a "nazi" label and pass on, García Lupo makes this basic assessment of the GOU:

> Aside from some foolish things they did, often on the advice of certain civilians, the men of the GOU [considered] that Argentina could not be a developed country without heavy industry and that there could be no heavy industry without a foreign market.[59]

This explanation, not merely repeating geopolitical concepts of German derivation, is what leads to better comprehending the problem of South American politico-economic leadership, for which Brazil and Argentina were contending at that time. The concepts of neutrality — in some cases the result of a tendency toward nazi-fascist excesses, but in others genuinely autonomous — implied that the military sectors backing this stand had a certain concern for the industrialization that the country was facing. Some of the motives impelling the young officers to practice neutralism domestically and, to a large extent, support the Axis abroad have been listed by Ramos:

> The tradition of the nation, very strong within the army, imposed upon the latter an attitude of noninvolvement in conflicts not having a bearing on Argentine security. The technical prestige of the German army, some of whose instructors had contributed to the professional training of the Argentine military cadres, also influenced this stand. It must be added that for the last ten years young military men had been faced with the gloomy spectable of the country's gradual colonization, attributable as much to the oligarchy as to British imperialism. This was why the army tended to sympathize, as did many nationalists, with the opponent of our age-old exploiter.[60]

Several proindustrialization nuclei were formed within the army. Gen. Manuel Savio, whom we have already met marching with the 6 September 1930 military column, was one of the most representative spokesmen for these groups. Some of the measures taken by the government that resulted from the 1943 coup also helped the process of industrialization, whatever may have been the concrete ideologies of those who signed the various decrees for the creation of the Industrial Credit Bank, the expropriation of the Natural Gas Company, the increase in military industries, the study conducted for the reevaluation of tariffs, the reactivation of the Trans-Andean Railroad, the expropriation of some public service companies in the interior (owned by American capital), and others. After this period, Savio drafted and had Congress approve "Law 12,709 creating the General Directorate of Military Manufacturing and Law 12,987 (known as the Savio Act), which provided the basis for Argentina's steel industry. Savio later was president of the Joint Argentine Steel Company, and he drew up the over-all plan for the establishment of our heavy industry."[61] The years 1943-45 also witnessed the taking over of political and economic functions by the military. Finer writes in this connection that:

> The Rawson-Ramírez-Farrell régime in Argentina, 1943-5, is a similar example of direct rule by the military. With one exception (the Finance Minister) everyone in General Ramírez's cabinet was a military man. In all the Provinces, the civilian administrators were removed and replaced by military men also, and most of the mayors of the cities were replaced by young colonels.[62]

The trend toward military intervention in spheres apparently outside their province — in economics, for example — was to be irreversible and constitutes one of the typical features of our recent history that have been accentuated since 1955. It should also be pointed out that the traditional political parties suffered a corresponding loss of prestige as administrators of national affairs. It is likely that many facts will not be understood if the above factors are not correlated.

The navy: a brief analysis

The role played by the naval forces in the 6 September 1930 movement has been recognized officially by General Order No. 107 (13 September 1930) of the Ministry of the Navy. The text of this important document reads as follows:

> Some days having elapsed since the one on which the morale of the Argentine people, inspired by a saving reaction, overcame its dejection, and the details of some episodes that occurred during that day having become known, the minister of the navy in the provisional government makes known to the personnel that the navy has faithfully fulfilled the requirements of the movement that has taken place. It was necessary from the beginning to indicate precisely the role corresponding to each of the three

groups that were taking part: the people, the army, and the navy. In this way, the apparently passive but very important role of remaining mustered on its ships and ready for the first call fell to the navy. It constituted a moral force of high value and a great material reserve that supported the popular movement by its presence and attitude, keeping itself united and at its post because this fitted in with the plans drawn up and because the General Leader of the movement so disposed. The impatience of some officers who wanted to disembark their personnel in order to take a more active part with them on the side of the people on that great day was very natural; but that would have drawn us away from our mission, and we would have violated express orders, at a time when more than ever we had to follow them because of the delicate situation. This cooperation, which obliged each one to control the strong natural impulse to take an active part in actions whose development was foreseen, has made evident collective qualities of great value which have allowed events to take their course without altering the calm discipline that characterizes seamen and has made it possible to appreciate the discretion with which in certain cases incidents have been avoided that might have had disagreeable consequences. The nation having returned to its normal equilibrium, the navy must take up its habitual activities again. The shock that the institution has experienced has led to a confirmation of previous beliefs relative to the need to work very seriously for the good of the navy. This will first of all require that each man belonging to it shall exhibit the highest degree of self-denial of which he is capable, so that the navy may tread the path of morality and decorum in order to have all efforts contribute to what is the most pressing objective at this moment, the solid improvement of all the services and of all their component parts, within the laws and regulations in effect.[63]

This General Order carried the signature of Uriburu's navy minister, Rear Adm. Abel Renard and Navy Cap. Eleazar Videla, chief of the Secretariat of the Ministry. At one time. Renard was considered the head of what was known as the "nationalist" group within the navy,[64] and Videla a few years later became minister of the navy in the cabinet of General Justo. Some authors have mentioned a document signed by the navy men on 5 September 1930 in which the position of that service was defined. The text read as follows:

(1) That they are not disposed to continue to support the government of Hipólito Yrigoyen. (2) That they request his im-

mediate resignation and that of his cabinet. (3) That they will not use the arms of the nation against the people, nor against their army comrades. (4) That with those same arms they will guard against any attempt at a civilian or military dictatorship. (5) That they will defend the faithful and strict fulfillment of the National Constitution, after the resignation of the present president and cabinet. (6) That they will not allow the movement of any ship out of Puerto Nuevo until such time as a new government is constituted and constitutional order reestablished throughout the country.[65]

García Lupo has summarized the role played by the navy within the country, especially in the political sphere:

The navy had been associated for a century with British diplomacy in the River Plate region. *A combination of close class spirit, romantic admiration for British naval greatness, and economic alliance with the Anglophile ruling oligarchy, placed the navy in the role of watching the development of the political crises of the country without taking part in them. . . .* The navy led a sheltered existence for a century and when it made known some corporative opinions, its point of view was always a minority one and was immediately repudiated by the majority of the country. In the 1941-43 period, the navy was belligerent, against the neutrality of the army and public opinion. On the surface, the navy invoked the need to support actively the cause of democracy; back of this lay the hope that the entrance of Argentina into the conflict would oblige the government to invest some millions in the acquisition of warships, even if it were only to use them as escorts for Argentine merchant vessels that carried on the exchange between this continent and Europe. In 1943, the navy remained completely marginal to the nationalist military outburst and within its cadres there smoldered the discontent that exploded when an admiral [Vernengo Lima] led the coup d'état against Perón, in October 1945. Perón never had the sympathy of the navy people, who at all times as a unit upheld conservative points of view with reference to government plans and, finally, also as a body, acted with decision to overthrow him.[66]

From the foregoing it may be deduced that the navy — a corporative body "where there are no internal disagreements, which periodically and in silence purges itself and lives cloistered"[67] — did not share in the complicated and varied history of the army during the thirties. Despite its "romantic admiration for British naval greatness," its effective contacts and close associations for over forty years have been with the United States. An American author acknowledges this to be common knowledge:

> The officers of the Argentine Navy, on the other hand, are reputed to be socially a cut above the Army officers and, beginning in the 1920s, they had as close ties with the United States Navy as did the Army officers with the German Army. In the early months of the military dictatorship set up in 1943 their influence was illustrated by the effort made under the leadership of Admiral Segundo Storni, then Foreign Minister, to align Argentina with the United States and its allies against the Axis; but circumstances forced Storni to couch his overtures in terms unacceptable to the United States, and Secretary of State Cordell Hull rebuffed him so sharply that he was forced to resign, whereupon pro-Axis elements gained complete control of the government at Buenos Aires.[68]

After this date the animosity of the navy against the powerful GOU and the official government policy grew. Edwin Lieuwen refers to the process as follows:

> Resistance to Perón had always been strongest in the navy, whose democratic traditions conflicted with Perón's increasing authoritarianism. The naval officer corps, unlike that of the army, tended to come from the rural oligarchy and the wealthy urban families, and hence was hostile to any regime bent on upsetting the nation's basic institutions. So unsympathetic was the navy to the GOU and its program, even in the very beginning, that the government after the 1943 revolution could find no high-ranking naval officer willing to accept the post of navy minister until March of 1944. As early as February of 1944 the navy launched a conspiracy to oust the Farrell-Perón regime. In August and September of 1945, high-ranking navy men were demanding and petitioning that Perón not be allowed to assume the presidency and that the "sovereignty of the people" be restored. And in October of that year the bulk of the navy joined a disgruntled army group that nearly succeeded in ousting Perón. Suppressed but not extinguished, the navy's resentment continued to smoulder as the regime lavished funds on the ground forces while refusing to purchase new naval combat units.[69]

In the events of 8 to 17 October 1945, the efforts of the navy (almost in its entirety) and of the military sectors headed by Avalos to remove Perón permanently from public posts culminated in a resounding fiasco. Bartolomé Galíndez, who has recounted many of the backstage happenings, describes the details of the meetings at the home of Adm. Domecq García, Navy Captain Gregores's liaison role with the army officers, the discussions of the navy's top brass at the Naval Center, the commissions of navy· and military men that interviewed President Farrell (the navy held that the government must be entrusted to the Supreme Court and in this respect spoke for most of the traditional political parties also), and the perusal by the leaders of the two services of the names that figured in the utopian cabinet set up by Juan Alvarez.[70]

The navy, especially after 17 October 1945, continued to be rabidly anti-Peronist, although some of its members such as Alberto Teisaire enjoyed the confidence of the president of the nation. The October 1945 situation would recur some years later, under different circumstances, after the abortive 16 June 1955 coup. In September 1955, the navy, together with a sector of the army and relying upon the tolerance of the air force, was the service that gave impetus to the "Liberating Revolution," and since that time the political function of the army cannot be understood without correlating it with that of the navy.

Rear Adm. Aníbal O. Olivieri was among the few whose stand was opposed to the official navy line during the early Peronist period. Olivieri — who in 1951 became navy minister in the national cabinet — acknowledges that since 1945 the majority of the three thousand higher ranking officers "were undeniably disaffected toward the government and the president, though they made no political display and did not deviate from the strict fulfillment of their professional obligations." He goes on to say that "there was only a small group of recalcitrant officers opposed to the president and the government; above all because they always considered themselves a sort of social elite within the navy. Given to contacts with persons and circles of a high socioeconomic position, these men never embodied the deep social significance of the navy before the people and its institutional responsibility to the nation"[71]

Olivieri gives his own version of the attraction Perón exercised over the masses, which of course is not shared by the anti-Peronist officer corps in the army and navy promoted to posts of political leadership after the September 1955 overthrow of the regime:

Perón was the hope of those who had given up hope when faced with the ineffectiveness of the politicians that had preceded him. If there had been solid political parties, if the politicians had not fallen into disrepute because of their own inability to give politics the meaning and the effectiveness that it has in the life of civilized countries, then it would have been impossible for someone unknown not only throughout the country but particularly among the working masses, to defeat the politicians irretrievably in the clean elections that carried him to the Presidency of the Republic.[72]

Though it was not to become evident until 1955, during the period from 1930 to 1946 the Argentine navy gradually worked out its position as a service which was "profoundly influenced by liberal ideiology."[73] This liberalism, transformed into *"gorilismo,"* was to be concretely expressed in the revolts of September 1962, and April 1963 that the navy inspired or participated in.

Army and politics: social composition, ideology

Once more we resort to Samuel Finer for a summary:

The class interest of the junior officers is of importance also in Latin American republics like Argentina and Brazil which are experiencing the growth of a middle class. Before the first world war the officers came mostly from the rural oligarchies, and when they intervened they did so in support of their economic and political position. Nowadays officers are drawn increasingly from the families of industrialists, civil servants and professional people. This partly explains the increased radicalism of junior-officer revolts in such countries. The Argentine army in 1943, for instance (the year of the first coup), was not connected with "the Oligarchy": "The army officers, generally speaking, had no place in society and did not come from the governing class of *estancieros,* successful professional men and big merchants." [Sir David Kelly, *The Ruling Few* (London, 1952)]. The naval officers did, and throughout the period of Perón's rule never gave loyal support to the régime, and in 1955 played the decisive role in his overthrow.[74]

García Lupo, although referring to a period later than that covered in this work, has with great insight pointed out that:

Nine of every ten officers of the armed forces come from the small bourgeoisie. In a country where it is not possible to speak of military castes and where a military man whose father or grandfather was one, too, is unusual, it is not an exaggeration to say that in 90 percent of the cases the reason for entering the military institutions was the desire for upward social mobility and to assure themselves of a certain standing in life. In the Argentine army, therefore, there are no national counterparts of the Prussian *Junkers* who became military men to defend their lands. For every Federico de Alzaga, for example, there are a hundred officers who are sons or grandsons of immigrants, with medium economic resources and a desire to achieve social consideration.[75]

This explains the fact that, starting in 1943, new names began to be noticed in the political arena and (the paradox is not as great as it may seem at first sight) that they came from the army:

. . . two or three dozen officers came to the surface with delightfully anonymous surnames such as Ramírez, Farrell, Perón, Mason, Pertiné, González, and Zavalla; the provincial middle class, the persevering officers who came from the military orphans' homes, the sons of devoted sergeants who had got their offspring into the Military College suddenly blossomed forth and seized power.[76]

Comparing the social background of General Uriburu and that of Colonel Perón, for example, useful conclusions may be drawn as to the situation existing in the army at the officer level in two consecutive but different periods: 1930 and 1943. Uriburu, first a conservative, and then a corporative, offshoot of the provincial patricians, was used by the oligarchy that, through Justo, recovered complete control of the state and the economy. Perón came from the middle class and was born in the province of Buenos Aires, but had no connections with the landowners.

[He]. . . alone among the 1943 revolutionary leaders, had been fully aware of the shift in the balance of economic power from the rural landowners to the urban industrialists and to labor. He was skillful enough to utilize the political potential of these latter groups. It was labor that had rescued him from a military purge in October of 1945, and once back in power he deliberately built up and used the trade-unions as a counterpoise to the armed forces, to deprive the latter of the role of sole arbiter of the political process.[77]

Objectively, the army between 1930 and 1943 served the specific interests of the oligarchy as a praetorian guard and as the sole effective support of the successive governments of Uriburu, Justo,

Ortiz, and Castillo. From 4 June 1943 on, events involved certain military sectors more closely with the political process from positions of responsibility, and Perón was the one who orchestrated their activities.

Professional politicians took a long time (it is not even certain that all of them were aware of the problem) to understand that the armed forces had to be considered something other than a convenient frame of reference within which it was possible to set up the usual arrangements for the perpetration of fraud and the frustration of the popular will. Their similar contempt for the labor movement only decreased the chances of victory for the traditional parties in 1946. Perón and his group understood the enormous importance of having military and union backing, and they made the most of the occasion.

The army, under the iron rule of General Rodríguez, improved its technical capacity and undeniably became "professionalized." For example, expenditures for military installations increased between 1932 and 1937 as show by table 18.

TABLE 18: EXPENDITURES FOR MILITARY INSTALLATIONS 1932 THROUGH 1937.

Year	Value in Argentine pesos
1932	3,800,000
1933	5,100,000
1934	7,300,000
1935	9,500,000
1936	12,950,000
1937	26,990,000

Another instance of this change within the military may be found in the great army maneuvers of October 1936. They took place in the provinces of Córdoba and San Luis and brought together 51 senior officers, 1.072 officers, and 20,000 enlisted men, besides 10,166 head of cattle and 1,200 vehicles. They represented the most important military exercises ever carried out by our army up to that time. As early as toward the end of 1932 some warning voices were already being raised about the situation within the army. Senator Palacios spoke about it as follows:

The internal condition of the republic is dangerous. After the confusion of 6 September many grudges have arisen and at one time seemed to be like the flames of a fire. What is more serious, the army has been divided; we cannot conceal it, our army, whose true title should be that which the Great Captain, now forgotten, bestowed upon it when he made it worthy of the illustrious name of "Liberating Army," setting it an unequalled example of abnegation and civic virtue with his retirement into solitude, rather than using power to subjugate his fellow citizens. . . . The 6th of September our army left its quarters, overthrew the president of the republic, and dissolved Congress. *It was a victorious uprising. Had it been defeated, perhaps I would raise my voice in this chamber to ask for amnesty for General Agustín P. Justo, the Chief Executive of the nation.*[78]

However, we were no longer in the nineteenth century and could not talk about the "liberating armies" that Palacios nostalgically seems to evoke; nor does it seem to us proper to employ such a hypothesis to identify Tyrians and Trojans. This somewhat utopian Socialist position, which led to applying the schema of an already vanished liberalism to the historical circumstances of the Argentine nation in the 1930s, was in evidence every time the national budget was considered by the Chamber of Deputies. The Socialist opposition advocated decreasing the appropriations for the army, as well as those for the clergy — and that was all. In 1934 Deputy José Luis Pena might be considered the official spokesman for that line of thought when he declared that:

I want to point out two traditional forces that burden the Argentine budget and have for a long time been complicating the Argentine economy by the financial demands they make, which increasingly obstruct national expansion. I refer to the church and the army.[79]

It was not strange, then, that the seed of European nazi-fascism, which provided a position opposed to the traditional politics of a more or less liberal cast, would sprout within the armed forces nor that it should attempt to replace the same with an authoritarian order. However, neither is it possible to interpret everything in the light of foreign influences and conclude that the copy is exactly like the original. Within the army itself there was quite a broad spectrum of ideological nuances: the distance that separated a trio such as Gens. Nicolás Accame, Francisco Fassola Castaño ("monarchical" and "fascist," according to Deodoro Roca)[80] and Juan Bautista Molina, passing through Perón and the colonels and majors of the GOU, and finally ending with Col. Roque Lanús, who corresponded cordially with Robustiano Patrón Costas, was enormous.[81] Though it may not always be possible to pigeonhole them exactly, there were "Germanophile," "neutralist," and "pro-Allied" military men. We have not even mentioned the officers with a Radical party background, such as Gregorio Pomar or Atilio Cattáneo, who were removed from active service and had no influence after 1943, nor, indeed, for sometime before that date.

Faced with the entry of the military establishment into politics (not as supporters of a regime, but as the regime itself), the traditional and leftist parties did not carry out the necessary task of analysis and critical evaluation of facts. They substituted convenient adjectives for ideas.[82] Some of them renounced their strongly antimilitaristic past and were already beginning to throw themselves into the conspiratorial mania with some military sectors during the Perón government. For this reason, the participation of the military in politics increased and became more powerful during Perón's first presidential term, eventually culminating after the 16 September 1955 coup in an as yet incomplete cycle. Despite the isolated voices that demand a "professionalization" of the officers,[83] which is nothing but a way of returning to the era when General Rodríguez guarded General Justo's back, what matters is to stress the importance of the military element in Argentine political history and not to postpone the urgent task of evaluating the same. Anything else will represent comforting but fruitless wishful thinking.

8 Economic Groups

Economic groups and politics: the problem of imperialism

The question of the pressure exerted by economic groups throughout the 1930-1946 period is probably the one that has been treated in greatest detail by authors of different schools of thought. This subject is usually treated within the more general framework of economic history and economic policy,[1] something that is not within the scope of this work. However, in practice, limitations are never so clear-cut as in theory, and for this reason the following paragraphs may have a somewhat hybrid appearance. The purpose here is to present certain milestones in a process that has not yet ended and that it is essential to take into account in order to understand the Argentine nation. Let us begin by reproducing Puiggrós's recapitulation of the state of Argentina at the beginning of World War II:

> The liberal state grew increasingly remote from the people and from national interests. Ignoring political liberalism, the people sought, through the promotion of leaders embodying national and popular concerns, a channel for the transformation of the country in the direction of economic liberation and social justice. This was the state of affairs in 1937-1939, on the eve of World War II. The economy was highly concentrated in the hands of foreign monopolies and the functions of the liberal state were highly centralized in the hands of the direct agents of those monopolies, but the people concealed beneath its contempt for the government and its distrust of the parties a mature awareness that it could not continue to lie under the liberal dogma, which sacrificed the opportunity for its own national development on the altar erected by an oligarchy without a country to the cosmopolitan masters of imperialist cartels and trusts.[2]

Under the title "invasion of the monopolies," Puiggrós also offers a survey of the economic and financial interests that had overriding influence within the Argentine state. Let us look at only a few of the examples on the very extensive list. In the field of foreign trade, there were four firms that exported 85 percent of Argentine grain and flax in 1936-1939. They were Bunge & Born, Luis Dreyfus, La Plata Cereal, and Luis De Ridder (the last two were subsidiaries of the first). The arrangement among those firms was like the one existing among the meat-packing concerns, though the latter case is more familiar because of de la Torre's accusations in the Senate. The true *private monopoly* mentioned above controlled the grain futures market, and its influence was felt in the political field. "Its power was so great that it appointed one of its attorneys governor of El Chaco Territory and another one mayor of Rosario."[3]

The railroad situation is also well known. The railroads had long been subject to the requirements of British capital.[4]

When, a few years before their concessions were to end, their monopoly was endangered by automotive competition and by the new transportation system created by native initiative, they demanded that General Justo's neoliberal government renew that monopoly on the country's whole transport system and issue a ruling which plunged the workers into the harshest exploitation. In many regions, the bus lines that made Argentine workers and entrepreneurs proud of their organizing ability disappeared, destroyed by the railroad companies. Transportation in the city of Buenos Aires, which had been recovered to a great extent through the efforts of small national capitalists, was again handed over to British capitalism, that is, to the Anglo-Argentine Company connected with S.O.F.I.N.A.[5]

The railroads also controlled the majority of the port concessions of that period; the efforts of imperialists to prevent Argentina's having a commensurate merchant fleet are well known. It is not strange that through the years prominent attorneys for the British railroad enterprises became presidents of the country, among them Manuel Quintana, Victorino de la Plaza, and Roberto M. Ortiz. The Ministries of Public Works and Finance were usually occupied by men in some way connected with foreign capital. The government banks, the autonomous government corporations, and the legislative bodies all included within their ranks politicians who stood for antinational interests. Is there any need to mention the CADE (Compañía Argentina de Electricidad) deal again?

The oil industry is a good example of how the interimperialists agreed to parcel out markets during the thirties. The American-owned Standard Oil Company granted its rival and colleague, the British-owned Royal Dutch, the Argentine consumer market (Paraguay and Uruguay were considered adjuncts of Argentina), and as a counter grant, the Royal Dutch ceded to Standard Oil the Brazilian consumer market. "The agreement immediately brought on a price war for the purpose of disorganizing the domestic markets, destroying independent competitors, and causing government intervention."[6] The Y. P. F., now long past the Mosconi era, also collaborated in the destructive work of the monopolies.[7] Both imperialisms had drawn fire from Mosconi himself, according to Raúl Larra in his biography of the "Oil General."[8]

On a certain occasion, when the Argentine Congress was debating the oil bill, I was asked which of the two trusts, the Anglo-Dutch Royal Dutch or the American Standard Oil was to be preferred because of its technical ability, working methods, and procedures. I replied that naturally both resulted from the special characteristics that distinguish European culture from the American. The American group is less scientific, more daring and impetuous, has at its disposal unlimited financial resources and for that reason displays great vigor in its enterprises. Since it belongs to a people that has grown extraordinarily wealthy within a short period, it exhibits the impulsiveness, posturing, and lack of concern (not to say contempt) for the feelings and customs of others that are typical of *nouveaux riches*. It does not recognize any barriers to the achievement of its objectives and it is this that gives rise to the reactions provoked by their harsh procedures; these procedures include everything from individual actions to ignoring and violating the sovereignty of other peoples. The European group is more scientific and in this respect has a longer tradition that the American; the latter generally speaks only its own language and ignores the contributions made by technical and scientific bibliographies compiled elsewhere. Since the former is less wealthy, it is more prudent, more methodical in its plans and its work habits; it is more gentle, so much so that at times it is not noticed, but this does not mean that it does not skillfully achieve the objectives it pursues, with all possible respect for the milieu and the environment within which it operates. When all is said, the two groups are alike and I would compare the American group to a hemp rope and the European to a silk one; so that, in reply to the question I was asked, I stated that if the two ropes, the rough and the smooth one, are going to be used to hang us, it would seem more intelligent to give both up and, by concentrating our wills and our abilities on this special problem, which presents such unique characteristics, solve it by our own efforts, thereby doing great good, for which coming generations will be grateful.[9]

The disturbing influence of imperialism is to be noted on various levels. Let us take a passing look at only two. José Luis Torres, who must not be overlooked in dealing with this subject, had this to say about the painful sequence of events:

> The projects initiated by the Argentines, no matter how good they might be, never were of any use to them, since whenever the energy and enthusiasm of some assured the initial success of an enterprise, it was not long before it was stifled by the interests created jointly by the malice of the rulers and the interests of international merchants, and the Argentines were forced to give up possession of whatever they themselves had created, for the benefit of those who had been and still are lying in wait to pounce like panthers upon any profit or anything that might afford sure profit. This was what happened in the only too well-known case of the first Argentine railroad, the Western, which had been built by the initiative and labor of Argentines; it was soon delivered over to foreign enterprises who obtained government concessions to lay their lines along the routes of the Western. The first telephones in the country were also Argentine and in general so were all the discoverers of the country's natural wealth and the founders of the first industries, from the leather tanneries and corned beef plants that preceded the meat-packing plants of supercapitalism, to the power plants that preceded the CADE, but were without its abominable characteristics.[10]

When Alfredo L. Palacios was a national senator, he gave a detailed account of the terrible "economic and financial situation of the subsidized provinces," the permanently *poor provinces* of our politico-institutional scene, before that legislative body, which had not been moved by Lisandro de la Torre's plea nor by the murder of Enzo Bordabehere. The imperialists and the governments that were their accomplices (the guilt is shared jointly) tolerated and fomented the macrocephalic growth of the port city and its zone of influence, as may be seen by simply rereading the history of Argentina since last century. This is how the federal capital, the province of Buenos Aires, a small part of La Pampa, a large part of Córdoba and Santa Fe, Entre Ríos and the south of Corrientes, with only 20 percent of Argentine territory, in 1941 comprised 67 percent of its population, almost 90 percent of the area planted in grain, 63 percent of the cattle, 46 percent of the sheep, 77 percent of the hogs, 54 percent of the railroad tracks, 61 percent of the telephones, 79 percent of the automobiles in circulation, and almost 80 percent of the capital invested in refining and manufacturing industries. Palacios summed up the tragedy of the forgotten interior in a characteristic paragraph: "I represent the capital of the republic. I was born in this cosmopolitan and luxurious city, which is unaware of Argentine suffering, of the desolation of the abandoned fields, and the tragedy of the men on the silent and deserted uncultivated lands."[11]

The preponderance of British interests during the thirties has already been suggested in the first part of this work and here we need only mention it. At the height of this imperialism, American imperialism began to increase its penetration. The struggles and rivalries between them in the area of meats and meat-packing plants, in oil, and in transportation should be kept in mind. World War II marked the turning point in the predominant influences. However, the way had already been paved some years earlier by the legal arguments of certain authors.

> There is a tendency to regard the growth of American capitalism in Argentina as dangerous, to such an extent that this has senselessly been made an issue in election campaigns. Much could be said to dispel this vulgar uneasiness; but wishing to be brief I want to express my opinion (which is also that of all those who look at the problem dispassionately), in this fashion: Argentina, so long as it has available effective laws for the protection of national sovereignty and the integrity of its natural wealth, should not fear that the United States, or any other great power, will treat this country without the consideration always due to every people that, aside from native arrogance, also has available an institutional organization that makes it respected within the assembly of civilized peoples. My work as a former judge and in my present legal profession has led me frequently to search in the constitutional sources of the United States for the solution to many of our public law problems.[12]

Can it seem strange that the author of the above lines should also be concerned with justifying, both constitutionally and ethically, the 6 September 1930 movement? Isn't one attitude the natural result of the other?

The 6 September 1930 movement was far from being the barrack riot that has done so much damage to the good name of the South American continent, but neither did it have the characteristics of the various other revolutions that have taken place in this country. *A government has been ousted — though it may sound paradoxical — in order to save the constitutional order.* It has properly been said at this time that it was the joint action of the people become the army and of the army become the people. This is undoubtedly the exact formula. *The improvement of democracy required the removal of an obstacle, and that obstacle has disappeared.* [13]

Quite accurately, Félix Luna has pointed out that:

On the economic level, the war brought an extraordinary change to Argentina. The currency drain was slowed as imports were reduced, new industries were created to make up for the products that could not reach us, and large gold reserves were gradually accumulated in our favor in.the belligerent countries, principally Britain. A slow but constant internal migration gradually peopled the great cities of the coast to fill the openings offered by new industrial activities. Unemployment ceased and a rapid circulation of goods was experienced. On the other hand, it is well to point out that the war caused the decline of British interests in the country, as their exports were reduced to a minimum and Britain became a debtor nation. The United States took advantage of the two years of peace that were left to it in order to intensify its relations with Argentina. A loan was granted, a commercial treaty materialized, a Corporation for the Promotion of Trade with the United States was created, and the Argentine travelers who had been accustomed to journeying through Europe began to look northwards, among them not a few important people such as Miguel Angel Cárcano and Federico Pinedo — who until then had followed an obsequiously pro-British line. The economic groups that guided the new industry began to have a part in political developments and the new urban proletariat began to gain an awareness of its future. [14]

The world conflict also gave rise to reactions from industrial groups who since 1935 had been consolidating their position. Enrique Rivera has explained it in this manner:

The 1930 agricultural crisis unexpectedly came to decide an old struggle in favor of the industrialists. The decline in the price of agricultural products and the lack of a market for them forced the oligarchy in power (Justo-Pinedo) to take a series of measures that amounted to enormous protection for industry, without their so intending it. The devaluation of the peso, the increase in customs duties, the control of foreign exchange with different rates for the purchase and sale of other currency, and, later, the requirement of previous authorizations for imports, although all manipulated by the oligarchs, gave impetus to the industrialization of the country. Later, when due to the war all these measures could have been abandoned because of the abundance of funds abroad, the war itself brought about the elimination of foreign competition. Under these circumstances, while the industrialists were confident of the eventual victory of the Axis or of a war that would exhaust its direct enemies, they secretly began to subsidize totalitarian nationalist elements. They carried on an intensive propaganda campaign within the state bureaucracy and especially within the officer corps of the army, which, for professional and class reasons, is very susceptible to all nationalist and authoritarian propaganda.[15]

This was another way in which economic groups intervened in politics. At the same time, of course, the sectors that dealt in the meat market were also exerting pressure. No one denounced their maneuvers with the calm — and the consciousness of how useless the endeavor was in such unresponsive surroundings — of Lisandro de la Torre. His ideas etch with fire the reality of a period:

> . . .I am alone facing a formidable coalition of interests; I am alone facing capitalist enterprises that are among the most powerful in the world; I am alone facing a government whose mediocrity when confronted with the cattle problem astonishes and saddens; and thus, alone, I shall battle to defend an impoverished and defenseless Argentine industry, as ten years ago I fought in defense of the *mate* industry, which two powerful ministers had condemned to death, and as I fought two years ago for the modest tomato industry which was barely beginning to develop in the regions of the republic most worthy of protection, when the Minister of Foreign Relations was already. . . offering it up as a burnt offering to one of his international concepts. . . I will fulfill my objective if I carry out a full, intensive, truthful, and courageous analysis of the process of subjection of the Argentine government to the norms traced for it by irresistible private interests: a process of subjection that impoverishes the country as much as it humiliates it.

In summarizing the "meat question" he said:

Investigation has demonstrated that the export of Argentine meats produces a profit solely for the middlemen, and that the government of the nation, instead of making an effort to change such an unfortunate situation, is at the service of the middlemen, has allowed them to establish a monopoly, and overwhelms them with favors in all the aspects of their activities, while it persecutes without quarter any attempt to organize Argentine enterprises controlled by the producers.

At the closing of an unfinished investigation, he made a final statement:

The determination, carried to the point of absurdity, to deny the truth and to find biased explanations for the most serious errors, gradually compromised the administration's position and ended by turning into an inrreparable government debacle an investigation that did not have such broad objectives. *The damage suffered by the prestige of the government would not amount to anything if in future it were possible to avoid the continuation of the other damage, the one that strikes a death blow at the most important source of wealth in the nation, deliberately subjected to the interests of foreign capitalism.*[16]

Institutions, tactics, and techniques

Pursuing the subject of meats — a key one during the period we are considering — we shall quote here the ideas voiced by Palacios in the Argentine Senate during its 12 and 13 September 1935 session:

The majority of the committee has demonstrated that the meat and meat by-products export business is carried out under a monopolistic system contrary to the interests of the country since it arbitrarily and for its own benefit tampers with the purchase price in Argentina; that the meat-packing plants have perpetrated numerous abuses due to the lack of rational cattle and meat classification and that they have violated the obligations imposed by the Commercial Code in the matter of records, all of which motivates the bills submitted by the majority, with reference to the classification of meats, their net-weight purchase, and the accounting procedures of the meat-packing plants, which are on the agenda and for which I will vote, even though I am far from believing that this legislation will solve this deplorable situation, which has its tragic aspects in relation to our sovereignty. . . .

> *For the minority that looks deeper into the problem, al-*
> *though it deals fully only with some aspects of the matter, the*
> *urgent need is to end the monopoly that causes the arbitrary*
> *prices; a monopoly that was created and endures because of the*
> *inaction of the Argentine government and of the cattlemen and*
> *that has been consolidated and legalized by the [Roca-Runci-*
> *man] London Pact.* [17]

The Socialist legislator also saw clearly into the transportation
problem:

> Instead, the project for urban coordination creates a corpora-
> tion that is known as the Transport Corporation of the City of
> Buenos Aires and which, given its organization, will be under
> the control of British capital. This corporation will have exclu-
> sive control of transportation and may expropriate all the auto-
> motive enterprises that refuse to join it. As was the case in
> national coordination, the struggle will be an unequal one: the
> "corporation" will absorb the small companies and the small
> owners, one after the other, and it may even establish better
> services at first. It is not unlikely that fares will not be increased
> in the early days in order to prevent adding the natural reaction
> of the population to the discontent of those directly injured.
> The rates will be increased later, when, in one way or another,
> the first voices raised in protest will have been silenced. Be-
> cause the final objective of this project is to allow the fixing of
> much higher rates than the present ones, as we will see when we
> analyze this. [18]

Many of the laws passed by Congress between 1932 and 1942
were responsive to antipopular interests and maneuvers. These
laws were enforced by the courts, since in many cases both the
judges and the lawyers, who were also the law professors and later
became ministers and high government officials (including an occasional president or vice-president of the nation), shared the economic and social advantages of those who brought the suits — the
powerful corporations and international consortiums. Ramón
Doll, a nationalist writer who is now almost forgotten, has
sketched with bold strokes the phenomenon known as the "three-
headed hydra: lawyer-judge-professor." We quote below a long
excerpt that gives a summary of his ideas:

> The enormous plutocratic forces that are undermining the foun-
> dations of our nationality need an instrument, a defending
> agent: the lawyer. But the lawyer alone, relying on his office, is

too weak for the defense of imperialism, and it is necessary that he have connections or influence with the judges; not occasional connections, but permanent ones; there is one place, one occasion when these physical, professional, or ideological connections grow strong, take root, are generated: the [University of Buenos Aires] Law School. This is the triangle of the bureaucratic oligarchy, this is the three-headed body of the most powerfully destructive organism that perhaps represents the main contingent of the plutocratic forces thrown against the country from abroad: *law office-judicial bench-Law School.* Notice especially that the surnames are always the same: these are the sons-in-law and the fathers-in-law, the brothers and the brothers-in-law. The lawyer for a railroad is always the professor at the Law School, who one day moves up to the bench or to a court of appeals, or the judge who moves up to an office well-subsidized by the Standard Oil and who just happens to be a professor at the Law School also. We all know intelligent and well-educated lawyers who are not professors at the Law School; they seldom play a part in the trilogy we have described. . . . We realize how easy it was for this perpetuation of families on the bench to create lasting ties of family, of solidarity, even of similar mentality among them. And let us remember that brilliant opportunities are open to almost all of them in the important Buenos Aires law firms when they retire, or without waiting for retirement. Of course, there is here a constant process of personal and ideological readaptation between the profitable law offices and the dynastic coteries of the courts. Sometimes, readaptation may require the opposite process as in the case of Juan González Calderón, who went from being an attorney for the railroads to the Federal Chamber [of Appeals]. . . .

The men [of the Radical party] most often confined themselves to ousting the powerful lawyers in order to occupy their places. Others, like Leónidas Anastasi who, because of the way he was elevated to public office, should have become the discreditor of our legal system, became instead its most devoted supporter by continuing a law journal established by [Tomás] Joffré, from which judges drew supporting arguments for their decisions.[19]

The CADE affair is one of the best examples of the intimate relationship analyzed by Doll. Torres, another nationalist author we have mentioned in previous chapters and who has devoted much time to this subject, mentions these incontrovertible facts:

The CADE continues to be a topic of current interest and to be the touchstone for testing the three branches of the state and, above all, the courts, which had been discredited during the [old] regime by shady dealings to serve SOFINA, Bemberg, the British railroads, and the most ferocious Jewish monopolies. If this is still not obvious, let us look at the following: [Juan A.] Bramuglia, the interventor of Buenos Aires Province, by an exemplary judicial decree dated 18 September 1945, imposed a fine of 8,776,733.91 Argentine pesos on CADE. . . The interventor who succeded him, General [Ramón] Albariños, by a decree of 22 December 1945, denied an appeal presented by CADE against Bramuglia's ruling and CADE paid the amount assessed and sued the province, demanding a full refund. The term to present evidence started on 25 March 1946, for the usual twenty days; on 6 April, at the request of CADE, the term was extended to forty days; on 7 November, at the request of CADE, it was again extended another thirty days; and on 9 December, at the request of CADE, it was again extended another sixty days. What is wrong? Is CADE continuing to play with the courts and compromise their prestige? It is to be hoped that the final decision will show that the justice of the revolution is not the justice of the [old] regime, and is therefore not at the service of the highly-placed financial delinquents who won with the complicity of a venal judiciary. If this is not so, another revolution will become necessary, since without justice there can be no social peace.[20]

This shows how a corporation associated with foreign capital enjoyed unusual privileges in the Argentine courts. It was not the only case, but it is valuable as a symbol. Torres goes on to state that:

CADE, as everyone knows, stands for *"Compañía Argentina de Electricidad."* But what everyone also knows is that it is Argentine in name only, although venal governments have accepted in a decree a malicious imposture for proven truth. The Investigating Commission presided over by Col. Matías Rodríguez Conde ascertained that all the stock of CADE belongs to SOFINA. But let us look at one of its boards of directors chosen at random: Chairman, Carlos Mayer Pellegrini, First Vice Chairman, Alberto Hueyo; Second Vice Chairman, René Brosens; Director Delegates, Andrés Bausili, Marcelo Deschamps, Zacarías Nürnberg, Rafael Vehils; Directors; Tito L. Arata, Roberto Fraser, Carlos M. Mayer, E. C. I. Meynell, Alejandro Shaw, Carlos Alfredo

Tornquist, César M. Vel. As may be seen, this list includes an overwhelming majority of native-born Argentine citizens, some of whom bear the most distinguished names of the gilded circles of upper-class society. But, still, who would dare say that this is an Argentine enterprise? Nevertheless, despite this, when CADE's false Argentinism is to be taken advantage of by SOFINA, the known lie is accepted officially as gospel truth, as it was during the past regime and as it still is being accepted.[21]

Torres does not fail to note another important consequence of the penetration of intellectual circles by the large companies or their best-known representatives:

CADE, or its leaders, and in this case they are one and the same, organized the *Editorial Sudamericana,* which publishes and distributes a so-called "Economic Orientation Series." Eric Johnston, the president of the United States Chamber of Commerce, by means of that press propagates throughout Argentina his views as a successful businessman in a curious book entitled *North America Unlimited* which is a hymn of praise to capitalism. The various chapters of this book attempt to demonstrate conclusively and exhaustively that the United States has the natural right, and even the obligation, to become the policeman of the world and to subject it to American directives in everything. That same press publishes books by José Figuerola, such as *La colaboración social en Hispano-América,* alternating with the one written by Harold G. Moulton entitled *Financial Organization and the Economic System,* in which American methods in both fields of endeavor are highly praised; Lionel Robbins's *Economic Planning and International Order,* in which this author edifies us with the same directives; Louis M. Hacker's *American Capitalism, Its Promise and Accomplishment* and J. B. Coudliffe's *La reconstrucción del comercio mundial,* advocating the limitation of nationalism to benefit Anglo-Saxon imperialism.[22]

The influence of CADE has continued to be felt since the time the concessions were renewed during the thirties, *by all Argentine governments up to the present time,* including those of Perón, Aranburu, Frondizi, and the rest. As for Perón, it will be enough to say here that no one has yet denied Juan Pablo Oliver's statement to the effect that:

On 27 May 1944 two proposed decrees, intended to recover for the state improperly acquired goods, were submitted to the executive branch by the Commission, to be offered to the people on the first anniversary of the Revolution, according to President Farrell's wish. *But these decrees were mysteriously held up due to steps taken by Vice-President Perón.* Minister of the Navy and of the Interior Rear Admiral Teisaire himself has openly said to me that the report will serve "to brand with a stamp the back of certain patriotic politicians," but that as far as the "plants" (read corporations) are concerned the solution would be to exploit the Iguazú Falls rationally. . . . Yet the directors or those close to the nefarious corporations, preen themselves complacently, telling anyone who will listen that all "danger" has been definitively averted. . . . I have no reason to get involved. The investigation was not decreed to be used against possibly corrupt persons who might not consent to follow the political twistings and turnings of the ruler of the day. *The purpose of the investigation was to put a stop to the permanent sources of corruption, which remain untouched, ready, now as ever, to pay well those who serve them.* I do not lend myself, therefore, to be an accomplice in decrees that the law does not authorize and reason and ethics condemn.[23]

Luna reinforces these arguments when he asserts that the said Commission

was created in August 1943, by the de facto government and, after arduous labors lasting almost a year and a half, it finished publishing its report in two thick volumes in a thousand-copy edition. The edition was seized by order of the then de facto vice-president, Col. Juan D. Perón, and only a few copies were saved. That organization had worked honestly and ably, since it had the best Argentine experts on the subject of electricity for its advisers.[24]

Later, Luna (perhaps without intending to do so) gives an example of political paradox which is still highly applicable:

We do not believe that Alvear had measured the true gravity of the CHADE (Compañía Hispano-Argentina de Electricidad) affair, which does not so much concern the bribing of municipal councillors by the company, as the attitude adopted by the Radical party and its directives vis-à-vis a typical example of corrupting imperialism. The handling of the whole deal, the subtle intervention of CHADE and SOFINA in the highest circles of national life, the disintegrating action exerted through various pressure media, clearly outline the danger arising from these voracious capitals. Alvear's mentality was not capable of seeing the danger. He thought that the country could not be governed without the consent of the great international powers. "Who is going to give me the money I will need to govern? Are you by any chance going to give it to me? " he exploded on one occasion in Arturo Frondizi's presence, his great bald head growing red with rage, while he struck the table with his fist. Frondizi had been urging him to take a firm stand vis-à-vis the CHADE scandal.[25]

After 1958, under Frondizi's government, which eventually also accepted the attitude that "the country could not be governed without the consent of the great international powers," an agreement was entered into converting the former CADE into SEGBA (Greater Buenos Aires Electrical Services), a subject that lies outside the chronological limits of the period we are studying, but which shows the continuing existence of the electric power monopoly throughout our politcal history. Such veteran officials as Enrique Butty are examples of continuity; he was an outstanding member of numerous CADE boards of directors and of the present SEGBA.

Among the economic institutions that influenced political decisions during the 1930-1946 period the Rural Society should not be overlooked. When the meat question was being debated, the society adopted a position defending the interests of the large cattle-owners. It is a well-known fact that these interests were precisely the same as those of British imperialism. And British imperialism came out of all the investigations and requests for reports unscathed, not through its own merits, but through the efforts of its representatives and associates.[26]

The Stock Exchange gained in importance as industrial growth brought a corresponding increase in the number and size of corporations and an increase in the volume of money in the market, as reflected in table 19.

An analysis of the Argentine Industrial Union's activities between the years 1930 and 1946 will permit us to make new contributions to the study of the connections between politics and the economy. For this purpose we will follow the unpublished work by Adolfo L. Pérez Zelaschi, which, after setting down the early history of the Industrial Union, points out that:

Now we come to 1930 and the Argentine Industrial Union, which has joined the anti-Yrigoyen policy of other groups representing interests opposed to its own, such as the Rural Society

TABLE 19: NOMINAL VALUE OF SHARES TRADED IN THE BUENOS
AIRES STOCK EXCHANGE, 1930-46

Millions of Argentine Pesos		Millions of Argentine Pesos	
Years	Trading	Years	Trading
1930	605.0	1939	1,106.9
1931	546.2	1940	1,173.1
1932	423.1	1941	1,686.2
1933	672.1	1942	1,490.0
1934	802.5	1943	2,096.0
1935	882.9	1944	2,681.7
1936	1,249.9	1945	2,291.5
1937	1,419.8	1946	2,973.5
1938	941.8		

Source: Prepared by the author from data published in Bolsa de Comercio de
Buenos Aires, *Boletín del Centenario (1854--10 de julio--1954)* Year 50, 155,
2565, 5 July 1954, p. 246.

and the Stock Exchange, and is getting ready to offer its collaboration to the new government without realizing (or perhaps
deceiving itself about it) that this government represents the
restoration of the old *agricultural exports-commercial imports*
ensemble which is favorable to British industry. On 11 September, Minister Pérez promises the AIU to revise import duties. Of
course, these were mere words. Soon the treaty negotiations
with Britain were to begin and the AIU, as in 1899, had to take
to the streets to organize a meeting of entrepreneurs and blue
and white collar workers.[27]

According to a contemporary account which has not been denied so far, Luis Colombo, who was president of the AIU from
1926 until his resignation in 1946, himself participated actively in
the events of 6 September 1930.

Luis Colombo, the president of the Argentine Industrial Union,
was able to enter the Executive Mansion with the first contingent of citizens who did so. Learning that Martínez was still
there, he went to the Executive Office, and was able to get to
the place where the about-to-be overthrown executive was.

Colombo informed Martínez of the prevailing situation and counseled him as a friend to present his resignation immediately.

What is more, the account adds that, due to errors in the original, Colombo himself "drew up the resignation that Martínez signed."[28] It must not be forgotten that Colombo (despite his protestations that he was a die-hard protectionist) continued to work as an "employee of the British banking and industrial firm of Leng, Roberts and Co."[29] Pérez Zelaschi goes on as follows:

In 1930 the AIU came out openly against President Yrigoyen. After the latter was overthrown, the AIU immediately put itself at the disposal of the revolutionary government and congratulated it "for its truly nationalist energy." The following year (Revista 753, September 1931), Colombo spoke at the Círculo Militar. He said, "We must organize parties with the most profound national feeling," meaning by this, parties with some sort of fascist organization. We have already pointed out the economic foundation for this sympathy and also the error in evaluation the AIU committed as to the real interests that motivated the revolution of 1930. The antidumping laws and those on draw-back, protective tariffs, and industrial credit, for which the AIU had been struggling for decades, were indefinitely postponed during the 1930-1940 decade and the situation was still the same at the beginning of 1943. In this year, due to an event that we are about to relate, the AIU acted as a. . . pressure group, as it had done in 1930, failing to realize where the *true* interests of those it represented lay.

In December 1943 (Boletín 900 XII-1943) Perón, already secretary of labor, paid a protocol visit to AIU that gives a glimpse of the already existing opposition. "It would be senseless," he said, "to set myself up against an institution such as this," but in fact his labor policy was obviously opposed to that of the industrialists. In December 1944 (Revista 913, January 1944) the AIU forwarded a note in which it. . . pointed out. . . the "truly strange manner" in which the relations between capital and labor were developing through the Secretariat of Labor. Perón apparently ingored the offer of collaboration made by the AIU and dealt directly with the companies or with industrial sectors. The AIU in its note had stated that formerly the life of the enterprises developed in an environment of "serenity and camaraderie;" but that now the agreements are signed under "not always serene" conditions, and this leads to the spread of "indiscipline in the plants" and to the unions using a "terminology wounding to the employers." A few days later, on 18 January 1945, Perón made a speech in which he left no room for doubt as to the fact that relations were strained. He said that "he had asked for collaboration" and had been answered "by silence, which, at this juncture, amounts to sabotage." "On one occasion," he went on, "I visited the AIU. . . after that I have requested a collaboration for which I am still waiting." What was that collaboration? Despite what might be expected, collaboration was not requested for formulating plans for labor improvements, social legislation, industrial development, and such like. It was requested for "the organization of economic forces so that they may not affect. . . the political state.". . . Perón's objective was much more limited: his intention was to convert the AIU — its structure, its legal status, its assets, its administrative and technical personnel *were already set up* and this would facilitate the task —into a counterpoise to the GCL, which was also being organized in similar fashion. The AIU was to be the basic entrepreneurial association, it was to become a "vast organism," as requested by a note from the Executive Office itself. Its Board of Directors answered evasively, accepting the idea of working toward "unity. . . in the study and solution of the industrial problems of the country." This was stated in its reply by four of the directors, Prati, Miranda, Friani, and Elizalde, "in the absence of the governing bodies." They offered also to include representatives from the military and other state organisms. The answer from the administration was harsh: the signers are "only four respectable gentlemen," not the Board of Directors of the entity, the reforms are mere "enunciations and proposed timid reforms" that do not assure *"collaboration with the state."* It demanded instead an opening up of the organization to new members, reform of the by-laws, resignation of the Board of Directors, and delivery of the entity into "impartial hands," appointment of a special commission made up of six members of the AIU, six industrialists not connected with the same, and three state representatives. This commission was to reform the by-laws with a view to promoting the "membership of all the industrialists," "effective collaboration," and "future functioning for the public good," and the establishing of the representation of the state since "it is necessary to move on to find solutions and to practical and efficient action." The AIU refused and the quarrel was left unresolved because Colonel Perón's power gradually deteriorated, leading to his resignation on 9 October 1945. From that moment on (and even earlier) the AIU enrolled as a pressure group against the Administration. Let us not forget that Colombo and Lamuraglia — the president and secretary of AIU — were arrested in October 1945. Immediately after the approval of Decree No. 33,302 — which provided for the payment of a Christmas bonus — the AIU, failing again, as it had in 1930, to grasp the true nature of the process, formed a Permanent Commission of Industry, Commerce, and Production together with the agricultural and commercial sectors. . . . The president of this Commission was Eustaquio Méndez Delfino. A rally was held at the Stock Exchange — the place and the speaker may be symptomatic — denouncing the "totalitarian methods" of the government. [The AIU] also maintained that the decree was "demagogic and vote-seeking," that the struggle going on was to be regarded in terms of "democracy against totalitarianism" and that it was carried on "for respect for human dignity." Finally, it declared that "the decree will not be complied with"; thus we have an attempt by a pressure group to take over political power. The AIU was already a holder of power and might have participated as such to a great extent if its appraisal of the situation had not been wrong. There are three reasons why this assumption cannot be considered unwarranted: a) the role played by the GCL in labor organization, to which, as we have seen, the AIU was meant to be a counterpoise; b) the insistence of the Peronist regime on organizing the entrepreneurs, something that it only partly achieved in 1952 through the creation of the General Economic Confederation; c) the fact that what the AIU did not achieve as an institution, that is, a share of political power during the Perón regime, was achieved by a group of industrialist that left the organization under the leadership of Miguel Miranda. Later, during the 1945-46 electoral campaign, came the episode of the AIU contribution to the Democratic Union funds by a check incredibly drawn *to bearer,* something that was at once used for Peronist propaganda purposes and, finally, the resignation of Colombo and the intervention of the AIU.[30]

The foregoing is an account of the important part played by the Argentine Industrial Union, an entrepreneurial organization that throughout the 1930-1946 period consistently opposed the passing of improved labor legislation, that followed Benito Mussolini's policies with growing interest and sometimes with open admiration,[31] and that proved that profascist sympathies were not actually incompatible with pro-British interests in prewar Argentina, as they were in other countries.

Imperialist agents and representatives in the government

Federico Pinedo, who was well versed in the subject, has explained the factors that led to lawyers and representatives of private enterprises occupying government posts. He recalls that "when Vice-President Castillo took charge of the government more or less permanently" in September 1940, he himself was asked to take over the Treasury portfolio for the second time, while others replaced the various ministers appointed by Ortiz.

> The cabinet thus formed, before it had taken a single step, was violently attacked as a "British cabinet" by the press and the so-called "nationalist" elements, typically profascist and pronazi, which as often happens, declared they were no such thing, but only "Argentine," as though we, the pro-Allied, were anything else. In this way "Argentinity," "Creoleism," and even "Hispanism" began to be monopolized by the strangest people, many of them of very exotic background and some with surnames unpronounceable in Spanish. We, the native Argentines, sons and grandsons of Argentines, some with many generations of ancestors born on our soil, with surnames made famous by worthy men since the days of the war of independence, the colony, and even the conquest, were denied our condition as Argentines by typically parvenu people, espousing a domestic and foreign policy most antagonistic to national traditions. . . .
> Because we repudiated "nationalism" and its implications; because we believed, as our elders had believed, in the beneficial effect of the activity of foreign men and capital, which had made a nation out of what had been the scene of raids by savage tribes, we were classified as "traitors to our country." Those who did not believe in the delights of economic self-sufficiency *were traitors to their country. Those who did not scream against the British domination under which the country was said to be groaning,* those who did not declaim against foreign imperialism, and who did not talk about "recovering" by violent means Argentine wealth and Argentine means of production and public services (which joint Argentine and foreign efforts, or exclusively foreign efforts relying on the Argentine promise to guarantee their rights had created in this country), were all traitors. Even to be known to be connected with those interests in open and freely acknowledged professional relations

was in itself to be a traitor and in this sense *the author of these lines was the very epitome of "a traitor to his country," in his role as attorney or financial adviser for various very important foreign firms or corporations, which, according to this strange nationalist concept, because they pay for specific and limited services, buy the conscience of those who render these services.* You can be an engineer for an electric power company, a doctor for a railroad, an agent for a grain company, a regular supplier of a meat-packing plant, an actuary in a bank or an insurance company, or a laborer or salaried employee or any of these, without losing your independence and retaining intact your nationality; but to be a legal or economic adviser to them, to help them draw up their contracts, guide them in their investments, or defend them in the courts of the country, according to this absurd concept, leads to the loss of independence and even of citizenship! National feeling should lead any patriotic Argentine to refuse such service. It would seem that it would be better for the proper protection of national interests that each company do without local counsel and bring its own foreign professionals to work within the country! [32]

Pinedo clearly rejects applying such unfair epithets to those who busy themselves in the defense of monopolies and trusts, invokes the national precedents established by illustrious figures, and even goes so far as to manifest his pride in belonging to a family of lawyers with traditions in such matters:

Almost all the large enterprises that at one time or another I have had the honor, as a professional, to sponsor or counsel were at some time the clients of my father, a partner of two Argentine presidents, Pellegrini and Sáenz Peña, or were clients of other prominent lawyers of the time, such as Rosa or Romero, Lucio or Alberto López, Julio García or Enrique García Merou, as in the preceding generation they had been the clients of my grandfather, whose name I bear, or of his relative and friend, don Bernardo de Irigoyen, or of Quintana, or of Domínguez, or of Ugarte. . . .

When President Castillo was informed of the connections his ministers had had with various companies in the normal exercise of their professions, he expressly stated that he did not see that this was any obstacle to their carrying on the functions he was entrusting to them, since he had no doubt that none of them would sacrifice national interests to those of their former employers, if a conflict arose between them. He repeated this statement in a categorical manner — at least insofar as it concerned me — when a question to this effect was brought up in the national Senate, and I have in my possession the letters that were exchanged on that occasion. *That opinion of the president is the same that would be held by any person of quality accustomed to treating with persons of quality, whom there is no right to suspect might place their official influence at the service of their former clients, as there is no right to suppose that they would place it at the service of their relations of any other sort.*[33]

This is what we were attempting to do: to prove that as far as Pinedo is concerned the whole problem of imperialism, of the representatives of the great companies who occupied — and who decades later continue to occupy — very important positions in the government, is merely a problem of personal decency, which is never questioned among "persons of quality." José Luis Torres felt otherwise:

I do not share the idea of Argentine political life just now made fashionable. . . and practiced by the administration, that affairs of state should be conducted by businessmen and that the latter are more useful in leading the country and more efficient in everything than other men, as is frequently proclaimed lately. I consider the opposite to this theory is closer to the truth. The government man should not be a man of business, but rather a man of thought and study, with a steady and calm judgment about everything, without marked bias for given industrial endeavors or for certain productive activities. *Only when the mind of the person who is charged with the highest and most unappealable decisions is not influenced by any consideration of advantage of a direct or indirect personal order related to his usual activities can he proceed with justice.*[34]

Is it necessary to point out that Torres's ambition practically failed to find effective application during the years between 1930 and 1946? It would be almost impossible, because of its length, to compile a complete list of advisers, ministers, and other key officials in the successive public administrations who at the same time retained important associations with private imperialist interests. We aim only to give a few examples. Beginning with Pinedo himself, the Rodríguez Conde report to which we referred earlier in this chapter, in analyzing the relations of the government and the companies (relations that were especially favored by some ministers), has this to say:

. . . That Pinedo, [Alberto Hueyo's] successor in the Ministry of the Treasury who persuaded the Independent Socialists to accept "conciliation" with the C.H.A.D.E., had been legal and technical adviser of that company, as shown by the special payments roll of the same (53,000 Argentine pesos according to vouchers Nos. 16,191, 17,522, 11,611, 3,986, and 355/380). On the other hand, it should be noted that Pinedo has come forward in the National Senate (17 December 1940 session, p. 1,546) to acknowledge implicitly being connected professionally with the SOFINA group.[35]

Federico Pinedo crossed the Jordan time and again with the same ease, on occasion defending the opposite position from the one he had upheld previously. Times — and the interests defended — also change.[36] Alberto Hueyo, who we have seen occupied high posts within the CHADE board of directors, was General Justo's first minister of finance. His own words give only a faint idea of his commercial connections in the Buenos Aires market in moments as difficult as those of the year 1932. At this time the minister called together in his office the managers of the principal Buenos Aires banks in order to ask them for a credit of fifteeen to twenty million Argentine pesos, for the purpose of easing the pressing economic situation of the public treasury.

I try to offer my listeners the strongest guaranties. For this purpose I bring up my business experience; *I also make clear my connections with some of the institutions represented at the meeting and the recent participation as chairman of the board it has been my lot to have in some of them,* and I affirm, on the word of an official and a gentleman, that I will make it my duty to set aside from the next collection of public revenues the funds necessary to repay the amount lent. [37]

The bank managers said no, and Hueyo as an "official" and as a "gentleman" concludes: ". . . I decided to impose a new sacrifice on government employees."[38] In a harsh polemical manner, José Luis Torres passes judgment on two officials who were not ministers, but enjoyed full powers in the conduct of the state's economic and financial affairs:

The economic structure of the [old] regime remained intact and the disciples of the classic interpreters of corruption in action against the country still held all the strategic spots in the Central Bank (which was not of the Republic), in the National Controller's Office, in the Income Tax Bureau, and in the autonomous government corporations, exerting effective control on the revolution itself. There was even talk of Raúl Prebisch's ministry and Ernesto Malaccorto's ministry; they were Federico Pinedo's best disciples. For a time they were more than ministers since they advised the latter, and imposed their own norms, relying on the incapacity of the incumbents.[39]

Lisandro de la Torre has confirmed this opinion:

The adviser to the Ministry of Agriculture is also the adviser to the Ministry of the Treasury, that is, Raúl Prebisch; he is the one charged with pulling both departments out of difficulties each time an unexpected emergency so requires.[40]

Referring to Prebisch's work as adviser to the minister of the treasury (Pinedo), he writes:

I am not fully convinced; I suspect that his [Pinedo's] wisdom is infused by Prebisch and that it sometimes happens that he forgets what Prebisch has said and contradictions occur then. Prebisch goes one way and the minister another. Prebisch writes all the messages, prepares all the bills, persuades him [Pinedo] to accept those he considers advisable, as in the case of the minimum price bill; he drafts all the interviews, prepares his memoirs, does all his figuring, even the one for that compensations' game, and from his strategic position as director of the *Revista Económica* of the National Bank, where he has a crowd of employees at his disposal, supplies [Pinedo] with all the material on bank and currency information that . . .[the minister] later exhibits as the fruit of his personal investigations.[41]

The presence of such advisers connected with the British imperialism of the time should not seem strange (here we are not considering Prebisch's later evolution and his international participation in the Economic Commission for Latin America beginning in 1945), when a president of the Republic, Roberto M. Ortiz, was as a former lawyer for the Western Railroad and other railroad companies and for the Telephone Company and the Tornquist enterprises. Scalabrini Ortiz offers much information on the various public personalities of Argentina and their connections with the large companies. Let us look at a few examples:

The embarrassment in the country became acute when Ezequiel Ramos Mejía, a local director of the British railroads, was named special ambassador to the Italian government and Guillermo Leguizamón, Chairman of the British Argentine Great

Western Railroad, was appointed chief adviser and factotum of the special mission sent to London. *In whose favor was Leguizamón going to plead? In favor of the British interests whose permanent employee he was or in favor of those (to him) transitory Argentine interests?* [42]

Pablo Calatayud, who had been minister of public works, had worked as a legal advisor to General Motors. This was back in 1931. During the Justo administration, Scalabrini Ortiz could not help asking himself the following question:

What sort of Argentinity and spontaneous national action can we expect from an administration when its ministers have been selected from among the most conspicuous attorneys for British enterprises, such as Saavedra Lamas, a consulting attorney for the railroads, in his private law practice and in his seat in the Chamber of Deputies a defender of the most indefensible British claims, such as the one for the acceptance of the obviously watered securities of the Western Railroad and for the sale of the Andean Railroad; or Cárcano, an employee of British steamship companies; or Alvarado, who would be a nobody as soon as the British withdrew their protection from him? [43]

Alvarado held his post as minister of public works for many years and was always favorably disposed to suggestions made by British interests. Though these are only a few of the cases we might mention, they are enough to indicate the extent of the problem.

Agricultural groups and industrial groups; reinvestment

The data compiled by Jacinto Oddone on the "owners of the land" in the province of Buenos Aires is still useful, although some of the figures may not be wholly up-to-date.[44]

TABLE 20: FAMILIES OWNING OVER 30.000 HECTARES AND CORRES—RESPONDING VALUATION ACCORDING TO THE GUIDE TO THE TAX—PAYERS IN THE PROVINCE OF BUENOS AIRES (1928)

Family	Hectares	Valuation in Argentine Pesos
Alzaga Unzué	411,938	111,826,700
Anchorena	382,670	67,101,350
Luro	232,336	21,413,500
Pereyra Iraola	191,218	47,467,800

Family	Hectares	Valuation in Argentine Pesos
Pradere	187,034	24,502,200
Guerrero	182,449	31,841,900
Leloir	181,036	26,823,200
Graciarena	165,687	22,464,800
Santamarina	158,684	41,019,720
Duggan	129,041	36,844,000
Pereda	122,205	32,194,600
Duhau	113,334	14,574,700
Herrera Vegas	109,578	25,038,200
Zuberbühler	105,849	9,748,400
Martínez de Hoz	101,259	23,840,150
Estrugamou	99,590	32,485,500
Días Vélez	97,598	23,799,900
Casares	94,897	24,186,600
Atucha	83,914	29,981,400
Drysdale	77,500	18,766,500
Cobo	77,500	18,766,600
Bosch	76,028	16,487,300
Drabble	75,797	17,345,100
Bunge	74,417	16,337,300
Pueyrredón	70,632	12,633,700
Ortiz Basualdo	69,506	19,137,600
Mulhall	63,457	2,175,000
Pourtalé	60,726	11,546,700
Llaudé	50,959	10,265,000
Saavedra	53,500	20,609,800
Deferrari	52,013	10,506,600
Crotto	51,141	5,002,000
Stegmann	42,842	10,637,900
Perkins	40,245	14,183,400
Otamendi	40,159	11,250,100
Maguirre	38,893	10,600,300
López Lecube	38,513	3,224,400
Taillade	38,451	2,305,900
Apellanis	38,381	1,891,700
Lastra	37,435	9,948,100
Alvear	36,698	12,944,700
Tornquist	36,419	2,750,200
Lyne Stivens	36,074	3,691,300
Fernández	35,403	4,556,100
Van Pannewitz	35,153	10,620,000
Fernández	34,755	6,504,860
Rooth	34,000	3,803,800

ECONOMIC GROUPS 249

Family	Hectares	Valuation in Argentine Pesos
Hale	32,389	11,526,800
Durañona	32,281	15,003,400
Parravicini	31,991	2,951,300
Totals	4,663,575	965,108,080

Source: Jacinto Oddone, *La burguesía terrateniente argentina*, pp.176-177.

In general the situation continues to be the same. For example, in accordance with an official survey made in 1942, it was found that in the province of Buenos Aires there were 221 owners who held 593 real estate parcels (total area: 4,130,021 hectares), with a total valuation for tax purposes of 673,787,900 Argentine pesos; and that 51 legally incorporated entities owned 153 real estate parcels (total area: 916,035 hectares), with a total valuation for tax purposes of 149,738,200 pesos.[45] On the basis of the figures for 1948, Jorge Vicien has estimated the value of the rural property owned by corporations to be 15 percent of the total within that category. Table 21 gives some examples selected from the country as a whole.

TABLE 21: LARGE LAND - OWNING CORPORATIONS IN ARGENTINA

Owner	Hectares
La Forestal (British)	1,250,000
Argentine States of Bovril Ltd. (British)	647,520
Río Negro Land Co. (British)	665,000
The Argentine Southern Land Co. (British)	647,000
Ganadera Gente Grande (British)	450,000
Leach Argentine States (British)	200,000
Bunge y Born Ltda.	500,000

Source: Marcelo Isacovich, *Argentina económica y social*, p. 38.

Despite Yrigoyen and Perón (and the timid experiments begun in 1958 by the governor of Buenos Aires Province, Oscar Alende), latifundia holdings have not ceased to exist within our agricultural structure. The links between the latifundia owners and the so-called "industrial bourgeoisie," which some authors invest with a mythically autonomous personality, were, and continue to be, close, due to a process known technically as *reinvestment*. Sometimes the profits derived from the rural properties are invested in industry; sometimes, the reverse is true. In addition to this, many industrialists personally have important landed interests. Is it strange that during the 1945-1946 period the Rural Society (to mention just one example) sometimes marched hand in hand with the Industrial Union in its opposition to Colonel Perón? In this, as in so many other cases, they had much more to bring them together than to keep them apart, as table 22 shows.[46]

TABLE 22: CONNECTIONS BETWEEN INDUSTRIAL AND AGRICULTURAL INTERESTS IN ARGENTINA

Name	Industrial Interest	Landholding Interest
Aguirre, Ernesto	OSRAM, AEG, Duperial, Diadema Argentina	Ganadera Las Mesetas
Anchorena, Alberto de, Enrique de, Nicolás de, and Nazar de	República, Comercial Industrial y Financiera Cía. Italo-Argentina de Electricidad INSUD-Hanomag	El Dorado, S. A., 380,600 hectares
Arata, Tito	CADE Tamet, Sudametal INDUSTRIA Colorín Fibrocemento Monolit Formio Argentina	Frigorífico La Negra, Victoria Cía. de Colonización, La Criolla, Argentino - Británica de Inmuebles
Atucha, Jorge de	Hiram Walker	83,900 ectares
Bacigalupo, Domingo	Manufactura Algodonera Arg. Crédito Industrial y Comercial Argentino Cervecería Palermo Safac	Santa Margarita, Vivina Cía inmobiliaria Argentina Sol
Baqué, Santiago	Philips Arg. Industrias Arg. del Papel	Crédito Inmobiliario Argentino

Name	Industrial Interest	Landholding Interest
Bracht, Federico	Crédito Industrial y Comercial Arg. Eternit	Estancias y Tierras del Pilaga, Estancia La Peregrima
Bunge & Born	Duperial La Química . Grafa CAICO, La Fabril Alba Financiera e Industrial Consorcio Industrial	Quebrachales Paraguayos, La Invernada, Vivorata, Estab. Agríc., Inmobiliaria del Río de la Plata, Fomento Territorial, Estancias Unidas, Media Luna Rural, Estancias Loma Alta, Comega Ganadera, CODEC Establec. Agrícolas, SAHICO Hipotecaria Rural, Estancias Estanar, Los Alfalfares, Cía. Rural
Braun-Menéndez Behety	Fármaco Arg. Atanor CADE Ferrum Cristalerías Rigolleau Sudamericana de Fosforos	Estancias Sara Braun, Los Ranqueles, Pastoril, Estancia Puerto Velaz, Ganadera Los Lagos, Ganadera Valle, Huemul, Ganadera Oriental, Ganadera M. Behety
Bruzzone, Horacio	La Cantábrica	3,200 hectares
Canale de María, E.	General Electric	La Vascongada
Calatayud, Pablo	Siam di Tella Aceitera Argentina Eternit S. K. F. Argentina, Cía. Argentina de Neumáticos	Punta Alta, Cía. Agrícola, Ganadera E Inmobiliaria
Crespo, R. G.	General Electric	Estancia Santa Catalina
Mendez Delfino, Antonio	CATITA	Estancia El Condor, Los Ranqueles
Di Tella family	Siam Siat	Cabaña Nogales

Name	Industrial Interest	Landholding Interest
Drysdale, Alejandro M.	CADE Vidriería Arg. Noel y Cía. Siam Eveready Philco Arg. Atkinson Ltda.	La Forestal Argentina, Quebrachales Asociados del Norte, La Inmobiliaria Agrìco- la Ganadera, El Yatay y Cía., Agrí- cola Ganadera, 77,500 hectares
Frazer, Roberto	Fca. Argentina de Al- pargatas CADE El Globo Ltda. Ferrum	La Forestal
Garavaglio y Zorraquín	SAIAR CAEBA	La Merced, S. A. Agrí- cola, Comercial y Fo- restal
Herlitzka, Mauro	Papelera Pedotti, Inyecta Arg.	La Austral, Cía. General de Bienes Raíces y Muebles
Lahusen, Christal	Sedalana	Industrias Rurales de Río Negro
Mayer, Carlos M.	CADE Duperial Química Ciba Industrias Argentinas del Papel	Frigorífico Armour, Los Naranjos, Inmobiliaria y Financiera Ltda.
Merlini Pedro	Cía. Argentina In- dustrial, Comercial, Agrícola y Ganadera	
Roberts, William R.	El Globo Fca. Argentina de Al- pargatas	Leach Argentine, The Smithfield Meat, La Rosario Agrícola
Robiola, M.	Siam	Estancias Argentinas «El Hornero»
Santamarina, Antonio	CATITA	158,00 hectares
Shaw, Alejandro	Cotécnica Ferrum Tamet	La Agraria Cía. Territorial Río de la Plata

Name	Industrial Interest	Landholding Interest
Tornquist, Carlos A., Eduardo A., Ernesto Martín	CADE Formo Argent. Piccardo y Cía. Fibrocemento Monolit Tamet Ferrum Cristalerías Rigolleau	La Criolla, Cía. Territorial Río de la Plata, 36,000 hectares, Crédito Territorial de Santa Fe

Source: Prepared by the author from data published in Milcíades Peña, "Rasgos biográficos de la famosa burguesía industrial argentina," *Estrategia*, No. 1, September, 1957, pp. 45-80, as updated by Gustavo Polit in *Fichas de Investigación Económica y Social*, vol. I, April 1964, pp. 60-80.

As Peña comments: ". . . remember that all those who appear are, but not all who are appear."[47] These examples are sufficient to indicate the extent of a problem that has not yet been studied in depth and should be dealt with in monographs. The question became more urgent after the emergence of the new industrial sectors during the Peronist regime and after the support given by part of the industry to the Intrasigent Radical candidate, Arturo Frondizi, during the 1958 presidential campaign.

9 The Labor Movement

Unions and politics: a backward glance

The period between 1930 and 1946 represents a stage in the history of the Argentine labor movement that has not been fully clarified. This may be due to the existence throughout this period of two at times contradictory factors. The first one was the attempt to establish a single labor confederation (this does not mean that it was representative in number or importance), to which the tactics of Socialists, Communists, and unionists "on the European model" (the anarchism of the Argentine Regional Labor Federation was by then clearly on the way out) contributed. The second was the irruption of growing masses of native workers, both from the urban and rural areas, who during the thirties started to make their impact felt on the social structure of Argentina. Colonel Perón used the second group as the basis for his new program for union organization, which he accomplished with the cooperation of the leaders who left the first group's internal squabbles to draw close to the mass of the workers ("an available mass," as French sociologist Raymond Aron has called them in similar cases). The years 1944 and 1945 were the key ones in the process.

Another seeming paradox in our political history is the fact that the laboring masses entered social life under the leadership of certain army sectors who responded to Perón's orientation, not under the guidance of the working class parties such as the Socialist and the Communist. Many of the Socialist proposals for labor legislation became a reality through decrees issued by the executive branch, under prodding by Secretary of Labor and Welfare Perón. Are the masses to be blamed because they did not keep dusty records in mind instead of the concrete realities? Are we simply to blame (and do nothing else) the authoritarian tendencies that developed in union organization in our country, considering that many of the bodies that should have been responsible for a more progressive orientation insisted on the "democracy-fascism" dichotomy, apply-

254

ing it *equally* to Europe and to Argentina, and were not listened to or understood by the hundreds of thousands of laborers who actually were experiencing improvement in their living conditions? This does not mean that the merits of many hard-working militants in the leftist parties should be ignored, but rather that attention must be called to the fact that the direction of their efforts was mistaken. Gino Germani, a sociologist who cannot be suspected of sympathetic views toward Peronism, in summarizing in 1950 some conclusions on the social repercussions of economic changes in Argentina from 1940 to 1950, said that:

> In fact, the net result has been the *transformation of a relatively undifferentiated urban and rural proletariat into an industrial working mass,* concentrated within the large urban centers, *imbued, in one way or another, with the feeling of its social rights* and accustomed to exercising them for several years, whether indirectly or directly by means of strikes; *a mass that is consequently ready to defend and to improve its standard of living, which, even within its restrictions, is undoubtedly higher than that enjoyed in earlier periods or in the rural zones from which it had migrated.*[1]

José Luis Romero has tried to understand the process by using a more specific approach:

> The perpetuation of the agricultural economic structure — with cattle-raising holding the first place — limited the horizons of the masses that were increasing numerically and in various ways were being redistributed throughout a country whose vitality transcended those limitations. In the northern and eastern regions the masses were at the mercy of the entrepreneurs who were at the same time the political leaders, especially in the mills, shops, the *mate* plantations, and the mines. This gave rise to a phenomenon that was to be of great importance: *the growth of a deep popular resentment against the ruling groups and of a marked political skepticism resulting in, and accompanied by, a clear awareness of certain social and economic rights that the masses considered to be elementary justice. In this way the masses came to abandon activity on the political level (which was alien to them) and took their places on the level of the social struggle. Only a favorable occasion was needed for this new attitude to be manifested, and that occasion arose after the 1943 military revolution.*[2]

The same author, after referring to the social consequences of the country's industrialization and urbanization process, adds that: "behind these phenomena there lurks another no less significant: *the undeniable advancement of the masses both in the amount of remuneration and in working conditions, with the resulting increase in their purchasing power and opportunities for enjoyment.*"[3]

The immediate and tangible advantages that the laborers achieved after 1943 are undeniable. This is the reason why the specious arguments of many observers who assert that the working class sold its independence of action for a "mess of potage" seem strange. In the final analysis, the professional leaders entrenched in the union organizations of the thirties had for years been promising that same "mess of potage." For example, the General Confederation of Labor in 1932 drew up a minimum program defining moderate rights that Argentine workers did not yet enjoy. This program was entered into the *Diario de Sesiones* of the Chamber of Deputies at the request of Francisco Pérez Leirós, then serving as a federal deputy in addition to his usual union duties. In its statement of principles the GCL warned that:

> As may readily be seen at a glance, the GCL minimum program does not contain extreme demands that by their extent may make legislative approval difficult or impossible. This program simply expresses the basic aspirations of the working class, which, while remaining only aspirations in our country, in others have been fully satisfied and have several years of experience behind them. But despite their being modest demands, we are certain that their incorporation into the social legislation of the country and their faithful enforcement will yield beneficial results for the workers and in some aspects will be an effective contribution to the solution of such acute and serious problems as unemployement.[4]

The following is a summary of the petition:

Recognition of the unions. By the mere fact of their existence, unions shall be considered public interest institutions, with authority to see to the enforcement of labor legislation.

Work hours and vacations. Eight hours of work for adults in day work and six in night work or in unhealthy industries. The work week shall be a maximum of five days. Annual vacations with pay.

Living wage and national insurance. Minimum salary periodically fixed by commissions made up of representatives of labor unions and employers' industrial or regional associations. Establishment of national unemployment, sickness, old age, and maternity insurance.

Workers' participation. Participation and control by the labor organization in various state organisms [National Department of Labor, Immigration Bureau, National Health Department, General Railroad Bureau, Administration of the State Railroads, General Bureau of Shipping and Ports, General Maritime Prefecture.]

Employment office. Elimination of private agencies; employment offices shall be established by the municipalities, and the unions shall have direct participation in their administration.

Maternity protection. Pension payments proportional to number of children under fourteen years old to any woman without a husband and without resources.

Childhood protection. Compulsory non-religious, free, public education, up to fourteen years old, the state also providing free food, clothing, and the necessary educational supplies.

Law No. 9,688 (labor accidents). Amendment of these aspects of the law: disability shall be computed from the time the accident occurs; extension of the law to all wage-earners without exception; increase of partial compensation benefits to 100 percent of salary; increase of maximum compensation to 15,000 Argentine pesos; elimination of salary limitations in order to be entitled to the benefits of the law. The state shall be in charge of accident insurance.

Job security and seniority for workmen employed by the state and other public entities.

Cost of living. Fixing of rural and urban rents in accordance with value; construction of low-priced dwellings for workers by the state and the municipalities.

Repeal of Law No. 4,144. [Deportation of undesirable foreigners]

These were the limited demands that the GCL presented to Congress for consideration. It is true that with the support of the Socialist legislators some urgently needed laws were approved during the 1932-1942 period, but their enforcement was limited by the courts. However, the overall situation of the workers (except in some very specific sectors, such as that of the railroad workers and the commercial white-collar workers) was tragic. We will cite only two examples that were presented before Congress in the thirties. During the debate on a draft resolution relating to "working and living conditions of the workers and employees in the meat industry," Socialist Deputy Guillermo Korn stated that:

All the laws protecting workers, without excluding those referring to maternity and childhood, are adroitly circumvented by
the meat-packing companies. Union organization is persecuted.
Work accidents are concealed. Professional people in the pay of
the companies usually take part in the skillful drawing up of
certificates intended to evade the affected parties' right to
indemnization, and the latter's ignorance of the laws and rudi-
mentary union organization often make them the victims of
unscrupulous and shrewd operators ready to deal with the companies behind the back of their clients.[5]

Korn's protest against the so-called *standard* work system that
was implemented in the Berisso, La Plata, Avellaneda, and Zárate
meat-packing plants, went so far as to charge that "the magnates
of the meat industry, from their boards of directors in foreign
countries, have codified the minutest details" of the labor system.
The words of the Socialist deputy were explicitly confirmed in the
note addressed in 1939 to the Chamber of Deputies by the Communist militant José Peter, then Secretary General of the Board of
the Meat Industry Labor Federation. In one paragraph he says:

> Since 1927 the meat-packing plants have been enforcing the
> so-called *standard* system. They established special bonuses
> called "prizes" on the highest productivity per work hours in
> order to stimulate the yield per worker. Beguiled by the incen-
> tive of greater gain, driven by poverty and insufficient wage, the
> workers pushed themselves to increase production, putting
> forth extraordinary and truly superhuman efforts. From the
> normal level the yield was raised to an exceptional degree and
> this exceptional level was fixed as the minimum. The "prizes"
> were abolished and instead of a scale of bonuses a scale of sus-
> pensions and penalties was established for those who do not
> comply with the fixed minimum.[6]

The second example of living conditions for large sectors of our
country's workers covers the sugar, lumber, textile, grape and
wine, and *yerba mate* industries in Argentina, at the time of the
debate on the draft bill covering the investigation of "the salary,
work-day, housing, dressing, hygienic, and safety conditions in the
places of work." (1936) Socialist Deputy Juan Antonio Solari
declared at the time that:

> On our investigation tours we have seen, at the Chumbicha sta-
> tion in Catamarca, those workers traveling in cars intended for
> freight and cattle. I still remember, and this memory is indelibly

imprinted on my mind, the passing of a "slave train" coming from Salta, obscenely overcrowded with a mass of men, women, and children, many of them drunk, under the command of a contractor, of a "slaver," as the sinister labor contractors of the north of Argentina are called, and our conscience as Argentine deputies has rebelled against so much injustice.[7]

His Socialist colleague Pérez Leirós saw deeper into the problem:

Why do I try to confine the work of this commission to only five industries? *Because most of them are protected industries that have been subject to legislation and that have, according to law, unusual benefits — we must see to it that these protected industries, too, have some consideration for their workers — and because, due to the scant legislation of this nature, these workers are the most defenseless.*[8]

Pérez Leirós view helps us to understand better the nature of the two sores that festered within the country after 1930, as Raúl Larra testifies:

. . . its colonial condition and the iniquitous and merciless exploitation of its laboring masses. When leftist legislators obtained a more or less favorable law, the courts took care to pare it down or twist it according to interpretations suited to each one's taste. Our social legislation was so far behind the times that it lent itself to all sorts of manipulations.[9]

We repeat: these are but two examples. The labor problem, despite some more or less isolated efforts, continued to grow worse as time went by. The very supplanting (as far as membership and importance goes) of some traditional unions (the railroads and printers) by the new industrial groups (metallurgical and textile, together with the embattled meat workers led by Cipriano Reyes), is a process that does not seem to have been clearly grasped by the interested parties nor by the employers, who continued to speculate on the basis of the old hedonistic principle and who blindly opposed gains that in most civilized countries were already accepted as rights, without realizing that times had indeed changed; nor by many union leaders who planned campaigns as though the working masses were solidly behind their claims. The masses were moving in other directions. The years from 1943 to 1946 mark the irruption of the labor forces at the political level, and even more, at the social level, but this process was not sudden nor unexpected.

The labor movement from 1930 to 1943; the GCL, rivalries, bureaucracy

It does not lie within the scope of this work to give a detailed account of the course of Argentine labor unions throughout the 1930-1946 period. Some works have begun to cover the vaccum existing in this field.[10] What we are interested in here is to emphasize the fact that from the moment, soon after the 6 September 1930 coup, when the GCL was organized, the latter became the scene of internal discord among the various groups that claimed representation of the labor sectors and that, as a body, it would almost without interruption take a complaisantly bureaucratic position vis-à-vis succeeding national governments, a position that cannot but make the contemporary observer ponder.

Diego Abad de Santillán, an anarchist writer who worked untiringly in union activities in both his homeland, Spain, and in Argentina, has emphasized with considerable bitterness the almost total passivity of the labor movement at the time of the 1930 military coup, despite isolated attempts by anarchist groups.[11] A brief outline will suffice to bring us up to the moment of fusion: around 1930 there were in Argentina three labor confederations:

> ... the Argentine Regional Labor Federation, which was faithful to the resolution passed at its fifth congress to propagate anarchic Communism within labor unions; the Argentine Labor Union, directed by labor unionists and anarchists opposed to having the union organization align itself with any specific ideology; and the Argentine Labor Confederation, with a Socialist orientation.[12]

The last two, the ALU and the ALC — the anarchists refused to participate — established the General Confederation of Labor on 27 September 1930. Their first press release stated that:

> The GCL of the Argentine Republic, which brings together over 200,000 workers, among whom are included the railroad, maritime, and urban transportation workers, stevedores and longshoremen at ports and stations, the industrial and rural workers, white-collar workers, and the rest, considers it its duty to confirm the autonomous nature of this working class organization that is independent of all political parties or ideological groups and therefore not involved in any action taken by them. As is stated in the association agreement, the GCL will immediately proceed to invite the unions not included within this agreement to come into its ranks. Since it is the greatest concentration of

workers registered in the annals of the Argentine labor movement up to the present time and since its establishment offers
the necessary guaranties of earnestness, the representatives of
the united labor organizations warmly urge their class brothers
to come into the bosom of the GCL, in this manner making a
reality of the fervent wish for unity that animates all workers
desirous of liberty and well-being.[13]

This type of "pure" unionism desirous of leaving the political
field to take refuge exclusively in union proposals will not seem
strange when we read in a work by Rubens Iscaro that "the union
associations adopted vis-à-vis the prevailing situation [the 6 September uprising] an attitude of non-involvement." The GCL, the
principal fruit of the .ALU-ALC union, did nothing except follow
the path of its predecessors.

This fusion of two organizations, to the exclusion of the class
movement [e. g., Communist] and of the autonomous unions
and without a fighting program that would mobilize the working class, could not awaken enthusiasm toward the new workers' association; this is the reason why the membership of the
GCL did not increase in the next few years.[14]

This is what makes the comment by Graciela Biagini on the
accomplishments of the GCL during the 1930-1933 period so fitting:

... it intervened in the solution of worker-employer conflicts in
an indirect manner. It sent ambiguous resolutions and petitions
to the minister of the interior or to the government in general
supporting the member unions that had problems, always provided it did not imply taking a clear position on economic or
political problems. In the same way, it recommended to the
working class "closing ranks" in order to avoid conflicts, which
means that at no time during this period, or in others we will
examine, did it decide through the cooperation of the member
unions and federations to solve any problem that might imply
adopting a specific position. It took shelter behind "uninvolve-
ment" and the apolitical nature of the labor association.[15]

Parallel with the development of these attitudes, an ossification
process set in within the ruling sectors that had *provisionally* set
up the GCL, through their repeated refusals to call a constituent
assembly. A labor activist with a Peronist background later came
to the harsh conclusion that: "The workers' association had
become another dead-end street that, like the Socialist and Com-

munist parties, was gladly accepted by imperialism; it sidetracked the few rebellious impulses that might crop up."[16] In the meantime, the general condition of the labor movement during the first years of the thirties may be summed up in the words of Juan José Real, who gives us a view of the other side.

> The labor union movement. . . , with the exception of the transportation organizations — railroad workers, locomotive engineers, and streetcar unions — only enrolled in its ranks a minority of the working class. The industrial unions — the metallurgical, textile, meat, and foodstuffs unions — contributed a small number of active members. The sugar industry workers were wholly disorganized; the rural workers' unions — unions of various trades — comprised small minorities. It was only after the 1935 strike that the construction union finally organized the majority of the trade under the leadership of militant Communists. The lumber industry was also organized after the dissolution of the Class Committee. However, in 1935 the industrial proletariat reached a figure of 534,000 workers; the agricultural sector had 800,000. Factionalism due to opposed (and sometimes irreconcilable) tendencies was added to disorganization. This factionalist struggle prevailed over every other preoccupation, including the main one of the union movement, that is, the organization and defense of socioeconomic interests. The dissolution of the Union Committee for Class Solidarity [Communist in ideology] contributed to the formal unity of the workers organized under the GCL, but the ideological struggle, though somewhat diminished, was carried over into the bosom of the workers' confederations.[17]

Around 1935 the situation began to be untenable for many of the unions affiliated with the GCL. The clamor from the rank and file made clear the opposition to the indefinite tenure of leaders who had not even been democratically elected to their posts. Then:

> . . . on 12 December 1935, in view of the intolerable situation prevailing in the labor organization, the most important members, the Railroad Union, the Locomotive Engineers, the Commercial White Collar Workers' Confederation, the Streetcar Union, the Municipal Workers' Union, and the State Workers' Association decided to depose the Central Committee of the GCL and took over its secretariats.[18]

The new Executive Board they set up was entrusted with completing the task of bringing together "the congress of the Confederation that had been convoked by the deposed authorities, but was
presided over by the ones self-appointed on the memorable night
of 12 December." At the same time, another division occurred in
the labor movement; a sector displeased with the manner in which
matters were being handled installed itself in the headquarters of
the Federation of Telephone Workers and Employees (located on
Catamarca Street 577, from which they were to take their name)
and in 1937 they reorganized the old Argentine Labor Union
(ALU), which held its first Congress in 1939. According to Sebas-
tian Marotta, "it was also the last. The tragic consequences of the
events of June 1943 within a short time brought about its disappearance. With it disappeared the last expression of an autonomous and independent union movement."[19]

To return to the GCL, its Constituent Assembly was finally held
on 30 March and 1 and 2 April 1936; it repudiated the conduct of
the deposed leaders, approved the activities of the provisional
Board and the by-laws of GCL, introducing some amendments in
the draft under discussion.[20] Iscaro explains that:

> At the time this constituent assembly of the GCL was held,
> there were important organized sectors in the union movement
> *even though the greater part of the immense urban and rural*
> *working masses was still unorganized.* The number of unions
> was less than it had been fifteen years earlier; of course, this was
> due to the transformation of the small trade unions into large
> industrial unions, a change that took place by virtue of the very
> process of industrial concentration and centralization.[21]

The new authorities were appointed on 10 June 1937. José
Domenech was the secretary general and the list of members of
the Executive Committee included such well-known names as
those of Angel Borlenghi and Francisco Pérez Leirós, whose subsequent careers were very different. The statement of objectives
restated the usual topics:

> Forty-hour week and paid annual vacations; establishment of
> mixed commissions in each industry to determine periodically
> wages and work rotation; minimum salary, job security and
> seniority for workers employed by the government and by pub-
> lic entities; enforcement of social legislation; national unem-
> ployment, disability, and old-age insurance; maintenance of the
> reforms of the Commercial Code approved by Congress. [Law
> 11,129]

Graciela Biagini, in analyzing a declaration by the GCL (18 February 1938) with reference to the transfer of presidential power (in which statements such as these were made: "We do not harbor any fear of lack of understanding of the spirit of social justice on the part of the president-elect"), comes to the conclusion that:

> ... it is the only [declaration]. . . that the GCL was to make publicly on the government and its conduct during the whole period. In it Justo's administration is criticized, but the interesting thing is that this criticism comes up now, when this administration ends, not at the moment when it would have been advisable to attempt to change and channel the attitude of the government. The activity of the GCL is again channeled, less pronouncedly, in the direction it projected before the events of December 1935. It confined itself to addressing circular letters to the unions and to the government. The number of activities organized by that organization decreased. [22]

In this way we come to the First Congress of the GCL, which took place on 13-15 July 1939.

> Militant Communist union members took an important part: they contributed to extending and giving impetus to the organization of the GCL throughout the country. The Congress discussed especially the situation of the workers in the meat-packing plants, in construction, textiles, *yerba mate* and sugar mills, who "are subjected to inhuman exploitation, with absolute disregard of labor legislation." It undertook the defense of Law 11,729, the work of women and minors, accident prevention, the forty-hour week, and others. Finally, on the motion of militant Communists, a resolution was passed entrusting to the leadership of the GCL the taking of joint measures with the ALU and other organizations for the purpose of working toward union within a single national association for the whole country. [23]

Despite the concrete proposals made by the ALU for the purpose of attempting to find points in common that would possibly lead to the achievement of unity, the GCL postponed action on the matter, giving only vague answers to any proposals for union. The Congress, in addition to approving a general declaration of democratic principles ("To reaffirm its most absolute adherence to democratic institutions and to express its intention of defending them everywhere. To express its firm purpose of working in favor of the fullest freedom of the press and of speech, assembly, and association. . .") acknowledged that the workers' organization had been unable to display greater activity because of the undue intervention of the authorities charged with public order, the unfavorable economic situation of the country, and the limited financial resources of the GCL, and approved some amendments to the by-laws.

In July 1940, (needless to say, the war was extending its influence over a large part of the globe) the GCL addressed the government on the subject of labor unemployment and the high cost of living in order to present a program for action that would offset these conditions. Among other things, the GCL proposed:

Construction of public works, especially those that will produce income or avoid payment of rents; development of national industries and increase in production, avoiding exorbitant profits; increase in international trade; facilities for the purchase or lease of lands; abolition of taxes on essential articles; and representation of the GCL on the agency created by Law 12,591. [24]

Around that time the Communists were struggling to strengthen the union association through setting a goal of "one million members" for the GCL. They did this with growing enthusiasm after the invasion of the Soviet Union by Nazi Germany. The one million mark was surpassed within a very few years, but through a totally different approach. A well-known Communist militant has explained the motives that led the labor union sector of the Communist party to support the policy of unity:

From 1940 to 1943 the Communists fought within the union movement to establish the unity of the working class as the main factor that would contribute to speeding up the process of democratic and antifascist consolidation and prevent our country's being drawn into the war on the side of the Rome-Berlin-Tokyo Axis, as the majority of those who later carried out the 4 June 1943 military coup d'état intended.

Again, as we have already had occasion to point out throughout this study, the international aspects filled the minds of many labor-unionists (and of many politicians). In the interval, the country continued to wait. The state of siege decreed by Castillo and the apparently complaisant attitude of a certain sector of the GCL leadership toward the policy of the chief executive are facts that help explain why the Central Committee of the GCL (an organ on which the Communists had some delegates who stubbornly persisted in asking for measures favorable to the breaking off of relations with the Axis countries) did not meet for two years, though the by-laws required that it meet every four months.

It was not until 13 October 1942 that the leadership of the GCL finally met, after repeated demands from Communist members and after Domenech's overweening power and his un-democratic methods had raised up a repudiation movement against him and he was booed at every public gathering where he appeared.

Note that after two years without a meeting, the resolution the Central Committee adopted was to petition the executive branch "to break off relations with Germany, Italy, and Japan, and with all those countries that in one way or another contribute to the maintenance of such systems of government."

On 15 December 1942, the Second GCL Congress commenced its sessions. The election of the officers showed that the Dome-nech group, supported mainly by the Railroad Union, was in the minority with regard to the rest of the delegates. Angel Borlenghi was elected chairman of the Congress. Among the resolutions the assembly approved was one stating that:

The GCL is beyond any partisan electoral or political interest, since it comprises within its ranks, without distinction as to ideologies, all the producers. It possesses the conditions essen-tial to promoting the national unity of all the political and economic sectors of the Republic that are ready to reestablish the electoral honesty that will make the leadership of the state accessible to the representatives of the authentic majorities that will guarantee the rule of constitutional public liberties for all the inhabitants of the country...[25]

A list of demands was also included: (1) to recommend that the CC [Central Committee] intensify the campaign of demonstrations against the high cost of living, denouncing the illicit activities of profiteers and the obvious unconcern of public officials in this connection; (2) to stimulate the working class struggle for the immediate achievement of an increase in wages; (3) to obtain speedy approval of the congressional proposals tending to establish a minimum wage for all the workers of the country; (4) to contin-ue to strive with the proper authorities for representation of GCL on the agency created by Law 12,591.

There was much activity before the election of the new Central Committee could take place, especially as a result of the changes that had taken place in recent years in the internal political background of the unions that made up the GCL. Iscaro describes them as being as follows early in 1943, at the time of the change in officers: "Communist: construction, lumber, meat, metallurgical, printing. Socialist: commercial white-collar workers, municipal workers, state workers, locomotive engineers. Labor Unionists: railroad, streetcar, and beer."[26] When the time came to elect the new CCC, two slates were submitted labeled No. 1 (headed by José Domenech) and No. 2 (by Francisco Pérez Leirós) for voting purposes. The agreements entered into before-hand seemed to assure Domenech's reelection, since he had been able to obtain formal commitments of support from half plus one of the delegates. In the voting, the Domenech slate was defeated by one vote: someone did not live up to the "deal."[27] Then the inevitable happened; sanctions were applied to the rebel leader, new elections were called; and the opposition slate refused to accept the anomalous situation. This meeting produced two GCLs, known as No. 1 and No. 2. The railroad, streetcar, and beer unions were the most important ones in the No. 1 GCL, while No. 2 had the National Federation of Construction Workers, the Locomotive Engineers, the Printers' Federation, the Federation of Commercial White-Collar Workers, the Foodstuffs Federation, the National Metallurgical Federation, the Municipal Workers' Union, the Government Workers' Federation and the Sole Union of Lumber Industry Workers.

This was the situation of what might be called the "official" labor movement on the eve of the 4 June military coup. Attention must be called to the fact that everything was not as straightforward as this account of events might seem to indicate. In addition to the statements made and the various administrative activities, the cliques that perpetuated the leaders in office, and the political rivalries that sometimes were extremely bitter, the period offers numerous examples of the combativeness of large sectors of the Argentine working class. Some of them were beginning to display two diverging views within the labor movement: the one that followed traditional tendencies has been discussed in this chapter; the other formed a nucleus for the workers that were to prove susceptible to the social and political phenomenon labeled "Peronism" for mere expository convenience. This group was itself to have considerable influence on that movement and after 1943 was to be the predominant sector in the history of union activities. From his own viewpoint, Alberto Belloni has given the following brief account of these opposing approaches:

Two well-differentiated wings were discernible among the workers at that time [1943]. Though the distinction has grown less
apparent, it has not been overcome even now. The old minority
sector, which had sprung from European immigration and had
always had Buenos Aires for its base of operations, was entrenched within some anemic unions. Their outlook was anarchis-
tic, "syndicalistic," and international. They were frozen within
the molds of classical reformism and led by an old bureaucracy.
With the exception of the few anarchists in the plumbers and
port workers trade unions, and a few others, the major part of
this sector was to be found in the public service unions such as
the gas, transportation, state, and printing and commercial
white collar workers' unions. Many of these workers belong to
the ranks of the old Argentine "social democracy": the Socialist
party. . . . This sector of the working class for decades was typical
of the Argentine labor movement, giving it an abstract schematic image. Unfortunately, the imperialists made use of this equiv-
ocal stand.

The other wing of the Argentine labor movement is made up
of the flow of the native youth, descendants of *Criollos* and the
gauchos of the *montoneras,* who descend on Buenos Aires.
They are the ones who are driven by the lack of housing to
erecting the so-called *Villas Miseria.* Their strong arms become
skillful on coming into contact with machinery and mechanical
tools. They possess a virgin intelligence, without great experience
or awareness of their place as a class within modern society.
Even the tradition of their forebears has been broken by the
victory of the Buenos Aires oligarchy that had devastated the
interior. Isolated in their backlands, facing away from the
nation, forgotten, disregarded by the capital city minority that
monopolized everything, they possess a great resilience that
when released shows the true visage of our people that has been
muffled for the last eighty years. The strength of these men
came from the very bowels of the earth and of the Argentine
people, and this enables them to set a new national course.[28]

Disregarding a certain bucolic idealism that does not affect the
core of the problem, this account describes a situation that seems
basic to an understanding of the process under consideration. During the 1930-1943 period numerous strikes took place, but an
account of them does not lie within the area of our central interest. We might mention by way of example those strikes of the
streetcar and agricultural workers (1932), that of the telephone

operators that same year, that of the lumber industry workers
(1934), that of the construction workers (which lasted ninety-six
days in 1936), that of the private bus drivers (1942).[29] The metallurgical workers' strike in 1942 merits special mention because of
the significance it had in itself and because of the confrontation it
involved between the old-line leadership (at the time controlled by
Communists such as Muzio Girardi) and the new unionists who set
up a separate organization.[30] It is no accident that this union soon
became one of the most fervent supporters of the labor policy
Colonel Perón initiated as secretary of labor and welfare. According to the official Comunist party view, the situation during this
interval was as follows:

... Since the working class organized in unions included in the
GCL had not taken part in the movement for democratic unity
because of its supposedly "apolitical" Socialist leaders, who
were reform- and syndicalist-minded; since certain Radical and
Socialist leaders concerned themselves more with deciding questions of electoral supremacy than with building up an antifascist
fighting front; and since the other democratic and antifascist
forces did not take into account the repeated warnings that our
Party had given of the danger of coups-d'état, the military and
civilian profascist conspirators were able to prepare and carry
out their coup-d'état and seize power on 4 June 1943.[31]

The Communists persisted in this attitude during the 1943-1946
period. From this stand to membership in the Democratic Union
there was but one step. Must we add that that step was taken and
very enthusiastically, too? Again we turn to Graciela Biagini for a
summary of the stages in the ossification process that overtook the
leading elites of the GCL. She says that:

... the GCL leaders continued to call themselves representatives
of the working class, but in reality their position at the top kept
them from seeing the problems of that class, since they were
not in touch with the rank and file except through interme-
diaries as a result of the bureaucratization process that had
come about because of the association's growth. The interme-
diaries could for various reason, both of a personal and of an
ideological or party nature, distort the rank and file's aspirations. The process of oligarchization had also taken the form of
resistance on the part of the reform leaders to the admittance of
new unions.[32]

This was the situation on the eve of events that were to be important in the political history of Argentina, as well as in union annals; that is, the relations between the laboring masses and Colonel Perón, as they exemplified an ideology and a technique.

The labor movement in critical years: Perón and the masses

We have already alluded to many of the questions involved in this complex problem of the masses who find a "charismatic" leader and the interaction of the two. In many ways the terminology used by Max Weber, though it has been much overworked by some social scientists, is useful in trying to understand this phenomenon. We preferred to devote a place to this question when we gave a survey of Argentine sociopolitical history (see chapter 4), since we believe that the separate presentation of certain specific aspects does not help to make things any clearer unless preceded by a view of the whole. We believe this to be the case here, so we first warned of the active presence of a sector relatively unnoticed until then (except when occasionally it made the front-page of newspapers, as it did during the "Tragic Week" under the Yrigoyen administration and on some other similar occasions) and we placed it within the total framework of the political events we tried to outline. Now it is time to be more specific in order to help clear up a scene usually painted in the exaggerated colors of partisan politics or pamphleteering; some overlapping is probably unavoidable. For labor unionists of the old school such as Sebastián Marotta, everything was touchingly simple:

The government subtly, *through decrees granting the workers fulfillment of long-held aspirations,* gradually captured the sympathy of some and the adherence of others. These decrees imposed payment for official holidays to the workers, granted them ten and fifteen days paid vacations, a right that had been denied them by employers despite the fact that Law 11,729 was in effect; the payment of a supplementary one-month salary under the guise of a Christmas bonus; the extension of social security to blue- and white-collar workers excluded until then. *What workers in other countries had been achieving through their actions was here granted by mere decree. . . .* In their eyes the government appeared as the moving force creating a new social reality. Henceforth the blue- and white-collar workers were to concern themselves only with "going from their homes to work and from their work to their homes." Some militants facilitated the governmental maneuver. Thus, the unions ceased to express the will of the workers. The lack of class spirit, on the one hand, and on the other, the material conditions under which the workers lived due to the employer's sordidness and lack of understanding, contributed to the success of these government objectives.[33]

Things were actually considerably more complicated. If we disregard the needs that the masses, *actually* felt and which the labor leaders, whether of the GCL or of other associations, did not even remotely satisfy and reduce everything to the easy game of the demagogue (viewed by some as a sort of Pied Piper of Hamelin with military trimmings) and his faithful followers, we run a grave risk of understanding almost nothing or next to nothing.

From the beginning of the government that resulted from the 4 June 1943 military coup, Perón and his team perceived the enormous reserves of power available by marshalling the support of the massive labor sectors. They were also aware of the constant internal strife and the occasional lack of representation existing among most of the unions affiliated with the GCL.

Going back to the two labor organizations existing before 4 June 1943, GCL No. 1 (Domenech) after the coup expressed its support of the government measures tending to curb the maneuvers that increased the cost of living for the people. It did not protest the closing of the Communist labor union quarters, nor the arrest of Communist leaders. GCL No. 2 (Pérez Leirós) was dissolved by the de facto authorities. The unions affected put on shows of strength.

In the month of August [1943], the Railroad Union and the Locomotive Engineers Union were intervened militarily. On the twenty-seventh of the same month the Executive Committee of GCL No. 1 resolved, in view of these interventions and of the meaning that the withdrawal of its members had for the Confederation, to give up its executive functions and appoint three trustees for the funds, pointing out that "the organizations that have not been affected by the said government measure can decide whether or not to continue this Confederation." The remaining unions decided to reconstitute the Central Committee "for the purpose of carrying on the union activities of the Confederation." The new members elected in the constituent assembly of the CCC on 11 September were: Secretary General, Ramón Seijas; Associate Secretary, Alcides Montiel; Executive Secretary, Alfredo Fidanza; Treasurer, Enrique Porto; Assistant Treasurer, Juan Pardo. This board was made up of a majority of

Socialist militants, many of whom later went over to Peronism.[34]

This fact has been confirmed by, among others, former Communist Real when he referred to the activities of the new Secretary of Labor and Welfare (whose department, as we know, was created on 27 November 1943):

Meeting followed meeting almost daily [between Perón] and labor leaders, and soon he found in some of them a favorable response to his propositions; on the other hand, he came up against the resistance of the leaders with Communist, anarchist, or Socialist tendencies. However, some of the latter, Borlenghi, Tesorieri, and others among them, then began to collaborate. Lt. Col. Domingo Mercante, the son of a railroad worker, was appointed interventor of both railroad organizations. There he found a nucleus that supported him in his task. Ample concessions were made to the railroad workers, printers, commercial white-collar workers, oil industry workers and other unionized workers. To these must be added a measure of some importance, the decrease in rents and later their freezing (Decree 6141/44).[35]

The state of mind of many workers at this time with regard to the policies openly favored by the administration is reflected in the following excerpt written by metallurgical worker Angel Perelman:

In 1944 we began to notice incredible things in our union work: labor laws not enforced before were now being enforced; there was no need to resort to the courts to obtain vacations; other labor provisions, such as the recognition of plant delegates, guaranties that they would not be dismissed, and so on, were immediately and strictly enforced. The nature of the internal relations between the employers and the personnel of the plants had changed completely. Internal democratization that we had established at the metallurgical workers' union had resulted in the plant delegates' becoming the hub of the whole organization and the direct expression of the workers' will in each establishment. The employers were as disconcerted as the workers were amazed and happy. The Secretariat of Labor and Welfare had become a factor in the organizational development and support of the working class. It did not operate as a state regulating agency that was above the classes within the union structure; it acted as a state ally of the working class. These were the actual circumstances that provided the background for the political choice made by the Argentine masses and manifested in the streets on 17 October 1945.[36]

Some of the elements in the process that led Colonel Perón to take an interest in the union movement have been summarized by Jorge Abelardo Ramos from his own point of view:

Without decreasing the intensity of the repressive action toward Socialist and Communist union elements, Colonel Perón fostered the formation of new leaders who later identified with his policies; he divided the unions where he could not detach them from their corrupt leaders; sponsored new ones where there were none; and encouraged the formation of large industry-wide federations that for the first time comprised millions of workers. Relying on the wave of war prosperity, he granted wide economic improvements to the sectors being mobilized, creating a structure of social laws that the proletariat made its own and got ready to defend. . . . Colonel Perón sought to achieve various objectives at the same time: to sweep out labor parties discredited within the labor movement, to create a popular base for himself, and at the same time subordinate labor organizations to the tutelage of the state. It must again be kept in mind that the earlier union movement, to which the large new sectors of the working masses did not belong, had for decades been under the influence of imperialism and its agents. Perón's policy, based on the triumphant expansion of industry, found its most unexpected support in the treason of the old parties and in the momentum given the struggle for union organization by the high labor occupational index.[37]

During these various stages, some of the leftist sectors showed signs of an alarming confusion vis-à-vis the new setup, a confusion that soon led them to contradictory attitudes. For example, Rubens Iscaro, writing in 1958, had this to say:

Immediately after assuming power, the de facto government drew up its plans to achieve control of the union movement. The then Col. Juan Domingo Perón called the labor leaders together at the Ministry of War to find out "how the workers were going to cooperate with the government." *The GCL leaders, formerly docile to the oligarchical Castillo government, showed themselves also docile to the government of the dictatorship.* They promised their cooperation in exchange for retaining their jobs. At the same time, the Secretariat of Labor and Welfare was beginning to attract labor leaders, both from the GCL and the ALU and the unions directed by the Socialists, *as well as from the parallel unions created with the support of that Secretariat.* [38]

These "parallel unions" are among the most important keys for an analysis of the Argentine labor problem during those years; if the incomprehension of the phenomenon found in contemporary accounts may be questioned, then it seems excessively indulgent not to comment on the judgments expressed almost fifteen years later. As so happens, those "parallel unions" were precisely the ones that held the working masses during those decisive moments; the others were left with their "leaders" and their traditional mental attitudes. The Communist party (it was not the only one, but it is mentioned by way of example) for some time had been struggling to bring about the Democratic Union, and it subordinated all its efforts, especially those in the labor field, to this end. Thus, we find that:

Also, the Democratic Union coalition, in uniting the Radical, Socialist, Progressive Democrat, and Communist parties, had the support of the independent unions, part of the peasants' organizations, and most of the democratic intelligentsia. This coalition was the result of common positions held earlier in the struggle against the military-fascist dictatorship and for a return to a democratic regime; against the profascist "neutralist" policy of the military governments that followed one another from 1943 on and for participation of the country on the side of the United Nations, in order to thrust our country toward a democratic and progressive outcome, so that, once the German-fascist hordes and their satellites were defeated, Argentina could participate in the construction of a better world. For this reason, *the formation of this coalition aroused great enthusiasm among the working class and the people* and opened up the possibility of winning the elections. [39]

As may be seen, there is not one single reference to raising the standard of living of the masses or to the concrete problems of national reality (save, perhaps, the allusion to the "return to a democratic regime") that might make intelligible to the people the "democratic and progressive outcome," that was desired. Elsewhere, in attempting to explain the electoral results of 1946, the assertion is made that:

Almost on the eve of the elections, realizing that the electoral balance was tipping toward the Democratic Union, Perón used the government to issue a series of decrees that fulfilled some of the workers' old demands (Christmas bonus, promises of profit-sharing, and so forth). This, added to the lack of revolutionary fervor with which certain sectors of the parties that made up the Democratic Union coalition carried on their propaganda, caused the upset in the electoral balance in favor of the Peronist coalition.[40]

The events that led to 17 October 1945 and subsequent political developments up to the election that ratified the choice of the Perón-Quijano presidential team, have been outlined on pp. 90-96 and 102-110 of this book, and we refer the reader to them. We believe that this brief account of the passing scene indicates the manner in which the labor movement was really incorporated into the political process from about the end of 1943.

Addendum

The problem of the labor unions and their relation to politics (specifically to Perón and the movement that later became known by his name) lies much beyond the chronological limits of this book. Suffice it to point out here that the Labor party (founded on 24 October 1945) and its later developments (Sole Party of the National Revolution and Peronist Party) as well as the opposition course that some of the initial leaders later followed (Cipriano Reyes, for example) have not been the subject of the detailed study they merit in works that should have treated the problem.[41]   Referring to the party, Belloni has said that:

The Labor party was the first national party of the organized working class, the turn-out into its ranks was massive and covered the whole country, and it was based on the unions. It came about as the product of repeated contacts that the union leaders had been maintaining since 1943, and that had set up a sort of interunion organization outside the leadership of the central labor associations.

Its program was based on the following; recovery of public services and basic industries; elimination of the latifundia and the partition of land; converting property to social ownership; tax on income, land, and inheritance; workers' participation in the profits of enterprises; full social welfare. The Labor party leaders came from all labor fields and from being union leaders they became the new political chiefs of the militant proletariat. They were Luis F. Gay, Telephone Union; Cipriano Reyes, Meat

Packers and others such as Monsalvo, Montiel, Argaña, Cleve, Andreotti, Garófalo, Ponce, Pérez, Tejada, and many more who until the day before had been socialists, syndicalists, and anarchists.[42]

Other authors, instead of searching out the causes that brought about such a grouping and the crisis in the traditional parties, prefer the comfortable way of gossip and jest. It is in this spirit that Reynaldo Pastor, who was a conspicuous figure within national conservative ranks, writes:

It was essential to set forth briefly the process of integration of that rowdy column which its creator christened with his own surname, in an innocuous display of personal aggrandizement, without doctrinaire transcendence. It has been called "the deluge," without this implying accepting the adjective "zoological" that cost the spirited Radical Deputy Sammartino his seat as a congressman. Besides, there is no need to offend the national fauna.[43]

Another example is *Ayer fue San Perón* by the versatile Raúl Damonte Taborda.

In otherwise valuable books, the emotional *parti pris* of the respective authors prevents their seeing all the aspects of a given situation clearly. We will end these practically random gleanings from our reading by giving an excerpt from Alfredo Galletti, who, in commenting on the events of 17 October 1945, says emphatically that:

It is obvious that the highest level of demagoguery had been reached, nearly unsurpassable. The heterogeneous mass (which was not only a *lumpenproletariat* in Marxist terms, but something more) felt itself in some way understood since it had been addressed in such language; in short, they were the good sort of people who grow emotional over the facile lyrics of a tango and who long for the stilled voice of their favorite singer [Carlos Gardel]. . . .[44]

To these deficiencies in interpretation are added those opinions (some of them presumably authoritative since they come from specialists in the field of political science and sociology) which in analyzing "Peronism" suggest basic identification with European totalitarian movements, something that, in our opinion, is not very convincing. For example, as prominent an author as Seymour M. Lipset does not hesitate to call Peronism the "fascism of the lower class." [45] With this he only succeeds in confusing the concepts still further. Arthur P. Whitaker, perhaps aiming at too thorough a synthesis, prefers to view matters from this other angle:

> We must be careful, however, not to exaggerate the extent of Perón's borrowings from abroad. These were heavy in matters of technique and organization, particularly in the fields of propaganda and control of labor, but he used them to strengthen a system deeply rooted in his understanding of the history of his own country and in his own observations of the successive regimes of Irigoyen, Uriburu, and the Conservative Restoration. He found in Rosas his slogan of discipline and order, and the strong-arm squads of the *Mazorca* to support it; in Rosas and Irigoyen a fervent nationalism spiced with anti-imperialism; in Irigoyen the popularity of attacks on the oligarchy; in Uriburu the Army's mission of national regeneration; and in the Conservative Restoration the demoralization of the chief political parties and the abandonment of laissez faire in favor of economic controls. [46]

We believe that any discussion in these terms is worthless, as are the indiscriminate praises by recent panegyrists. In our judgment, the point from which we must start has been summarized by Carlos S. Fayt in these words: "With Peronism the working masses and strata of the Argentine proletariat come upon the scene. *The Argentine worker acquires a social status and a share of the wealth and the political power until then unknown.*" [47] This author goes on to explain that all this was achieved "at the price of its liberty." Ezequiel Martínez Estrada, commenting apocalyptically on 17 October, seems to place things in their proper perspective when he asks in connection with the "subproletariat of poor workers": "*How can we reproach him for not feeling the loss of his liberty and dignity when he had never had them?*" [48]

10 Past and Present

Balance Sheet

The first part of this work attempted to give a condensed account of what had happened in Argentina between the years 1930 and 1946. Using the surnames of each period's principal figure, the four chapters in that section were entitled respectively "Uriburu," "Justo," "Ortiz-Castillo," and "Perón" and were intended to refresh the reader's memory by citing episodes illustrative of certain trends or developments. In the present chapter we will recapitulate certain constants typical of the period.

Chapter 1 deals with the overthrow of the Yrigoyen government by a military conspiracy and with how the conspiracy had been precipitated by civilian activities such as Conservative, Antipersonalist Radical, and Independent Socialist agitation as well as by the tolerance or neutrality shown by other groups. This tactical and strategic lesson has been repeated in contemporary Argentine history, but in the end the armed forces have been the final beneficiaries. The deterioration of the old *caudillo* and his administration was also analyzed, as was the work done by Uriburu – promises versus accomplishments – during his tenure of office and the pressures that led to the *Concordancia,* imposing Justo's candidacy. Formally, this led to the triumph of the Conservative restoration vis-à-vis the possibility of a corporate state that the nationalists and General Uriburu himself had already started to dream about.

Chapter 2 deals with the economic dependence of Argentina on its British metropolis and with the juridical aspects of this dependence ("the legal expression of colonialism"). The meat problem held a preferential place in the imperialist complex. Emphasis was also laid on the industrial growth evident and measurable at least since 1935 and on some concomitant and interrelated phenomena such as internal migrations, the emergence of new professional specializations, the geographic and industrial concentration in the coastal area and especially in metropolitan Buenos

Aires. During this period certain "preconditions" of what in the next decade was to be Peronism became evident. James W. Rowe, a keen foreign observer, lists these preconditions as being the nationalist reaction, internal migrations, and union organization prior to Perón, all elements that have been dealt with in this· book.[1]

Fraud — manipulation of elections, federal intervention of certain provinces, legislative approval of fraudulent credentials — is the other outstanding characteristic of the period under consideration up to 1943, in addition to domestic and foreign economic privileges. After 4 June, the government was at first dominated by the Catholic nationalists, but later Colonel Perón, supported by key military and labor sectors, consolidated his power as the outstanding leader within the regime. However, stress was placed on the political skepticism during the thirties of large sectors of the Argentine people who had witnessed the Radicals' abstention up to 1935 and their later acceptance of participation within the system imposed from the top, the recurring violence (the uprisings, the murders of Guevara and Bordabehere) and the placing of the country in a position of virtual vassalage to Britain.

The *Concordancia* early crossed swords with a respectful opposition in Congress made up of Socialists and Progressive Democrats, the Civil Alliance having been defeated in 1931. The Socialist and Progressive Democratic parties knew that they benefited from the abstention of the Radicals as far as the number of seats they occupied was concerned and through holding those seats they thought they would be able to counteract the excesses of the regime. When the Alvear Radicals gained a governorship (in Córdoba Province) and reentered the electoral picture, they were the principal opponents of the *Concordancia*. However, again thanks to well-organized fraud, the Ortiz-Castillo ticket defeated the Alvear-Mosca team. The leader of the Radicals was in the end the chief victim of the system in which he had agreed to participate.

At the international level this was the high point of the American Good Neighbor policy, formally accepted at the Montevideo (1933) and Buenos Aires (1936) Conferences by all the nations of the hemisphere. Although Argentina continued to look to Great Britain, it was already becoming more directly aware of its position within the inter-American world, an awareness that was to intensify with the beginning of World War II. It was this widespread conflict that lent the Ortiz-Castillo government (chapter 3) its characteristic quality, since the war aggravated previously existing conditions (some had started to be felt at the time of the 1929 crisis) such as the crisis in exports and in state finances, the industrialization to make up for the lack of imports, the domestic market affected by the lack of imported products, the need to keep the British market open for Argentine grains, wool, meat, and hides. [2]

Political disintegration was evident and reflected especially in the collective bodies that claimed to represent public interests, such as the Municipal Council of the capital, and in the scandal of the electrical concessions endorsed in 1941 by a resolution of the Chamber of Deputies. This resolution was signed by both Conservatives and Radicals, in an attempt to clear those implicated in that doubtful business of any guilt or responsibility. The fact that the SOFINA international monopoly gave generous financial support to *both* the 1937 presidential contenders (Ortiz and Alvear), as was documented by the Rodríguez Conde report, is a case in point.

The bankruptcy of the Conservative restoration was made clear by the disagreements that disturbed the relations of Ortiz and his team-mate. Although we do not share their opinion, many authors believe that this demonstrates a lingering "democratic" urge on the part of the ailing president, which did not manifest itself in other fields such as economics and social welfare. Alvear himself only desired more or less free elections that would allow him to return to power, but his own economic ideas did not go beyond a utopian return to the "outward growth" that the country had experienced between 1880 and 1914. [3]

Surprisingly, the Socialists won a majority of the Chamber of Deputies seats allocated to the national capital in the 1942 elections. This can be considered a repudiation by the majority of the Buenos Aires voters of the *Concordancia* and of the Radicals' policy of acting as "His Majesty's loyal opposition." However, it was too late. "Deals" and corruption in the administration were the usual order of business. Castillo, first as vice-president acting for Ortiz and later as president, attempted to patch things up during the 1940-1942 period, but without abandoning his favorite political prescription for governing, the "unanimity of one" (Castillo himself), a revised and enlarged version of the solo-show of Julia A. Roca and Miguel Juárez Celman in the late nineteenth century. He fostered the merchant marine and nationalized the Port of Rosario while at the same time he closed the Buenos Aires Municipal Council, declared a state of siege, and in general earned the resentment of all the parties. In the international field, he developed his version of "neutrality," to which the so-called democratic forces applied the derogatory phrase "favorable to the Axis powers," which actually explained only one of the reasons for his attitude. The other one, of course, was his desire to keep open the channels for commercial communication with Britain and to attempt to build up better relations with the United States, at least until the latter entered the war on 7 December 1941. On 14 October 1941 the first commercial treaty between Argentina and the United States in ninety years was signed. The fluctuating relations among Argentina, the United States, and Great Britain, besides the Nazi penetration of South America, made understandable the difficulties of neutrality in a marginal and semi-dependent country.

Castillo had finally come to the conclusion that by periodic luncheons and leisurely speeches, he had won the goodwill of the armed forces — the army, really — toward his domestic and foreign policies. However, during this period the army decided that it would arrogate to itself the decisions which it considered more appropriate to the current state of the war. The conflict was approaching its turning point and a German victory no longer seemed as certain and inevitable (except to the fanatical military partisans of the Axis and to the noisy nationalist groups) as it had during the period of the overwhelming *blitzkrieg*. On 4 June 1943, the praetorian guard seized direct control. the "power behind the power" had become simply the political power. The army ruled.[4]

The decisive years between 1943 and 1946 (chapter 4) continue to be very significant for those studying Argentine contemporary problems, especially in order to avoid the pitfalls presented by the recurrence of the same problems under different conditions. Erratically and sometimes contradictorily, the 1943 de facto regime alternately issued statements influenced by Catholic nationalism and attended to the concrete demands of the popular sectors. All the political parties without exception took notice only of the first phenomenon and ignored the second. This blurred their perspective, already somewhat wearied by the various phases of the war. Emphasizing abstract slogans of the "democracy vs. nazifascism" type (which made sense on an international level) and their domestic repercussions was not enough to explain completely the complexity of the Argentine situation, which required attention to its own needs and its own solutions.[5] The efforts to form the Democratic Union (to a great extent a projection of the antinazi and antifascist struggle) did not include also paying attention, for example, to the emergence of a new type of workers' party such as the Labor Party (which was to be one of the main

pillars supporting Perón's electoral victory)[6] nor to understanding
the deep significance of the measures promoted by the ambitious
colonel from his Labor Ministry post, all of which went much farther than the facile opposition labels of demagoguery and opportunism took into account.

The October 1945 crisis brought the above two factions face to
face. On the one hand was the legalistic faction (which was to
reappear innumerable times later) whose principal idea was that
the government should be entrusted to the Supreme Court, as
though recourse to a legal technicality might work miracles in solv-
ing a burning issue, and on the other the until then unorganized
mass that demanded Perón's return to public life since it believed
that many of its demands could be articulated through him. The
strength of the second faction lay in the labor rank and file of the
industrial belt around the city of Buenos Aires, but it also had the
active support, or at least the acquiescence, of a certain sector of
the army and security forces.[7] The open intervention of the
American State Department in the Argentine political process
suited the designs of the Democratic Union; the Braden case is
merely an example among many.[8] Instead of producing the expected result, it strengthened the aggressive nationalism that Perón
flaunted during his political campaign.

The second part of this study is devoted to the principal actors
in this period of Argentine history. Chapter 5 deals in detail with
political parties and other political forces which in accordance
with the traditional theory of industrialized countries, such as
Great Britain and the United States, should be the dynamic agents
of the development process. It is our opinion that in Argentina things
happened in a very different way. First, the much discussed "Parliamentary crisis," common to all great nations with functioning
legislatures,[9] in Argentina seemed to be aggravated by both domestic and foreign factors such as the structure and organization
of the parties themselves, by electoral fraud, fraudulent credentials, the "crime in the Senate" (an incident that cannot be classi-
fied merely under the category of police news), the preponderance
of the executive branch as the head of a state that intervened progressively more and more in society, the spread of this crisis to
lower-level corporate bodies (the provincial legislatures and the
Buenos Aires Municipal Council), and the reaction that this parliamentary decay provoked in other sectors or pressure groups. All
this contributed to making the Congress fulfill its specific functions less effectively. The army, which closed Congress in 1930
and 1943, and the nationalists, who made it the butt of their

taunts and bitter tirades, prepared the climate of opinion that led
to the discrediting of the institution.

As we have already stated, the congressional crisis is also the
projection of the structural and ideological crisis of the political
parties themselves. After all, the Congress, the provincial legislatures, and the municipal councils should afford the most favorable
field for the activities of professional politicians, outside the
national or provincial executive branches. To prove our contention,
we presented in this chapter of the book the members of the *Concordancia* coalition (the Conservatives, the Anti-personalist Radicals, and the Independent Socialists), Alvear and his Radical
party, the Socialist party, and the Progressive Democratic party,
all of whom chose to participate in Congress during the "infamous
decade." In all cases, personalist and factionalist elements existed
within each group and ideological differences were more evident in
the general statements of objectives than in specific practical cases
where reversals of the official stands often occurred.[10] Divisions
and schisms are another constant characteristic, together with the
coalitions that actually took place or were merely proposed: the
attempts at a popular front, the union of the "law-abiding" parties, that is, the Radical party, the Progressive Democratic party
and the Socialist party, encouraged by the latter, the 1931 Civil
Alliance, and the efforts that finally culminated in the 1945
Democratic Union.[11] Argentine communism continued to orient
its work "toward the outside," that is, the external model of the
Soviet Union under Stalin continued to be a basic preoccupation,
and this tendency has been sharply criticized by Rodolfo Puiggrós.[12] Starting in 1935, the Communist party directed its best
efforts toward becoming integrated into a system that rejected it.
This included both the *Concordancia* and its congressional opposition.

The brief analyses also dealt with the FORJA movement, its
crucial position because it had originated within a party with a
popular background, its impotence because it could not form a
substantial autonomoous political group, and its dissolution when
faced with the newly emerging but still unorganized Peronist element; with the nationalists, who in their ultramontane and reactionary zeal were better able than most to detect the bankruptcy
of the political parties and the rise to power of the army; and with
the university movement, all of which seems to us to help round
off the picture of the "crisis of the political parties" during this
period. From this we went on to consider the political function of
certain pressure groups and power factors whose activities between

1930 and 1946 contribute to a better understanding of the reasons behind the party crisis. These were the army, the church, and the labor movement mobilized from the top by the state machinery. This means that other groups were taking the place of the parties in carrying out similar functions, as a result of party inactivity or stagnation. Consequently, though it is proper to speak of a crisis of the parties, it is also right and even imperative to refer at the same time to the *politicization* of the armed forces.

In accordance with this view, we focused on the church (chapter 6) in order to describe its tactics and activities in the political field, for we did not wish to resort to facile anticlericalism. Its *modus operandi* was different during the thirties and after 1943 (the date of the Catholic nationalist irruption into politics), but was always based on two themes; the opposition to divorce legislation and religious instruction in the schools. In general, it can be asserted that the church maintained cordial relations with all the goverments that succeeded each other during the 1930-1946 period and that it sought to improve its positions of influence. Two well-differentiated sectors are also to be found within the Catholic clergy in Argentina. One had fascist-falangist tendencies and the other (the minority one) was devoted to the so-called "social Catholicism" concepts — two wings of the same strategy, with the hierarchy as the final balancer.

The study of the armed forces (chapter 7) categorically confirms our thesis on the rise of pressure groups and power factors to carry out the functions that the parties should have performed. A glance at the history of the Argentine army between 1930 and 1946 proves the continuing political activity of the army as a whole or of characteristic sectors which took the lead in shaping events. This happened not only in the case of successful uprisings, but also throughout the whole period known as the "infamous decade." The professionalist doctrine fostered by Rodríguez justified having the army effectively guard the regime and become its sole disciplined base of support, other than the *Concordancia.* During this interval, industrialist tendencies emerged in the army. These stressed the need for heavy industry for "national defense," but also that as a by-product it might provide raw materials to middle-sized and small entrepreneurs. In fact, these groups took the place of the unresponsive industrial sectors, especially between 1943 and 1946, though the groundwork was laid in the preceding decade.[13] However, in the 1943-1946 period the army was already governing directly, as it had done in 1930 and was again to do in 1955, and ideological confrontations were common. The

GOU embodied the tradition of the military lodges [14] and became the first instrument for consolidating Perón, one of its members, in power.

The influence patiently exerted in previous years bore ephemeral fruit for oligarchical nationalism, which for a short time clambered back into office and then was left by the wayside. Here we need only repeat that Uriburu (though only relatively), Justo, and Perón are the three most important political figures of their period, and their background is well known.

The role of the economic groups (chapter 8) is perhaps the most familiar because of the extensive bibliography available on the subject. Their activities in channeling the political process are abundantly documented by authors of very different ideologies. In our chapter we only noted certain points bearing on the always current problem of imperialism, initially British and then American. This interplay continues to be another constant essential to the understanding of Argentine politics and economy; the country is at least physically part of South America, it is remote geographically from the Caribbean where the United States has been lord and master (at least until an exception occurred in Cuba in 1959), and since it gained its independence it has maintained special relations with Great Britain. We then mentioned very briefly some cases of tactics and techniques employed by privileged economic groups to influence or control a certain type of governmental decision, by means of direct agents or by outright bribery. We again brought up the example of the electric monopoly's continuing activity and (through the writings of the almost forgotten Ramón Doll) presented the phenomenon known as the "three-headed hydra: lawyer-judge-professor," both of which show the penetration of the large economic interests into other levels of society. We added a brief catalog of imperialist agents in government, without aiming at exhaustive treatment of the subject and a note on reinvestment between the agricultural-ranching and industrial groups.[15]

Chapter 9 is devoted to the labor movement. From 1930 until 1943, we witness on the one hand the formation and operation of a central labor organization (not always the only one) to unite the workers of the traditional branches of industry and, on the other, the emergence of new sectors as a result of industrial growth, internal migrations, and other factors, as well as the spectacle of the rural wage-earner ignored until the enactment of the "Statute of the Rural Worker." It was this forgotten worker who within a few years was to constitute a massive foundation for Peronism. These two trends developed separately. The first group believed that the other existed on the basis of handouts and lack of class awareness encouraged by the military government through its Secretariat of Labor; the second was profoundly disillusioned by the bureaucratization and the inactivity of organized labor groups such as the GCL (into which the Socialist and Communist parties carried their quarrels and their differences) and devoted itself, thanks to support from the top, to forming new unions, to taking over the existing ones or to forming "parallel unions" that by achieving exclusive union representation pushed the traditional trade unions out of the picture. The masses — and the army — supported the Peronist regime for ten year (1946-1955). But that is another story, one that urgently needs to be told again and to be cleared of the gratuituous accretions that have grown up about it and that make it difficult to separate facts from biased interpretations.[16]

Conclusions

What we are interested in doing in this section is to identify certain lines and trends that began to manifest themselves between 1930 and 1946, and during the last twenty-five years have projected themselves upon our political processes; that is, we wish to point out what the lessons of the thirties seem to be when viewed from our present vantage point and to indicate some of the most important consequences to be derived from them. Perforce, we cannot give a finished picture, but only a sketch. It is advisable, before taking up the main theme, to make certain statements about the branches of the government and the constitutional framework within which the play of the parties and of other groups of Argentine society should fit theoretically. We believe that this will bring about a better understanding of the crisis within which we are living at the beginning of the 1970s.

Some of the factors that explain this political crisis, a crisis that affects not only the parties but also large areas of the liberal system established by the Constitution of 1853, are to be sought in the increased functions of the state and especially (to establish a tentative date) from 1930, in the growing preeminence of the executive branch in relation to the other two branches, the legislative and the judicial. The decline of Congress and the Supreme Court can be clearly traced from 1930 up to the present. In the case of Congress, the well-known closing of that body in 1930 and 1943 was repeated in 1955, in 1962 (at which time the "representatives of the people" practically ceased to function after a few months of much-discussed maneuvers), and *sine die* in 1966. On each occa-

sion the time elapsed between closings becomes less as may be
seen from the following
> Between 1930 and 1943: 13 years
> Between 1943 and 1955: 12 years
> Between 1955 and 1962: 7 years
> Between 1962 and 1966: 4 years

The problem of how representative each Congress has been
should also be taken into account in evaluating the crisis of this
institution. These restrictions on representativeness include the
banning of Peronism from elections ever since 1955, the shift to
limited participation of that party in Congress during Illia's administration, the proportional representation system since 1963,[17]
and other factors, all relevant to the question. The short-lived
experiment with the National Advisory Board (1955-1957) indicated more than ten years ago just how serious the crisis was. Established by the military government and chaired by Adm. Isaac F.
Rojas, then the nation's vice-president, it sought to surround the
"Liberating Revolution" with a certain kind of popular backing by
means of advisers drawn from the various political parties with the
exception of Peronism and Communism. Toward the end of April
1957, "since the government did not have new matters to submit
to the Board, the body [entered] into a prolonged recess."[18]

The Supreme Court has continued, as in 1930 and 1943, to follow the conservative judicial line of accepting and validating *faits
accomplis* in the political field (especially those concerning de
facto governments or governments of force), perhaps with the
hope of thus assuring its own survival as a body and the often proclaimed "independence" of the Judicial Branch. However, this
process has acquired a different aspect in the last decades. First of
all, the justices of the Court (with the exception of Casares) were
removed from office by the Peronist legislative majority in 1947
through impeachment proceedings carried out with all due forma-
lities but with the obvious partisan intent of replacing those justices with supporters of the regime.[19] In 1955 the members of the
judicial branch had their tenure suspended and the justices of the
Supreme Court as a whole were removed from their posts and replaced. It was one of the first measures Lonardi took to "de-
Peronize" the judiciary. Shortly thereafter, the new magistrates
signed a decision legalizing the palace coup that raised Pedro Eugenio Aramburu on 13 November 1955 to the post of successor to
the September leader of the movement:

Buenos Aires, on the sixteenth day of the month of November, 1955, the Chief Justice of the Supreme Court of the Nation, Alfredo Orgaz, and Justices Manuel J. Argañarás, Enrique V. Galli, and Carlos Herrera, Jorge Vera Vallejo being absent on leave, and Attorney General Sebastián Soler meeting in extraordinary session in order to consider the communication addressed to this Court as of yesterday by the National Executive Branch, reporting that "the armed forces of the nation, which took charge of the government of the republic left vacant by the defeat of the tyranny, have entrusted to Gen. Pedro Eugenio Aramburu, as Provisional President, the mandate of the public government in order to carry out the revolutionary program for the reestablishment of the rule of law and the return of the country to an authentic democracy."

Whereas: As a result of the note received, the apointment of the person exercising the provisional presidency has been carried out without changing the objectives that the victorious revolution originally envisaged.

Whereas: said communication contains an express declaration that the office has been conferred in order to achieve the "reestablishment of the rule of law and the return of the country to an authentic democracy";

Whereas: this self-imposed limitation is in accordance with the terms of the oath taken by members of this Court, the Attorney General of the nation, and the lower courts, to carry out their duties "well and legally and in conformity with the principles, rights, and guarantees of the National Constitution";

Now, therefore, be it resolved: that the receipt of the said communication be acknowledged to the National Executive Branch, by means of a copy of this resolution.[20]

In 1962 there was a much-discussed intervention in politics by the highest tribunal of the land when it administered the oath of office as president of the nation to José María Guido (29 March) in order to resolve the very serious institutional situation brought about by the overthrow and subsequent arrest of President Arturo Frondizi by the armed forces' high command.[21] The Court decided the matter by referring to its traditional posture relative to "political or nonjudicial questions" (which it is not within its jurisdiction to consider since they appertain exlusively to the executive branch) and establishing that the "acephalous situation of the Republic" is obvious because of "the absence of any president and vice-president of the nation" and it does not behoove the Supreme

Court to pronounce decisions on the causes determining this "absence."[22] Even if these "causes" were an open armed insurrection against the national Constitution and its authorities!

However, it was on 28 June 1966, as a result of the so-called "Argentine Revolution," that the Supreme Court suffered the most obvious loss in recent times of its self-proclaimed "independence." Not only were the justices removed and replaced by others directly named by Lt. Gen. Juan Carlos Onganía,[23] but it was also decided that since the government was "under the obligation of being guided by what is prescribed by the Revolutionary Objectives, the Statute of the Revolution and the National Constitution, it is essential to have a Supreme Court whose members have sworn to respect those norms."[24] The decline of the judicial branch and of the very Constitution on which its decisions are based is obvious.

The executive branch has itself been growing stronger vis-à-vis the other two branches in various ways. Here we will only point out the proliferation of "decree-laws" whenever the Congress has not been functioning. For example, consider the profound changes introduced into legislation by the 1943-1946 and 1955-1958 military governments (in the case of the "Liberating Revolution," as we shall see later, the changes "by decree" even affected the Constitution). However, from 1966 on, "decree-laws" ceased to be known as such and became simply "laws." This implies a more far-reaching change than one of terminology alone, since it reflects the decline of the legislative bodies within the last few decades, as power has come to be concentrated in the executive branch.[25] What is abnormal (the issuing of "decree-laws" by the executive in emergency cases) becomes the normal (the executive issues its own "laws"). This seems to be one of the logical presumptions of the Onganía military regime.

The executive branch also has benefited from another significant change in terminology, which is the clear reflection of a manifest tendency toward administrative centralization and de facto unitarianism, which increases as time passes. What were always called "federal interventors" either under military governments or under the pertinent clauses of the Constitution, now become "governors" plain and simple. A "governor" *sui generis* of course, since the federal administration appoints him in complete disregard of provincial autonomy and of the principle of popular elections, which are basic requirements of even a modestly federalist system. The temporary and exceptional again becomes the "normal" under this concept of government.

The National Constitution has also had the scope of its application and its theoretical supremacy reduced. It was amended in 1949 in accordance with the procedure established by its own clauses. Objections of a formal nature were raised by the opposition with regard to the quorum necessary for Congress to approve the bill in question.²⁶ A decree (or "revolutionary act") of 27 April 1956 declared the Constitution of 1853 in effect with the amendments made in 1869, 1866 and 1898, *but excluded the 1949 amendment.* The same de facto government, by a decree of 12 April 1957, declared it necessary that the Constitution of 1853, together with its three accepted amendments, be studied with a view to partial amendment and called a convention for this purpose. A number of articles were submitted to it that were considered open to amendment in order to assure the following: (a) the establishment of a more adequate electoral system; (b) the reinforcement of the federal system of government; (c) the protection of individual liberty and the expression of individual and social rights; (d) the strengthening of municipal autonomy; (e) the internal balance between the branches of the federal government, giving the legislative branch functional independence and supervisory powers, and defining the powers of the executive branch, including the appointment and removal of public employees, and the strengthening of the judicial branch as a whole; (f) a proper system for the control and development of natural sources of energy.²⁷ The constitutional convention met in the city of Santa Fe and did not succeed in discharging its obligations. It was left without a quorum "after whole months during which everything except reform was discussed," thus proving the existence of unbridgeable gaps between the parties that had sent representatives to the convention. The Peronists were prevented from running their own candidates for convention delegates and cast a blank ballot in the election held to choose them. The convention only succeeded in approving the insertion after Article 14 of the National Constitution of a new text referring to the rights of workers (including the right to strike) and to social security, and left open the possibility that Congress might issue a Work and Social Security Code as an amendment to Article 67, Section 11. This did not materialize.²⁸

In contrast with the wide range of subjects that *were not considered by the Convention,* the government resulting from the "Argentine Revolution," on 28 June 1966, issued important official documents that disclosed the constitutional crisis to which the country had long been subject. This is apparent from the resolutions in the "Statement of the Argentine Revolution," which reads as follows:

(1) To set up a Revolutionary Junta composed of the commanders in chief of the three armed services of the nation, to assume political and military power in the Republic. (2) To remove from their posts the president and vice-president of the Republic and the governors and lieutenant-governors of all the provinces. (3) To dissolve the National Congress and the provincial Legislatures. (4) To remove from their posts the members of the Supreme Court and the Attorney General of the Nation. (5) To dissolve all the political parties of the country. (6) To make known to the people of the Republic the principal causes that have motivated the Revolutionary Action, the text of which is appended hereto as Appendix 1 of this Statement. (7) To put into effect the Statute of the Argentine Revolution, appended hereto as Appendix 2 of this Statement. (8) To define the Political Objectives of the Nation, which are appended hereto as Appendix 3 of this Statement. (9) To appoint the members of the Supreme Court and the attorney general of the Nation. (10) To have the members of the Supreme Court take the oath of office from this Revolutionary Junta, having them swear to carry out their duties, administering justice well and legally and in accordance with what is prescribed by the Revolutionary Objectives, the Statute of the Revolution, and the Argentine Constitution. (11) To offer the office of president of the Republic to Lt. Gen. Juan Carlos Onganía, who, on accepting the same and taking possession of his office shall receive the oath administered by this Revolutionary Junta in the following words: "I swear by God our Lord and the Holy Scriptures, faithfully and patriotically to fulfill the office of President of the Nation, faithfully to observe the Revolutionary Objectives, the Statute of the Revolution, and the Constitution of the Argentine Nation. Should I fail to do so, may God and the Nation call me to account." (12) To issue the decrees necessary for carrying out the provisions of this Statement. (13) To notify the diplomatic missions accredited to our country of what has been resolved for the purpose of normal relations with their respective countries. (14) To consider this Revolutionary Junta dissolved at the time the new president of the Republic is sworn into office.[29]

From 1966 on, the Constitution was relegated to the third place within the legal order of precedence in Argentina, coming after the

"Revolutionary Objectives" and the "Statute of the Argentine Revolution." This is the last major indication of the profound institutional crisis of liberalism, the outlines of which had already begun to appear in 1930.[30] The political parties reflected this crisis, each in its own way. Here, the most important phenomenon is the consolidation of the Peronist party in power, after having gone through two crucial stages; at first, the Labor party and the Radical party (Renewal Board) coexisted and then they were fused into the Sole Party of the National Revolution, the immediate predecessor of the Peronist party.[31] This group, despite the overwhelming preponderance it had in Congress, did not make itself felt on the national scene as an autonomous force, was for several years intervened within its principal districts, and after 1955 was the victim of proscriptions, persecutions, and also suffered from schisms. Peronism as a party does not yet have a detailed history of its development nor of its relations with the union wing of the movement.[32]

As for the rest of the parties that we have known since the 1930-1946 period, new schisms and fragmentations have occurred again in all of them in one way or another, either because of personalities or because of ideological differences. For example, the Radicals were the principal and most numerous opponents of Peronism in Congress and attempted to act as a counterweight in the legislative process. The Intransigent sector predominated in the Radical leadership as is shown by the Ricardo Balbín-Arturo Frondizi ticket that opposed Perón's reelection in 1951. After 1955 the old Radical main stem divided into several branches. Two of these were the Intransigent Radical party and the People's Radical party (1956), which arose as a result of the simultaneous presidential ambitions of Frondizi and Balbín, who were to oppose each other in the 1958 elections. In 1963, the Intransigent Radical party insisted on retaining its candidate Oscar Alende, while the sector led by Frondizi and Rogelio Frigerio preferred to throw its lot in with the "National and Popular Front" vetoed by the administration shortly before the 7 July elections. Shortly thereafter the latter group formed the Movement of Integration and Development and cut off many of its ties with traditional Radicalism, whose heir was to be the People's Radical party when Arturo Illia became president of the republic.

The Conservatives united in a fluid National Federation of the Center parties, but a schism also occurred in their ranks when the Popular Conservative Democratic party was formed under the leadership of Vicente Solano Lima, who attempted without success a rapprochement with the Peronist sectors. Solano Lima was designated by Perón as the presidential candidate of the "National and Popular Front" which, as we have seen, was prevented from taking part in the 1963 elections.

Schisms were rife within the Socialist party, particularly after 1958 when its two wings were known as the Democratic Socialist party (Ghioldi and Repetto were left as the leaders of this conservative Socialism on the European model) and the Argentine Socialist party, with Palacios at its head. The Argentine Socialist party was later to suffer new schisms motivated either by questions of tactics (positions vis-à-vis Peronism) or of ideology (Castroism, the Soviet Union-People's Republic of China confrontation, and the attitude that should be followed in this situation by "revolutionary Socialists").

Indigenous Communism, which had seemed to be so monolithic under the prolonged leadership of Victorio Codovilla (who headed the party until his recent death), was weakened, especially during the 1960s, by the departure of its best young intellectuals and also by the break with the official apparatus of the Young Communist League, which had some influence within the university movement and the Argentine University Federation.[33] While the enfeebled Argentine Communist party debated subjects such as the Sino-Soviet dispute (as the Socialists did), Castroism, the position toward, and assessment of, Peronism, and the functions of an authentic revolutionary party within our society, the government of the "Argentine Revolution" persisted in the practice we have known since the thirties (for instance, the bill to curb Communism introduced by Senator Matías G. Sánchez Sorondo) of attempting to suppress ideologies by decree. An example in point is the anti-Communist "law" issued in 1967, which does not even define the offense it creates and penalizes in its articles.[34]

Other political groups appeared between 1955 and 1966 and there is no point in trying to mention them all in this brief summing up. They include the Christian Democratic party with both "liberal" and "populist" wings, and a moderate electoral following; the Federal Union party; the Independent Civic party; the Movement of National Liberation; as well as the various provincial "neo-Peronist" groups and the Socialist party of the National Left.[35] This proliferation of labels is, if you will, another proof of the crisis affecting Argentine political parties during the last decade or two.[36] It is common knowledge that the 1966 military government attempted to cut this Gordian knot by dissolving all political parties in the country, a somewhat bizarre way of placing

Peronism on an equal footing with other parties by proscribing them all; it is not yet possible to hazard a guess about the permanent viability of this measure.

As for the nationalists, as we had already indicated in treating the events in 1930 and 1943, they came on the scene again at Lonardi's side in 1955 (Amadeo, Goyeneche, Etchecopar, and others) until they were displaced in November of that year by the liberal-leaning "coup within the coup."[37] In 1966 they applauded and joined the military government which, in their judgment, was putting into practice many of their old tenets such as the dissolution of the parties, hierarchical and authoritarian government, the closing of Congress, and a preeminent role for the armed forces and the church in the administration of public affairs. However, nationalist support is not unanimous; Marcelo Sánchez Sorondo and his group have opposed that "treason" and are still looking themselves for the fortunate military man of whom they have always dreamed. The Atheneum of the Republic is an intellectual group considered very influential by the press and general report. It seems to be devoted, through officials who may be affiliated with it, to promoting vague "corporative" and "communitarian" reforms within the "Argentine Revolution." In this they are only following the tradition of Uriburu's frustrated advisers.[38]

To end these observations on the decline of the parties in contemporary Argentina, we would like to refer to a type of mentality that is largely responsible for the state of affairs. It is a mentality that refuses to accept or assimilate (even critically) the recent, and the not so recent, past. This difficulty is found to exist in men of the most diverse affiliations and contributes to the political disintegration and fragmentation that has been mentioned by so many authors as characteristic of our country within the last few decades. Adm. Isaac F. Rojas, in a speech commemorating the thirteenth anniversary of the "Liberating Revolution," the extreme wing of which he had led, affirmed that:

> The Republic has known only three liberating movements: the May Revolution, which was the fountainhead of our nationhood; the one that was victorious at Caseros when it overthrew the first tyranny; and the one that culminated thirteen years ago in the overthrow of the second despotic regime.[39]

The resemblance of the above remarks to those made in 1930 by Matías G. Sánchez Sorondo when he pioneered what later came to be known as "the Mayo-Caseros line," is remarkable.[40] Yrigoyen's Radicalism and Peronism do not exist for Rojas despite their electoral victories, and neither do the military movements of 1930 and 1943. These failures of perception compound the present Argentine crisis and continue to obstruct the urgent political and ideological synthesis that the nation needs.

Now we need only summarize the corresponding trends (in many cases a continuation of the events of the 1930-1946 period) evident in the other power factors, in accordance with their presentation in the text: the church, the armed forces, the economic groups, and the labor movement. The statement that the Catholic church, through its hierarchy, has maintained cordial relations with all Argentine governments since Yrigoyen's first term must be qualified by mention of the exception to this rule represented by the conflict between the church and Perón in 1954 and 1955, typified by the belligerency of the Catholic faithful, the demonstrations, the exile of Bishops Manuel Tato and Ramón Novoa, the "burning of the flag," Perón's excommunication, the legalization of divorce, the bills allowing officially supervised prostitution, the elimination of religious instruction from the schools, and the attempts to reform the national Constitution in order to separate church and state.[41]

However, these events did not have lasting effects. Catholicism was the cohesive element in the civilian-military movement of September 1955, together with the loudly proclaimed opposition to the oil contracts that Perón was about to sign with American corporations. Sectors of the army, the traditionally "liberal" navy, old anticlerical parties such as Socialism, and nationalist groups, all acted together brandishing the banners of both nationalism and liberalism. After the short-lived Lonardi interregnum and after the coup d'état that placed Aramburu in the presidency, the church returned to its normal good relations, which only varied in degree, with the government of the day, whether Aramburu himself, Frondizi, Guido, Illia, or Onganía.

The divorce law was filed away; in 1968 only some archaic impediments to the separation of bodies by mutual consent were actually changed. From 1958 on, the church has been allowed to organize private but legally recognized universities; its influence on public administration, through high officials in the field of education, has become increasingly felt since 1966.[42] After the sudden death of Bishop Fermín Lafitte, the "Peronist Cardinal" Antonio Caggiano, became Archbishop of Buenos Aires and primate of the Argentine church. Cardinal Santiago Luis Copello, too exhausted by his direct contacts with Perón between 1946 and 1955, followed the easy path of diplomatic exile by occupying an important post in the Vatican Foreign Office for several years.

Despite the evidences of opposition visible on a world level since Vatican Council II between precouncil and postcouncil Catholics, in our milieu the hierarchical balance of power continues to tip in favor of traditionalism, as shown by the much-discussed episode of the removal of the "progressive" Bishop of Avellaneda, the Most Reverend Jerónimo Podestá, during Onganía's military government. The Argentine Catholic church no longer presents, as it did in the 1930-1946 period, the strategy of the two wings to which we referred in chapter 6. Now it is rather a question of a hierarchy that wishes to continue to have the privilege of communicating with those holding political power, in order to continue to influence them from above. They are faced with groups of young priests and laymen who, for example, support Camilo Torres, the guerrilla priest, and persist in joining the destiny of militant Catholicism to that of the revolution which, in their judgment, is required not only in Argentina but also throughout Latin America. In the last analysis, these progressive sectors are the ones that are bringing into evidence (only this time they do so *from within* Catholic doctrine and thought) the crisis of the nation's upper clergy. This crisis had been foreshadowed decades earlier, but it has been aggravated by the postwar and cold war world, and by the more or less peaceful "coexistence" between East and West, with the attendant dichotomy between evolution and revolution which must be rethought in Argentina.

From 1946 to 1970 the predominant function of the armed forces, and especially of the army, in the Argentine political process has undergone nearly all possible changes. These include massive support of the Peronist regime, though not without some exceptions such as isolated countercoups like that of General Benjamín Menéndez in 1951 and the 16 June 1955 rebellion (aided by naval aviation); the military refusal to accept the vice-presidential candidacy of Eva Perón and the refusal by the Ministry of the Army to honor the request by the GCL for weapons destined for the workers' militias envisaged during the last few weeks of the Perón government; direct control of the state between 1955 and 1958, during the "Liberating Revolution," with the navy playing a growing role in politics.[43] The pace of the historical process speeds up after these dates.

Frondizi won the 23 February 1958 elections thanks to Peronist support, since this movement had been barred from presenting its own candidates. The armed forces turned the government over to him conditionally, as has been graphically pointed out by Tulio Halperín Donghi when he speaks of the Intransigent Radical party

as the "tolerated opposition."[44] This becomes obvious with the
demands (over thirty during the period of his unfinished term)
that the army presented to him in the exercise of their self-
assumed right to veto the decisions of the civilian administration
whenever they considered it necessary to do so. This stage came to
a head toward the end of March 1962, when the commanders in
chief of the three services deposed and arrested the president of
the republic (as they did again with Illia less than four years later),
and then reluctantly accepted the nominal presidency of José
María Guido, who was supported by the Supreme Court. Until the
elections of 7 July 1963, the Guido administration was the typical
case of a "puppet or captive government" under military control.

Before this date, the serious domestic crises of September 1962
and April 1963 had been surmounted when the most extreme anti-
Peronist elements of the navy and a small army group attempted
to establish a government of force *sine die* with support of willing
civilian advisers. The elections of 1963 (in which, as we know, the
National and Popular Front was prevented from participating) led
to the electoral college victory of the People's Radical party candidate, Arturo Illia, who had obtained a plurality, but not a majority
of the popular vote. He continued to head the administration until
28 June 1966; on this date, the commanders in chief of the three
services (the Revolutionary Junta) overthrew Illia and handed the
highest public office to General Onganía, who as commander in
chief of the army from the end of 1962 to November 1965 had
reactivated Rodríguez's "professionalization" doctrine in order to
fight the dangerous deliberations going on within the Army. Again
the 1930 policies resurfaced in the sixties. While the new chief
executive insisted repeatedly on his phrase "the armed forces do
not govern," in reality this was a mere statement of intentions, not
supported by the supremacy the military sector acquired within
the political system. What emerges is a peculiar type of autocracy,
with Onganía as the sole depositary of formal authority as long as
he could count on the backing of the services.[45]

Complementing all this, the army, the navy, and the air force
differ in their use of some techniques which were barely discernible in 1930. The preparatory "psychological action" of 28
June 1966 surpasses anything known until then, since part of the
mass communications media, together with the propaganda services of the three branches of the armed forces, contributed to the
creation of a climate favorable to the coup.[46]

The integration of the military with the economic groups is
becoming greater, a trend that has increased especially since

1943.[47] The supremacy of the military in the country's political
leadership is obvious because of their employment as representatives and promoters on behalf of important national and foreign
interests in the field of economics, finance, and industry. This is
but another symptom of the decline of the remaining organized
sectors of society.[48]

A phenomenon which is crucial to a proper understanding of
the action of economic groups in Argentina in recent years is represented by the emergence of two, not always mutually exclusive, policies during the sixties. The first is that of a monopolistic
concentration of Argentine industry to the detriment of medium
and small producers. Here we are only interested in transcribing
the conclusions arrived at in a detailed and informative study on
the subject published in 1965:

> (a) The economic structure of Argentina was very early and
> rapidly controlled "from within" by imperialism in association
> with the upper or oligarchic bourgeoisie. This situation has not
> changed. (b) This fact does not mean that the *entire* economic
> apparatus is in the hands of the monopolies. Side by side with
> these, independent producers continue to exist, but their situa-
> tion is one of relative weakness and subordination. In any case,
> this is typical of a monopolistic structure, which implies control
> of the market, not the exclusive existence of monopolies. (c)
> Monopolization in Argentina is the function of the foreign
> monopolies, directly and in association with the upper bour-
> geoisie. (d) Foreign capital was preferentially invested until
> 1930 in agriculture or in related fields, so that the economy was
> predominantly agrarian. However, even before 1930 it had also
> penetrated industry and had come to control the larger enter-
> prises. After 1930 foreign investment became oriented toward
> industry, coinciding with the change in our economic structure.
> (e) Monopolistic control is therefore constant and the indepen-
> dent or relatively independent bourgeoisie always occupies only
> the lower levels of the medium cattle-ranchers and the medium
> industrialists; the top is always occupied by foreign monopolies
> and the upper bourgeoisie associated with them. This explains
> the weakness of bourgeois nationalist attempts such as Yrigoye-
> nism and Peronism. (f) The concentration of capital is constant:
> it simply becomes more acute during times of internal crisis.
> This concentration of capital (monopolization) in our country
> has its own characteristics typical of a dependent country such
> as ours, which does not fall within the classical colonial model;
> it takes place with the overwhelming and decisive participation,

and for the benefit of, the imperialist monopolies associated with the local upper bourgeoisie.[49]

The second policy is to a great extent complementary to the first. It is called "denationalization" of Argentine industry, something that has been documented in 1968 from numerous sources. Not only is there evidence of "a significant increase in the rhythm of incoming foreign capital [but also] that it is applied more to the acquisition of already-established national enterprises rather than to the creation of new ones." The process is particularly pronounced in the banking sector.[50] Thus, if both trends are taken into account, the avowed purpose of the military government of the "Argentine Revolution" appears to be extremely contradictory insofar as it relates national defense (through the National Security Council) to the economic development of the country (National Development Council), since the "internal front" that it seeks to consolidate is increasingly in alien hands. Also, the "liberal" economic policy of the regime ("to buy from those who buy from us") brings the country back to outgrown historical eras when Great Britain was our exclusive metropolis, something that is no longer so at a time when even Yugoslavia replaces Argentina as the most important provider of meats for Great Britain, other than the members of the Commonwealth. This sort of economic policy is in conflict with the attitude of the popular sectors that still remember a different stage in the slow process of transforming their aspirations (which Perón in his day knew how to interpret so well) into concrete realities, rather than the one that prevailed between 1930 and 1943.[51]

Organized workers cannot be left out of any government scheme in the way the bureaucratized GCL often was during the 1930s; an attempt was made to make them "participate" nominally in government strategy, while their wages continued to be frozen and the more combative sectors of the proletariat were repressed. However, the labor movement has gained a different dimension and a different image within the Argentine political process, and it constitutes one of the two great forces (the other, of course is the military) active in recent years in the life of the nation.[52] We have already said that this subject requires a more thorough analysis and a more serious interpretation than the mere partisan or sentimental labels that are frequently used in trying to study it. Rather than stressing the policies that are a carry-over from the thirties or such outward, but misleading, similarities as that between the 1943 GCL No. 1 and 2 and the 1968 GCL of Azopardo Street and that of Paseo Colón Avenue, for instance, it is essential to emphasize the enormous differences that separate the two periods; we are living in a period of mass unionization that seeks to channel its demands by diverse routes and not, as was the case earlier, through a single "union aristocracy" locked in internal struggles while around it a new proletariat sprang up. A military diagnosis of the "dramatic and dangerous emergency" existing in Argentina in 1966 claimed that:

> ... the disastrous conduct of public business by the present government, as the culmination of many errors by those that preceded it during recent decades, of structural failures, and of the application of inadequate systems and techniques to contemporary conditions, has brought about a breakdown of the spiritual unity of the Argentine people, a general feeling of discouragement and skepticism, apathy and loss of national consciousness, the chronic deterioration of economic and financial life, the crumbling of the principle of authority, and a lack of order and discipline that are translated into deep social unrest and a notorious disregard for law and justice.[53]

This simplistic way of looking at matters reduced everything indefinitely to a regime that emphasizes authority, order, and discipline, always as abstract concepts that are not applied to the solution of the great national problems of Argentina and to the incorporation of the labor sectors into a true common endeavor in which they can feel they truly participate, as they did during Peron's administration. While a country cannot be governed forever as though it were a barrack, neither can it be governed by traditional ward politics, nor the management methods of foreign enterprises. The future must show us what new routes the organized groups of Argentine society will follow by assimilating and then improving upon the lessons of the past in order to arrive at a goal with a strong egalitarian content.

Notes

FOREWORD

1. The question of support for the Radical party is by no means a clear issue. Former President Frondizi claims that it went way beyond the urban middle class; see Arturo Frondizi and others, *Introducción a los problemas nacionales; curso dictado en el Centro de Estudios Nacionales* (Buenos Aires: Centro de Estudios Nacionales, 1965), pp.55-60. Imaz confirms this assertion, but only in reference to the party leaders and up to 1930; see José Luis de Imaz, *Los que Mandan (Those Who Rule)*, trans. Carlos A. Astiz with Mary F. McCarthy (Albany: State University of New York Press, 1970), pp. 199-207. On the other hand, Scobie seems to emphasize the native middle class as the sole source of reform; see James R. Scobie, *Argentina: A City and a Nation* (New York: Oxford University Press, 1964), pp. 189-214.

2. To what extent elected officials actually controlled Argentine politics between 1916 and 1930 is an open question; in regard to the military establishment, see Robert A. Potash, *The Army and Politics in Argentina, 1928-1945; Yrigoyen to Perón* (Stanford: Stanford University Press, 1969), chaps. 1 and 2; and Juan V. Orona, *La Logia Militar que enfrentó a Hipólito Yrigoyen* (Buenos Aires: Editorial Leonardo Impresora, 1965), passim.

3. The 1853 constitution provides in Art. 77 that the president and the vice president may not be reelected until a full term (six years) has elapsed.

4. See the *Acta de la Revolución Argentina*, Arts. 3 and 7. The military officers who installed the Onganía regime qualified their commitment to the Constitution by indicating that its provisions would be respected as long as they did not oppose the ends outlined in the above mentioned *Acta*. This reservation also applies to the Levingstone and Lanusse administrations. See Instituto de Ciencia Política, Universidad del Salvador, *La "revolución argentina"; análisis y perspectiva* (Buenos Aires: Ediciones Depalma, 1966).

5. For supporting view, see Diego Abad de Santillán, *Historia institucional argentina* (Buenos Aires: Editora Tipográfica Argentina, 1966), p. 491 ff.

6. For a comprehensive discussion of this topic, see Juan A. González Calderón, *Curso de derecho constitucional* (Buenos Aires: Editorial Guillermo Kraft, 1963), chap. 6.

7. The legal authority can be found in *Estatuto de la Revolución Argentina*, Art. 9.

CHAPTER 1

1. "Testimonio," *Revista de Historia* (Buenos Aires), no. 3, 1958 (issue devoted to the "Crisis of 1930"), p. 112.

2. *En Tiempos de la República,* (Buenos Aires: Mundo Forense, 1946), 1:66. For a study of a provincial stituation and of the relations between a Mendoza caudillo and Yrigoyenismo, see Dardo Olguín, *José Néstor Lencinas* (Mendoza: D. Accurzio, 1962).

3. As examples, compare the versions of the Socialist schism given by Pinedo, *En tiempos de la República*, 1:53-62, and Joaquín Coca, *El contubernio (Selección)* (Buenos Aires: Coyoacán, 1961). pp. 41-64. On Antiperson-

alist Radicalism there is much material in Gabriel del Mazo, *El radicalismo (Ensayo sobre su historia y doctrina),* vol. 2 (Buenos Aires: Gure, 1959); Rodolfo Puiggrós, *Historia crítica de los partidos políticos argentinos* (Buenos Aires: Argumentos, 1956); and in Ricardo M. Ortiz, "El aspecto económico-social de la crisis de 1930," *Revista de Historia,* no. 3, 1958, pp. 41-72.

4. "Manifesto of the 44," in *La Nación,* 10 August 1930; this statement was signed by Conservative and Independent Socialist legislators. It was followed by a similar pronouncement, signed by six Antipersonalist senators and all its congressmen, and published in *La Nación,* 21 August 1930.

5. "Declaración del Dr. D. Antonio De Tomaso," in José María Sarobe, *Memorias sobre la revolución del 6 setiembre de 1930* (Buenos Aires: Gure, 1957). The meeting was attended by Mariano de Vedia y Mitre, Antonio Santamarina, Rodolfo Moreno, Carlos A. Astrada, Leopoldo Melo, De Tomaso, and Lt. Col. Bartolomé Descalzo. See also Rodolfo Moreno, "La colaboración conservadora a la Revolución. Antecedentes y acción del partido," in Diez Periodistas Porteños, *Al margen de la conspiración* (Buenos Aires: Biblos, no. 8), p. 395.

6. Pinedo, *En tiempos de la República,* 1: 42.

7. Del Mazo, in *El radicalismo,* 2: 151, states that:

People were also beginning to collect in the waiting room to his office, and, unfortunately, an unscrupulous gang of low-level secretarial officials made deals in granting appointments. Also, clear-cut stands by the Radical party were lacking. The leadership of the latter seemed to have become fossilized, and they did not respond flexibly to the requirements of those very difficult times.

For an account by an anti-Yrigoyen Radical — later to be a "unionist" — of the events that brought about the fall of the government, see Jorge Walter Perkins, *¿Qué ha hecho crisis en la Argentina?* (Buenos Aires: Rosso, 1931).

8. See Roberto Etcchepareborda, "Aspectos políticos de la crisis de 1930," *Revista de Historia,* no. 3, 1958, especially pp. 36-40, and Arturo Torres, *Elpidio González, biografía de una conducta* (Buenos Aires: Raigal, 1951), pp. 107-10

9. See Diego Abad de Santillán, "El movimiento obrero argentino ante el golpe de estado del 6 de setiembre de 1930," *Revista de Historia,* no. 3, 1958, an excellent analysis from an Anarchist point of view.

10. In this we follow Sergio Bagú, in his contribution to *Tres Revoluciones* (Buenos Aires: Emilio Perrot, 1958), pp. 18 ff., who deals separately with the civilian sector of the conspiracy; and José Luis Romero, *Las ideas políticas en Argentina,* 3d ed. (Buenos Aires: Fondo de Cultura Económica, 1959), who speaks of "fascism" and "fraudulent democracy," pp. 228 ff. See also: Carlos Ibarguren, *La historia que he vivido* (Buenos Aires: Peuser, 1955), pp. 384 ff.

11. General Uriburu, a relative and personal friend of Ibarguren, had made the following statement to him:

My intention is to effect a real revolution that will change many aspects of our institutional regime, modify the Constitution and avoid the repetition of the demagogical control which is now upsetting us. I am not going to

lead an uprising to benefit politicians and change the men in the government, but rather a transcendental and constructive rebellion disregarding
the parties. [*La historia que he vivido*, p. 384]

12. *Memorias*. . . , p. 63.

13. "Lo que yo vi, de la preparación y realización de la revolución del 6 de
septiembre de 1930," draft notes appearing in the appendix to Sarobe's
Memorias. . . ,pp. 281-310, the authorship of which has not been denied. It is
also reproduced — together with articles on the 1943 and 1955 coups d'état —
in Juan Domingo Perón, *Tres revoluciones militares* (Buenos Aires:
Escorpión, 1963).

14. *Memorias* . . ., pp. 125-26.

15. *Orígenes de la revolución del 6 de septiembre de 1930 (Rosas e Irigoyen)* (Buenos Aires, 1930), p. 10.

16. *Memorias...*, p. 160.

17. In Quesada, *Orígines*. . . , pp. 107,108. In this speech, Sánchez Sorondo
also foreshadowed the line later to be followed by the regime that replaced
Juan Perón; this regime claimed to be a continuation of the independence
movement of May 1810 and of the overthrow of dictator Juan Manuel de
Rosas at the battle of Caseros.

18. Quesada says that:

From that ministry came one of the twenty-four civilians who were in
contact with the Military Junta of the Revolution during the organizing of
the 6 September movement: Matías G. Sánchez Sorondo. The others were
Daniel Videla Dorna, Alberto Viña, Raúl Guerrico, Juan Carulla, Guillermo
Peña, Santiago Rey Basadre, Raúl Zimmermann, Alejandro Zimmermann,
Jorge Zimmermann, Enrique H. Zimmermann, Félix Gunther, Félix
Bunge, César J. Guerrico, Alberto E. Uriburu, Nicolás E. Rodríguez, Carlos
R. Ribero, Detlef von Bülow, Roberto Hossmann, Horacio Kinkelin, David
Uriburu, Rodolfo de Alzaga Unzué, Luis González Guerrico. [*Origines. . .,*
pp. 109-10].

The list contains only twenty-three names. Perhaps Lugones was missing.

19. *Vida de Hipólito Yrigoyen (El hombre del misterio)* (Buenos Aires,
1939), p. 449. Two Radical analyses on Yrigoyen appear in Félix Luna,
Yrigoyen, el templario de la libertad, (Buenos Aires: Raigal, 1954), and
Silvano Santander, *Yrigoyen* (Buenos Aires: La Fragua, 1965).

20. *Jurisprudencia Argentina,* vol. 34, pp. 5-13. Gabriel del Mazo *(El radicalismo,* 2: 156- 59), supports the theory of official pressure on the members
of the Supreme Court, by threats of removal from tenured status [Spanish, *en
comisión,* which in Argentine administrative law means that they can be dismissed without cause] together with the whole judicial branch. The arguments are credible.

21. *Derecho Constitucional,* 3d ed. (Buenos Aires: Depalma, 1959), pp.
857-59. Bielsa writes:

If, when faced by a takeover of the government by force, constitutional
rule ceases in regard to the executive and legislative branches and autho-

rity, what can be done judicially? The French Council of State – an adjudicating organ within the executive branch – at the time of the coup d'état by Napoleon III, made a statement of protest and the members of the Council resigned their posts.

22. Argentine Senate, *Diario de sesiones,* 20 January 1932 session, debate on the powers of that body, pp. 13-14 (emphasis added).

23. On the creation of the National Democratic Federation see Pinedo, *En tiempos de la República,* 1: 80-104.

24. Ibarguren, *La historia que he vivido,* p. 412 (emphasis added). His attitude confirms a certain distaste for electoral procedures: "From that moment (8 September 1930), some impromptu orators, as though obeying a signal, announced immediate elections in imprudent speeches: 'Votes, yes; arms, no,' was the loud cry of those who thus proceeded with impertinent officiousness and without official representation" (p. 387).

25. This point is documented in his article, "Otra página de historia," *Obras de Lisandro de la Torre,* vol. 1, 2d ed. (Buenos Aires: Hemisferio, 1952), pp. 222-37.

26. *Obras de Lisandro de la Torre,* vol. 5 (Buenos Aires: Hemisferio, 1954), p. 119.

27. *Cartas íntimas* (Buenos Aires: Futuro, 1951), pp. 29-30. In the letter of 16 February 1934 (p. 34), de la Torre insists on Uriburu's preference for him as a candidate to succeed the general in power "before the revolution triumphed."

28. This is stated by Félix Luna in *Alvear* (Buenos Aires: Libros Argentinos, 1958), pp. 86-87.

29. In a letter dated 16 February 1934, reproduced in *Cartas íntimas,* p. 35, Lisandro de la Torre wrote: "After the Buenos Aires Province defeat, Uriburu had ceased to be master of the situation and was held prisoner by a *military clique* which forced him to turn the Interior Ministry over to a person committed to Justo's candidacy." The changes in the cabinet were as follows: Interior Ministry, Octavio S. Pico; Justice and Public Instruction, Guillermo Rothe; Treasury, Enrique Uriburu; Agriculture, David Arias; Public Works, Pablo Calatayud; Navy, Vice Admiral Carlos Daireaux. Shortly thereafter Adolfo Bioy took charge of the Ministry of Foreign Relations.

30. Sergio Bagú, *Argentina en el mundo* (Buenos Aires: Fondo de Cultura Económica, 1961), p. 86.

31. *En tiempos de la República,* vol. I, pp. 108-14.

32. Ibid., p. 112.

33. *Criterio ,* No. 192, 5 November 1931, p. 170.

34. *Mi paso por la política (De Uriburu a Perón)* (Buenos Aires: Santiago Rueda, 1957), p. 20.

35. Matías G. Sánchez Sorondo, "6 de setiembre de 1930," *Revista de Historia,* no. 3, 1958, p. 103.

36. Carlos Ibarguren, *La historia que he vivido,* p. 391.

37. *Mensaje del Presidente Provisional de la Nación, teniente general José F. Uriburu, al Pueblo de la República, La obra de gobierno y de administración del 6 de septiembre de 1930 al 6 de septiembre de 1931* (Buenos Aires:

Cámara de Diputados, 1931), p. 3. The most complete account of the Uriburu administration is that of J. Beresford Crawkes, *533 días de historia argentina* (Buenos Aires: Imprenta Mercatali, 1932). See also, *La palabra del general Uriburu* (Buenos Aires: Roldán, 1933).

38. Del Mazo, *El radicalismo*, 2:196.

39. Ibid.,

40. *La historia que he vivido*, p. 433.

41. "Testimonio," *Revista de Historia*, no. 3, 1958, p. 118 (emphasis added).

CHAPTER 2

1. *Las ideas políticas en Argentina*, p. 237. The term "infamous decade" (which covers the years between 1930 and 1943) was originally coined by José Luis Torres, though it has acquired currency in the political language of Argentina. See his book *La década infame* (Buenos Aires: Editorial de Formación "Patria," 1945).

2. The changes that occurred during the 1932-38 period were as follows: Interior: Ramón S. Castillo, Manuel R. Alvarado (provisionally); Treasury, Federico Pinedo, Roberto M. Ortiz, Carlos A. Acevedo; Justice and Public Instruction, Ramón S. Castillo, Jorge de la Torre; War, Gen. Basilio B. Pertiné; Navy, Navy Capt. Eleazar Videla; Agriculture, Luis Duhau, Miguel A. Cárcano.

3. *La historia que he vivido*, pp. 446-47.

4. "Situación presente y perspectivas futuras del comercio exterior," *Cursos y conferencias* (Buenos Aires). Year 10 no. 4, July 1941, p. 399.

5. *Obras de Lisandro de la Torre*, vol. 2, 2d ed. (Buenos Aires: Hemisferio, 1952), p. 44 (28 July session).

6. Ibarguren, *La historia que he vivido*, p. 447.

7. *Obras de Lisandro de la Torre*, 2: 128 (18 June 1935 sessions).

8. Argentine Senate, *Diario de Sesiones*, 21 June 1935 session, pp. 255-56.

9. See Rodolfo Puiggrós, *Libre empresa o nacionalización en la industria de la carne* (Buenos Aires: Argumentos, 1957), especially pp. 149-52; and *La democracia fraudulenta* (Buenos Aires: Jorge Alvarez, 1968), pp. 131-82.

10. *Obras de Lisandro de la Torre*, 2: 507.

11. Arturo Jauretche, *F. O. R. J. A. y la década infame* (Buenos Aires: Coyoacán, 1962), pp. 41-42. For Scalabrini Ortiz's views, see *Política británica en el Río de la Plata*, 3d ed. (Buenos Aires: Fernández Blanco, 1957).

12. Argentine Senate, *Diario de Sesiones*, January 22, 1935 session, p. 585.

13. *En tiempos de la República*, 1: 100 (emphasis added).

14. *La historia que he vivido*, p. 443.

15. Del Mazo, *El radicalismo*, 2: 267.

16. Art. 2, sec. (a), of Law N⁰ 12,137 provided for the "promotion of the destruction, insofar as necessary, of wine-producing grapevines, through the payment of compensation"; art. 9 of Law N⁰ 12,236 placed a tax of four Argentine pesos on each new *mate* plant; art. 6 of Law N⁰ 12,137 provided for a one-thousand-peso tax per hectare on new plantings of wine-producing

grapevines. See Arturo Frondizi, "Régimen jurídico de la economía argentina," *Cursos y conferencias,* Year 10 no. 2-8-9, October-November-December 1941, pp. 858-956. Frondizi outlines the problem of "liberal" interventionism as follows:

The international and national factors that provoked the crisis of 1929 in Argentina, in affecting cattle raising, agriculture, land exploitation, that is, the groups directing the country's economy, produced a total change of positions. The principle of economic freedom that had served to retard progress in labor legislation was no obstacle to the rapid relinquishing of economic liberalism. Once the country entered this road, the state was allowed to do everything and anything that might contribute to overcoming situations in themselves difficult, without limiting the means; not even the zealous defenders of provincial autonomy, which was reduced to a minimum by the fiscal and economic advances of the federal government, expressed themselves. That is to say that, when the crisis seriously menaced those social groups that rule the country, the two great principles that inspired the Argentine Constitution, liberalism and economic federalism, rapidly disappeared. And the country then surrendered without an effort to this new policy in which the state was visibly placed in the forefront. [p. 949]

17. Del Mazo, *El radicalismo,* 2: 268.

18. Ibid.

19. Argentine Chamber of Deputies, *Diario de Sesiones,* 11 September 1935 session, p. 611.

20. Argentine Senate, *Diario de Sesiones,* 28 September 1936 session, p. 468.

21. As an introduction, the following may be consulted: Arturo Frondizi, *Petróleo y política* (Buenos Aires: Raigal, 1954); Jorge del Río, *Política argentina y los monopolios eléctricos* (Buenos Aires: Cátedra Lisandro de la Torre, n. d.); and Rodolfo Puiggrós, *Historia crítica de los partidos políticos argentinos,* chap. 32.

22. Marcos Kaplan, *Economía y política del petróleo argentino (1939-1956)* (Buenos Aires: Proxis, 1957), p. 22.

23. Argentine Chamber of Deputies, *Diario de Sesiones,* 28 February and 1 March 1935 session, p. 181.

24. Argentine Chamber of Deputies, *Diario de Sesiones,* 26 and 27 September 1933 session, p. 412.

25. Alfredo L. Palacios in Argentine Senate, *Diario de Sesiones,* in the meat industry investigation, 12 and 13 September 1935 session, p. 265.

26. "Historia económica del Noroeste argentino," in *Cursos y Conferencias,* Year 16, 187-188, October-November 1947, p. 43.

27. Adolfo Dorfman, *Evolución industrial argentina* (Buenos Aires: Losada, 1942), pp. 100-101.

28. Argentine Chamber of Deputies, *Diario de Sesiones,* 17 August 1933 session, p. 255.

29. Argentine Chamber of Deputies, *Diario de Sesiones,* 14 July 1938 session, p. 769.

30. *Criterio,* 559 (17 November 1938), p. 228.

31. "El desarrollo de la industria argentina," in *Cursos y conferencias,* Year 10, nos. 1-2-3, April-May-June 1941, p. 144.

32. Armando Ulled, "La industria textil," ibid., p. 169.

33. The expression belongs to Sergio Bagú, *Argentina en el mundo* (Buenos Aires: Fondo de Cultura Económica, 1961), p. 91.

34. "Régimen jurídico de la economía argentina," p. 954.

35. *La cuestión democrática* (Buenos Aires, 1937), pp. 81-82 (emphasis added).

36. *Ibid.,* pp. 106, 134, and 200.

37. *La patria y su destino* (Buenos Aires, 1947), pp. 172-74.

38. Argentine Chamber of Deputies, *Diario de Sesiones,* 6 September 1933 session (Tribute to the revolution of 6 September 1930), pp. 950 ff.

39. *Mi paso por la política (De Uriburu a Perón),* p. 25 (emphasis added).

40. Argentine Chamber of Deputies, *Diario de Sesiones,* 4 September 1935 session, p. 381.

41. Ibid, 18 June 1936 session, pp. 50-51.

42. Ibid., 25 July 1934 session, p. 623.

43. Ibid., 22 and 23 August 1934 session, p. 605

44. Atilio Cattáneo, *Plan 1932 (el concurrencismo y la revolución)* Buenos Aires: Proceso, 1959), p. 68.

45. Lisandro de la Torre gave the details:

Bordabehere's mother was not admitted as a plaintiff, thus changing the traditional precedent of the federal courts; the main witness, the chief of police of the Argentine Congress, who declared a few instants after the deed, before some senators and before the Senate under secretary, that he had admitted Valdez Cora to the floor because of a special request or order, was not indicted for withholding information nor for perjury; the Senate personnel withdrew into absolute silence; nor has Duggan, who had gone to the stenographic office to plead for magnanimity toward the former minister of agriculture, not for Valdez Cora, and to ask them to testify falsely that they had seen a gun in Senator Bordabehere's hands, been indicted for withholding information nor for perjury, when in reality his statement requesting magnanimity for the former minister of agriculture and not for the actual author of the deed seriously compromised [the high official]; and the former minister of agriculture, convicted of perjury by the testimony of four trustworthy witness, had not been indicted either. Of these four witnesses, two declared that they had seen the minister greet Valdéz Cora at the door of the antechamber, and the two others declared that they had seen Valdéz Cora in the doorway of [the minister's] house talking with him and receiving instructions. All this, which in an ordinary case would have been more than enough in Argentine justice as circumstantial evidence of the crime and as the basis for a writ of preventive detention, in this exceptional case has been ruled out and misrepresented. [Argentine Senate, *Diario de Sesiones,* 6 August 1936 session p. 748]

46. Argentine Chamber of Deputies, *Diario de Sessiones,* 5 August 1936 session, p. 643.

47. Luis María Mattos, Progressive Democrat Deputy, in the questioning of Interior Minister Ramón S. Castillo (Melo's successor) on the federal intervention of Santa Fe, Argentine Chamber of Deputies, *Diario de Sesiones,* 6 June 1936 session, p. 524.

48. *En tiempos de la República,* 1: 176 (emphasis added).

49. *Cartas íntimas,* p. 42 (8 October 1935 letter).

50. Ibid., p. 57 (8 March 1937 letter).

51. Repetto, *Mi paso por la política (De Uriburu a Perón),* p. 81.

52. Luna, *Alvear,* p. 261.

53. *Cartas íntimas,* pp. 116-17 (2 August 1938 letter).

54. Argentine Senate, *Diario de Sesiones,* 10 December 1936 session, p. 202.

55. From the request for permission to carry out a mission for the executive branch; see Argentine Senate, *Diario de Sesiones,* 18 May 1937 session, p. 61.

56. Argentine Chamber of Deputies, *Diario de Sesiones,* 5 July 1933 session, p. 7. On Yrigoyen and his era, see Rodolfo Puiggros's important book, *El yrigoyenismo* (Buenos Aires: Jorge Alvarez, 1965).

57. *El Paso de los Libres,* 2d ed. (Buenos Aires: Coyoacán, 1960), p. 37.

58. *El radicalismo,* 2: 270.

59. Luna, *Alvear,* pp. 161-65, gives an account of the incident.

60. Argentine Chamber of Deputies, *Diario de Sesiones,* 16 September 1937 session, p. 1192.

61. This author in *Mi paso por la política (De Uriburu a Perón),* states that "the railroad worker José Domenech and Marcelo T. de Alvear, Lisandro de la Torre and Nicolás Repetto" spoke (p. 199). The official Communist version is different: "... José Domenech spoke for the GCL; Paulino González Alberdi for the Communist party; Arturo Frondizi for the Radical party; Lisandro de la Torre for the Progressive Democratic party; Mario Bravo and others for the Socialist party," *Esbozo de historia del Partido Communista de la Argentina,* drawn up by the Commission of the Central Committee of the Argentine Communist party (Buenos Aires: Anteo, 1947), p. 84. These discrepancies about concrete facts may be explained by the phenomenon of "revisionism" of recent history undertaken by professional politicians.

62. *En tiempos de la República,* 1: 181 (emphasis added).

63. Luna, *Alvear,* p. 179.

64. Pinedo, *En tiempos de la República,* 1: 181.

65. Raúl Scalabrini Ortiz, *Política británica en el Río de la Plata,* p. 248. For other views on the subject, see pp. 243-258.

66. *Argentina en el mundo,* p. 16. This work reiterates certain schemas in the treatment of the international relations of our country; we do not always share its conclusions.

67. *The Memoirs of Cordell Hull*, 2 vols. (New York: Macmillan Co., 1948). For Argentine-United States relations during the period covered by our book, Harold F. Peterson, *Argentina and the United States, 1810-1960* (Albany: State University of New York Press, 1964), may be consulted; also Alberto Conil Paz and Gustavo E. Ferrari, *Argentina's Foreign Policy, 1930-1962* (Notre Dame: University of Notre Dame Press, 1966). A more realistic and penetrating view of the problem may be found in Rogelio García Lupo, *Historia de unas malas relaciones* (Buenos Aires: Jorge Alvarez, 1964).

68. *Memoirs*, 1: 308.

69. *Argentina en el mundo*, p. 84.

70. *Memoirs*, 1: 319.

71. Hull mentions the documents that had not been ratified: the Treaty to Avoid or Prevent Conflicts Between the American States signed at the Fifth Pan American Conference at Santiago, Chile, in 1923; the Kellogg-Briand Pact of 1928; the Convention of Inter-American Conciliation and the Convention of Inter-American Arbitration, signed at Washington in 1929; and the Anti-war Pact of Saavedra Lamas, signed by six Latin American countries at Rio de Janeiro on 10 October 1933.

72. *Memoirs*, 1: 329.

73. Ibid.

74. Ibid., p. 331 (emphasis added).

75. *En tiempos de la República*, 1: 146 (emphasis added).

76. *Memoirs*, 1: 329; 2: 1724.

77. *The Time for Decision* (New York and London: Harper & Brothers Publishers, 1944), p. 205.

78. See *Prontuario (Una autobiografía)*, 2d ed. (Buenos Aires: Gure, 1956), pp. 191-92.

79. *Memoirs*, 1: 497.

80. Ibid., p. 499.

81. Ibid., p. 500.

82. *Yankee Diplomacy (U. S. Intervention in Argentina)* (Dallas: Southern Methodist University Press, 1953), pp. 30-31.

CHAPTER 3

1. Later, Cosme Massini Ezcurra would replace Padilla as minister of agriculture, and Luis A. Barberis would take Alvarado's place as minister of public works (Barberis had been head of this department during the Justo Administration).

2. Translator's Note: This is an accurate, although not a literal, translation of the expression "cabecitas negras" used by those residing in the Buenos Aires metropolitan area to identify the migrants who came from the interior when openings became plentiful. The reference to the color should not be understood literally, since althought the migrants' skin was somewhat darker than that of the inhabitants of Buenos Aires, they were unquestionably white. C. A. A.

NOTES 311

3. *Evolución industrial argentina*, p. 359.

4. *Estructura social de la Argentina*, p. 57.

5. Ibid., pp. 76-77.

6. Ibid., p. 77

7. Argentine Chamber of Deputies, *Diario de Sesiones*, 13 March 1941 session, p. 629 (emphasis added).

8. This note may be found in Argentine Chamber of Deputies, *Diario de Sesiones*, 16 August 1939 session, pp. 118-21.

9. Cipriano Reyes was the leader of the meat-packing plant workers in the mid-1940s and one of the key members of the Labor party which supported Perón early in the latter's political career. C. A. A.

10. Argentine Chamber of Deputies, *Diario de Sesiones*, 19 November 1941 session, p. 793.

11. Reproduced in Raúl Larra, *Lisandro de la Torre (Vida y drama del solitario de Pinas)*, 4th ed. (Buenos Aires: Hemisferio, 1950), p. 312.

12. The original text may be found in José María Monner Sans, *Pirandello (Su vida y su teatro)* (Buenos Aires: Losada, 1947), p. 182.

13. Argentine Chamber of Deputies, *Diario de Sesiones*, 16 January 1939 session, p. 538.

14. Argentine Senate, *Diario de Sesiones*, 11 January 1939 session, p. 452.

15. Ibid., p. 454.

16. Martin Aberg Cobo, "La revolución de 1943" in *Cuatro revoluciones argentinas (1890-1930-1943-1955)* (Buenos Aires: Club Nicolás Avellaneda, 1960), p. 81 (emphasis added).

17. Ibid.,

18. Argentine Senate, *Diario de Sesiones*, 24 August 1940 joint session, p. 345.

19. *La historia que he vivido*, p. 485.

20. Argentine Senate, *Diario de Sesiones*, 28 April 1942 session, p. 30. An absorbing account of a political event in the history of Buenos Aires Province may be found in Norberto Folino, *Barceló, Ruggierito y el populismo oligárquico* (Buenos Aires: Falbo, 1966). This book is essential to understand the Conservative party of that district.

21. Cf. Repetto, *Mi paso por la política (De Uriburu a Perón)*, pp. 204-11.

22. *Alvear*, pp. 268-69.

23. Gustavo Gabriel Levene (dir. and coord.) *Presidentes argentinos*, with the collaboration of Alberto Palcos, Boleslao Lewin, Ricardo Rodríguez Molas, and Félix Luna (Buenos Aires: Fabril, 1961), p. 188. The author acknowledges Alberto Palcos (one of Levene's collaborators in the book) as the source. The latter probably obtained this version from those close to Mario Bravo.

24. *Alvear*, p. 252. For another partisan evaluation of Alvear, see Manuel Goldstraj, *Años y errores (Un cuarto de siglo de política argentina)* (Buenos Aires: Sophos, 1957), passim.

25. Enrique Ruiz Guiñazú would replace Roca in Foreign Relations; Carlos A. Acevedo would take Pinedo's place in the Treasury Ministry (both in

1941); General Pedro Pablo Ramírez replaced Tonazzi in the Ministry of War toward the end of 1942.

26. *En tiempos de la República*, 1: 186.

27. Ibid., p. 189.

28. Ibid., p. 192.

29. *Alvear*, p. 283.

30. *La revolución que anunciamos* (Buenos Aires: Nueva Política, 1945), p. 148.

31. Franklin Lucero, *El precio de la lealtad* (Buenos Aires: Propulsión, 1959), pp. 15-19.

32. Argentine Chamber of Deputies, *Diario de Sesiones*, 3 June 1942 session, p. 510.

33. Reproduced in Argentine Chamber of Deputies, *Diario de Sesiones*, 27 June 1942 session, p. 343.

34. *Alvear*, p. 302.

35. The text has been reproduced many times. We have taken it from *El Reformista* (a publication of the Reformist Movement of students of the University of Buenos Aires Law School), no. 1, October 1957.

36. *La Revolución que anunciamos*, p. 249.

37. "La revolución de 1943," in *Cuatro revoluciones argentinas*, pp. 85-86. Cf. Ibarguren, *La historia que he vivido*, p. 498.

38. *Memoirs*, 1: 607 (emphasis added).

39. Bagú, *Argentina en el mundo*, p. 89.

40. *Memoirs*, 1: 825-26 (emphasis added).

41. *Argentina en el mundo*, p. 93.

42. *Yankee Diplomacy*, p. 51.

43. *Memoirs*, 2: 1150. Foreign Minister Enrique Ruiz Guiñazú's position may be found in his book, *La política argentina y el destino de América* (Buenos Aires: Huemul, 1944).

44. *Yankee Diplomacy*, pp. 66-67.

45. Marcelo Sánchez Sorondo, *La revolución que anunciamos*, p. 120.

46. *Argentina en el mundo*, p. 91. Though Bagú's statement is correct, this author seems to forget the "internal" consequences of neutrality, namely, that the nation does not participate (in lives and goods) in a world war. It is possible that the majority of Argentine public opinion may have been pro-Allies, but it cannot be asserted that that same majority favored actual entrance into the conflict. In this connection, cf. Smith, Jr., *Yankee Diplomacy*, p. 54.

47. *Memoirs*, 2: 1409.

48. Ibid.

49. See *The Time for Decision*, p. 238.

50. This chapter, under the title *El poder detrás del trono*, has been translated and published in Argentina (Buenos Aires: Coyoacán, 1962). It is most interesting to compare the versions given by Cordell Hull (in his *Memoirs)* and by Kelly in reference to Argentina's foreign policy. Cf. also Courtney Letts de Espil, *La esposa del embajador (10 años en la embajada argentina en Washing-*

NOTES

313

ton, 1933-1943) (Buenos Aires: Jorge Alvarez, 1967), an interesting account of social life in the American capital.

51. Sir David Kelly, *The Ruling Few* (London: Hollis and Carter, n. d.), p. 293.

CHAPTER 4

1. *La revolución que anunciamos,* p. 16.

2. Cf., for example, Ibarguren, *La historia que he vivido,* pp. 497 ff.; Bonifacio del Carril, *Crónica interna de la Revolución Libertadora* (Buenos Aires: n. p., 1959), p. 24 (they speak of "Grupo Obra de Unificación"). The following refer to "Grupo de Oficiales Unidos": Arthur P. Whitaker, *The United States and Argentina* (Cambridge, Mass.: Harvard University Press, 1954), p. 115; John J. Johnson, *Political Change in Latin America* (Stanford, Calif.: Stanford University Press, 1958), pp. 137-38. Edwin Lieuwen, *Arms and Politics in Latin America,* rev. ed. (New York: Frederick A. Praeger, Publisher, 1961), pp. 67-68; Alfredo Galletti, *La Política y los partidos* (Buenos Aires: Fondo de Cultura Económica, 1961). Carlos S. Fayt's *La naturaleza del peronismo* (Buenos Aires: Viracocha, 1967) must be consulted when studying the origins of Peronism in both its military and political aspects. (Two recent contributions to these subjects are Juan V. Orona, *La Logia Militar que derrocó a Castillo* (Buenos Aires: n. p., 1966) and Robert A. Potash, *The Army and Politics in Argentina, 1928-1945; Yrigoyen to Perón* (Stanford: Stanford University Press, 1969), particularly chap. 7. (C.A.A.)

3. *Cronicá interna de la Revolución Libertadora,* p. 28.

4. Aberg Cobo, "La revolución de 1943," in *Cuatro revoluciones argentinas,* p. 6.

5. Ibid., p. 89.

6. Ibid., p. 90.

7. *Yankee Diplomacy,* p. 81.

8. The changes that had occurred up to the time of Ramírez's ouster were as follows: Vice-President Sueyro died and Farrell occupied his office; the members of the cabinet were: Interior, Gen. Luis C. Perlinger; Foreign Affairs, Gilbert; Treasury, César Ameghino; Justice and Public Instruction, Gustavo Martínez Zuviría; War,Col. Juan D. Perón; Navy, Rear Adm. Alberto Teisaire; Public Works, Ricardo Vago and, later, Gen. Juan Pistarini.

9. *La patria y su destino,* pp. 213-14.

10. *En tiempos de la República,* 1: 193-94 (emphasis added).

11. *Mi paso por la política (De Uriburu a Perón),* p. 207.

12. "Prólogo" to *Cuatro revoluciones argentinas,* p. 8.

13. *El radicalismo (El Movimiento de Intransigencia y Renovación, 1945-1957)* (Buenos Aires: Gure, 1957), 3: 30-31.

14. *La política y los partidos,* p. 148.

15. *Peronismo y frondizismo* (Buenos Aires: Patria Grande, 1958), p. 45.

16. *Crónica interna de la Revolución Libertadora,* p. 26.

17. *Esbozo. . . ,* p. 108.

18. The complete text may be found in Jauretche, *F. O. R. J. A. y la década infame,* pp. 101-102.

19. In *Jurisprudencia Argentina,* 1943-II, pp. 522-23. For an analysis of the decisions of the Supreme Court on de facto governments, cf. Segundo V. Linares Quintana, *Tratado de la ciencia del derecho constitucional,* vol. 6 *(Forma de gobierno–Hecho y derecho de la revolución)* (Buenos Aires: Alfa, 1956), pp. 402-73. Also, "Atribuciones de los gobiernos *de facto* según la jurisprudencia de la Corte Suprema de Justicia de la Nación," *Boletín del Seminario de Ciencias Jurídicas y Sociales de Buenos Aires,* nos. 130-134, April-August 1943.

20. For example, the opinion of Federal Court of Appeals Judge Juan A. González Calderón, dated 14 September 1943, in the case of Victorio Codovilla:

The present national government is considerably more than the executive branch of a regular constitutional regime. This government was set up by the triumphant revolution of 4 June 1943, and has been recognized by the Supreme Court decision of 7 June 1943. In its pronouncement, the Supreme Court fully admitted the validity of the acts *the present government* has carried out to attain the objectives it envisages. [*Jurisprudencia Argentina,* 1943, 3: 882]

21. The text appears in Bartolomé Galíndez, *Apuntes de tres revoluciones (1930-1943-1955)* (Buenos Aires, n. p., 1956), p. 35.

22. *Anales de Legislación Argentina, Decretos,* 1943, 3: 459-61.

23. *Mi paso por la política (De Uriburu a Perón),* pp. 308-9 (emphasis added).

24. *Esbozo...* p. 114 (emphasis added).

25. Cf. *Criterio,* no. 827, 6 January 1944 editorials (emphasis added).

26. "Un *grave problema argentino* imaginario," *Criterio,* 830, 27 January 1944, p. 81.

27. Cf. Torres, *La patria y su destino,* pp. 225-28.

28. Part of the last editorial of *Nueva Política,* August 1943. It is reproduced in *La revolución que anunciamos,* pp. 258-59.

29. *Revolución y contrarrevolución en la Argentina,* 2d. ed. (Buenos Aires: La Reja, 1961) p. 399.

30. Ibid., p. 399.

31. *The United States and Argentina,* p. 128. Whitaker was writing in 1954.

32. *Crónica interna de la Revolución Libertadora,* pp. 30-33.

33. The list of those who figured in Farrell's cabinet from 1944 to 1946 is as follows: Interior, Luis C. Perlinger, Alberto Teisaire, J. Hortensio Quijano, Eduardo J. Avalos, Bartolomé Descalzo, Felipe Urdapilleta; Foreign Affairs, Orlando I. Peluffo, César Ameghino, Juan I. Cooke; Treasury, César Ameghino, Ceferino Alonso Irigoyen, Armando G. Antille, Eduardo J. Avalos, Amaro Avalos; Justice and Public Instruction, Gustavo Martínez Zuviría, J. Honorio Silgueira, Alberto Baldrich, Rómulo Etcheverry Boneo, Antonio J. Benítez, Héctor Vernengo Lima, José María Astigueta; War, Juan D. Perón, Eduardo J. Avalos, José Humberto Sosa Molina; Navy, Alberto Teisaire, Héctor Vernengo

Lima, Abelardo Pantin; Agriculture, Diego I. Mason, Amaro Avalos, Pedro S. Marotta; Public Works, Juan Pistarini. The secretariats that were created had the following incumbents; Industry and Commerce, Julio C. Checchi, Mariano Abarca, Joaquín I. Sauri, Rolando Lagomarsino; Aeronautics, Bartolomé de la Colina, Edmundo Sustaita; Labor and Social Security, Juan D. Perón, Domingo A. Mercante, Héctor F. Russo.

34. *Mi paso por la política (De Uriburu a Peron)*, p. 288.

35. The text may be found in Repetto, *Mi paso por la política (de Uriburu a Perón)*, pp. 292-97.

36. Ibid., p. 307.

37. *La política y los partidos*, p. 172. Del Mazo *(El radicalismo*, vol. 3, p. 50) recalls that: "When the 'march' took place, the people could observe in the ranks, together with high Radical leaders, well-known figures of the old oligarchic and fraudulent 'regime' as well as the most noted adversaries of Radicalism, leaders of political parties."

38. Félix Luna, *Presidentes argentinos*, p. 244.

39. *Revista de Economía Argentina*, 26: 315, September 1944, p. 280.

40. Ibid., p. 283.

41. Bernardo Rabinovitz, *Sucedió en la Argentina, 1943-1956 (Lo que no se dijo)* (Buenos Aires: Gure, 1956), p. 60. Another journalistic version of the situation in Argentina around the mid-forties is the one by Ruth and Leonard Greenup, *Revolution before Breakfast* (Argentina 1941-1946) (Chapel Hill: University of North Carolina Press, 1947).

42. Galíndez, *Apuntes de tres revoluciones*, p, 46.

43. Ibid., p. 47.

44. Ibid.

45. *La patria y su destino*, pp. 243-44.

46. *Apuntes de tres revoluciones*, p. 46.

47. *Tres revoluciones*, pp. 62-63.

48. *Del anarquismo al peronismo (Historia del movimiento obrero argentino)* (Buenos Aires: A. Peña Lillo, 1960), p. 53.

49. See the account of 17 October 1945 written by a militant Peronist union leader in Angel Perelman, *Cómo hicimos el 17 de octubre* (Buenos Aires: Coyoacán, 1961), especially pp. 71-79. Another account may be found in Emilio Morales, "El 17 de octubre de 1945," *El obrero*, second period, 1, 1, November 1963, pp. 19-42. The best documented work on the year 1945 is Félix Luna, *El 45 (Crónica de un año decisivo)* (Buenos Aires: Jorge Alvarez, 1969).

50. Galíndez, *Apuntes de tres revoluciones, p. 48*.

51. Perelman, *Cómo hicimos el 17 de octubre*, p. 77.

52. *Ayer fue San Perón* (Buenos Aires: Gure, 1955), p. 66 (emphasis added).

53. *Esbozo. . . ,* p. 121.

54. Ibid.

55. *Las ideas políticas en Argentina*, p. 247 (emphasis added). In an unpublished work by Adolfo L. Pérez Zelaschi entitled "Cronología e interpretación del 17 de octubre" which we have been able to consult through the good offi-

ces of Norberto Rodríguez Bustamante, the three most widespread interpretations of the significance of that day's events are summarized as follows:

a) The people, by a spontaneous movement – or, according to a variant in vogue during Evan Perón's life, quietly led by Eva Perón – gathered in the Plaza de Mayo to free its leader, benefactor, guide, or *caudillo*, deposed and incarcerated by a treacherous maneuver of the oligarchy;

b) The mercenary masses were paid and mobilized by salaried activists, using official means of transportation, and fully protected by the police, in accordance with a rational, calculated plan carried out by high leaders devoted to Perón: Borlenghi, Estrada, Mercante, Reyes, Eva Perón, and others, for the purpose of demonstrating Perón's political power;

c) The people, in an absolutely spontaneous movement, disorganized and incoherent, gathered in the Plaza de Mayo, coming together in a barbarous but genuine protest movement against the status quo and the political and social norms in effect until that moment. In this interpretation, Perón is only the catalytic agent in a protest with social roots. [pp. 12-13]

Pérez Zelaschi calls these various interpretations "Peronist," "anti-Peronist," and "populist," respectively. To take their place, he proposes one of his own, which to some extent coincides with the one we develop in our text, using *partial* truths contained in all three: "...I believe two things took place on 17 October; careful management from above of a latent feeling of frustration, to which the masses responded from below, unconsciously and without realizing that they were being used" (p. 15).

56. The details may be found in Lucero, *El precio de la lealtad*, pp. 30-38.
57. *The Ruling Few*, p. 310.
58. *Memoirs*, 2: 1384.
59. Smith, Jr., *Yankee Diplomacy*, p. 84.
60. Whitaker, *The United States and Argentina*, p. 124.
61. *Memoirs, 2: 1390* (emphasis added).
62. *Yankee Diplomacy*, pp. 100-101.

During the two weeks following the issue of the *ruptura* decree, the Ramírez administration carried out several anti-Axis measures which were pleasing to the U. S. State Department. Commercial and financial intercourse with the Axis countries was ordered to cease, while telecommunications with Germany and Japan were ended. A large number of Axis agents were arrested, and Foreign Minister Gilbert promised Washington that other actions would soon be taken. Relations between Washington and Buenos Aires improved perceptibly during this brief period, but Cordell Hull continued to be apprehensive over the future of the Ramírez regime.[pp. 101-2]

63. "In all possible ways the Farrell regime sought to install a Fascist dictatorship in Argentina by controlling the press, courts, schools, and key institutions, and nullifying or impairing basic civil rights" *(Memoirs, vol. II, p. 1396)*.
64. *Memoirs*, 2: 1397.
65. Smith, Jr., *Yankee Diplomacy*, p. 111.

66. *Memoirs,* 2: 1413-14. Cf. also p. 1411.

67. Quoted in Hull, *Memoirs,* 2: 1412.

68. Ibid., p. 1413

69. Ibid., p. 1414.

70. Ibid., p. 1415.

71. *The Ruling Few,* p. 303.

72. *The Time for Decision,* p. 236 and pp. 236-67.

73. *Yankee Diplomacy,* pp. 124-25.

74. Cf. Sumner Welles, *Where Are We Heading?* (New York: Harper, 1946), pp. 205-206.

75. Smith, Jr., *Yankee Diplomacy,* p. 133. Hull complains of the decision:

At the Mexico City Conference the Farrell regime obtained, as I feared it would, an entering wedge into the United Nations organization. As a condition thereof, the other American Republics agreed that Argentina should accept the common policy pursued by the Republics and make full use of her resources in the war against the Axis. This was easy enough for the Farrell regime to agree to, for the war against the Axis was now virtually over, and the victorious Axis star to which the Castillo, Ramírez, and Farrell Governments had hoped to hitch Argentine hegemony of South America was now falling. [*Memoirs,* 2: 1405]

76. For example, 2: 1407-8.

77. *Memoirs,* 2: 1408.

78. Smith, Jr., *Yankee Diplomacy, p. 143* (emphasis added). A lively account of Braden's politicoeconomic activities, before and after 1945, may be found in Rogelio García Lupo, *La rebelión de los generales,* 2d ed. (Buenos Aires: Jamcana, 1963), pp. 110-36.

79. Statements to the press in Rabinovitz, *Sucedió en la Argentina, 1943-1956,* p. 63.

80. Smith, Jr., *Yankee Diplomacy,* pp. 145-46.

81. *La patria y su destino,* p. 239. The references are on pp. 239-40.

82. The complete text is in Jauretche, *F. O. R. J. A. y la década infame,* p. 117. Del Mazo speaks of the offer by General Avalos to Amadeo Sabattini to have the latter form a cabinet (events of the eighth to the seventeenth October 1945), which the National Committee of the Radical party rejected out of fear of the Intransigent faction (*El radicalismo,* vol. III, pp. 57-58).

83. The complete text is given in Jauretche, *F. O. R. J. A. y la década infame,* p. 118.

84. *Mi paso por la política (De Uriburu a Perón),* p. 310.

85. Whitaker, *The United States and Argentina,* p. 146.

86. *Esbozo. . . ,* p. 121.

87. Galletti, *La política y los partidos,* p. 173.

88. *The United States and Argentina,* pp. 64-65.

89. *Where Are We Heading?,* p. 226.

90. Rabinovitz, *Sucedió en la Argentina, 1943-1956,* p. 65.

91. *Mi paso por la política (De Uriburu a Perón),* pp. 312-13.

92. Rabinovitz gives an account of the episode in *Sucedió en la Argentina, 1943-1956*, pp. 69-70.

93. *The Ruling Few*, p. 311.

94. Smith, Jr., *Yankee Diplomacy*, p. 156. The complete title of the document is *Consultation among the American Republics with Respect to the Argentine Situation* ["Blue Book"].

95. *Yankee Diplomacy*, p. 159.

96. Galletti, *La política y los partidos*, pp. 184 and 184-85.

97. Rodolfo Ghioldi, *Tres revoluciones*, especially pp. 73-75.

98. *Esbozo. . .*, p. 125.

99. *Historia de la Universidad de Buenos Aires* (Buenos Aires: Eudeba, 1962), p. 183.

100. *Tres revoluciones*, p. 63.

101. Smith, Jr., *Yankee Diplomacy*, p. 155.

102. Whitaker, *The United States and Argentina*, p. 149.

103. See other statements of opposition politicians in *La Prensa*, 25 February 1946; *La Razón*, 25 February 1946; and *El Mundo*, 26 February 1946 on the electoral purity of the 24 February voting; also, *Las Fuerzas Armadas restituyen el imperio de la soberanía popular* (Buenos Aires: Ministerio del Interior, 1946).

CHAPTER 5

1). Argentine Chamber of Deputies, *Diario de Sesiones*, 12 June 1930 session, pp. 33 and 34 (election of deputies from the federal capital district). At the 16 July 1930 session (p. 460 of the *Diario de Sesiones*), Oyhanarte returned to the same subject:

> Let us be reconciled to each other within legality, I said some days ago in this room, as the expression of a deep longing, fervently felt. Gentlemen, I now repeat, let us become reconciled to each other within legality, if we do not wish to hurl the country into an abyss of no one knows what unfortunate and terrible hours. This is why, when I vote for setting aside these credentials, as I shall vote for the rejection of the San Juan and the Mendoza elections, I do so because of the supremacy of legality, that is, to safeguard the seriously compromised health of the moral patrimony of the Republic.

2. Argentine Chamber of Deputies, *Diario de Sesiones*, 28 July 1930 session, pp. 530 - 31 (election of deputies for the San Juan electoral district).

3. Ibid., pp. 534 and 536 - 37.

4. Ibid., pp. 538 - 39.

5. Ibid., pp. 532 - 33.

6. *Facundo*, selection by Horacio Sanguinetti, epilogue by Santiago Montserrat (Buenos Aires: Perrot, 1959), p. 43.

7. Ibid., p. 47.

8. *El difícil tiempo nuevo* (edited and with an introduction by Gregorio Bermann) (Buenos Aires: Lautaro, 1956), p. 168.

9. *La patria y su destino*, p. 22.

10. Ibid., pp. 189-91. The *petite histoire* of the Congress and its men in Ramón Columba, *El Congreso que yo he visto*, 3 vols. (Buenos Aires: Columba, 1948).

11. "Un dilema para el Congreso: reforma o fracaso," *Revista Argentina de Ciencia Política*, 1,2, July-December 1960, pp. 210-11. For similar appraisals, see Rafael Bielsa, *Derecho constitucional*, p. 864 (note); Mario Justo López, "Poder Legislativo," in *Argentina 1930-1960* (Buenos Aires: Sur, 1961), pp. 108-16. See also Carlos Cossio, *La política como conciencia (Meditación sobre la Argentina de 1955)* (Buenos Aires: Abeledo-Perrot, 1957), pp. 55-68. For the first analysis of the "basic sociological characteristics — education, socioeconomic status, and ethnic origin — of the Argentine legislators in three different moments of the evolution of democracy in this country," see Darío Cantón, *El Parlamento argentino en épocas de cambio: 1890, 1916 y 1946* (Buenos Aires: Editorial del Instituto Torcuato di Tella, 1966).

12. For example, Uriburu's decree reads as follows: "The President of the Provisional Government decrees; Art, 1º: The present Congress is hereby declared dissolved. Art. 2º: At the proper time the necessary measures will be taken for the constitution of the new Congress. Art. 3º: Let it be communicated and published." On the criticism of the Argentine political system of the 1940s, consult César Barros Hurtado, *Hacia una democracia orgánica* (Buenos Aires: Impulso, 1943).

13. *La política y los partidos*, especially pp. 105-10.

14. Interview in *Leoplán*, Year 29, 666, 6 March, 1963, p. 14 (emphasis added). Fresco himself, some years earlier, had faced the Socialist benches and addressed them in rhetorical terms: [Argentine Chamber of Deputies, *Diario de Sesiones*, 7 December 1932, p. 24]

> If some time in the august silence of the night we are able to hear the vibrant note of the clarion call of liberty, we shall be in the vanguard to render supreme homage to the endangered fatherland; but also, if in some uncertain and sorrowful hour of the national destiny that red rag of yours, of the wilderness and of the steppe, and the blue and white one that Belgrano pledged allegiance to on the banks of the river of the same name should face each other, the clashing of their lances will be so fierce and so apocalyptic the sound of the melée, that the ground will open up in a deep fissure to swallow up the one, then rise up to a peak so that on the smoking remains of the red one, the other, ours, the one of the May sun, which is worth a thousand and one times more to us than all the other pennants of the earth, may be planted!

15. Federico Pinedo, *En tiempos de la República*, 1: 102. Pinedo was one of the most enthusiastic promoters of the Federation.

16. Cf. Galletti, *La política. . .* , pp. 104-5.

17. Reynaldo Pastor, Argentine Chamber of Deputies, *Diario de Sesiones*, 30 June and 1 July 1938 session, p. 565.

18. Argentine Senate, *Diario de Sesiones,* 28 April 1942 session, p. 10.

19. Pinedo, *En tiempos. . . ,* pp. 61-62 (emphasis added).

20. Nicolás Repetto, who opposed bilateral agreements in general, went so far as to say during the debate on the Roca-Runciman treaty that: "Of course, our vote will not imply a reflection upon the diplomatic endeavors of Julio A. Roca in London. We proclaim, and we have publicly so declared, our support because of the very discreet manner, because of the truly exemplary perseverance, and because of the high dignity which our mission was able to maintain at all times in the exercise of their high mandate" [Argentine Chamber of Deputies, *Diario de Sesiones,* 18 July 1933 session, p. 285].

21. Argentine Chamber of Deputies, *Diario de Sesiones,* 1 December, 1932 session, p. 118.

22. Argentine Chamber of Deputies, *Diario de Sesiones,* 4 August 1933 session, p. 811.

23 Galletti, *La política y los partidos,* p.111.

24. *Ideas de gobierno y política activa* (Buenos Aires; Gleizer, 1938), pp. 302-3.

25. On the abortive revolutions by the Radical party, consult the above mentioned Jauretche, *El Paso de los Libres;* and Cattáneo, *Plan 1932.*

26. *Alvear,* pp. 262 and 280-81. The conclusions of the report made by the lower house committee that studied the problem of the electrical concessions — to which Luna alludes in the quotations — is reproduced on p. 59 of this book.

27. Flier of the Democratic Union.

28. Leonardo Castellani, S.J., "A modo de epílogo o epílogo intruso," epilogue to Marcelo Sánchez Sorondo, *La revolución que anunciamos,* pp. 265-66.

29. Argentine Chamber of Deputies, *Diario de Sesiones,* 15 June 1932 session, pp. 172-73.

30. *El radicalismo,* 2: 260-61 and 263 (emphasis added).

31. Evidence is provided, among others, by Atilio Cattáneo, *Plan 1932 (El concurrencismo y la revolución),* especially pp. 228 ff.

32. On Alvear's part in the CADE business, consult Jorge del Río, *Política económica y los monopolios eléctricos,* especially pp. 145 ff.

33. *Alvear,* pp. 213-14 (emphasis added).

34. *La revolución que anunciamos,* pp. 103-4.

35. Those who joined Peronism include Arturo Jauretche, a "strong radical," member of FORJA, and others like him; also, some of the signers of the "Avellaneda Declaration" that resulted in the Intransigence and Renewal Movement, such as Armando Antille, Bernardino Horne, Jorge Farías Gómez, Natalio Carvajal Palacios, and Ricardo San Millán. Those who joined the Intransigence Movement include Arturo Frondizi, Amadeo Sabattini, and Ricardo Balbín. On this topic see Juan José Real, *30 años de historia argentina (Acción política y experiencia histórica)* (Buenos Aires-Montevideo: Actualidad, 1962), pp. 84-85.

36. *Ideario democrático (A través de la República)* (Buenos Aires: Gleizer, 1937), pp. 132-33.

37. A partial critical anthology of Socialist thought, with interesting documents on the 1930-55 period, is that of José Vazeilles, *Los socialistas* (Buenos Aires: Jorge Álvarez, 1968).

38. Argentine Chamber of Deputies, *Diario de Sesiones*, 10 April 1932 session, pp. 191-92.

39. Argentine Chamber of Deputies, *Diario de Sesiones*, 27 September 1940 session, p. 923.

40. Argentine Senate, *Diario de Sesiones*, 17 September, 1935 session, p. 338. The resolution appears in Argentine Chamber of Deputies, *Diario de Sesiones*, 15 January, 1942 session, p. 822, and was inserted at the request of Deputy Julio V. González. Palacios was not formally affiliated with the Socialist party in 1930, but he returned to the fold later and represented that party in the Senate. His position is clear from the following paragraphs of the above mentioned resolution:

1. To express that recognizing a government junta imposed by the army and whose mission the people thought consisted only in handing over the government functions to the constitutional authorities is contrary to the Constitution and to the democratic spirit that informs it. 2. That a return to institutional normalcy that will allow the development of our country within democracy is a fervent and patriotic aspiration and that for this purpose power should be handed over to the official upon whom it constitutionally devolves, so that he may immediately call elections.

Palacios's "constitutional and democratic" revolutionary stance is confirmed by a previous resolution of 5 September 1930, in which he demanded Yrigoyen's resignation.

41. *Mi paso por la política (De Uriburu a Perón)*, p. 28.

42. Repetto said in 1942:

How is it possible, Mr. Speaker, that in our international policy we should treat a country such as the United States, which is the most important democratic republic in the world, which is one of the most powerful countries with whom we will have to have increasingly close ties in the future in order to build the Western Hemisphere we all desire? How is it possible to treat the United States with that feeling of undissembled hatred and thoughtlessness which is daily and hourly manifested in the attitudes of our government? It is a senseless and incomprehensible policy. [Argentine Chamber of Deputies, *Diario de Sesiones*, 24 September 1942 session, p. 736]

For a schematic review of the work of the Socialists during this period (as well as in early and later ones), see Juan Nigro, *La obra del socialismo argentino* (Buenos Aires: Amaurota, 1956).

43. Américo Ghioldi, Argentine Chamber of Deputies, *Diario de Sesiones*, 15 June 1932 session, p. 199.

44. *Principios y orientaciones* (Buenos Aires: Gleizer, 1939), p. 242.

45. *Ideario democrático*, p. 102.

46. *The United States and Argentina*, p. 63.

47. John J. Johnson, *Political Change in Latin America*, p. 109 (emphasis added).

48. Marcos Merchensky, *Las corrientes ideológicas en la historia argentina* (Buenos Aires: Concordia, 1961), pp. 191-92.

49. Galletti, *La política y los partidos*, p. 115.

50. Joaquín Coca, *El contubernio* (Buenos Aires: Coyoacán, 1961), pp. 77-79 (emphasis added). This author had an unusual career in Argentine politics; he was a shoemaker and identified himself as "the son and grandson of militant proletarians" (p. 12). As a member of the Socialist party, he was conspicuous for his opposition to the official leadership, a stance that later led him to the Socialists Labor party (a party that did not last very long), and finally to the movement led by Perón, under whose banner he became presidential elector in 1946. In the late 1930s, when Coca was a congressman, he commented that:

> It is not as a boast that I am going to say now that before 6 September, immediately after the oligarchic victory in the federal capital in March 1930, in view of the events that were taking place: agitation in the barracks, the subversion of the Police Department, the attitude of the seditious press of the extreme Right, I was one of the few citizens who at that time proclaimed the necessity for democratic unity in order to defend our institutions, or, to be more specific, the need for an understanding between the Radical party and the Socialist party in order to oppose oligarchic reaction. Since then, we have continued to defend the same point of view within the Socialist party, promoting within it the need of defending by means of a popular front the union of the democratic parties. And this afternoon it behooves me in the name of the Socialist Labor party to state that we here defend the same ideas, that we uphold the same procedures to oppose the present reaction, which is merely the continuation of what has been done against our liberties, against our rights, and against our institutions since 6 September 1930. [Argentine Chamber of Deputies, *Diario de Sesiones*, 30 September 1937 session, pp. 1217-18]

It does not seem necessary to give a more detailed picture of the political scene of the period by discussing the Socialist Labor party or the Workers' Concentration party (with a small nucleus active in the federal capital) or the minute and sometimes mutually irreconcilable Trotskyite sectors. They would add nothing new to the sketch attempted.

51. Lisandro de la Torre, *Cartas íntimas*, pp. 39-40 (letter of 1 June 1934) and pp. 41-42 (letter of 21 August 1935). See, also, *Obras de Lisandro de la Torre*, 2d ed., vol 4 (Buenos Aires: Hemisferio, 1960), especially p. 304.

52. Galletti, *La política y los partidos*, p. 99.

53. Ibid., p. 102.

54. Democratic Union flier.

55. Carlos Strasser (ed.), *Las izquierdas en el proceso político argentino* (Buenos Aires: Palestra, 1959).

56. *Tres revoluciones*, pp. 73-74.

57. "La crisis política argentina," reproduced in *Doce años de política argentina*, 2d ed. (Buenos Aires: Praxis, 1958), p. 44.

58. Quoted in del Mazo, *El radicalismo*, 3: 64.

59. *Estructura social de la Argentina*, p. 260. The entire chapter 16 may be profitably consulted.

60. *El otro rostro del peronismo (Carta abierta a Mario Amadeo)*, 2d ed. (Buenos Aires, 1956), pp. 304-31. Two books of memoirs, written by Communist party activists more than twenty years after the 1946 elections, exemplify the traditional position of the Communist Left on Perón. They are *El recuerdo y las cárceles (Memorias amables)* by an attorney, Rodolfo Aráoz Alfaro (Buenos Aires: Ediciones de la Flor, 1967); and *Crónicas proletarias* by union leader José Peter (Buenos Aires: Esfera, 1968).

61. *Esbozo...*, pp. 70, 71, 74, and 77, respectively.

62. *Esbozo...*, p. 79.

63. Repetto, *Mi paso por la política (De Uriburu a Perón)*, p. 199 (emphasis added). The euphemism "law-abiding" was indirectly addressed solely to the proscribed Communist party.

64. "Nevertheless, Marcelo T. de Alvear, during the last few years of his life (he died in 1942), fought great battles for the reestablishment of democratic liberties." [*Esbozo... p. 76*] "Ortiz was a supporter of constitutional normalcy and his presence in the first place [of the presidential ticket] tended to disarm the democratic forces. In the elections of 1937, Ortiz was elected through fraud. Nevertheless, his first steps in the government showed his intention to enforce respect for the guarantees and rights of the citizens." [p.86]

65. *30 años de historia argentina*, p. 57. See also: Jorge Abelardo Ramos, *El Partido Comunista en la política argentina (Su historia y su crítica)* (Buenos Aires: Coyoacán, 1962), pp. 136-44. For a critique of the Socialist and Communist parties, see also Rodolfo Puiggrós, *Las izquierdas y el problema nacional* (Buenos Aires: Jorge Alvarez, 1967) and *La democracia fraudulenta*, passim.

66. With suitable caution, Victorio Codovilla, *El significado del "giro a la izquierda" del peronismo* (Buenos Aires: Anteo, 1962) may be consulted. Another symptom of the internal crisis the Communist party had respecting its approach to Peronism and the national reality is represented by the splinter groups of young intellectuals and university students during the 1960s.

67. "Our party did not conceive of unity as a mere association for electoral purposes — as the other democratic parties wanted it to be — but rather as an ambitious movement [the activities of] which would be projected on the life of the nation for a long period to come, in order to permit the transformation of Argentina from a backward, semifeudal country, dependent on the imperialist powers, into an advanced, democratic, and independent country." [*Esbozo...*, p. 100]

68. Rodolfo Ghioldi (7 November 1945), quoted in *Esbozo...*, p. 124.

69. Argentine Senate, *Diario de Sesiones*, 1 September 1932 session, pp. 37-41.

70. Argentine Chamber of Deputies, *Diario de Sesiones*, 10 June 1936 session, pp. 677-80.

71. Argentine Chamber of Deputies, *Diario de Sesiones,* 20 December 1938 session, p. 699.

72. Declaration reproduced in Jauretche, *F.O.R.J.A. y la década infame,* p. 118. This is the testimony of one of the militants in the movement, who followed fairly faithfully the stages indicated. See also, Juan José Hernández Arregui, *La formación de la conciencia nacional (1930-1961)* (Buenos Aires: Hachea, 1960), pp. 291-402, where the author makes a long value-loaded study of FORJA to confront it with the concepts of the "abstract Left." Enrique Rivera critizes the *forjistas* very sharply in *Peronismo y frondizismo* (Buenos Aires: Patria Grande, 1958). pp. 62 ff. Gabriel del Mazo is very brief in *El radicalismo,* 3: 17-22.

73. *La formación de la conciencia nacional,* p. 299.

74. From the founding Manifesto, quoted in Jauretche, *F.O.R.J.A. y la década infame,* p. 66.

75. *La formación de la conciencia nacional,* p. 305 (note).

76. Jauretche, *F.O.R.J.A. y la década infame,* p. 37 (note).

77. *La formación de la conciencia nacional,* p. 316. "In its extensive ten-year political and pamphleteering literature, only once and in a purely incidental way is the word 'proletarian' mentioned, the term 'working class,' never. F.O.R.J.A. preferred to talk of 'the people' by an idealizing generalization, which is the ideological alibi employed to avoid (precisely because of petit-bourgeois class fears) [admitting] the existence of social classes and their real antagonisms." [p. 401]

78. Statements by Arturo Jauretche, quoted in *F.O.R.J.A. y la década infame,* p. 109.

79. Statement reproduced in *F.O.R.J.A. y la década infame,* p. 118.

80. Hernández Arregui, *La formación de la conciencia nacional,* p. 400. He recounts the intervention of Jauretche in the drawing up of the Statute of the Rural Worker on p. 395.

81. *Alvear,* p. 195. However, Luna does not fail to point out that "today's Intransigent Radicalism is to some extent the child of F.O.R.J.A." (Ibid). On the personality of Dellepiane, consult Jorge I. Koremblit, *Luis Dellepiane y su pensamiento político* (Buenos Aires: Raigal, 1953).

82. *Historia crítica de los partidos políticos argentinos,* p. 411.

83. The best synthesis of the subject, because of the abundance of information and the critical approach, is found in the work of Marysa Navarro Gerassi, *Los nacionalistas* (Buenos Aires: Jorge Alvarez, 1968). See also, Juan José Hernández Arregui, *La formación de la conciencia nacional,* chapter III, pp. 165-289; Jorge Enea Spilimbergo, *Nacionalismo oligárquico y nacionalismo revolucionario* (Buenos Aires: Amerindia, 1958); Oscar Troncoso, *Los nacionalistas argentinos* (Buenos Aires: SAGA, 1957); Ismael Viñas, "Orden y progreso," *Contorno,* 9-10, April 1959, pp. 31-40; Jorge Abelardo Ramos, *Revolución y contrarrevolución en la Argentina,* especially pp. 333-37 and 387-96. Among the nationalist works that may be consulted profitably, there are: Carlos Ibarguren, *La historia que he vivido;* Marcelo Sánchez Sorondo, *La revolución que anunciamos;* Mario Amadeo, *Ayer, hoy, mañana* (Buenos Aires: Gure, 1956); José María de Estrada, *El legado del nacionalismo,* 2d ed.

(Buenos Aires: Gure, 1956); and Mario Martínez Casas, *El país, el dinero, los hombres (Relato de una experiencia)* (Buenos Aires: Theoria, 1957).

84. See, as an example, the opinions of Hernández Arregui, *La formación de la conciencia nacional,* p. 400, and of Noé Jitrik, *Leopoldo Lugones, mito nacional* (Buenos Aires: Palestra, 1960). Also the reevaluation by Dardo Cúneo, *Leopoldo Lugones* (Buenos Aires: Jorge Alvarez, 1968), thirty years after the death of the nationalist pioneer.

85. Carulla, a revolutionary in 1930, in 1937 ended by supporting the Ortiz-Castillo ticket, which, among other things, was responsive to British interests. Consult Adrián C. Escobar, *Ideas de gobierno y política activa,* pp. 226-30.

86. *La historia que he vivido,* pp. 439 and 465, respectively. For a summary of the nationalist thought according to this author, see pp. 465-66.

87. *La revolución que anunciamos,* p. 180. (The original article was written in 1942.)

88. *Ayer, hoy, mañana,* p. 114.

89. Ibid., p. 124.

90. "Orden y progreso," *Contorno,* p. 35.

91. *Revolución y contrarrevolución en la Argentina* p. 391.

92. *Ayer, hoy, mañana,* p. 19 (emphasis added).

93. *El legato del nacionalismo,* p. 77.

94. Ibid., p. 63.

95. *La revolución que anunciamos,* pp. 251 and 258-59 (emphasis added).

96. Spilimbergo, *Nacionalismo oligárquico y nacionalismo revolucionario,* p. 34. On the role of nationalism in colonizing and colonized countries, see Hernández Arregui, *La formación de la conciencia national,* pp. 199 ff.

97. At the funeral of Roberto de Laferrère, Marcelo Sánchez Sorondo, referring to his comrade in ideas, said: "Roberto de Laferrère was an Argentine who owned his country by the irrefutable titles of possession and inheritance" *(Segunda República,* Year 3, no. 42, 6 February 1963).

98. *La historia que he vivido,* pp. 431-32.

99. Argentine Chamber of Deputies, *Diario de Sesiones,* 7 December 1932 session, p. 193. See also: Juan Antonio Soari, Argentine Chamber of Deputies, *Diario de Sesiones,* 11 May 1932 session, pp. 253-58.

100. *La historia que he vivido,* p. 463.

101. *La formación de la conciencia nacional,* p. 289.

102. See Torres, *La oligarquía maléfica* (Buenos Aires: Centro Antiperduélico Argentino, 1953), pp. 119-22, for a favorable opinion of the author on Manuel Fresco.

103. Consult Gregorio Bermann, *Juventud de América (Sentido histórico de los movimientos juveniles)* (Mexico: Cuadernos Americanos, 1946); Gabriel del Mazo, *Estudiantes y gobierno universitario* (Buenos Aires: El Ateneo, 1946); Alfredo L. Palacios, *La universidad nueva* (Buenos Aires: Gleizer, 1957). Alberto Ciria, Horacio Sanguinetti and Arnoldo Siperman eds. *La Reforma Universitaria (1918-1958)* (Buenos Aires: FUBA, 1959); Bernardo Kleiner, *20 años de movimiento estudiantil reformista 1943-1963* (Buenos Aires: Platina, 1964); Alberto Ciria and Horacio Sanguinetti, *Univer-*

sidad y estudiantes (Buenos Aires: Depalma, 1962) and *Los reformistas* (Buenos Aires: Jorge Alvarez, 1968).

104. Ciria and Sanguinetti, *Univerisdad y.estudiantes,* p. 11.

105. Halperín Donghi, *Historia de La Universidad de Buenos Aires,* p. 151.

106. On "interpretations and currents of the University Reform," see Bermann, *Juventud de América,* 11: 191-208.

107. It is clear that:

Gónzález thought that the conditions existed for organizing a great popular party with a reform base — such as the Peruvian APRA — which would have the organic doctrine, tradition, and even experienced leaders; but his failure is explained by the distrust of youth for 'great politics,' by the somewhat paternalistic and messianic position of the university man of the period with relation to the rest of society, and basically because it began to become evident that there was a crisis in the political parties, which did not in any way represent either the interest or the will of the people any longer. In short, a new bourgeois party was being created (very similar to those already existing), which, had it caught on, far from uniting, would have fostered new minority divisions. [Ciria and Sanguinetti, *Universidad y estudiantes,* pp. 46-47]

108. Ciria and Sanguinetti, *Universidad y estudiantes,* p. 16.

109. Ibid., p. 17.

110. See, for example, Richard J. Walter, *Student Politics in Argentina (The University Reform and its Effects, 1918-1964)* (New York: Basic Books, 1968), especially chap. 6, pp. 119-54; it is the first American book devoted especially to the subject of the reform movement in Argentina.

111. *El difícil tiempo nuevo,* pp. 125-26 and 340.

112. See Santiago Montserrat, ed., *Las obras y los días,* introduction by Saúl Alejandro Taborda (Buenos Aires: Losada, 1945).

113. Roca, *El difícil tiempo nuevo,* p. 148.

114. Epitaph on his grave in the cemetery of Unquillo, Córdoba Province.

115. *Facundo,* p. 35. The subject of "Federalist communalism" is discussed on pp. 35-40.

CHAPTER 6

1. John J. Kennedy, *Catholicism, Nationalism, and Democracy in Argentina* (Notre Dame: University of Notre Dame Press, 1958), p. 12.

2. Argentine Chamber of Deputies, *Diario de Sesiones,* 22 September 1932 session, pp. 438-39. The divorce bill introduced by deputies Bernardo Sierra, Silvio L. Ruggieri, Enrique Dickmann, and Carlos G. Colombres was being discussed.

3. Argentine Chamber of Deputies, *Diario de Sesiones,* 23 and 24 September 1932 session, pp. 490-91. The partial reforms in the provisions for legal separation (not for actual divorce) introduced by the government of General Juan Carlos Onganía in 1968 continued to indicate the strength of the anti-divorce current inspired by the church in Argentina.

4. Argentine Chamber of Deputies, *Diario de Sesiones,* 22 September 1932 session, p. 427.

5. "El culto a María Santísima en la tradición argentina," *Criterio,* Year 16, no. 808, 26 August 1943, p. 398.

6. *Criterio,* Year 18, no. 923, 22 November 1943, p. 497.

7. "A los católicos de la provincia de Santa Fe," *Criterio,* Year 18, no. 893, 26 April 1945, p. 369.

8. Hernán Benítez, "La enseñanza religiosa ante la Cámara," *Criterio,* Year 19, no. 974, 14 November 1946, p. 459.

9. "La avalancha comunista," *Criterio,* Year 9, no. 462, 7 January 1937, p. 14.

10. "Ateísmo," *Criterio,* Year 9, no. 947, 9 May 1946, p. 431. The "deist" unity disappears when there is a conflict of interests, as the collective pastoral letter against Protestant missions within Argentina shows:

> The civil liberty of religion and the tolerance of the religion of all guaranteed by our Constitution for the inhabitants of the country is a very different thing from the absolute religious liberty which is claimed by Protestant missionaries who consider us an inferior mission people, whom they have dared to calumny by classifying us as 'idolatrous,' ignorant, and devoted to a degenerate religion, in order to lead away from the Catholic church those who belong to it by a centuries-old tradition. [*Criterio,* Year 17, no. 883, 1 February 1945, pp. 115-22]

11. "Hay que dejarlos solos," *Criterio,* Year 9, 465, 28 January 1937, p. 81. The church had already been concerned about the Progressive Democratic party and its founder, as Lisandro de la Torre himself pointed out: "The country priests in Santa Fe, and I don't know whether here in Córdoba, too, propagate from the pulpit all manner of falsehood intended for simple women and uneducated men. They tell them that if the Alianza wins we are going to burn churches and profane cemeteries, and the poor people cross themselves in horror" *(Obras de Lisandro de la Torre,* 5: 158; cf. also p. 127).

12. "Cuesta abajo," *Criterio,* Year 13, no. 656, 26 September 1940, p. 80 (emphasis added).

13. Juan B. Justo, *Discursos y escritos políticos* (Buenos Aires: Jackson, n.d.), p. 198.

14. Argentine Chamber of Deputies, *Diario de Sesiones,* 20 and 21 September 1933 session; p. 671 (emphasis added).

15. Angel M. Giménez, on the background of this bill, in Argentine Chamber of Deputies, *Diario de Sesiones,* 5 September 1932 session, p. 388. Another Socialist deputy, Julio C. Martella, took pains to make known the statistics on the entrance into the country of "priests and other religious personnel" up to 1933. See Argentine Chamber of Deputies, *Diario de Sesiones,* 20 and 21 September 1933 session, p. 693.

16. The amusing verbal duel between Iriondo and Ghioldi appears in Argentine Chamber of Deputies, *Diario de Sesiones,* 27 and 28 September 1934 session, pp. 442-80. The forest could not be seen for the trees, and the Socialist representative takes pains (for example) to ascertain whether in the "Osvaldo

Magnasco" Professional School for Women the Eucharistic hymn was or was not sung or part of the opera *Norma* "in which the Almighty is invoked" (p. 557).

17. Cf. Argentine Chamber of Deputies, *Diario de Sessiones,* 28 June 1934 session, pp. 55-60; and 19 July 1934 session, pp. 509-25.

18. A single example, José Luis Pena, Argentine Chamber of Deputies, *Diario de Sesiones,* 26 and 27 December 1934 session, pp. 387-89.

19. Argentine Senate, *Diario de Sesiones,* 2 August 1932 session, pp. 1010-11 (emphasis added). Correa's statements alluding to the *modus operandi* of certain Catholic sectors are interesting.

20. "El Congreso," *Criterio,* Year 7, no. 345, 11 October 1934, p. 218.

21. "La oración del presidente," *Criterio,* Year 7, no. 347, 25 October 1934, p. 245.

22. "Nacionalismo," *Criterio,* Year 6, 290, 21 September 1933, p. 56.

23. "Epilogue" in Marcelo Sánchez Sorondo, *La revolución que anunciamos,* p. 271.

24. *Historia de la Argentina (1515-1957),* 3d ed. (Buenos Aires: A. Peña Lillo, 1960), vol. II, p. 387 (emphasis added).

25. *Napal (El escritor, el orador, el apóstol)* (Buenos Aires: Stella Maris, 1941), p. 149 (emphasis added).

26. *La política y los partidos,* p. 161 (note).

27. In *Notas sobre Maquiavelo, sobre política y sobre el Estado moderno,* introduction and translation by José M. Aricó (Buenos Aires: Lautaro, 1942), pp. 207 ff.

28. "El nuevo acuerdo," *Criterio,* Year 4, no. 184, 10 September 1931, p. 326 (emphasis added).

29. *Criterio,* Year 4, no. 162, 9 April 1931, p. 68.

30. *Catholicism, Nationalism, and Democracy in Argentina,* p. 180.

31. Ibid., p. 181.

32. *Criterio,* Year 9, no. 431, 4 June 1936, p. 112 (emphasis added).

33. "El concepto de la Acción Católica," *Criterio,* Year 10, 101, 2 February 1930, p. 171.

34. *Criterio,* Year 16, no. 796, 3 June 1943, p. 115.

35. See Deodoro Roca's sharp comment in *El difícil tiempo nuevo,* pp. 53-54.

36. *Criterio,* Year 16, no. 834, 24 February 1944, pp.173-76 (emphasis added).

37. *Catholicism, Nationalism, and Democracy in Argentina,* p. 212 (emphasis added).

38. Ibid., pp. 171 and 177 (emphasis added).

39. "Por la dignidad nacional," *Criterio,* Year 6, no. 270, 4 May 1933, p. 104.

40. Franceschi, "Estado totalitario; Estado cristiano," *Criterio,* Year 6, 278, 29 June 1933, p. 296.

41. Franceschi, "El jefe" (in memory of General Emilio Mola), *Criterio,* Year 10, no. 485, 17 June 1937, p. 151.

42. *Criterio,* Year 10, no. 480, 13 May 1937, p. 151.

43. Franceschi, "Iglesia y Estado," *Criterio*, Year 7, no. 357, 3 January 1935, p. 9 (emphasis added).

44. Franceschi, "Gobernar," *Criterio*, Year 5, no. 227, 7 July 1932, p. 8.

45. Franceschi, "Antisemitismo," *Criterio*, Year 6, no. 306, 11 January 1934, p. 34.

46. Franceschi, "Catolicismo y nacional-socialismo," *Criterio*, Year 10, no. 541, 14 July 1938, p. 256.

47. Franceschi, "Totalitarismo, liberalismo, catolicismo," *Criterio*, Year 13, no. 662, 7 November 1940, p. 223.

48. "Ideas políticas de Monseñor de Andrea," *Revista Argentina de Ciencia Política*, Year 1, no. 2, July-December 1960, p. 175.

49. *Catholicism, Nationalism, and Democracy in Argentina*, p. 141.

50. "Una entrevista con el general Uriburu," *Criterio*, Year 3, no. 137, 16 October 1930, p. 500 (emphasis added).

51. "El manifesto del gobierno provisional," *Criterio*, Year 3, no. 136, 9 October 1930, p. 461. *Criterio's* editorial regarding the 5 April 1931 elections in the province of Buenos Aires clearly shows its position: "Thus, the Buenos Aires contest may have followed the democratic model, according to the eulogists of the system, but it obviously demonstrates that the citizen still has not acquired full consciousness of the value of his vote" *(Criterio*, Year 4, no. 163, 16 April 1931, p. 100).

52. *Criterio*, Year 4, no. 188, 8 November 1931, pp. 37-38 (emphasis added).

53. "Mensaje del Presidente Provisional de la Nación, Teniente General José F. Uriburu, al Pueblo de la República," *La obra de gobierno y de administración del 6 de setiembre de 1930 al 6 de setiembre de 1931* (Buenos Aires: Imprenta y encuadernación de la H. Cámara de Diputados, 1931), p. 18.

54. "Congreso Eucarístico y política," *Criterio*, Year 7, no. 362, 7 February 1935, p. 127 (emphasis added).

55. "La Iglesia y los partidos," *Criterio*, Year 9, no. 465, 28 January 1937, p. 79.

56. República Argentina, *Poder Ejecutivo Nacional, (Período 1932-38)*, 10 vols. (Buenos Aires: Kraft, 1938), vol. 8, no pagination.

57. *Criterio*, Year 16, no. 800, 1 July 1943, p. 197.

58. "Hacia la revolución," *Criterio*, Year 15, no. 740, 7 May 1942, p. 9 (emphasis added).

59. "Consideraciones sobre la revolución," *Criterio*, Year 16, 798, 17 June 1943, p. 153.

60. Franceschi, "Nuevas consideraciones sobre la revolución," *Criterio*, Year 16, no. 800, 1 July 1943, p. 200.

61. *Criterio*, Year 17, no. 860, 24 August 1944, p. 179.

62. Galíndez, *Apuntes de tres revoluciones*, pp. 19-20. The author alludes later on to the so-called democratic tendencies of the Argentine clergy, and, as might be expected, cites the example of Bishop de Andrea.

63. "Epilogue" in Marcelo Sánchez Sorondo, *La revolución que anunciamos*, p. 280.

64. *Nuestros vecinos argentinos* (Santiago de Chile: Editorial del Pacífico, 1956), pp. 181-82. See the single quotation from Manuel Ordóñez urging support for the Tamborini-Mosca team, on p. 182.

65. *Catholicism, Nationalism and Democracy in Argentina,* pp. 197 and 207 (emphasis added).

66. Franceschi, "La pastoral colectiva del Episcopado," *Criterio,* Year 18, no. 923, 22 November 1945, p. 487.

67. Magnet, *Nuestros vecinos argentinos,* p. 187.

68. *Catholicism, Nationalism, and Democracy in Argentina,* p. 165.

69. *La política como conciencia,* pp. 148-49 (emphasis added). See also pp. 23-28 and 96-117 for Cossio's personal view on the subject of church and politics. The "Argentine Revolution" of 1966 also offers an excellent opportunity to study the complex relations between the church and politics, along the lines traced by Cossio.

70. See the study of "organized religion" in José Luis de Imaz, *Los que mandan* (Albany: State University of New York Press, 1970), chap. 9, as an example of the difficulty the author had in separating scientific objectivity from subjective evaluation. A notable critique of this work has been published by Francisco J. Delich in *Pasado y presente* (Córdoba), Year 2, nos. 7-8, October 1964-March 1965, pp. 232-40.

CHAPTER 7

1. *The Man on Horseback: The Role of the Military in Politics* (London: Pall Mall Press, 1962).

2. Finer (Ibid., pp. 87-88) considers that there is a high political culture when:

> (1) the *"political formula,"* i.e. the belief or emotion by virtue of which the rulers claim the moral right to govern and be obeyed, is generally accepted. Or, to say this in another way, where (2) the complex of civil procedures and organs which jointly constitute the political system are recognized as authoritative, i.e. as duty-worthy, by a wide consensus. Or again in other words, where (3) public involvement in and attachment to these civil institutions is strong and widespread.
>
> The criteria by which we can assess this attachment to and involvement in the institutions of the régime are three. We must ask: (1) Does there exist a wide public approval of the procedures for transferring power, and a corresponding belief that no exercise of power in breach of these procedures is legitimate? (2) Does there exist a wide public recognition as to who or what constitutes the sovereign authority, and a corresponding belief that no other person or centre of power is legitimate or duty-worthy? (3) Is the public proportionately large and well-mobilized into private associations? i.e., do we find cohesive churches, industrial associations and firms, labour unions, and political parties?

Where all these conditions are satisfied the level of political culture may be said to be high; to the extent that they are not, it is correspondingly low.

3. "Les Militaires et le Pouvoir," *Revue Française de Sociologie,* vol. 2 no. 2, April-June 1961, pp. 75-87. The quotations are from pp. 81, 82, and 87, respectively.

4. Argentine Senate, *Diario de sesiones,* 3 May 1932 session, p. 273.

5. *En tiempos de la República,* 1: 81.

6. Cf. *Memorias sobre la Revolución del 6 setiembre de 1930,* passim.

7. Published in *Crítica,* 21 February 1932 and reproduced in *Plan 1932* by Atilio Cattáneo, pp. 427-32. The quotation appears on pp. 427-28, 430, and 431 of this edition.

8. Félix Luna in Gustavo Gabriel Levene, ed., *Presidentes argentinos,* (Buenos Aires: Fabril, 1961), p. 204.

9. *Alvear,* pp. 58-59. The account is confirmed by Justo's son:

My father had for some years been a member of the Círculo de Armas and to this fact, his brilliant work as director of the Military College and an attitude of covert resistance to the previous government of Hipólito Yrigoyen should be added. This background, together with his friends from that Circle and from the Jockey Club – the only individuals whom my father considered "decent people" – made his appointment possible. His most serious rival, Gen. José F. Uriburu, was rejected because during the 1914-1918 war he had been openly Germanophile. [Quebracho (Liborio Justo), *Prontuario,* p. 41 (note)]

10. Luna, in Levene, ed. *Presidentes argentinos,* p. 217.

11. *En tiempos de la República,* vol. I, p. 171.

12. *Prontuario,* p. 181 (note). (Emphasis added.) Carlos Ibarguren – an intimate friend of Uriburu – states that:

General Justo, who declined to cooperate with Uriburu in the military leadership of the uprising, saying that he would only be "one soldier more," opposed the tendency of the latter; Justo led politicians and many military men in the sense of not giving the movement any other meaning and objective than that of turning over the government, as soon as possible, to the opposition parties, calling for immediate elections. In this way this senior officer, who enjoyed great prestige in the army and favor among politicians, saw himself as the future president of an Argentina returned to normalcy, in view of Uriburu's refusal, solemnly formulated in his first proclamation, to accept any possible candidacy to that office. [*La historia que he vivido,* p. 391]

13. Luna, in Levene, ed., *Presidentes argentinos,* p. 210.

14. For these and other data on Perón's military career, we have employed with reservations and comparing it with other sources, the propagandistic book by Enrique Pavón Pereyra, *Perón (Preparación de una vida para el mando, 1895-1942),* 9th ed., rev. and enl. (Buenos Aires: Espiño, 1953).

15. *Doce años de política argentina,* pp. 16 and 34 (emphasis added).

16. Bonifacio del Carril, *Crónica interna de la Revolución Libertadora,* p. 34. Some well-know names: Col. José M. Mayora, Col. Juan Pistarini, Lt. Col. Alvaro Alzogaray, Lt. Col. Juan Bautista Molina, Lt. Col. Pedro Pablo Ramí-

rez, Ltd. Col. Juan N. Tonazzi, Lt. Col. Emilio Kinkelín, Maj. Angel Solari, Maj. Humberto Sosa Molina, Capt. Urbano de la Vega, Capt. Juan D. Perón (Cf. Sarobe, *Memorias...*, pp. 40 ff.; see also, Perón's "draft notes" which appear as an appendix to Carril's book, especially pp. 290 ff.).

17. The names have been taken from the extensive list that appears in *Al margen de la conspiración* (Buenos Aires: Biblos, n.d.) pp. 224-29.

18. Ibid., p. 200.

19. The text appears in Quesada, *Orígenes de la Revolución del 6 de Septiembre de 1930*, p. 103.

20. Jauretche has this to say:

General Justo has used the conspiring Radical leaders and, through Alvear, he has put himself at their head when, immediately after the Pomar uprising in Corrientes, Uriburu tottered; Justo, supported by the Lodge he had formed in his Ministry of War, gave the Provisional President the alternative [of accepting] his candidacy or having the revolution succeed. Uriburu gave way and Justo betrayed the Radicals, with whom he later came to an understanding by dispensing ambassadorships that served to pacify them. [*Ejército y política (La patria grande y la patria chica)*, monthly suppl. no. 6-7 of *Qué* 2 (February 1958): 33]

21. *Historia crítica de los partidos políticos argentinos*, p. 321 (note).

22. Ibid., p. 321 (emphasis added).

23. *Plan 1932*, pp. 233-34 (emphasis added). See also the whole of chap. 9. Ernesto Palacio is equally positive:

The state of military conspiracy [December, 1933] was general. Numerous garrisons were engaged therein, though they conditioned their participation on the giving of an order by the leader of the party. After much vacillation Alvear refused to give it, for which reason the garrisons abstained, and the movement was condemned to failure. This was no obstacle to having the Radical leaders accused of moral complicity; many were detained or confined... in the south. *(Historia de la Argentina, 2: 383]*

24. *Plan 1932*, p. 12.

25. One of its paragraphs reads as follows:

Vis-à-vis the dictatorship of General Justo, the dictatorships of the Standard Oil, Bunge & Born, Dreyfus, the Meat-Packing Association, Transportation, the Telephone Company, and so forth. Vis-à-vis this foreign dictatorship, vilely masquerading under the colors of our flag, which only civilians and military men who have fallen into the ignominy of treachery to their country can support, we proclaim the revolution with the objective of reconquering for the Argentine people the sum of their abused rights and liberties, chained by the miserable legion of fascists of the Jockey Club and Círculo de Armas, who have not hesitated to sell our nationhood in exchange for the satisfaction of their bastard and mean personal ambitions, both political and commercial.

The complete text may be found in Cattáneo, *Plan 1932*, pp. 250-51.

26. Argentine Senate, *Diario de sesiones*, 12 May 1932 session, p. 319.

27. Argentine Senate, *Diario de sesiones*, 12 May 1932 session, p. 360 (emphasis added).

28. Argentine Senate, *Diario de sesiones*, 13 May 1932 session, p. 418.

29. Argentine Senate, *Diario de sesiones*, 13 May 1932 session, p. 427.

30. Argentine Senate, *Diario de sesiones*, 19 April 1932 session, p. 589.

31. Argentine Senate, *Diario de sesiones*, 13 June 1932 session, p. 115 (emphasis added).

32. For example, Senator Bravo said that:

Much matériel has been acquired for trench warfare and for siege warfare. In accordance with what I have read with reference to war contingencies for the Argentine Republic, there is no possibility that at any time during such military operations trench warfare will be carried on nor is there any possibility that siege matériel may be used, since in most of the continent there are no sufficiently fortified strongholds to be demolished by the high caliber artillery acquired by the Argentine army. [Argentine Senate, *Diario de sesiones*, 19 May 1932 session, p. 593]

The Socialist Deputy Juan A. Solari in 1941 again returned to the subject of the irregularities in some military bureaus. (See *Diario de sesiones*, 14 March 1941 session, pp. 634-42.)

33. Argentine Senate, *Diario de sesiones*, 21 May 1932 session, p. 634 (emphasis added).

34. The complete text of the dispatch appears in Argentine Senate, *Diario de sesiones*, 12 September 1934 session, p. 158.

35. Argentine Senate, *Diario de sesiones*, 12 September 1934 session, pp. 158-59. The words "errors and" were introduced by Laurencena (Argentine Senate, *Diario de sesiones*, 30 September 1934 session, p. 939).

36. Argentine Senate, *Diario de sesiones*, 30 September 1934 session, p. 943.

37. Argentine Senate, *Diario de Sesiones*, 30 September 1934 session, p. 938.

38. *Historia política del ejército argentino (De la Logia Lautaro a la industria pesada)* (Buenos Aires: A. Peña Lillo, 1959), p. 64. See also the collection of articles, *Ejército y semi-colonia* (Buenos Aires: Sudestada, 1968), by the same author.

39. Letter from 1st Lt. (ret.) Miguel J. Rojas to Gen. Benjamín Rattenbach, Secretary of War of the Nation, dated 19 October 1962, published in the daily *El Mundo*, 3 November 1962. Rojas was private secretary to President Justo (1932-1938).

40. Argentine Chamber of Deputies, *Diario de sesiones*, 23 and 24 December 1932 session, p. 614.

41. Pp. 26-27 (emphasis added).

42. In *Aquí se aprende a defender la patria*, monthly supplement No. 2-3 of *Qué* 1 (March 1957): 18. The 1935 text is reproduced in its entirety in another article (dated 1955) entitled "¿Estaremos soñando? ".

43. *Ideario democrático*, p. 61.

44. *Alvear*, p. 283.

45. Silvio Frondizi, *Doce años de política argentina*, p. 29.

46. "Una logia poco conocida y la revolución del 6 de setiembre," *Revista de Historia*, 3: 73-94. Subsequently, Juan V. Orona has published two well-documented books in which he expands the subject of the article: *La Logia Militar que enfrentó a Hipólito Yrigoyen* (Buenos Aires: Editorial Leonardo Impresora, 1965) and *La revolución del 6 de Septiembre* (Buenos Aires: Editorial Leonardo Impresora, 1966). A good account of the military lodges in Argentina, in journalistic style, may be found in Rogelio García Lupo, *La rebelión de los generales*, chap. 7, pp. 50-63.

47. Both texts — "Bases" and "Razón de ser" — may be found in the appendix to the Orona article, "Una logia poco conocida...," pp. 92-94. "Nuevas bases para el G.O.U." may be found in appendix III to García Lupo's *La rebelión de los generales*, pp. 228-38.

48. "La revolución de 1930." *Cuatro revoluciones argentinas*, p. 57.

49. Orona, "Una logia poco conocida...," pp. 79, 84, and 87.

50. *Plan 1932*, pp. 27-28.

51. *La rebelión de los generales*, pp. 50-51. For a detailed analysis of the GOU see Fayt, *La naturaleza del peronismo*, pp. 45-64; the following may also be consulted: Gontrán de Güemes, *Así se gestó la dictadura: el G.O.U.* (Buenos Aires: Rex, 1956); and Juan V. Orona, *La Logia Militar que derrocó a Castillo*.

52. Bonifacio del Carril, *Crónica interna de la Revolución Libertadora*, p. 29.

53. *Frente al totalitarismo peronista* (Buenos Aires: Bases, 1959), p. 97. Cf. to this position Whitaker, *The United States and Argentina*, pp. 115-16.

54. Argentine Chamber of Deputies, *Diario de sesiones*, 11 September 1941 session, p. 334.

55. *Al servicio del ejército* (Buenos Aires, n.p., 1946) pp. 90 and 127.

56. Ibid., p. 9.

57. *The Man on Horseback*, pp. 120-21.

58. *La rebelión de los generals*, p. 57. Cattáneo has tried to draw a detailed parallel between the two lodges (cf. *Plan 1932*, pp. 31 ff).

59. *La rebelión de los generales*, p. 58.

60. *Revolución y contrarrevolución en la Argentina*, p. 386.

61. Ramos, *Historia política del ejército argentino*, p. 69.

62. *The Man on Horseback*, p. 176. Whitaker has written that:

Once his position was secure, however, ... [Perón] lavished funds upon the regular armed forces, including the common soldiers, and gave political preferment to the officers, who were given posts in the cabinet, as interventors in the provinces, and as managers in government-controlled enterprises in industry and mining. From the start he made it clear that so long as the military supported him, he would take care of them and share the conduct of public affairs, civil as well as military, with them. [*The United States and Argentina*, pp. 142-43]

63. *La obra de gobierno y de administración del 6 de setiembre de 1930 al 6 de setiembre de 1931*, pp. 37-38.

64. For an analysis of his position, see Scalabrini Ortiz, *Política británica en el Río de la Plata*, pp. 251-52

65. In Quesada, *Orígenes de la Revolución del 6 de Septiembre de 1930*, p. 97. See also, *Obras de Lisandro de la Torre*, 1: 224. ("Otra página de historia"); and *Al margen de la conspiración*, p. 135.

66. *La rebelión de los generales*, pp. 38-39 (emphasis added).

67. Ibid., p. 40.

68. Whitaker, *Argentine Upheaval* (New York: Frederick A. Praeger, 1956); p. 67. Cf. García Lupo, *La rebelión de los generales*, especially pp. 37-42 and 137-44.

69. *Arms and Politics in Latin America*, p. 71. It should be pointed out, however, that Lieuwen has never provided any hard data to support his assertion. The only data available shows only slight differences in social background between army, navy, and air force officers; see Imaz, *Los que Mandan*, and Carlos A. Astiz, "The Argentine Armed Forces: Their Role and Political Involvement," *Western Political Quarterly*, 22, December 1969, pp. 862-78.

70. *Apuntes de tres revoluciones (1930-1943-1955)* (Buenos Aires; n.p., 1956), pp. 42 ff.

71. *Dos veces rebelde (julio 1945-abril 1957)*, 2d ed. (Buenos Aires: Sigla, 1958), pp. 15 and 16. On the attitude of some top leaders opposing Perón, see the interesting backstage disclosures on pp. 25-27.

72. Ibid., p. 25.

73. Mariano Montemayor, *Presencia   política de las fuerzas   armadas* (Buenos Aires: Sigla, 1958), p. 44.

74. *The Man on Horseback*, pp. 42-43.

75. *La rebelión de los generales*, p. 89. See the entire chapter XIII as a synthesis of themes cogent to the one discussed here.

76. Ibid., p. 90.

77. Lieuwen, *Arms and Politics in Latin America*, p. 69.

78. Argentine Senate, *Diario de sesiones*, 27 September 1932 session, pp. 440-41 (emphasis added).

79. Argentine Chamber of Deputies, *Diario de sesiones*, 26 and 27 December 1943 session, p. 387. On p. 389, however, Pena makes the following observation: "The fact of the financial gravitation of the army is translated into a growing political intervention. It cannot be ignored that the army, for some time past, has had an increasing political intervention in the life of Argentina."

80. *El difícil tiempo nuevo*, p. 142. See also Scalabrini Ortiz, *Política británica en el Río de la Plata*, p. 250.

81. See Lanús, *Al servicio del ejército*, pp. 93-97. The following quotation exemplifies the concept of the army held by this author: "... an army that is not taught pride in the traditions of its country and respect for its patriciate, which is one of the aspects of love of country, carries within it the fatal germ of anarchy." (pp. 36-37).

82. See Montemayor, *Presencia política de las fuerzas armadas*, pp. 38-39.
83. For example, Lt. Gen. Banjamín Rattenbach in his *Sociología militar (Una contribución a su estudio)* (Buenos Aires: Perlado, 1958). Another parallel analysis is that of Mario Horacio Orsolini, *La crisis del ejército* (Buenos Aires: Arayú, 1964).

CHAPTER 8

1. For the period before 1930 Ricardo M. Ortiz, *Historia económica de la Argentina (1850-1930)*, 2 vols. (Buenos Aires: Raigal, 1955), is important. Some other useful works for an in-depth study of economic problems and related matters in Argentina are Raúl Scalabrini Ortiz, *Política británica en el Río de la Plata;* Alejandro E. Bunge, *Una nueva Argentina* (Buenos Aires; Kraft, 1940); José Boglich, *La cuestión agraria* (Buenos Aires: Claridad, 1937); Bruno A. Defelippe, *Geografía económica argentina* (Buenos Aires: Losange, 1959); Leopoldo Portnoy, *Análisis crítico de la economía* (Buenos Aires: Fondo de Cultura Económica, 1961); Jaime Fuchs, *La penetración de los trusts yanquis en la Argentina*, 2d ed. (Buenos Aires: Cartago, 1959) and *Argentina: su desarrollo capitalista* (Buenos Aires: Cartago, 1965); Rodolfo Puiggrós, *Libre empresa o nacionalización en la industria de la carne* (Buenos Aires: Argumentos, 1957); Jorge del Río, *Política argentina y los monopolios eléctricos* (Buenos Aires: Cátedra Lisandro de la Torre, n.d.); Adolfo Dorfman, *Evolución industrial argentina* (Buenos Aires: Losada, 1942); Jacinto Oddone, *La burguesía terrateniente argentina*, 2d ed. (Buenos Aires: n.p., 1936); Marcelo Isacovich, *Argentina económica y social* (Buenos Aires: Quipo, 1961); Silvio Frondizi, *La realidad argentina*, vol. I, 2d ed. (Buenos Aires: Praxis, 1957); Aldo Ferrer, *The Argentine Economy* (Berkeley: University of California Press, 1967); Benito Marianetti, *Argentina: realidad y perspectivas* (Buenos Aires: Platina, 1964); Enrique Silberstein, *Los economistas* (Buenos Aires: Jorge Alvarez, 1967); Guido Di Tella y Manuel Zymelman, *Las etapas del desarrollo económico argentino* (Buenos Aires: Eudeba, 1967); Dardo Cúneo, *Comportamiento y crisis de la clase empresaria* (Buenos Aires: Pleamar, 1967).

2. *Historia crítica de los partidos políticos argentinos*, pp. 469-70. On foreign imperialism and our economy, see Eduardo B. Astesano, *Historia de la independencia económica* (Buenos Aires, n.p., 1949); Rodolfo and Julio Irazusta, *La Argentina y el imperialismo británico* (Buenos Aires: Tor, 1934); Julio Irazusta, *Balance de siglo y medio* (Buenos Aires: Theoría, 1966); José V. Liceaga, *Las carnes en la economía argentina* (Buenos Aires: Raigal, 1954); Ricardo Olivari, *El comercio exterior argentino* (Buenos Aires: Edinorte, 1963); Ysabel F. Rennie, *The Argentine Republic* (New York: Macmillan, 1945); and Félix J. Weil, *Argentine Riddle* (New York: The John Day Company, 1944).

3. Puiggrós, *Libre empresa*, p. 471. Deodoro Roca adds that:
Bunge & Born, a many-headed monster, has converted the Argentine Chaco into a province of the World Cotton Empire. Its general manager,

Hirsch, is the Viceroy of the Chaco. Isaac Libenson is the secretary and guiding spirit of the National Board for the Defense of Production. He intelligently directs a vast movement for the protection of the cotton producers, iniquitously exploited by Bunge & Born. He succeeds. He spoils the latter's plans. Peacefully he prevents the Monopoly from continuing to throttle the Chaco planters. The Chaco is a territory subjected without any control to the power of the federal government. The governor is the master. The territory is naturally shaped for that type of governor; and the governor is precisely Bunge & Born, the monopoly-holder and exploiter of the Chaco, since the incumbent [of the governorship] is a salaried lawyer of that company. The Chaco is thus a satrapy where there is no other law than that of Bunge & Born. The lawyer Castelles is appointed governor. Since then the peaceful movement has taken on a bloody character. Bunge & Born declares the exploited planters outlaws. It kills, murders, jails. Martial law for the territory. The members of the National Board for the Defense of Production, who are doing an Argentine, a patriotic and humane job, are imprisoned. Those who are foreign-born have their citizenship papers revoked by the judges... [El difícil tiempo nuevo, p. 158]

4. Cf. Ricardo M. Ortiz, El ferrocarril en la economía argentina, 2d ed. (Buenos Aires: Cátedra Lisandro de la Torre, 1958).

5. Puiggrós, Historia crítica de los partidos políticos argentinos, p. 472.

6. Ibid., p. 478.

7. Cf., among others, Arturo Frondizi, Petróleo y política; Marcos Kaplan, Economía y política del petróleo argentino (1939-1956).

8. Mosconi, general del petróleo (Buenos Aires: Futuro, 1957).

9. Speech delivered in Colombia (1 March 1928), reproduced in Enrique Mosconi, La batalla del petróleo (Buenos Aires: Problemas Nacionales, 1957); pp. 230-31.

10. La patria y su destino, pp. 180-81.

11. Argentine Senate, Diario de sesiones, 27 August 1941 session, p. 429.

12. Clodomiro Zavalía, "La hora de Estados Unidos," Revista de Economía Argentina, Year 13, 25, 146, August 1930, pp. 143-44.

13. Clodomiro Zavalía, "El cambio de la situación política," Revista de Economía Argentina, Year 13, 25, 147, September 1930, p. 171 (emphasis added).

14. Alvear, pp. 265-66.

15. Peronismo y frondizismo, p. 44.

16. Obras de Lisandro de la Torre, vol. II, pp. 112-13, 379, and 507 (emphasis added).

17. Speech reproduced in Nuestra América y el imperialismo (Buenos Aires: Palestra, 1961), pp. 223-25 (emphasis added). A general account of cattle-raising in Argentina may be found in Horacio Giberti, Historia económica de la ganadería argentina (Buenos Aires: Hachette, 1961).

18. Palacios, Nuestra América, p. 259. The part quoted corresponds to the 1936 debates.

19. Ramón Doll, Acerca de una Política Nacional (Buenos Aires: Difusión, 1939), pp. 51-55. The lawyers mentioned by Doll also became university pre-

sidents, thus enlarging their field of action and the circle of their influence. Vicente Gallo and Carlos Saavedra Lamas of the University of Buenos Aires are examples. Gallo and Clodomiro Zavalía, then dean of the Law School, represented CHADE before the Supreme Court (cf., for example, Jorge del Río, *Política argentina y los monopolios eléctricos,* p. 107).

20. *La patria y su destino,* pp. 128-29 (note). Torres, like Doll, falls frequently into elementary anti-Semitism; in this case arbitrariness is joined to prejudice.

21. Ibid., pp. 342-43.

22. Ibid., pp. 83-84.

23. From the "preliminary warning" included in the pamphlet "La C.A.D.E. y la Revolución" (Buenos Aires, 1945), reproduced by Jorge del Río, *Política argentina y los monopolios eléctricos,* pp. 211-12 (emphasis added). Let us bear in mind that Oliver, together with Juan Sábato, was part of the "Investigating Commission of the Public Electricity Services of the City of Buenos Aires," created by decree No 4910 of 6 August 1943 under the chairmanship of retired Col. Matías Rodríguez Conde.

24. *Alvear,* pp. 198-99. "Colonel Rodríguez Conde, having a presentiment that the copies of the Report would not be distributed, gave a restricted number of copies to people he honored with his confidence so the country would not be deprived of information on this matter; among others, the author of this book received a copy."(Jorge del Río, *Politica argentina...* p. 83). Cf. in this connection Silvio Frondizi, *La realidad argentina,* 1: 238 ff.

25. *Alvear,* pp. 215-16.

26. On the Sociedad Rural, consult Jorge Newton, *Historia de la Sociedad Rural Argentina,* 2d ed. (Buenos Aires: Goncourt, 1966).

27. "La Unión Industrial Argentina (Grupo de Interés — Grupo de Presión)," paper presented at the seminar dealing with pressure groups in Argentina, held during the second semester of the 1962 academic year at the department of sociology of the University of Buenos Aires, under the direction of Professor Noberto Rodríguez Bustamante, p. 18. The assistance given by Professor Rodríguez Bustamante in gaining access to this paper is deeply appreciated. On the same subject, also see Cunéo, *Comportamiento y Crisis de la Clase Empresaria,* pp. 129-46 and 167-90.

28. *Al margen de la conspiración,* pp. 333 and 335.

29. Scalabrini Ortiz, *Política británica en el Río de la Plata,* p. 153. Hernández Arregui confirms that:

> The AIU, led by Luis Colombo, was linked to the oligarchies of the interior. He owned wine cellars in Mendoza, was president of the *Bodegas y Viñedos Tomba* Corp. and connected his operations with the banks that regulated the production of wine and with Mr. William Roberts, agent for foreign banks and president of *Bodegas y Viñedos El Globo.* Luis Colombo was Vice-President of *Bodegas Arizu,* and also member of the board of the Leng, Roberts Ltd. company. One newspaper called him "a representative of the foreign banks." He was adviser to the Wine Industry Regulating Board and also a director of the Central Bank, representing national industry, and his business deals were linked with the British railways. Luis

Colombo took part in the appointment of Minister Pinedo. [*La forma-ción de la conciencia nacional*, p. 295]

30. "La Unión Industrial Argentina," pp. 64-68.
31. Ibid., pp. 48-49, and the quotations of 54-55.
32. *En tiempos de la República*, I: 186-87 (emphasis added).
33. Ibid., pp. 187-88 (emphasis added).
34. *La patria y su destino*, p. 409 (emphasis added).
35. Cited in del Río, *Política argentina y los monopolios eléctricos*, p. 89.
36. Compare Pinedo's book, *El fatal estatismo*, 2d ed. (Buenos Aires: Kraft, 1956), with the policy of "state intervention" carried out during the presidency of General Justo — supported by his minister of the treasury, Pinedo himself — and what we mean will be clearly apparent. Pinedo, be it said in passing, when he was an Independent Socialist deputy in 1932, was known to be influential in the upper echelons:

Mr. Pinedo is the *deux ex machina* of this budget, Mr. President. His connection and collaboration with the treasury minister of the de facto government is obvious and notorious. His connection with and his work of collaboration with the present minister are known. His activities on the Budget Committee are known. His participation in the government councils with the congressmen of the majority is public knowledge and notorious. And if there should be anything lacking to stamp him as a member in solidarity with this majority, he himself has offered it precisely in his speech of Saturday when he said that he was not separated from the majority by any disagreement in the matter of expenditures, his disagreement was in the matter of taxation. [Adolfo Dickmann, Argentine Chamber of Deputies, *Diario de sesiones*, 18 April 1932 session, p. 250]

37. "La política financiera argentina (desde el 20 de febrero de 1932 al 20 de julio de 1933)," *Cursos y conferencias*, Year 6, vol. 11, no. 1, April 1937, p. 14 (emphasis added). See also Alberto Hueyo, *La Argentina en la depresión mundial (1932-1933)* (Buenos Aires: El Ateneo, 1938).
38. "La política financiera argentina...", p. 15.
39. *La patria y su destino*, pp. 231-32.
40. *Obras de Lisandro de la Torre*, 2: 165. See also, pp. 200-202, on Prebisch's stand on the meat question.

The great progress that the present form of budget and its division into various titles represents is not generally appreciated. An outstanding member of Congress has predicted that this would be changed, and I harbor the hope that this may not be the fate of the productive, earnest, wearisome labor of the great public official who carried it out and whose name I mention because it honors Argentine administration, Raúl Prebisch, who has collaborated in a work of true classification of the budget... [Federico Pinedo, Argentine Chamber of Deputies, *Diario de Sesiones*, 16 April 1932 session, p. 219]

41. *Obras de Lisandro de la Torre*, 4: 419. On Malaccorto, see ibid., 2: 222 and 418 ff.

42. Scalabrini Ortiz, *Política británica en el Río de la Plata*, p. 42 (emphasis added). See also p. 247.

43. Ibid., pp. 247-48. On another minister of the treasury of the nation, Carlos A. Acevedo, see p. 248.

44. The table gives the figures shown in the provincial taxpayers' guide for 1928. Oddone adds: "As the reader will understand, in no case do we refer to the properties that families mentioned own in the cities and towns, since if this were done the capital of each family would increase enormously. Our purpose is simply to show what they own in the way of rural property." *(La burgesía terrateniente argentina*, p. 177). The table is also given in Argentine Chamber of Deputies, *Diario de sesiones*, 26-27 April 1932 session, p. 914, at the request of the Socialist Deputy Pena.

45. *Criterio*, Year 15, 751, 23 July 1942, p. 312.

46. On the relationships between imperialism and the "industrial bourgeoisie," see Dorfman, *Evolución industrial Argentina;* and Fuchs, *La penetración de los trusts yanquis en la Argentina*, passim.

47. Milcíades Peña, "Rasgos biográficos de la famosa burguesía argentina," *Estrategia* 1 (September 1957): 49.

CHAPTER 9

1. "Algunas repercusiones sociales de los cambios económicos en la Argentina (1940-1950)," *Cursos y conferencias*, Year 20, 40: 238-40, January-March 1952, p. 577 (emphasis added).

2. *Argentina: imágenes y perspectivas* (Buenos Aires: Raigal, 1956), pp. 35-56 (emphasis added). The quotation is from a paper originally written in 1951. See also, José Luis Romero, *El desarrollo de las ideas en la sociedad argentina del siglo XX* (Mexico: Fondo de Cultura Económica, 1965), passim;

3. Romero, *Argentina, imágenes y perspectivas*, p. 36 (emphasis added).

4. 16 April 1932 session, p. 338.

5. Argentine Chamber of Deputies, *Diario de sesiones*, 28 September 1936 session, p. 694.

6. Argentine Chamber of Deputies, *Diario de sesiones*, 16 August 1939 session, p. 119. The insertion was requested by Deputy Mario Castex; Peter adds this statement on the living conditions of the worker in the meat industry:

Food is poor and scarce. When this results in illness, there is no money for medicines or treatment. Living quarters are even worse: shanties made of tin and wood, narrow, dirty rooms, uncomfortable and cold; rooms where the worker worn out by weariness will not be able to sleep because the noise from adjoining rooms will reach his as though through an amplifier. There is neither air, nor sun, nor sanitation. On the contrary, the most propitious conditions for tuberculosis and all manner of diseases are present. [pp. 119-20]

The novel *Sin tregua* by Raúl Larra (Buenos Aires: Futuro, 1959), dedicated to José Peter, "whose life partly inspired this fiction," gave terrible descriptions of work in the meat-packing plants. In this case, fiction is a burning reflection of reality; Peter himself testified to the facts in his later *Crónicas proletarias* (Buenos Aires: Esfera, 1968).

7. Argentine Chamber of Deputies, *Diario de sesiones*, 29 and 30 September 1936 session, p. 813.

8. Ibid., pp. 820-21 (emphasis added).

9. Introduction to Lisandro de la Torre's *Cartas íntimas*, p. 15.

10. We consulted the following texts: Graciela Biagini, "La Confederación General del Trabajo como grupo de presión," paper presented at the seminar dealing with pressure groups in Argentina, held during the second semester of the 1962 academic year at the Department of Sociology of the University of Buenos Aires: Rubens Iscaro, *Origen y desarrollo del movimiento sindical argentino* (Buenos Aires: Anteo, 1958); Alberto Belloni, *Peronismo y socialismo nacional* (Buenos Aires: Coyoacán, 1962); Alberto Belloni, *Del anarquismo al peronismo (Historia del movimiento obrero argentino)* (Buenos Aires: A. Peña Lillo, 1960); Angel Perelman, *Cómo hicimos el 17 de octubre* (Buenos Aires: Coyoacán, 1961); Sebastián Marotta, "Organizaciones obreras," *Argentina 1930-1960* (Buenos Aires: Sur, 1961), pp. 150-58. For the period before 1920, see Marotta, *El movimiento sindical argentino. Su génesis y desarrollo*, 2 vols. (Buenos Aires: Lacio, 1960-1961). There is useful material on the labor movement in Jacinto Oddone, *Gremialismo proletario argentino* (Buenos Aires: La Vanguardia, 1949); Enrique Dickmann, *Recuerdos de un militante socialista* (Buenos Aires: La Vanguardia, 1949); Luis Cerruti Costa, *El sindicalismo, las masas y el poder* (Buenos Aires: Trafac, 1957); Roberto Carri, *Sindicatos y poder en la Argentina* (Buenos Aires; Sudestada, 1967); and Samuel L. Baily, *Labor, Nationalism, and Politics in Argentina* (New Brunswick: Rutgers University Press, 1967).

11. See "El movimiento obrero argentino ante el golpe de Estado del 6 de setiembre de 1930," *Revista de Historia*, 3, first quarter 1958, pp. 123-32. A serious study of the relations between the worker and his socioeconomic environment up to the 1929 crisis may be found in José Panettieri, *Los trabajadores* (Buenos Aires: Jorge Álvarez, 1968).

12. Marotta, "Organizaciones obreras," p. 150.

13. The complete text may be found in Biagini, "La Confederación General del Trabajo. . . ,"p. 6.

14. *Origen y desarrollo del movimiento sindical argentino*, pp. 144 and 146.

15. "La Confederación General del Trabajo. . .," p. 30.

16. Belloni, *Del anarquismo al peronismo*, pp. 41-42. In a source with a different ideological tendency, the *Esbozo*... of the Communist party, there are comments on the fact that some leaders of the GCL "devoted themselves systematically to discouraging strikes and supported Uriburu and later Justo's administration" (p. 78).

17. *30 años de historia argentina*, p. 40.

18. Iscaro, *Origen y desarrollo*. . . , p. 153.

NOTES

19. Marotta, "Organizaciones obreras," p. 154.

20. A copy of the original text may be found in Biagini, "La Confederación General del Trabajo. . . "p. 16.

21. *Origen y desarrollo. . .*, p. 158 (emphasis added). On the same page he provides some figures: "According to Department of Labor data, the GCL in 1936 comprised 317 unions and 262, 630 dues-paying members; the ALU, 31 unions and 25,093 dues-paying members; the FACE [Catholic Federation of Female Clerks], 25 unions and 8,012 dues-paying members; and the independent unions were 83 with 72,834 dues-paying members."

22. Biagini, "La Confederación General del Trabajo. . . ," p. 37.

23. Iscaro, *Origen y desarrollo. . .* p. 166. The complete text of the resosolution may be found on pp. 166-67.

24. Biagini, "La Confederación General del Trabajo. . . ," p. 39, "Theoretically the program was not bad; on the contrary, its implementation would have served to alleviate the economic difficulties of the working class; but the GCL did not take any steps, either great or small, to see that it was carried out" (pp. 39-40).

25. The preceding quotations are from Iscaro, *Origen y desarrollo...,* pp. 167 and 170. The complete text of the resolution is reproduced on pp. 176-77.

26. Ibid., p. 179.

27. This petty and not very edifying process may be followed in Biagini, "La Confederación General del Trabajo. . . ," pp. 40-42; and in Iscaro, *Origen y desarrollo. . .* pp. 178-80. The spirit of fraud and intrigue had tainted even the union field, as a reflection of a whole era.

28. *Peronismo y socialismo nacional,* pp. 12-13.

29. Iscaro records that ". . . in the 1931-39 period [the number of strikes] reached 565 with 286,00 workers participating" [*Origen y desarrollo. . .*, p. 160]. Further data on strikes may be found in *Esbozo. . .*, passim.

30. See the graphic account of the strike by Angel Perelman, *Cómo hicimos el 17 de octubre,* pp. 31-33 and 43 ff. The Communist version is given in *Esbozo. . .*, p. 99 (note).

31. *Esbozo. . .*, p. 107.

32. "La Confederación General del Trabajo. . . ," p. 45. The interesting conclusions on which the author bases her thesis that the GCL operated in a practically uninterrupted manner during the years 1930 to 1943 as a covert government "pressure group," always receptive to suggestions from the administration (to whom it periodically addressed petitions for a "minimum program" of improvements), seem convincing to us (see especially pp. 43-45).

33. "Organizaciones obreras," p. 155 (emphasis added). Also see, for some less simplistic analyses, Rodolfo Puiggrós, *El proletariado en la revolucion nacional* (Buenos Aires: Trafac, 1958) and Torcuato S. Di Tella, *El sistema político argentino y la clase obrera* (Buenos Aires: Eudeba, 1964).

34. Biagini, "La Confederación General del Trabajo...," pp. 42-43. See Iscaro, *Origen y desarrollo. . .*, pp. 226 ff.

35. *30 años de historia argentina,* p. 66. For details on the part played by Borlenghi and Mercante, see Rabinovitz, *Sucedió en la Argentina*

(1943-1956), pp. 22 ff. After referring to Decree 28,169/44 (Statute of the Rural Worker) the above-mentioned Real proceeds with this enumeration:

This social policy reached other strata of the workers up to then disorganized and "submerged," namely, the field and sugar-mill workers, from which arose the powerful Federation of Sugar Industry Workers. It also affected the tenant farmers: Decree 14,001/43 froze leases under the rates in effect on 1 July 1940; it meant a substantial reduction. Later the reduction was extended to include leases of the milk producers. This social policy was placed within the framework of an economic policy with a pronounced industrializing tendency, which started with the creation of the Industrial Bank (Decree 8,537/44) and had a nationalist orientation: the Natural Gas Company and the grain elevators were immediately nationalized. [*30 años de historia argentina*, pp. 66-67]

36. *Cómo hicimos el 17 de octubre*, p. 46. The most important decrees on labor matters (1943-1946) may be found in the corresponding volumes of *Anales de Legislación Argentina*.

37. *Revolución y contrarrevolución en la Argentina*, pp. 401-402. On Perón's contacts with the political parties (including the Communist), see Real's opinion in *30 años de historia argentina*, pp. 68-69.

38. *Origen y desarrollo...*, p. 228 (emphasis added). The text recalls almost verbatim that of a 1947 official Communist publication which reads as follows:

For this reason, Perón set himself a tactical plan which he fulfilled step by step. First, he tried by every means to prevent the functioning of independent unions, putting them in a position of illegality, imprisoning their leaders, beginning with the best-known Communist union leaders, in order to break their contact with the working masses; then by various means he bribed a considerable number of old reform leaders of the GCL, who placed themselves unconditionally at his service; and, at the same time, he publicized demagogically certain slogans deeply felt by the working class and the people, and in this way he tried to remove the masses from the influence of the democratic parties in general and of the Communist party in particular, and to win their support for the domestic and foreign policies of the military-fascist government. [*Esbozo . . .*, p. 114].

Compare the above excerpt with the following quotation from Perelman, *Cómo hicimos el 17 de octubre*, p. 63:

. . . we, the organizers of the 1944 and 1945 unions, came mostly from the old traditional sectors of the labor movement; among us there were many syndicalists, communists, Trotskyites, socialists, members of FORJA (like Libertario Ferrari), activists who in one way or another understood very clearly the duel that at that moment was taking place in the country and the significance of Perón's political and historical generalizations. To us it meant the recovery of an old lost language, the reestablishment of a fundamental historical line, the most appropriate for a national and popular movement. For the thousands of activists, delegates, and leaders of unions, mostly from the interior, who had never taken part in politics or in unions, it was a veritable discovery of national and international problems.

39. *Esbozo. . .* , p. 122 (emphasis added).

40. Ibid., p. 125.

41. Galletti, *La política y los partidos,* is a good example of this. See an excellent first step toward an analysis of the Labor party's genesis in Fayt, *La naturaleza del peronismo,* especially pp. 114-54.

42. *Del anarquismo al peronismo,* p. 56. The author states immediately after this that:

The Labor party was to be Perón's best political support in those days when all the old parties, the Supreme Court, the Stock Exchange, the Rural Society, the university, the banks, the state bureaucracy, the Industrial Union and the press were against the popular trend. Only one organized and centralized power, that of the army, was taking its place as a power factor on the side of the workers. *After Perón's accession, the Labor party, which had consolidated that victory on the basis of producing a great labor and popular political platform, was to be supplanted by professional politicians until it was dissolved.* [emphasis added]

The testimony of a former Labor party member who ended as a rabid opponent of Perón may be found in Walter Beveraggi Allende, *El Partido Laborista, el fracaso de Perón y el problema argentino* (Montevideo, 1954).

43. *Frente al totalitarismo peronista,* p. 116. Among many other references, see also pp. 118-19.

44. *La política y los partidos,* p. 177. See also p. 152.

45. In *Political Man (The Social Bases of Politics)* (Garden City, N. Y.: Doubleday & Co., 1960), pp. 170-73. William Kornhauser says that Peronism is a "mass movement similar to fascism," *The Politics of Mass Society* (Illinois, The Free Press of Glencoe, 1959), p. 156. For a critical analysis of the Peronist "doctrine," see Alberto Ciria, *Perón y el justicialismo* (Buenos Aires: Siglo Veintiuno Editores, 1971).

46. *The United States and Argentina,* p. 120. At the sociological level consult Gino Germani, *Política y sociedad en una época de transición (De la sociedad tradicional a la sociedad de masas)* (Buenos Aires: Paidós, 1962), chapters 8 and 9.

47. Lecture reproduced in José S. Campobassi and others, *Los partidos políticos (Estructura y vigencia en la Argentina* (Buenos Aires: Cooperadora de Derecho y Ciencias Sociales, 1963), pp. 49-50 (emphasis added).

48. *¿Qué es esto? (Catilinaria),* 2d ed. (Buenos Aires: Lautaro, 1956), pp. 32-33 (emphasis added).

CHAPTER 10

1. In his "Argentina's Durable Peronists: A Twentieth Anniversary Note (Some Preconditions and Achievements)," *American Universities Field Staff*

Reports (New York: East Coast South America Series, 12, 2 (Argentina, April 1966), pp. 5-18. See also pp. 18-19 for some intelligent comments regarding the achievements of the Peronist administration.

2. "Before the beginning of the Second World War, the bases for the industrial development of Argentina had already been laid, with its share of pros and cons, with its social implications. *The war did not start this development;* the war added elements which tended to emphasize it; the war, undoubtedly, accelerated it." Dardo Cúneo, *El desencuentro argentino 1930-1955* (Buenos Aires: Pleamar, 1965)., p. 40 (emphasis added).

3. For an analysis revealing the Conservative and Radical attitudes vis-à-vis the industrialization process through which the country was passing during the first part of the 1940s, see Miguel Murmis and Juan Carlos Portantiero, "Crecimiento industrial y alianza de clases en la Argentina (1930-1940)," *Documento de Trabajo No 49* (Buenos Aires: Centro de Investigaciones Sociales, Instituto Torcuato Di Tella, 1968), especially pp. 17-28. Alfredo Parera Dennis, "Una década decisiva en la formación de la moderna clase obrera argentina: 1935-1945," *Fichas de investigación económica y social,* 1, 3, September 1964, pp. 53-61, may also be read profitably.

4. Tulio Halperín Donghi sums up as follows in *Argentina en el callejón* (Montevideo: Arca, 1964), p. 43:

The army reappeared at this moment. Strictly speaking, it had never disappeared; it was the tutelary force of our governments, which owed their continued existence only to its support. Now it was withdrawing [this support] from Castillo: a military stroll through the center of Buenos Aires ended, amidst leaden indifference, what had been started thirteen years earlier by another more warmly received parade. Was it really ending?

5. On the "two proclamations" by the army on 4 June 1943, evidence of the complex situation, see Cúneo, *El desencuentro argentino,* pp,. 79-80.

6. See some of the basic documents of the Labor party in Fayt, *La naturaleza del peronismo,* pp. 118-19 and 121-30.

7. A critique from within the fold of the attitude of the parties of the Left between 1943 and 1945 may be found in Juan José Real, 'La izquierda y el 4 de junio de 1943," in Carlos Astrada and others, *Claves de historia argentina* (Buenos Aires: Merlín, 1968), pp. 223-45.

8. A tardy and weak defense of Braden's mission in Argentina is to be found in Thomas F. McGann, "The Ambassador and the Dictator: The Braden Mission to Argentina and Its Significance for United States Relations with Latin America," *Centennial Review of Arts and Sciences,* 6, 2, Summer 1962, pp. 343-57.

9. For example, see the article by T. R. B., a prestigious regular columnist of the liberal weekly, *The New Republic,* 20 July 1968, p. 4, where statements like the following are made: "Congress has steadily lost power for 25 years. It is still stacked for the conservatives. You look to it often with despair."

10. See Murmis and Portantiero, "Crecimiento industrial...," on the respective positions of the parties with reference to the debate on the "Economic

Reactivation Plan," presented by Minister of the Treasury Federico Pinedo (1940), approved by the Senate, but never considered by the Chamber of Deputies (pp. 22-28). For an important critique of the Radical Civic Union as a party representing the middle class, see Peter Smith, "Los radicales argentinos y la defensa de los intereses ganaderos,1916-1930," *Desarrollo Económico*, 7, 25, April-June 1967, pp. 795-829.

11. For a searching analysis of the motivation of the "democratic unions," see Cúneo, *El desencuentro argentino*, p. 51.

12. In his book, *La democracia fraudulenta*, pp. 61-96, one of many works by this author.

13. See Cúneo, *El desencuentro argentino*, especially pp. 46-47, 82-83, and 99; Jorge Abelardo Ramos, *Revolución y contrarrevolución en la Argentina*, 3d ed., vol. II (Buenos Aires: Plus Ultra, 1965), pp. 622-24 and Rogelio García Lupo, "Lo que pensaba el general Savio de nuestro acero," *CGT*, Year 1, 21, 19-IX-68, p. 6.

14. On this subject, the information gathered in three books by Juan V. Orona, *La Logia Militar que enfrentó a Hipólito Yrigoyen* (Buenos Aires: Editorial Leonardo Impresora, 1965); *La revolución del 6 de Septiembre* (Buenos Aires: Editorial Leonardo Impresora, 1966); and *La Logia Militar que Derrocó a Castillo* (Buenos Aires: Editorial Leonardo Impresora, 1966) is indispensable.

15. For a recent reader on politics and economics between 1930 and 1943, consult Alberto Ciria and others, *La década infame* (Buenos Aires: Carlos Pérez, 1969).

16. See some partial contributions to that study in Roberto Carri, *Sindicatos y poder en la Argentina* (Buenos Aires: Sudestada, 1967); Puiggrós, *El proletariado en la revolución nacional* (Buenos Aires: Trafac, 1958); and José Luis de Imaz, *Los que Mandan* (Albany: State University of New York Press, 1970), chap. 11, pp. 215-41.

17. The proportional representation system employed was "D'Hondt's variant" (explained at some length in Rafael Bielsa, *Derecho constitucional*, 3d ed. (Buenos Aires: Depalma, 1959), pp. 225-26, and in reality it was first applied in Argentina during the election for constitutional convention delegates (1957) in order to count only the votes of the parties that participated, thus ignoring the proscription and consequent blank ballots of the Peronists.

18. Pablo Guissani, "La Junta Consultiva," *Extra*, Year 1, 5, November 1965, p. 30. This is a caustic and penetrating analysis of that body.

19. See Alan T. Leonhard, "The 1946 Purge of the Argentine Supreme Court of Justice," *Inter-American Economic Affairs*, 17, 4, Spring 1964, p. 77. He wrote: "The judges on the Court at this time were Chief Justice Roberto Repetto, and Justices Antonio Sagarna, Benito Nazar Anchorena, Francisco Ramos Mejía, and Tomás Casares. Repetto resigned immediately, and Casares, because of his dissenting opinion in many of the contested judgments, was excused from prosecution" (p. 74).

20. Argentine Supreme Court, *Fallos*, vol. 233, 1955, pp. 15-16.

21. The texts of Guido's message to the Supreme Court and of the oath he

later took before the latter, may be found in *El Derecho,* vol. 2, 1962, pp. 4 and 5.

22. In the Luis M. Pitto case (Supreme Court, 3 April 1962), *El Derecho,* 2, (1962): 2.

23. See·Decrees No. 3 and No. 7 (both dated 28 June 1966) issued by the Revolutionary Junta, by which, respectively, the following Supreme Court Justices *are deprived of their offices:* Aristóbulo D. Aráoz de Lamadrid, Luis María Boffi Boggero, Pedro Aberastury, Ricardo Colombres, Esteban Imaz, Juan C. Zavala Rodríguez; also the attorney general, Ramón Lascano; and the new members of the Supreme Court are appointed *by the President of the Nation* (Eduardo A. Ortiz Basualdo, Roberto E. Chute, Marco A. Risolía, Luis C. Cabral, and Guillermo A. Borda — later replaced by José F. Bidau — and the new attorney general, Eduardo H. Marquardt). The texts appear in *Anales de Legislación Argentina,* 1966, 26-B, pp. 759-60.

24. Preamble of the "Statute of the Argentine Revolution", in *Anales de Legislación Argentina,* 1966, 26-B, p. 756. On the relations between the judicial branch and the executives created by force, see Zulema Julia Escobar, "Antecedentes jurisprudenciales argentinos en materia de revolución," in Instituto de Ciencia Política, Universidad del Salvador, *La "Revolución Argentina" (Análisis y prospectiva)* (Buenos Aires: Depalma, 1966), pp. 41-61.

25. Bear in mind Decree No. 773 of 18 April 1943 of the Ramírez administration, providing that the "word *provisional* be struck from the resolution constituting the present government and from the official documents on which it may have appeared, and it is hereby forbidden to apply it to the authorities of the Government of the Nation."

26. See Argentine Chamber of Deputies, *Diario de sesiones,* special session of 13-14 August 1948, p. 2710 and passim, in the debate on the need for constitutional reform.

27. See Bielsa, *Derecho constitucional,* pp. 134-35 ff. For a collection of disparate opinions on the timing and extent of this frustrated 1957 reform, see the symposium on the constitutional reform edited by Arnoldo Siperman, in which the opinions of Bonifacio del Carril, Carlos S. Fayt, Silvio Frondizi, Segundo V. Linares Quintana, Benito Marianetti, and Alberto Antonio Spota appear. It was published in *Revista de Derecho y Ciencias Sociales,* Year 3, 5, Winter 1957, pp. 77-112.

28. Bielsa, *Derecho constitucional,* pp. 140-41 and 140 (note).

29. *Anales de Legislación Argentina,* 1966, 26-B, pp. 753-54. Of the Statement transcribed, four copies were signed for recording, publication, and eventual lodging in the archives of the Executive Office of the President and the offices of the commanders of the three branches of the armed forces. The signers of the documents are the respective commanders in chief of the three services: Lt. Gen. Pascual A. Pistarini, Admiral Benigno I. Varela, and Air Force Gen. Adolfo T. Alvarez.

30. The text of "Revolutionary Objectives" and of "Statute of the Argentine Revolution," is found in *Anales de Legislación Argentina,* 1966, 26-B, pp. 757 and 756, respectively. See Ernesto J. Miqueo Ferrero, "Leyes

fundamentales argentinas," in *La "Revolución Argentina,"* pp. 199-210, for a favorable comment on this vertical and authoritarian structure.

31. For a keen commentary on this process, see George I. Blanksten, *Perón's Argentina* (Chicago: University of Chicago Press, 1953), pp. 334-35.

32. There has been no in-depth study of the broadening of electoral participation during Perón's presidential terms: granting of voting rights to women, conversion of national territories into provinces, and others, and the relation of this to the numerical increase of the "three branches" of the Peronist party: male, female, and organized labor.

33. On the university movement and its problems from 1943 to the present time, consult Ciria and Sanguinetti, *Los reformistas* (Buenos Aires: Jorge Alvarez, 1968), especially pp. 113-239; also Luisa Brignardello, "Argentina: dos años de malas relaciones," *Mundo Nuevo,* Buenos Aires, 26-27, August-September, 1968, pp.25-37.

34. It must be emphasized that the Communist party has been a polemical object of study for authors such as Ramos, *El Partido Comunista en la política argentina* (Buenos Aires: Coyoacán, 1962); and Puiggrós, *Las izquierdas y el problema nacional* (Buenos Aires: Jorge Alvarez, 1967) and *La democracia fraudulenta* (Buenos Aires: Jorge Alvarez, 1968), as we have already indicated, but in our judgment the overall perspective has been wrong since its real significance in the political process of Argentina has been exaggerated.

35. The *National Left* despite the intentions of its principal exponents – Ramos, Hernández Arregui, Jauretche, and younger disciples – constitutes an interesting intellectual restatement of many myths of the Argentine past and present, rather than a political mass movement. On the crisis of the "Left" in Argentina, see Ismael Viñas, "Hora cero de la izquierda: organización política y fuerza revolucionaria," *Nueva Política,* Year 1, 1, December 1965, pp. 21-53.

36. In relation to the numerous parties between 1955 and 1960, see Galletti, *La política y los partidos,* pp. 228-46.

37. See Halperín Donghi's remarks on the nationalists in 1955 in *Argentina en el callejón,* p. 77.

38. For an extreme interpretation of "communitarism," see Jaime María de Mahieu, *El Estado comunitario* (Buenos Aires: Arayú, 1962).

39. *La Razón* (Buenos Aires), 15 September 1968, p. 5.

40. The statement by Sánchez Sorondo has already been reproduced in chap. 1, p. 8. For a discussion of the ideologies in vogue in the 1930s and 1940s, see José Luis Romero, *El desarrollo de las ideas en la sociedad argentina del siglo XX,* chap. 4.

41. Cf. Halperín, *Argentina en el callejón,* pp. 71-73.

42. The disproportionate influence that Catholic laymen, with the tolerance and at times the support of the hierarchy, exercise as members of boards of censors of public spectacles (which periodically gives rise to true *causes célèbres*) also is very evident. This is another tradition that we have noted since the time of the Justo administration.

43. In that 1955-1958 period the divisions within the armed forces regarding Peronism and the subsequent delivery of the government to civilians

hardened. But when the occasion arose, uprisings against the military government were repressed with unwonted firmness (9 June 1956), including the execution of the actual or presumed opponents of the official policy. See Rodolfo J. Walsh, *Operación Masacre*, 3d ed. (Buenos Aires: Jorge Alvarez, 1969), a masterpiece of political journalism.

44. In *Argentina en el callejón* p. 92, where this author compares the Intransigent Radical party with the 1931 Civil Alliance.

45. This interpretation — written in 1968, at the time the second Spanish edition of this work appeared — was proved correct by events. The increasingly authoritarian tendencies of Onganía, his arrogant exercise of power, which prevented the institutionalization of the regime on the basis of popular consensus, among other factors, gave rise to a keen concern within the high commands of the armed forces. The latter deposed him on 8 June 1970 in a quick "coup within the coup" which raised Gen. Roberto Marcelo Levingston to the presidency of the nation through appointment by the junta of commanders in chief of the three forces.

Onganía's deterioration was evident from at least the middle of 1969, when active discontent of the opposition sectors became acute in Argentina. Characteristic instances were the assassination of the most important Peronist labor leader, Augusto T. Vandor, the acts of terrorism, the attacks on the banks, and the military and police barracks, and other places carried out from that time on by various clandestine groups (with Marxist, and even Peronist tendencies) engaged in armed struggle and, especially, by the explosion of collective anomic violence mixed with elements of urban guerrillas that took place in the city of Córdoba toward the end of May 1969 and made the military regime totter. On Córdoba as a microcosm of Argentine society in crisis, see Franciso J. Delich, *Crisis y protesta social-Córdoba, mayo de 1969* (Buenos Aires: Ediciones Signos, 1970).

The kidnapping 29 May 1970) and subsequent assassination of General Pedro E. Aramburu, a political event that has not yet been clarified definitely, was the spark that ignited Onganía's personalist and repressive apparatus and precipitated his fall.

46. On the subject, in general, consult Carlos A. Florit, *Las fuerzas armadas y la guerra psicológica* (Buenos Aires: Arayú, 1963). For concrete examples during the first half of 1966, see the weeklies *Confirmado* and *Primera Plana.*.

47. Rogelio García Lupo, *Contra la ocupación extranjera*, 3d ed. (Buenos Aires: Editorial Centro, 1971), contains worthwhile information on this and related matters.

48. For a personal and penetrating appraisal of Latin American "golpismo" see José Nun, "América Latina: la crisis hegemónica y el golpe militar," *Desarrollo Económico*, 6, 22-23, July-December, 1966, pp. 355-415.

49. Susana Fiorito, José Vazeilles, and Ismael Viñas, "Concentración monopolista e historia industrial," *Nueva Política*, Year 1, 1 December 1965, p. 64. See also, *Fichas de investigación económica y social*, Year 1, 1, April 1964 (issue devoted to industrial evolution and the Argentine entrepreneurial class); and Ismael Viñas, "¿Existe la burguesía nacional? ," *Revista de pro-*

blemas del Tercer Mundo, 1 April 1968, pp. 9-43. A useful storehouse of data on "entrepreneurial" organizations (ranchers, industrialists, and businessmen according to the author) is Dardo Cúneo, *Comportamiento y crisis de la clase empresaria.* For example, interesting details on the origins and activities of the General Economic Confederation (GEC) from 1952 on (pp. 191-214, 229-44, and 257-66), as an instance of the not very pronounced solidarity of interests among the various representatives of the Argentine industrial sector.

50. *Comercio Exterior* (Mexico), 18, 9, September 1968, p. 808. The same publication points out that "The sector that has received the greatest influx of capital... has been the banking one, a situation facilitated by the following two circumstances: (a) the provisions of the Argentine Central Bank which restrict the amount local banks may pay by way of dividends; and (b) the favorable disposition of Argentine government circles toward the entrance of foreign capital." Data on outstanding examples of transfer of ownership of Argentine enterprises to foreign capital between 1962 and 1968 can be found in *Primera Plana,* Year 6, 297, 3 September 1968, p. 67; the figures mentioned there include nine banks, four cigarette producers, fourteen makers of automobile parts, two home furnishings factories, and one automobile manufacturer.

51. Beginning in October 1970, and with the support of his minister of economics, Aldo Ferrer, General Levingston began a superficial modification of the policies followed by Onganía; through numerous laws that did not solve the problems of monopolistic concentration and imperialist penetration discussed in this chapter, it was attempted to "Argentinize the economy" and "develop with justice." The by-product of these measures was an increase in social tension and in inflationary pressures which started early in 1971. Since Levingston was also searching for "the deepening of the Argentine Revolution" (that is to say, to remain in power for a number of years while his economic blueprint brought positive results and to structure a supporting political movement) this strategy forced him into a confrontation with the commanders in chief of the three branches of the armed forces, increasing the threat of a split within the military. The results were negative and on 23 March 1971, the commanders in chief deposed him; shortly thereafter, Army Commander Lt. Gen. Alejandro A. Lanusse took over the presidency. Levingston had repeated in a shorter period of time Onganía's mistakes. The political, economic, and social future of Argentina is still an open question.

52. See the synthesis in the article by Rogelio García Lupo, "La doble década de los militares y las masas," *Lyra,* Year 20, 189-191, 1963 (no paging).

53. Preamble to "Statement of the Argentine Revolution" (28 June 1966), *Anales de Legislación Argentina,* 1966, 26-B, p. 753. It may be useful to compare this military description with the situation in Argentina at the beginning of the seventies after five years of the "Argentine Revolution."

Index

354